THE POLITICS OF FORCE

Bargaining During International Crises

"This book presents a very useful, sound, and skillful analysis of one of the most important contemporary modes of power politics below the threshold of war. The subject is exceedingly well chosen and well defined. Its subtleties are managed in an orderly but sensitive fashion. The hypotheses are constructive, the data effectively related to the hypotheses, and the conclusions soundly derived. In general, I have nothing but praise for the whole project."—*Robert E. Osgood (of The Washington Center of Foreign Policy Research)*

How is international influence acquired by nations and used to achieve political objectives during crises? What effect do crises actually have upon the stability of the international system, and upon the nature of bargaining itself under these conditions?

To answer such questions about the role of organized coercion in the overall international system requires the development of increasingly sophisticated concepts and perspectives which can

OF FORCE

d the demands of comparative l analysis. The author's pur- his book is to formulate a re- trategy that moves between ostract conceptualizing on the onal system and purely induc- iry.

gh an analysis of several cases rlin crises of 1948-1949 and Taiwan Strait crisis of 1958, Cuban missile crisis of 1962— or elucidates various inter- nd highly politicized forms of nal coercion. The analysis w insights into the stability ernational system and the role ed force in international poli-

earlier book, *The Interme-* e author dealt with the role ies can play in the termina- ises. Focusing on bargaining ditions of crisis, this book Professor Young's penetrat- ation of the nature of con- he role of coercion in inter- fairs.

Oran R. Young is an Assistant Professor in the Department of Politics and a Faculty Associate in the Center of International Studies at Princeton University.

Published for the
CENTER OF INTERNATIONAL STUDIES,
PRINCETON UNIVERSITY.
A list of other Center publications
appears at the back of this book.

THE
POLITICS OF FORCE

Bargaining During

International Crises

BY ORAN R. YOUNG

PRINCETON, NEW JERSEY
PRINCETON UNIVERSITY PRESS
1968

To Harold Sprout

Preface

There are periods in the study of many subjects in which conceptualizing activities unaccompanied by systematic empirical analysis are both justifiable and fruitful. This is often true when a new area of research is just beginning to open up, or when drastic changes in the empirical referents of a subject necessitate far-reaching intellectual adaptations. In recent years the latter case has been exemplified, to a considerable degree, in analyses of the determinants of the role of organized coercion in international politics and international stability. Under such circumstances, the use of empirical materials for research tends to focus on: attempts to generate new thoughts, concepts, and questions by browsing widely in the field; efforts to develop sweeping, unstructured generalizations; and attempts to illustrate points so as to establish their relevance to the real world. As Schelling aptly phrases it in the preface to *Arms and Influence*: "I have used some historical examples, but usually as illustrations, not evidence."[1]

In the analysis of intrinsically empirical subjects, however, a point is almost inevitably reached at which this kind of relatively unadorned conceptualizing becomes increasingly unsatisfactory. First, attention begins to focus on overly subtle nuances and excessive conceptual hair-splitting rather than on efforts to match concepts and realities. Second, debates about intrinsically empirical points begin to focus on the confrontation of sweeping but largely unsubstantiated generalizations championed on an *ex cathedra* basis. Third, there is apt to be a growing emphasis on the construction of simple inventories of previously formulated concepts, questions, hypotheses, and so forth. There have been striking developments along these lines in recent studies of the determinants of the role of organized coercion in international politics and international stability.

Such developments do *not* indicate that these subjects should

[1] Thomas Schelling, *Arms and Influence* (New Haven: Yale University Press, 1966), p. vii.

be abandoned for greener pastures, a solution that may recommend itself too easily to those committed to conceptualizing activities unaccompanied by systematic empirical analysis. Conditions of this kind do indicate, however, a substantial need to formulate a new relationship between conceptual and empirical work based on a more systematic approach to empirical analysis and the development of a two-way flow between conceptualization and empirical analysis. It is of critical importance that conceptual work not be deemphasized and allowed to wither away. Even a brief experience with the problems arising from the application of inductive procedures without devoting sufficient attention to the relevant conceptual issues is sufficient to make this clear.[2] What is needed instead is an upgrading of empirical analysis relative to conceptual work, and a conscious effort to combine the two activities in fruitful ways.

The development of a viable combination of this kind, applicable to the analysis of many aspects of international politics, is a major objective of the present study. Most of this book is devoted to systematic and comparative analyses of patterns of coercion in specific cases of international crisis. But this empirical work is organized in terms of, and rests squarely upon, an extensive effort to develop an integrated set of concepts, questions, and hypotheses about bargaining under conditions of crisis.

This procedure nevertheless raises additional questions about the functions of empirical analysis in a study of this kind. The use of empirical materials, even in a highly systematic fashion, rarely leads to absolute "proofs" of hypotheses about empirical relationships in any formal sense. This is true of analyses in the natural sciences as well as the social sciences—in contrast to such nonempirical subjects as logic and mathematics. As a result, absolute proof is seldom the key objective of analyses in the empirical disciplines. Such analyses therefore tend to

[2] For a fuller discussion of the problems attendant upon the application of inductive procedures without devoting adequate attention to conceptual problems of an antecedent nature, consult Oran R. Young, *Systems of Political Science* (Englewood Cliffs, N.J.: Prentice-Hall, 1968), Chap. 7.

focus more on efforts to raise the level of confidence in generalizations about empirical relationships, and on attempts to provide satisfying explanations of observed phenomena.

At the same time, the use of empirical materials on a systematic basis fulfills other specific functions. First, systematic empirical analysis exerts pressures to integrate concepts, questions, and hypotheses into a coordinated, coherent whole rather than leave them as an unstructured and only vaguely related collection of ideas. Second, empirical analysis serves as a sounding board and corrective for abstract conceptualizing which might otherwise degenerate into mere proliferation of logically plausible categories. Third, systematic empirical application of a given set of hypotheses often leads to novel conclusions, new questions, or new concepts and patterns of explanation. Fourth, the test of empirical application is often useful in developing guidelines for discriminating between fertile and arid channels for further research.

The present study thus has important epistemological and substantive objectives. From an epistemological perspective, the book attempts to formulate a research strategy between the extremes of unadorned conceptualizing (or unstructured generalizing) and puristic induction which may be useful in the analysis of many aspects of international politics. On the substantive side, this volume constitutes a continuation of my earlier work on the nature of conflict and the role of coercion in international politics. Whereas my earlier book[3] focused on problems associated with the termination of conflict, this one deals with problems attendant upon the acquisition and utilization of influence to achieve political objectives in crises.

This study was conceived under the aegis of the Center of International Studies at Princeton University and supported by that institution throughout. I therefore have the pleasure, once again, of expressing my gratitude to Klaus Knorr, director of the Center, as well as to Jane McDowall and the Center's outstanding secretarial staff. I also wish to take this opportunity to offer my thanks and appreciation to colleagues,

[3] Oran R. Young, *The Intermediaries: Third Parties in International Crises* (Princeton: Princeton University Press, 1967).

acquaintances, and students who listened patiently while I developed my ideas on the topics treated in this volume, despite the fact that those ideas frequently emerged in bits and pieces or only in embryonic forms. Finally, it is a pleasure to thank William McClung and Roy Thomas of Princeton University Press for their assistance in my efforts to make the prose in this book readable.　　　　　　　　　　　O. R. Y.

Princeton, New Jersey
February 1968

Contents

CONTENTS

PART I
CRISES AND BARGAINING

Introduction

This book is about bargaining under conditions of international crisis. It is an attempt to analyze regularities in bargaining processes characteristic of international crises and to spell out how bargaining during crises differs from bargaining in other contexts.

Crises are recurrent and influential phenomena in international politics that are both complex and ambiguous. This leads to substantial difficulties in developing definitions that help to distinguish crises from the ordinary flow of international politics. Moreover, there are several fundamentally divergent perspectives from which to analyze international crises. The present study treats crises primarily as processes of interaction among the actors in international politics rather than as determinants of the internal politics of individual states. Focusing on interaction in this way does not at all imply a decision to ignore questions dealing with decision-making processes within individual states. It does, however, imply an analysis of the phenomenon of international crisis primarily as a topic in international politics rather than as a topic in the internal politics of individual states.

This focus on bargaining under conditions of crisis stems from two broader sets of interests to which the phenomenon of crisis is distinctly relevant. The first centers on the problem of stability in the international system as a whole. It is logically plausible that the international system could break down precipitously and decisively as a result of an all-out "strike from the blue," especially in periods when the destructive capacity of the component actors relative to the dimensions of the overall system is great.[1] Nevertheless, the disin-

---

[1] It is important to emphasize there are two elements in this calculation —the level of destructive capacity and the dimensions of the international system. While the contemporary revolution in military technology is impressive, many discussions of the impact of these developments concentrate on changes in destructive capacity to the exclusion of changes in the dimensions of the system. Careful analysis would in fact almost certainly indicate that the relative influence of destructive capacity was equally impressive in various past periods in which international politics was not based on a global system.

centives associated with strikes of this kind have always been sufficiently great in modern history to make disruption of this kind relatively improbable. At the same time, the international system has manifested sufficient resilience to remain fundamentally stable except under the impact of violence of extreme proportions. Under these conditions, crises assume a major role in determining the stability of the system. A crisis per se is unlikely to disrupt the international system. But a severe crisis involving the great powers or a series of interlocking and amplifying crises represents one of the most plausible ways for the stability of the international system to be seriously challenged.

This interest in the problem of international stability has important implications for the selection of specific crises for detailed analysis. The present study deals mainly with crises of sufficient magnitude to generate potential challenges to the stability of the international system. The most important and relevant cases are therefore those directly involving the superpowers, or having the potential to produce such an involvement, and those in which the participants possess relatively high levels of destructive capacity. Crises of lesser magnitude are likely to be conducted on a less constrained basis precisely because the links between such crises and the stability of the international system are weaker.

The second set of underlying interests concerns the role of force in international politics. In general, there is a substantial need for more highly developed and sophisticated concepts in this area, particularly in the middle ground between the strictly military and the predominantly nonmilitary aspects of *coercion* in international politics. Unfortunately, work in this area has been severely hampered by a number of fundamental images, prevalent throughout recent history, of the role of force in international politics. The insistence on a sharp dichotomy between war and peace and the tendency to think of highly coercive situations as contests of physical strength, for example, make it difficult to think sophisticatedly about intermediate forms of coercion.[2] As a result, there is at present a great need for new conceptualization about: the dif-

[2] Such distinctions may lead, moreover, to further dichotomies of

ferences between violent and nonviolent techniques of coercion; the pursuit of coercive objectives in highly politicized contexts; the utilization of contingent actions for coercive purposes; and the achievement of coercive goals through efforts to define the basic context of a clash in contrast to the more straightforward application of physical force.

A study of bargaining under conditions of crisis is particularly well-suited to the development of new concepts, questions, and hypotheses concerning intermediate forms of coercion in international politics. Crises tend to become highly coercive, but they generally develop in ways that emphasize the distinctions between coercion in general and violent coercion. They are therefore *not* apt to be dominated from the outset by the imagery of overt warfare or contests of physical strength. At the same time, crises virtually always develop into highly politicized clashes. They are often clearly visible in the flow of international politics as well as influential watersheds in the history of international politics.

---

dubious validity such as the contrasts between politics and force or between unconditional victory and unconditional defeat.

1. Crises in International Politics

There is no accepted definition of international crisis or even of crisis in general. This lack of consensus is one of the most striking impressions to be gained from a perusal of previous work in the field. Part of the difficulty lies in the diffuse and variable subject matter that has from time to time been lumped under the convenient heading of crisis. Further explanation may be found in the problem of diverging perspectives on crises. The orientation of the observer thus makes considerable difference in his perception and definition of what constitutes a crisis. For example, there is frequently a large gap between the perspective of an individual state and the perspective of the overall international system in assessing the nature and workings of crises. Within a given state, it is common to speak of crises in the cities, in programs of economic development, or in agricultural production. But all these situations are limited by the fact that they occur within the confines of an operative political community. Moreover, events constituting a serious crisis for an individual state within the international system may never reach the level of crisis from the perspective of the system as a whole. Throughout modern history the international system has been highly decentralized and capable of withstanding major reorganizations within its subsystems; many crises within its component units, therefore, have had little effect on the system as a whole. Severe international crises, on the other hand, raise special problems, both because of the absence of well-developed control mechanisms operating above the participants and because of their potential for catalyzing large-scale destruction.

Toward a Definition of International Crisis

There are several distinguishable level of abstraction at which it is possible to approach the problem of defining international crisis. It seems appropriate to begin with a discussion of several generic or "essential" definitions. In general terms a crisis can be thought of as an acute transition in the

6

state of a certain system or, to be even more specific, as a decisive or critical stage in the flow of events that together constitute an acute transition: for example, the events preceding the outbreak of war in August 1914 and the reoccupation of the Rhineland by Germany in March 1936. This definition has the advantage of preserving the original Greek conception of a crisis as a turning point, an event or period after which specified relationships are qualitatively altered from their previous state.[1]

There are, however, important difficulties in utilizing this definition of crisis in analyses of international politics. First, there has been little agreement on the essential nature of the international system itself, let alone its exact specifications at any given point in time. With the exception of certain radical types of change, therefore, it is generally impossible to get agreement on what would constitute an acute transition in the state of the system. Second, the international system has long been characterized by a marked capacity to retain its essential dimensions as a states' system, even under the impact of large-scale upheavals. It is hard to deny, for example, that the two world wars of the twentieth century were born in crisis and that they altered a great many political relationships in the international system. Nevertheless, a decentralized, states' system with no effective higher authority is just as evident today as it was in the second half of the nineteenth century. Third, the international system has, at the same time, sustained rapid and extensive changes in a number of areas.[2] Such changes have undoubtedly resulted in important transitions from time to time, but this leads directly into a debate over the meaning of "acute" transition and "critical stage."

[1] For the etymology of the word crisis consult *The Random House Dictionary of the English Language* (New York: Random House, unabridged edn., 1966), p. 344.

[2] The nature of change in international politics during various periods of time offers a fruitful subject for analysis. It has been argued, for example, that the current era has witnessed a shift from discontinuous patterns of change to the dynamism of a constant flow. Similarly, interest in change has focused on environmental shifts in some periods while in other periods the emphasis has been more on movements affecting the nature of the actors in international politics. Nevertheless, substantial changes of one kind or another have been characteristic of international politics during most periods.

7

In general, however, an evolutionary flow of developments that ultimately exercises a widespread impact on political relationships can hardly be classified as a crisis without excessively stretching word meanings. Fourth, it is often impossible to evaluate the overall impact a crisis will have on the international system until a long time afterward. In fact, the effects of individual crises tend to ramify through the system over time. It is one thing to speak of the 1914 crisis as an acute transition, but what of the more recent clashes focusing on Suez, Quemoy, and Cuba? Each of these situations is commonly described as a crisis, yet it is still too early to make confident judgments about their role in changing the state of the international system.

Another generic definition of crisis is based on the notion that a crisis occurs when a small change or disturbance produces disproportionate effects on the system. This definition evokes an image of powerful but opposing forces in a delicate balance that can be decisively tilted in one direction or another by an otherwise limited upheaval.[3] In this connection an intrinsically circumscribed event may be a catalyst for far-reaching changes. The assassination of the Austrian archduke at Sarajevo in 1914, for example, is often interpreted in this context.

This definition of crisis, however, also causes serious difficulties for empirical analysis. In the first instance, it is *sui generis* in the sense that it does not derive from the original meaning of the term crisis. Beyond this there are greater difficulties, many reminiscent of the problems discussed above in connection with the first definition. The fundamental resilience of the international system in the face of events commonly labeled crises and the frequent delay before the effects of a crisis clearly manifest themselves make it difficult to assess the proportionality of the consequences of individual crises. Moreover, the basic notion of a delicate balance of

---

[3] It would thus be important to analyze the "crisis potential" of any given configuration of forces in international politics. In addition, a definition of this kind leads to questions about the types of precipitating events that could touch off a crisis in specific situations.

opposing forces and of disproportionate change is ambiguous. The delicacy of any given balance of forces in international politics is generally open to debate. In the contemporary international system, for example, this is a subject on which there is little or no consensus.[4] The extensiveness and proportionality of changes are sensitive, among other things, to the level of generality at which they are analyzed. As suggested above, the persistence of a states' system may be taken as evidence that even large-scale wars can occur without causing fundamental or disproportionate changes in the basic qualities of the international system. On a lower level of abstraction, however, it is evident that crises frequently do have far-reaching political repercussions. But even here it is often difficult to determine whether such consequences are actually disproportionate to the original crisis.

These generic definitions are helpful in thinking about the essential qualities of crisis. But the difficulty in applying them to empirical situations indicates that, for the purposes of this book, they do not provide adequate criteria to identify international crises. Thus, it is necessary to consider additional means for the operational identification of crises. The following paragraphs outline the key characteristics, from a nominalist perspective, of the forms of interaction in international politics to be designated crises. These characteristics do not add up to a definition of crisis in a generic or "essential" sense. Nevertheless, their enumeration is useful both in specifying the subject matter of the present study and in selecting specific cases of crisis for extended analysis in later chapters.[5]

First, a crisis is a *process* of interaction involving two or more actors in the international system which is characterized by higher levels of perceived intensity than non-crisis periods. This basic characteristic contains two major elements.

[4] For a presentation of divergent views together with references to the literature in this area, see Richard A. Falk, Robert C. Tucker, and Oran R. Young, *On Minimizing the Use of Nuclear Weapons*, Center of International Studies, Princeton University, Research Monograph No. 23, 1966.

[5] For a famous discussion of the differences between "essentialism" and "nominalism" in social science research, see Karl R. Popper, *The Poverty of Historicism* (New York: Harper Torchbook, 1964), pp. 26-34.

Crises occur in relations between actors; they are not games against nature or inanimate forces. Though crises often involve more than two participants, there is generally a primary axis of conflict separating the participants into two sides.[6] Within this general framework, two types of third party are possible. Sometimes third parties relatively impartial to the principal participants in a crisis enter the arena of conflict primarily to facilitate a termination of the crisis.[7] On other occasions there are third parties whose interests lead them to favor one side over the other and who therefore intervene in behalf of the favored side.[8]

The second element of this first characteristic concerns levels of perceived intensity. Crises are situations perceived by the participants as much more competitive than the ordinary flow of international politics. As a result, the question of levels of intensity can be thought of in terms of balances of competitive and cooperative interests. While there are virtually no situations of pure conflict in international politics, non-zero-sum situations vary markedly both in terms of actual balances of competitive and cooperative interests and in terms of the acuteness with which these balances are perceived by decision-makers.[9] In this connection, the onset of a crisis tends to shift the attention of decision-makers toward an issue or issues which incline sharply toward competition rather than cooperation.[10]

[6] The primary axis of conflict is sometimes obscured by ambiguities. For example, a crisis may draw in additional actors whose interests diverge significantly from those of the principal participants. Also, dual crises sometimes occur in which conditions of crisis emanating from different situations emerge more or less simultaneously and interact with each other in important ways.

[7] Third parties of this kind are the principal subject of Oran R. Young, *The Intermediaries: Third Parties in International Crises* (Princeton: Princeton University Press, 1967).

[8] Activities of this kind form the focus of the literature on *intervention* in international law and in theoretical work on the management of power in international politics.

[9] For a conceptual discussion of the problems of competition and cooperation in non-zero-sum situations, see *infra*, Chap. Two.

[10] In absolute terms, crises generally produce cooperative incentives as well as competitive pressures. The point here is that the balance of interests tends to shift markedly toward the competitive end of the

A second important characteristic of crises arises from their tendency to produce sharp breaks in the ordinary flow of international politics. Though specific cases are seldom entirely unambiguous, it is usually possible to discern a marked discontinuity in the regular flow of events owing to the onset and the termination of a crisis. There is therefore an important difference between general international stresses and strains —though they may get worse—and crises. A crisis is usually distinguishable from the pre-crisis and post-crisis period. General international stresses and strains, on the other hand, tend to form seamless webs whose boundaries are rather obscure and whose consequences are discernible only over a long period. The population problem in the contemporary period, for example, constitutes a stress on the system that appears to be increasing in severity. It does not constitute a crisis, however. This matter of discontinuity becomes more complex when the focus shifts from the onset of a crisis to its termination. In particular, it is important to emphasize that crisis and war are different phenomena in international politics and an attempt to equate them will only lead to confusion. Crisis can terminate either violently or nonviolently. Thus a crisis may be a catalyst for war, as in 1914, but, as shown by the Berlin crisis of 1961, it need not result in organized violence.

Further consideration of different levels of analysis leads to additional complexities. A crisis can, for example, occur within a prolonged war when a sudden break in the existing pattern of interaction produces far-reaching effects on the outcome or characteristic instrumental modes of the clash. From another perspective it is possible to think of a war occurring within a crisis. If, for example, one treats the long political struggle associated with the Napoleonic bid for supremacy as a crisis of the European states' system, it is obvious that wars can take place within periods of crisis. Similarly, the juxtaposition of these different levels of analysis makes it possible to

scale with the onset of a crisis. Among other things, it is this phenomenon that accounts for the fact that efforts on the part of noninvolved parties to emphasize the common or overlapping interests of the protagonists in a crisis sometimes play a significant role in terminating crises.

think of specific crises occurring *within* broader periods of crisis.

These considerations raise several important problems concerning levels of abstraction in the conceptualization of crises, and relevant time scales for the analysis of crises. The two problems are in fact closely related. Assuming a broad historical perspective makes it possible to assess the struggle over the Spanish succession at the opening of the eighteenth century, the clashes surrounding the Napoleonic bid for supremacy, and the showdown between Imperial Germany and the other European powers culminating in the First World War as crises affecting the prevailing international system of the time. At this level of abstraction, each of these examples is a well-demarcated turning point with far-reaching consequences for international politics. If, however, the analysis focuses on the period after the Second World War, the problem of identifying cases of international crisis is substantially different. In this more limited period, outstanding confrontations such as Berlin, Suez, and Cuba have been less disruptive and less prolonged but, treated proportionally, they seem to deserve the label crisis. There are no final answers for these problems raised by different levels of analysis. Still, it is important to keep these problems in mind since the confusion arising from attempts to make comparisons that cut across levels of abstraction can be destructive to the value of the analysis in question.

Crises at all levels of analysis, however, emerge as fundamentally short-term phenomena. This point is frequently missed in the confusion caused by different levels of abstraction in dealing with international crises. The years covered by both the Napoleonic bid for supremacy in Europe and the showdown involving Imperial Germany, for example, appear as long spans of time from the perspective of the contemporary flow of international politics. But in the light of the broader flow of modern history, these crises appear as short periods of acute transition during which events occurred that greatly changed the subsequent flow of international politics. In the postwar period, on the other hand, crises have generally lasted for a number of weeks or a few months at most. At this level of analysis also, crises emerge as phenomena of short duration but extensive influence in shaping the subsequent course of events. Thus, crises may be solved, allowed to touch off open warfare, terminated without a solution of the main issues, or simply permitted to lead to the routinization of new levels or modes of conflict, but they do not continue for indefinite periods. This combination of clearcut discontinuity with preceding and subsequent events and shortness of duration constitutes one of the key identifying characteristics of crisis in the international system.

Within this framework, some additional points about the pace of crisis interactions should be emphasized. As indicated above, crises tend to "flare up" and to produce sharp breaks in the ordinary flow of international politics. It would be a mistake, however, to expect the shift from non-crisis to crisis to occur so suddenly that the transition could be labeled with pinpoint accuracy. The individual components of a crisis are frequently present in the international setting for some time prior to the onset of the crisis, and there is generally a period of buildup to crisis in which it is difficult to determine whether a full-fledged crisis will ensue. The relevance of the notion of a "strike from the blue" that would cause an instantaneous shift from non-crisis to crisis conditions is almost as restricted now as it was in earlier eras.[11] In addition, there are variations in the clarity of crises' inception. The sudden intensification of the Chinese shelling of the Quemoy islands on August 23, 1958, clearly marks the onset of the 1958 crisis in the Taiwan Strait. The Berlin crisis of 1948-1949, on the other hand, was characterized by a period of buildup between March and June that makes it more difficult to specify the actual beginning of the crisis. Nevertheless, these boundary questions should not be overemphasized. Even in a somewhat ambiguous case such as the Berlin crisis of

---

[11] This point can be elaborated on at various levels of abstraction. In proximate terms, crises are generally preceded by significant, though often rather nebulous and ambiguous, periods of buildup. More generally, the genesis of crises is often traceable in lesser antecedent problems occurring among the relevant actors during the normal flow of international politics. For a discussion of some related problems, consult Bernard Brodie, *Escalation and the Nuclear Option* (Princeton: Princeton University Press, 1966), pp. 25-35.

1948-1949, it is possible to restrict the point of inception to a relatively short period so that the distinction between crises and stresses or strains remains meaningful.

Assessments by contemporary observers about the onset of a crisis, however, are sometimes affected by a "recognition problem."[12] Situations occasionally arise in which decision-makers, assessing the climate of international politics, conclude that there exists a significant possibility a crisis will "flare up" in the near future. Yet they frequently fail to recognize the buildup of a crisis for what it is, and the assessments of different decision-makers are apt to vary considerably in this regard. Fundamentally, this "recognition problem" stems from the fact that observers generally perceive and interpret empirical developments on the basis of deeply entrenched world views, assumptions, and explanatory devices.

A third characteristic of crisis concerns the probabilities that violence of major proportions will break out.[13] That is, the onset of a crisis is generally accompanied by a pronounced rise in the *perceived* prospects that violence will break out or that previously unacceptable modes or levels of violence will be utilized.[14] This point explicitly refers to subjective perceptions about the prospects of violence rather than to a more objective measure of the probability of violence. In fact, it is desirable not to prejudge the latter point. The feeling that violence is increasingly likely is often sufficient to catalyze actions leading either to the termination of a crisis or to the development of "rules" and procedures to keep it manageable.

Finally, though it clearly flows from the generic definitions

[12] For some interesting comments on the "recognition problem," see Harry B. Williams, "Some Functions of Communication in Crisis Behavior," *Human Organization*, Vol. 16, No. 2 (Summer 1957), 15-19.

[13] Violence should be clearly distinguished from the broader category of coercion. While violence may in fact be a form of coercion in a given situation, it refers specifically to the physical destruction of valued objects in ways that are painful to the possessor. For a discussion of a number of important nuances in the distinction between coercion and violence, see Thomas Schelling, *Arms and Influence* (New Haven: Yale University Press, 1966), pp. 2-18.

[14] While crisis is distinguishable from war, violence is not necessarily absent in conditions of crisis. The point here concerns the prospects that *large-scale violence* will break out. On the relationship of violence to crisis, see *infra*, p. 17.

of crisis, it should be stressed that crises are processes of inter-action having important implications for the stability of some system or subsystem (or pattern of relationships) in interna-tional politics. This concept of stability refers to the capacity of a system or subsystem to sustain disturbances without breaking down or undergoing qualitative changes. Degrees or levels of stability can therefore be conceptualized in terms of the types and intensities of disturbance that a system or sub-system is able to survive intact.

Several additional points about stability are useful in the effort to identify crises in international politics. Within the in-ternational system crises may occur at various system levels, ranging from isolated local situations between two small states to extreme systemwide upheavals involving several states. Many crises in international politics occur at levels low enough so that their destabilizing impact upon the interna-tional system, or even on its major subsystems, is never serious. The decentralized quality of the international system tends to give it a high degree of crisis tolerance and allows sub-stantial reshuffling to occur at the local level without signif-icantly undermining the stability of the system as a whole. Moreover, to determine the impact of crises upon stability, it is often useful to distinguish between proximate conse-quences and long-run potentialities. A crisis that does not di-rectly undermine the stability of a given system or subsys-tem (or pattern of relationships), for example, may still cause potential instabilities of far-reaching significance by touching off repercussions which, if unchecked, could eventually de-stroy it.

To sum up, then, a crisis in international politics is a proc-ess of interaction occurring at higher levels of perceived in-tensity than the ordinary flow of events and characterized by: a sharp break from the ordinary flow of politics; shortness of duration; a rise in the perceived prospects that violence will break out; and significant implications for the stability of some system or subsystem (or pattern of relationships) in international politics. These characteristics, though not add-ing up to an "essential" definition of crisis, do provide useful criteria for the empirical identification of crises for analysis.

Related Concepts

The preceding discussion is directed toward the identification of crises in international politics. There are, however, several additional aspects of international crisis that require conceptualization in analyzing bargaining under conditions of crisis. A number of lists and surveys of concepts relating to international crisis have appeared over time.[15] But these efforts do not, unfortunately, have any cumulative significance, and their inadequacies, at least for constructing theoretical statements concerning crises, are extensive.

Several additional points concerning the links between crisis and intensity levels or degrees of conflict deserve comment. It is a mistake to think of crisis springing from a setting characterized by absence of conflict among the relevant participants. All relations among states in international politics are fundamentally competitive-cooperative in nature, meaning that elements of conflict and potential conflict in such relations are present at all times. Moreover, balances between competitive and cooperative interests tend to fluctuate dynamically and to produce complex interpenetrations of diverging interests. For this reason, conflict and even crisis are not "abnormal" conditions in international politics. It is therefore important to conceptualize crisis as a merging, intensification and acceleration of the "normal" or everyday patterns of conflict in the relations of actors in the international system.

Usually, crises do not end in such a way as to produce entirely cooperative relations among the participants. Although solutions are occasionally found for the substantive issues underlying a crisis, and although crises sometimes lead to overt warfare, crises more commonly "end" by *de facto* subsidence with the substantive issues unresolved or by the routinization of new forms of conflict.

The place of crisis in relations among states can be seen in the diagram below. Here the zone of crisis, la-

---

15 For convenient reference, consult C. F. Hermann, ed., *Contemporary Research in International Crises* (forthcoming), and A. J. Wiener and H. Kahn, eds., *Crisis and Arms Control*, Hudson Institute, HI-180-RR, 1962.

in straightforward descriptive terms, dividing the crisis into several time periods separated by events of particular salience.[18] Unfortunately, the value of this procedure for the more analytic requirements of this book may be limited. While the temporal dimension is an important one, it is also necessary to treat the problem of phases in terms of underlying shifts of analytic significance rather than simple sequential descriptions.

Among the principal problems associated with conditions of crisis are those related to the controllability of crisis interactions. There is great controversy concerning the extent to which the participants' control over events declines, if at all, with the onset of a crisis.[19] But there is little doubt that decision-makers commonly believe their ability to control events is substantially lowered during crises. The possibilities of an escalating conflict as well as of a sudden "explosion" to large-scale warfare appear more plausible under conditions of crisis. Moreover, the perceptual proximity of potential physical destruction may increase, and decision-makers commonly acquire a sense of personal responsibility for such matters during crises. Particularly important in shaping perceptions apropos of control are characteristics of crisis tending to emphasize the uncertainties associated with the situation and to underline the interdependent nature of the international bargaining process. Under these circumstances, normal problems of prediction in international politics are often accentuated, making systematic or fully rational planning extremely difficult.[20] For all these reasons, it is not unusual during crises

[18] The logic of prevailing historical methodologies has frequently dictated such an approach in studies of crises written by historians. Moreover, by their very nature journalistic reconstructions of contemporary crises are apt to be primarily descriptive.

[19] The idea of decline in control capabilities has been developed especially by the Stanford group in various analyses of the 1914 crisis. Consult, *inter alia*, R. C. North, O. R. Holsti, M. G. Zaninovich, and Dina A. Zinnes, *Content Analysis: A Handbook with Applications for the Study of International Crises* (Evanston, Ill.: Northwestern University Press, 1963). For a cogent argument disputing this idea, see Albert and Roberta Wohlstetter, *op.cit.* Available evidence in this complex area suggests that it constitutes a fruitful one for additional research.

[20] Schelling, in fact, appears to take this as a defining characteristic of crisis. See his argument that "The essence of . . . crisis is its unpredict-

for perceptions to develop that the situation has acquired a certain self-sustaining force or impetus of its own and that the ability of individual actors to exercise control over the course of events has therefore declined.

The distinction, which has arisen at several points, between the "actual" course of events and perceptions of them is an important one in analyzing international crises.[21] Various actors may well perceive the same sequence of events differently. One party may place the beginning of a crisis at a different time than other parties or even, in extreme cases, perceive no crisis where others do. And the events surrounding a crisis may achieve substantially different levels of visibility for various actors. Also, during the actual crisis, it is even more common for perceptual divergences to occur about levels of intensity or conflict, problems of risk and controllability, and the existence of relevant options or programs of action.

Perceptual divergences can obviously have far-reaching effects on bargaining processes in any crisis. When the underlying conflict is especially severe, asymmetries of this kind may occasionally be utilized in the interests of keeping the situation within manageable proportions.[22] They may, for example, operate to obscure certain irreconcilable positions or to open the way for third parties to influence the course of the

---

ability. The 'crisis' that is confidently believed to involve no danger of things getting out of hand is no crisis: no matter how energetic the activity, as long as things are believed safe there is no crisis. And a 'crisis' that is known to entail disaster or large losses, or great changes of some sort that are completely foreseeable, is also no crisis; it is over as soon as it begins, there is no suspense." (Schelling, *op.cit.*, p. 97). This argument is obviously an interesting one. Its value appears, however, to be limited for definitional purposes since few serious candidates for the label crisis would fail to pass the test set by these criteria.

[21] The word actual is placed in quotations here to avoid the classic argument over the existence and nature of reality. The distinction in this instance refers to definitions or descriptions of events as they might be formulated by an impartial observer on the one hand and by an involved party on the other.

[22] For a particularly interesting discussion of utilizing asymmetries of this kind for regulatory purposes, see Carl Stevens, *Strategy and Collective Bargaining Negotiation* (New York: McGraw-Hill, 1963), Chap. VII.

interaction.[23] But at the same time, perceptual divergences may allow considerable scope for tactical manipulation on the part of the principals.[24] An actor appearing to have fewer worries about the risks and dangers associated with a crisis, for example, will tend to acquire important advantages by being able to adopt more intransigent postures than its adversaries. Up to a point, an asymmetrical distribution of fears of this kind will even operate to protect the intransigent side via an amplifying feedback process.[25] On the other hand, advantages sometimes accrue to a party that appears "unreasonably" exercised over the dangers in a situation, therefore projecting a credible image that it cannot be counted on to act calmly or cautiously under the circumstances. Even more simply, there are occasionally advantages to be had from a mere demonstration of inability to perceive certain important aspects of a situation at all. These perceptual problems do not affect the existence of a crisis in any objective sense. But they do emphasize the central position of bargaining in conditions of crisis as well as in the more general flow of international politics.

Finally, in preparation for the systematic comparative analysis of later chapters, it is of some interest to explore the possibility of constructing classifications or typologies of crisis. There is a wide range of potential classificatory variables, including: the types and numbers of participants; geographical location and scope; substantive issues involved; type of initiating or opening sequence; existing levels of conflict at the outset of crisis; and ceiling and floor levels of coercion and violence. In general, classifications along these lines

[23] For a discussion of problems along these lines formulated specifically in terms of international crisis, see Young, *op.cit.*, Chap. I.

[24] One of Schelling's most important contributions lies in the exploration of perceptual phenomena from this perspective. For a very provocative treatment of a wide range of examples, consult Thomas Schelling, *The Strategy of Conflict* (Cambridge: Harvard University Press, 1960).

[25] In other words, the more intransigent B becomes, the more A's fears concerning the dangers of the situation are likely to rise. Thus, B's initial acts of intransigence may increase his leeway to act in a similar fashion subsequently. For a related discussion of this sort of behavior, see *ibid.*, Chap. 8.

21

are apt to be particularly useful in determining the conditions under which various hypotheses concerning crisis will hold. Several specific classificatory schemes seem especially relevant to the present study.

To begin with, the initiating sequence of a crisis can greatly affect the distribution of bargaining advantages among the principals, the prospects that major violence will ensue, and the stability of the overall interaction process associated with a crisis. Many distinguishable initiating sequences stand out from this perspective. First, there is the situation that arises when one side is discovered in the act of preparing a *fait accompli* designed to alter a significant balance of forces without touching off overt hostilities. This is what happened with the American discovery of the Soviet move to deploy offensive missiles in Cuba in 1962. Second, a crisis is possible when side A responds to important political or economic actions of side B indirectly but in such a way as to place great pressure on side B. A clearcut example of this is the blockade of Berlin in 1948, which the Soviets imposed in response to the initiatives of the Western powers in the Western zones of Germany. Third, a crisis will develop when side A responds to severe but nonviolent provocations on the part of side B with a limited application of military force in some form. This appears to have been the sequence of events at the outset of the Sino-Indian clash of October 1962. Fourth, a crisis is likely when one side employs military force to conduct a probe (without an overt invasion) which the opponent refuses to permit without a struggle. An example of this sequence occurred during August 1958 with the start of the Taiwan Strait crisis. Fifth, a crisis will develop almost immediately following a significant invasion by side A into side B's territory, which is resisted by B. The invasion of Egyptian territory by an Anglo-French expeditionary force in the autumn of 1956 constitutes a fairly good instance of this sequence.[26] Sixth, two parties can, through various processes,

26 Other developments, however, make this specific case a complex one. It is, for example, quite plausible to treat the clash between Israel and Egypt during the same period as a war. Nevertheless, the elements of circumspection and restraint in the confrontation between the Anglo-

become involved in a crisis with each other as a consequence of mutual intervention in an upheaval that originated as an internal problem within a given country. The 1958 crisis in the Middle East, for example, had characteristics of this kind. But this last category covers a variety of specific processes through which an international crisis can occur.

There is also a more abstract classification scheme that seems interesting in the context of the present study. Here the principal focus is on significant differences in the underlying dynamics and fundamental processes of crises. A number of basic types or classes of crisis emerge from this perspective.[27] A *positive feedback* crisis is a pattern of interaction based on a series of sequential, mutual, and amplifying responses. This is the basis of most escalation processes, arms races, and "security dilemmas." An *overload* crisis is a situation in which too many demands are placed on a given system in too short a time, leading either to complete breakdown or to serious short-circuiting. The reverse of the overload crisis, and less common in political situations, is a *starvation* crisis, which results from an inadequate supply of inputs: for example, when a pattern of relationships begins to disintegrate following a decline in political or economic support. Failures of negative feedback procedures or mechanisms can generate a *steering* crisis resulting in a loss of ability to select appropriate responses in situations requiring decisions. Finally, *adaptation* crises can occur when marked changes in some aspects of the international system are not accompanied by proportionate changes in other aspects of the system. Rapid changes in critical political balances or military technologies, for example, frequently generate adaptation crises in international politics.

Given the highly decentralized quality of the international system, there is good reason to suppose that positive feedback crises and adaptation crises will probably constitute the

---

French expeditionary force and the Egyptians indicate that at least certain portions of the events of 1956 in the Middle East can be accurately construed as a crisis.

[27] For a somewhat lengthier effort to work out the features of a classificatory scheme along these lines, consult Young, *op.cit.*, Chap. I.

predominant patterns of crisis affecting the overall system. In short, the other types of crisis are more common in situations characterized by the presence of relatively formal political institutions. This is not to argue that crises of these latter types are impossible in the international arena. It does, nevertheless, suggest a significant difference between the international system and the political systems of most individual states. This separation of crises into various classes also provides useful guidelines in distinguishing between relevant and irrelevant concepts for the analysis of international crisis.[28]

[28] In particular, this procedure offers a useful perspective on the so-called correspondence problem. It is therefore helpful in distinguishing between concepts whose fit with the substantive matters under analysis is good and concepts whose fit is poor. On this subject consult Martin Landau, "Due Process of Inquiry," *The American Behavioral Scientist*, IX, No. 2 (October 1965), 4-10.

2. The Bases of International Bargaining

The second focal element of this book concerns the processes of bargaining among the actors in the international system. It should be reemphasized that the study is based squarely on the proposition that international politics contains few significant zero-sum situations in the sense that the gains and losses of the participants add up to zero.[1] Not only do the parties involved in international bargaining generally possess specific common interests, several features of the overall system itself tend to infuse some cooperation into specific bargaining situations. The iterative aspects of international politics make it necessary for participants in any given situation to consider the effects of their immediate actions on their future relationships. The multiplicity of actors in the system causes the bargaining relationship of any two to be constrained by their interest in later dealing profitably with the others. Moreover, while the international political system is highly decentralized and noninstitutionalized, certain basic elements of society, in the sense of a normative substructure setting up at least minimal rules of the game, support international politics.[2]

The fact that international politics is not for the most part composed of zero-sum situations has important implications for the present study. In the first place, extensive bargaining is peculiarly characteristic of the "limited adversary" relationships that arise in non-zero-sum situations.[3] The closer a situa-

[1] This proposition has been explored sufficiently in a number of recent analyses, so it is unnecessary to offer a review of the evidence in support of it here. See, *inter alia*, Thomas Schelling, *The Strategy of Conflict* (Cambridge: Harvard University Press, 1960); Kenneth Boulding, *Conflict and Defense* (New York: Harper and Row, 1962); and Raymond Aron, *Peace and War* (Garden City, N.Y.: Doubleday, 1966).

[2] For interesting discussions concerning the elements of society underlying political interactions in the international system, see Hedley Bull, "Society and Anarchy in International Relations," in *Diplomatic Investigations*, eds. Herbert Butterfield and Martin Wight (London: Allen and Unwin, 1966), pp. 35-50; and C.A.W. Manning, *The Nature of International Society* (New York: John Wiley, 1962).

[3] The phrase "limited adversary" is Marshal Shulman's. For develop-

tion approaches the pole of pure conflict, in which the participants have no common or overlapping interests at all, the more likely it is to devolve into a straightforward contest of physical strength with little (if any) room for bargaining. In extreme cases of conflict it becomes difficult to maintain even minimal rules of the game, let alone to stimulate more substantive common interests. The more a situation becomes one of pure cooperation, on the other hand, the more likely it is to produce joint planning designed to maximize community benefits rather than debate between the participants over the distribution of payoffs. Between these two limits the relative weights of competitive and cooperative interests vary greatly among individual bargaining situations, constituting an important determinant of international bargaining. It is the very mixing and interpenetration of these two elements which produce the characteristic processes of bargaining in international politics.

In addition, it is fundamentally erroneous to conceptualize bargaining as an alternative to coercion, for they do not occupy the same level of generality let alone the same conceptual axis. While bargaining refers to certain types of interaction processes involving two or more actors, coercion refers to one of the principal *modes* such processes can take. Bargaining in international situations does in fact frequently involve the use of both various forms of violence and coercive pressures short of physical force. Nevertheless, important bargaining activities occur regularly all along the spectrum from persuasion without coercion to the most violent forms of coercion. Activities in these different modes often interact to make specific bargaining relationships extremely complex.

Since bargaining is essentially an interaction process, the nature of the interaction itself forms the basic focus for analysis, and here it is important to distinguish certain aspects of the overall interaction process. There is a difference between the scope and domain of a bargaining situation. Following Lasswell and Kaplan, scope refers to the issues or values at stake in a bargaining situation while domain designates the

ment of this notion in the context of evolving Soviet-American relations, see his *Beyond the Cold War* (New Haven: Yale University Press, 1966).

actors or groups of actors in the interaction process.[4] Next is the phenomenon of mode, referred to above. In analyzing bargaining under conditions of crisis, the distinction between coercion and violence is a particularly important one.[5] Coercion is a broad category encompassing all efforts to shape the decisions or actions of others actors against their wills. There is a direct contrast, therefore, between coercion and persuasion.[6] Violence, on the other hand, refers to the painful destruction of human and physical values. Violence employed as a rational means to achieve political objectives becomes a subset of coercion.[7] In general, crises tend to produce highly coercive forms of bargaining in international politics, but they also frequently impose important restraints on the use of violence for coercive purposes. This opens up another major element of bargaining processes—the employment of tactical maneuvers and devices. The notion of tactics in this context is a complex one since it refers to a wide variety of ways actors can combine, deploy, and manipulate tangible and intangible resources to increase their bargaining strength vis-à-vis other participants in a given interaction process. The impact of conditions of crisis on the relevance and utility of various bargaining tactics is a major subject for analysis in this book.

The interaction processes characteristic of bargaining occur in a broad *setting* apt to influence significantly particular bargaining situations. In general, the distribution of power within the international system at any given time may play a major role in shaping the basic nature and course of specific bargaining processes. A bipolar situation involving rigid blocs,

[4] For further discussion of these concepts, see Harold Lasswell and Abraham Kaplan, *Power and Society* (New Haven: Yale University Press, 1950), pp. 77-78.

[5] See Thomas Schelling, *Arms and Influence* (New Haven: Yale University Press, 1966), pp. 2-18.

[6] For a conceptual discussion of international coercion (contrasted with persuasion), see Myres McDougal and Associates, *Studies in World Public Order* (New Haven: Yale University Press, 1960), pp. 247-272.

[7] Violence does not always produce rational results, however. Calculated violence sometimes backfires in the sense that it causes the adversary to stiffen his posture. In addition, violence is sometimes carried out in a nonrational fashion in the sense that it bears no discernible relationship to purposive actions.

for example, will create a setting for bargaining quite different from that produced by a more fluid multipolar system. Similarly, the underlying normative structure of the international arena and the operative arrangements for regulating power in international politics importantly affect bargaining processes. The significance of these factors frequently originates from asymmetries and peculiarities that provide opportunities for manipulative bargaining as well as from the more basic regularities shaping the interaction processes. Various contextual factors also generally condition the interaction processes of bargaining. The quality of the technological environment, for example, often profoundly influences political interactions. Moreover, the setting of any given bargaining situation is usually conditioned by the prior relationships among the participants. An atmosphere marked by positive feelings of friendly association or by the hostility of cold war can greatly affect the development of attitudes, predispositions, expectations, and evaluations in a given interaction process. Finally, the domestic political climate within the states involved is frequently an important factor in international bargaining. While this is not a primary focus of the present study, it should be kept in mind when analyzing bargaining under conditions of crisis.

Competitive-Cooperative Bargaining

Non-zero-sum bargaining relationships[8] are characterized both by a fundamental interdependence among the participants and by a mixing of the motives of each. Interdependence arises from the fact that no participant can exercise full control over the course of the interaction.[9] As a result, each must take into account both the actual and potential actions of the others in deciding upon its own. Such bargaining relationships are therefore contingent by nature: the policies of the participants usually take the form that "if party X does A,

[8] Zero-sum situations are substantially simpler in conceptual terms than non-zero-sum situations and have been analyzed much more systematically. Increasing attention has been devoted to non-zero-sum problems, however. Schelling's *The Strategy of Conflict*, *op.cit.*, at present remains the single most important work in this area.

[9] There are, of course, degrees of interdependence. See *ibid.*, Chap. 4.

then we must respond with B," or that "we must initiate action C in the hopes of eliciting response D from party X." Under these circumstances, expectations about other parties, the projection of expectations about one's own state, and various bargaining tactics tend to become criticially important.

The phenomenon of mixed motives does not refer to a situation in which the motives of individual participants are ambiguous or confused,[10] but to the fact that in competitive-cooperative bargaining each party generally has motives indicating both competitive interests and cooperative interests as far as its relationships with each of the others are concerned. Problems of calculation and communication in this area sometimes arise from a tendency to formulate competitive and cooperative interests at different levels of generality. But the basic nature of the bargaining situation in a non-zero-sum relationship comes from multiple motives creating divergent pressures with regard to the substantive outcome of the interaction but also interacting extensively with each other.

Even in simple and straightforward cases of competitive-cooperative bargaining many outcomes are likely to be plausible. Most simply, the relationship can revert to the *status quo ante* with no gains or losses being registered on either side. This in fact happens regularly in international bargaining, though there is a tendency for it to shade gradually into a second type of outcome characterized by some degree of loss for both sides. This second type has been analyzed in detail in its pure form under the heading of the prisoner's dilemma.[11] A number of analysts have argued that problems of this kind are almost always a serious impediment to constructive bargaining in a highly decentralized system such as the international system.[12] Another outcome of a specific interaction may be that one side loses while the other gains.

[10] *Ibid.*, p. 89.

[11] For extended discussions of the prisoner's dilemma, see Anatol Rapoport and Albert M. Chammah, *Prisoner's Dilemma* (Ann Arbor: University of Michigan Press, 1965).

[12] Kenneth Boulding has argued this position with particular vigor. For a recent example see his "The Learning and Reality-Testing Process in the International System," *Journal of International Affairs*, XXI, No. 1 (1967), 1-15.

The relative proportions of gains and losses may vary greatly, depending upon the structure of the relationship and the bargaining skills of the participants. A variation of this type includes cases in which the value position of one side remains unchanged while the other side either gains or loses. Finally, most competitive-cooperative bargaining relationships can lead to gains for both sides as well as mutual losses. It is noteworthy, however, that only a small fraction of the possible outcomes resulting in mutual gains in a given bargaining situation will also produce a symmetrical distribution of gains. The problem of distributing gains, therefore, can generate a kind of secondary competition even in essentially cooperative bargaining relationships.

But this simplified picture of competitive-cooperative bargaining contains a fundamental structural symmetry which limits its descriptive applicability. Thus, it is necessary to introduce several distinguishable forms of variability that frequently shape bargaining relationships of this kind. As has been noted, the relative weights of competition and cooperation in the overall relationship may vary substantially. Where all the participants are strongly competitive, the proportion of possible outcomes characterized by mutual gains will be small. Mutual orientation toward cooperative interests, on the other hand, will produce the opposite result, shifting the bargaining away from primary competition involving the fundamental nature of the relationship and toward secondary competition associated with the distribution of benefits. Next, asymmetries may often exist in a bargaining process in regard to the balances between competitive and cooperative orientations of the individual parties. Some participants may perceive a given situation much more competitively than others. Individual balances of this kind frequently vary considerably during the course of a specific bargaining process. And these asymmetries among individual participants may interact with variations in the relative weights of competition and cooperation in the overall relationship, mentioned above, to increase the number of plausible patterns for specific cases. In addition, certain *ad hoc* problems can lead to variability in competitive-cooperative bargaining processes. Nonrational perceptual rigidities or various physical limitations, for example, may arbitrarily or artificially exclude some of the logically plausible outcomes in a given bargaining situation. Such a development has important implications for bargaining since it can either increase or reduce the scope for "cooperative haggling."

Within this broad framework, analyses of bargaining generally focus on: the actual processes through which a specific bargain is achieved; the determinants of gains and losses for the various participants; and the consequences of the outcome, in specific cases of bargaining, for the broader patterns of relationships within which bargaining occurs. The complexities introduced into assessment of these questions by the coexistence of competitive and cooperative interests are often made even more difficult, however, by the problem of interdependent utilities.[13] Stated by way of example, the critical problem here is to determine whether party X treats a gain by party Y as a loss for itself requiring compensation or as a gain for itself to be responded to with a reduction in its own expectations. Or to consider the opposite case, it is important to know whether X will accept a greater loss itself if it is clear this will also produce an increase in Y's losses. In formal game theory, this set of problems is frequently avoided essentially by openly prescribing a rule that an actor should never take interdependent utilities into account in making decisions about its own course of action.[14] In international bargaining, however, compartmentalization of this kind is frequently impossible to sustain.

Bargaining Contexts and Processes

In concrete cases, bargaining relationships usually become more complex than in abstract discussions. The interpenetration of competitive and cooperative interests often becomes so subtle and ambiguous that it is extremely difficult to assess

[13] A provocative treatment of some aspects of this problem is given by Stefan Valavanis, "The Resolution of Conflict When Utilities Interact," *Journal of Conflict Resolution*, II, No. 2 (June 1958), 156-169.

[14] In the discussion of side payments, game theorists often allow some of the problems associated with interdependent utilities to reenter by the back door. The general prescription against considering interdependent utilities, however, remains.

during the actual course of bargaining or to reconstruct for *ex post facto* analysis. Among other things, the exact nature of this interpenetration can shift substantially throughout the interaction process in response to participants' volatile perceptions about the changing character of the relationship itself as well as about alterations in their relative bargaining strength. Moreover, the fact that there are major advantages to be gained in bargaining from the manipulation of interests, information, resolve, and rationality adds to the difficulties of assessing the true dimensions of a bargaining situation.

Within the range of outcomes for specific situations resulting in gains for both sides, virtually every point represents an outcome such that each side could afford to settle for less and still emerge from the bargaining with a favorable bargain. Similarly, for virtually any point within the range of outcomes constituting mutual loss there is at least one alternative that would result in reduced losses for both sides. These facts illustrate the interdependent and contingent nature of competitive-cooperative bargaining. At the same time, they emphasize the competitive aspects of bargaining, even within a range of essentially cooperative outcomes: participant X will try to achieve an outcome as close as possible to his maximum benefit while participant Y tries to do the same for himself. But behavior along these lines can reintroduce zero-sum qualities into the interaction process. As a result, the more a party attempts to obtain its maximum benefits, the more it will be necessary to adopt policies based on delicate balances of tactical manipulations, coercion, and uncertainties. Moreover, attempts to pursue such gain-maximizing policies are highly likely to require commitments involving substantial risks. And this in turn raises the problem of attitudes toward risk-taking in bargaining situations.[15]

There are several ways to handle the problems of making decisions in the face of uncertainties and significant risks. Two procedures in particular deserve mention in the context of international bargaining. One is the procedure of maximizing

[15] For numerous analytical comments on this problem, see Anatol Rapoport, *Fights, Games, and Debates* (Ann Arbor: University of Michigan Press, 1960), Pt. II.

"expected value," a figure calculated by multiplying the utility of a given outcome by the probability of its occurrence.[16] The other is a more conservative procedure based on loss-minimizing calculations. In this case, insuring against major losses is given priority over achieving large gains in any given situation.[17] There is no *a priori* method of choosing between these procedures and no strictly rational reason why an individual actor should opt for one rather than the other. Moreover, the available evidence indicates that the actors in international politics seldom make systematic efforts to assess the nature of a specific bargaining situation in selecting the decision-making procedures to be employed in handling it.

A number of contextual factors generally influence decision-making processes, at least on a *de facto* basis, in specific bargaining situations. First it may be helpful to clarify some points about asymmetries. There are important differences, for example, among asymmetries arising from structural position, questions of orientation on issues of values, and matters of resolve. And there are frequent opportunities for trade-offs among these types of asymmetry. A classic case in international bargaining as well as in other contexts concerns the substitution of intensity of feeling or strength of resolve for deficiencies in numerical strength or physical capabilities. Another significant distinction involves differences between natural, or preexisting, and induced asymmetries. A natural asymmetry is a divergence antedating a given bargaining situation and is therefore part of the relevant context while an induced asymmetry is the result of deliberate efforts to cause a divergence within the framework of a particular bargaining situation. In a sense, then, the distinction can be reduced to one of time scale.[18] In a particular bargaining

[16] Any standard work on utility theory or game theory will deal with the concept of expected value. Consult, for example, Duncan Luce and Howard Raiffa, *Games and Decisions* (New York: John Wiley, 1957).

[17] For some interesting points concerning decision-making procedures of this kind, see Herman Kahn, *On Escalation: Metaphors and Scenarios* (New York: Praeger, 1965), pp. 244-45.

[18] This is to say, a natural asymmetry may in fact be alterable over the long run even though it is treated as a given in a specific bargaining situation. An induced asymmetry, on the other hand, can be created in the short run.

situation, however, much effort is frequently expended to create induced asymmetries while natural asymmetries are generally treated as givens and utilized accordingly.

Another contextual factor affecting decision-making in bargaining processes stems from the complicated problem of information levels. In a situation characterized both by the restriction of relevant variables to a small number and by the existence of "perfect" information[19] with regard to these variables, decision-making is simplified since the principle problem concerns the choice of values to be maximized. This reduces the role of uncertainty to a minimum. Most cases of international bargaining, however, produce the opposite characteristics. The relevant factors are apt to be many and complex. And information regarding these factors is frequently patchy, of doubtful accuracy, and ambiguous. Under the circumstances, there are apt to be extensive opportunities for the employment of manipulative tactics. Many of the tactics to be analyzed later, for example, at least partially depend on the existence of "soft areas" with regard to information available to the participants in bargaining. At the same time, there is considerable controversy over both the nature and the consequences of changes in relevant information levels during international crises. And it is worth noting here that certain bargaining moves are often adopted just to acquire information.

There are significant differences between "one-shot" bargaining situations and iterative processes. A bargaining situation unlikely to be repeated or to have important implications for future cases is likely to be fundamentally less restrained than an iterative one because the parties do not have to worry about retaliation in subsequent situations and because they need not establish a framework of expectations to deal with each other in the future.[20] An iterative process, on the other

[19] The concept of perfect information refers to an ideal situation in which decision-makers have at any given time accurate readings for all the variables relevant to a specific issue.

[20] For an interesting discussion of differences between "one-shot" and iterative situations in the context of the prisoner's dilemma, consult Rapoport and Chammah, *op.cit.*, Chap. 5.

hand, introduces additional considerations.[21] To begin with, the prospect of iteration makes it much easier to utilize "expected value" calculations on a rational basis. But at the same time, iteration raises new problems for analysis. Precedent generally becomes an important determinant of perceptions and decision-making in an iterative process. Among other things, this is likely to lead to the establishment of minimal rules of the game for the interaction process. In addition, analogic reasoning may become a major influence on decision-making in iterative situations. Once a participant recognizes the first elements of a familiar sequence, he is likely to project its future course on the basis of past experience. The phenomenon of reputation is another important consideration in iterative processes. Over a series of similar cases, any participant who acts with reasonable consistency either as a result of deliberate efforts or as a consequence of a stream of actions that can be interpreted meaningfully by others will acquire a reputation.[22] Reputation, then, is an important determinant of bargaining in that it serves to shape expectations and is often subject to significant manipulation in the hands of a skilled practitioner. The trick from the latter perspective is not to convince oneself but to project forcefully certain characteristic behavior patterns that an adversary will take into account in selecting his own course of action in a given bargaining situation.

Most international bargaining processes, however, are semi-iterative. There are almost always substantial differences among specific cases of bargaining with regard to such matters as the actors involved, the particular issues, and the nature of the political and technological setting. Nevertheless, there is usually a sufficient sense of iteration in international bargaining that the participants are strongly influenced

[21] For some useful concepts dealing with the qualities of iterative processes, see Fred Iklé, *How Nations Negotiate* (New York: Harper and Row, 1964), especially Chaps. 5, 10, and 11.

[22] The development of reputation does not always occur on the basis of conscious effort. Many influential elements of reputation, both desirable and undesirable from the possessor's point of view, commonly develop inadvertently.

by factors such as precedent, analogic reasoning, and reputation. In addition, bargaining processes in international politics are generally interdependent rather than iterative in a simple mechanical or independent fashion. This combination makes the analysis of bargaining particularly difficult. Because the past is a major determinant of perceptions, expectations, and so forth concerning the present and the future, specific bargaining situations cannot be neatly encapsulated or treated on an *ad hoc* basis. Moreover, the fact that such processes are not repetitious in a simple mechanical sense impedes efforts to discover regularities among individual cases. As is true with other aspects of competitive-cooperative bargaining relationships, the degree to which any specific situation constitutes an iteration of past cases is frequently subject to manipulative treatment. Perceptions of the similarities and differences between a current situation and past ones often help to determine the relative bargaining strength of the participants. Under the circumstances, crises are apt to be focal points in the debate over the iterative qualities of international politics because they are highly visible and because they stem from a merging and intensification of the elements of conflict in the normal flow of international politics.

Strategic Bargaining

In the preceding, bargaining has been analyzed for the most part on the assumption that the basic dimensions of the interaction process for any particular situation can be treated as given. In complicated cases, however, it is frequently necessary to relax this assumption. In fact, the distinction should be made here between "simple" bargaining and "strategic" bargaining. The critical variable in this connection concerns the differences between acceptance of a given bargaining context and efforts to alter the context as part of the bargaining process. Simple bargaining therefore refers to situations in which the activities of the participants consist primarily of: straightforward assessments of existing bargaining positions; more or less direct procedures for exchanging information about these positions; and efforts to strike a bargain on this basis.[23] In strategic bargaining, on the other hand, the participants attempt, by various bargaining tactics, to achieve at least temporary alterations either in the dimensions of the bargaining process or in the perceptions of the other parties concerning these matters.

While the fundamental nature of the distinction is clear, real cases of bargaining in international politics can fall anywhere between the most straightforward case of simple bargaining and the most complex case of strategic bargaining. Moreover, many specific techniques can be employed in bargaining strategically. Here questions on the uses of commitments, threats, promises, distortions, and dissimulation become particularly important.[24]

Strategic bargaining is extremely prevalent and influential in international bargaining processes, especially those that are more coercive than persuasive. The manipulative aspects of strategic bargaining are particularly compatible with coercive objectives in shaping the decision-making processes of other actors. This is why it is important to analyze the links between strategic bargaining and conditions of crisis, which will be treated at considerable length in later chapters.

The prevalence of strategic bargaining in international politics tends to create an atmosphere heavy with confusion and ambiguity. As a result, various impediments to bargaining often arise in the course of specific interaction processes. Such impediments generally fall short of posing full-fledged dilemmas, in the sense of logical insolubility,[25] but can be severe enough to hamper or downgrade specific bargaining processes.

[23] It can be argued logically that this extreme type of "simple" bargaining does not amount to bargaining at all since the relationship involves virtually no effective elements of competition. Indeed, few, if any, empirical situations of this kind actually arise. Nevertheless, the concept is very useful as an anchor for one pole of an important conceptual spectrum, the other being strategic bargaining.

[24] See Schelling, *The Strategy of Conflict, op.cit.*, Chap. 5.

[25] By definition, a dilemma poses logically incompatible requirements so that there is no rational method of choosing between them. The concept of bargaining impediments is used in this study to refer to problems which are not logically insoluble but which do raise serious difficulties in regard to rational choice.

Three general classes of bargaining impediments appear to be of major importance in international bargaining. First are problems arising essentially from ignorance, lack of understanding, or inability to characterize accurately the basic dimensions of a bargaining situation. This class encompasses unintentional rather than feigned problems, but it covers a variety of possibilities. The participants, for example, may not be able to agree on the state of their relationship at the outset of bargaining. They may not even be able to agree on the underlying issues at stake. Or there may be disagreement over the nature and distribution of payoffs associated with various plausible outcomes. One or more of the participants may not be able to specify what it would consider a gain for itself in a given situation. (To do so, in fact, requires an ability to draw certain utility curves which in turn presumes at least some general agreement on national interests. As a result, this class of bargaining impediments opens up the difficult problems connected with this controversial subject.)

A second class deals with emotional distortions and ideational divergences. The key problem here concerns gaps between "realities" and perceptions of them which arise from a variety of essentially nonrational sources. The consequences of such gaps for bargaining, whether they stem from emotional distortions or ideological incompatibilities, can be far-reaching. In extreme cases where the participants are seriously blocked by emotional rigidities or informed by incongruent world views, meaningful bargaining may be impossible. Moreover, asymmetries in the influence or pretended influence of such nonrational factors often provide good opportunties for manipulation to achieve certain bargaining advantages. There are, however, occasional times when divergences along these lines actually facilitate meaningful bargaining among the participants since a more accurate mutual awareness of the situation would necessitate recognition of the full extent of their incompatibilities. In general, impediments of this class are apt to be influential in international bargaining, but whether or not they are likely to become more severe under conditions of crisis remains an open question.

The third class of bargaining impediments covers problems

arising from extended uses of bargaining tactics and may well be the most complex of the three conceptually. Some of these problems have been referred to in the course of this chapter, but it seems desirable to attempt here a more general formulation. The basic source of impediments in this class stems from the fact that many bargaining tactics rely upon distortion or dissimulation with regard to motives, expectations, physical capabilities, resolve, and so forth.[26] The principal goals of such tactics are clear enough. They include the creation of favorable attitudes and expectations on the part of adversaries and outsiders and the manipulation of the bargaining situation so as to maximize one's bargaining strength. When both sides employ these tactics at the same time, however, the result is often both confusion over important elements of reality and rigidities emanating from a desire to maintain outward appearances. In this context certain problems become relevant: neither side, for example, may be willing to initiate conciliatory actions for fear of indicating weakness; both may be anxious to avoid moves which could be construed as concessions; and, since the premiums for projecting an image of inflexibility are sometimes substantial, the parties may generally seek to avoid any action that might cast doubt on their future bargaining skill.[27] Moreover, it is possible to become so caught up in the intracacies of strategic bargaining that the underlying dangers associated with outcomes of mutual loss are, at least temporarily, obscured in the decision-making processes of the participants.

A number of points in this chapter about the complexities of international bargaining may be clarified in a discussion of bargaining tactics.[28] The starting point in this context must be the concept of bargaining strength since an increase in

[26] Distortion and dissimulation can be tactically employed in efforts to project both one's own perceptions of reality *and* one's evaluations of the perceptions of other parties.

[27] A detailed discussion of impediments of this kind appears in Oran R. Young, *The Intermediaries: Third Parties in International Crises* (Princeton: Princeton University Press, 1967), especially Chaps. 1 and 6.

[28] One of the principal strengths of Schelling's work is his imaginativeness in spelling out tactical possibilities in bargaining situations. For numerous examples consult both Schelling, *Arms and Influence, op.cit.*, and Schelling, *The Strategy of Conflict, op.cit.*

relative strength is the ultimate objective in employing tactics. The concept of bargaining strength emphasizes both the interdependent nature of bargaining and the importance of relative as opposed to absolute influence. The strongest participant is the one able to persuade, trick, or coerce an adversary into accepting some desired outcome, not the one possessing the most physical instruments of power.

While tactics are of some significance in most bargaining situations, their role often becomes increasingly prominent as strategic bargaining becomes more extensive. In the first instance, it is sometimes possible to alter the underlying structure of a bargaining process as a means of changing relative bargaining strengths. A participant may, for example, be able to manipulate the context of a given bargaining process in such a way that certain logically plausible alternatives can no longer be considered. Such procedures are sometimes referred to as "bridge-burning" tactics. Similarly, it is sometimes possible to achieve advantages by deliberately manipulating the dangers of destructive outcomes or the general controllability of a given situation. Within this framework, bargaining frequently turns into a competition of will or a "war of nerves" between the sides. The role of tactics in this connection generally focuses on the achievement of credible commitments and on the creation or exploitation of influential asymmetries. Procedures of this kind frequently yield important bargaining advantages, but may also generate the characteristic dangers of a "competition in risk-taking," leading to rigid mutual commitments and postures which do not constitute a viable bargain.[29]

Tactics are often closely associated with problems of communication. In rather abstract terms communication can be viewed as the basis of all bargaining, and a clever participant can gain proximate advantages through the manipulation of communications processes. Sheer silence, for example, is sometimes a powerful way to induce another participant to adopt certain conclusions about the nature of a bargaining situa-

[29] The phrase "competition in risk-taking" is Schelling's. The problems of escalation associated with relationships of this kind are dealt with in *ibid.*, Chaps. 9 and 10.

tion. Beyond this, the whole phenomenon of signaling, which stems from a desire to communicate with other parties more actively, has important tactical implications in bargaining. Signaling is apt to acquire particular significance: when more direct forms of communication are inadequate owing to physical incapability or distrust; when a participant desires to launch a trial balloon concerning possible terms for a bargain without prejudicing his position; or when it seems desirable to communicate with only some of the parties composing the opposing side. Signaling may therefore become particularly important in the later stages of bargaining when the atmosphere has become somewhat confused from the affects of strategic bargaining and as the sides become increasingly interested in reaching some conclusion.

One way to define the objective of bargaining tactics is in terms of the notion of inducing, at a point favorable to the side employing the tactics, a coordination of perspectives and expectations about the outcome of the bargaining. To put it simply, the problem is to get the other side to see things your way as much as possible and to agree on a concrete bargain you consider favorable. Specific tactics may fail entirely or even backfire, but these maneuvers by the various participants frequently account for much of the dynamics associated with interaction processes of this kind.

3. The International Setting

As is true in most areas of empirical analysis, efforts to match abstract hypotheses about crises with specific examples raise diverging pressures between the desire to claim the widest possible application for hypotheses on the one hand, and concern about the commensurability of the realm of pertinent cases on the other.[1] The twin problems of validity and significance must be taken into account here as elsewhere. Although the application of hypotheses about empirical phenomena requires a commensurate universe of cases, it does not mean that individual examples must be absolutely similar. On the contrary, there are substantial premiums in analytic work to be had from discovering significant relationships common to superficially disparate phenomena. Still, international crises are substantially conditioned by the nature of the setting in which they occur. In fact, several types of links between individual crises and their settings are worth noting.

The problems of time scale and perspective, discussed in Chapter One, are relevant here. Both the sequence of clashes associated with the Napoleonic bid for supremacy in Europe and the Cuban missile crisis of 1962, for example, can be treated as crises in international politics. At the same time, these cases clearly involve time scales so drastically different that, for most purposes, attempts to make comparisons between them would be confusing and essentially meaningless. In short, the problem is similar to the difficulties encountered with different levels of generality in areas where the time factor is not important.

Many key aspects of international crises are closely linked to the qualities of their technological, political, and cognitive settings. With regard to technology, the extent to which the

[1] This chapter deals with the problem of delineating those cases to which the hypotheses of the present book apply as well as with the selection of specific crises for extended analysis. Such material is frequently omitted or greatly compressed in studies of this kind. Since this one has epistemological as well as substantive objectives, however, the discussion of these issues is presented in full in this chapter. For further comments on the epistemological issues raised, consult Appendix A.

setting is nuclear or nonnuclear,[2] for example, will have a substantial bearing on the perceptions of decision-makers concerning such matters as the danger of escalation, the desirability of proceeding cautiously, and the importance of restraint concerning the initiation of violence. Similarly, in terms of perceptions there are likely to be striking contrasts between a setting characterized by superior offensive technology and one characterized by defensive superiority. Various elements of the political setting also frequently affect the basic dimensions of an international crisis. A crisis involving the core powers in a rigid system of opposing blocs, for example, differs markedly from one involving lesser powers in a system with more fluid alliance commitments. And the extent to which parties not directly involved in a crisis are able to exercise their influence over the protagonists can be a major determinant of the course of any given crisis.[3] In addition, an influential, though somewhat intangible, determinant of the dimensions of a crisis is frequently its cognitive setting. The fundamental concepts and images concerning the uses of force in international politics which are prevalent among the decision-makers of the participating powers, for example, generally play an important role in defining the specific rules of the game for a given crisis. So do long-standing expectations about the probable behavior of other actors, which decision-makers inevitably bring to a given crisis.

Finally, though crises are recurrent phenomena in international politics, they do not recur in mechanically exact or independent patterns. International crises vary so much with regard to participants, issues, settings, and so forth that they can at best be only semi-iterative. No crisis, therefore, ever comes close to being an exact replica of any of its predecessors in the sense that iteration is sometimes achievable in controlled experiments. In addition, international crises are usual-

[2] In this study the concept nuclear setting refers to any situation in which two or more actors are capable of delivering nuclear explosives to enemy targets, though they may not in fact do so.

[3] In the contemporary international system, this is one of the most influential differences between crises involving the superpowers and those among lesser powers in which the superpowers are, in effect, peripheral actors.

ly interdependent in important ways. In most areas of international politics, the past often greatly influences the present and the future both directly in terms of proximate political relationships and indirectly in terms of such intangibles as analogic perceptions, learning capacity, and reputation. The resultant contrast between interdependent and independent patterns of recurrence tends to be particularly clear with regard to international crises.

All this does not mean there are no significant regularities among cases of crisis in international politics. On the contrary, the present study deals at length with such regularities. It does indicate, however, that it is important, in efforts to substantiate hypotheses about international crisis empirically, to specify clearly the relevant universe of cases, and that full-fledged comparisons between crises occurring in fundamentally different settings are apt to raise serious difficulties for analysis. At the same time, this discussion suggests the importance of distinguishing between fully developed efforts of empirical substantiation and more circumscribed analytic operations designed merely to produce insights concerning international crises. Such operations include the use of empirical analysis: to refine hypotheses for further research; to produce new ideas with regard to concepts, questions, and perspectives concerning crises; and to supply guidelines for subsequent research. Procedures of this kind are less powerful analytically than those leading to empirically substantiated propositions, but they lend themselves well to more far-reaching comparisons since they pose much less stringent requirements with regard to the commensurability of cases.

The position adopted in the present study on these issues is a mixed one. The main chapters attempt to develop hypotheses which can be substantiated empirically for a specific universe of cases. It is therefore possible to argue that the results of the study constitute propositions that are valid with regard to certain types of crisis. But the results clearly do not warrant the label propositions in all cases of crisis in international politics. At the same time, an effort has been made to organize the study so as to indicate the relevance of its findings for other universes of cases and for subsequent research on international crises.

The discussions of specific hypotheses in the main chapters include statements concerning the conditions under which they can be expected to hold. In general, however, the hypotheses of this study are oriented toward crises occurring in international systems characterized by high degrees of decentralization (or autonomy among the component units), the existence of two or more superpowers, the presence of weapons of massive destruction, and at least some superiority of offensive over defensive military technology. In addition, the hypotheses are geared toward crises involving the major powers in such systems.

The Postwar Setting

The specific hypotheses should be regarded, therefore, as applicable to any international setting exhibiting the characteristics elaborated in the preceding paragraph. The empirical focus of this book, however, encompasses the pattern of international politics that emerged in the aftermath of the Second World War. That is, the crises occurring within this period are focused on for purposes of assessing the match between abstract hypotheses and empirical realities. The specific cases of crisis selected for systematic empirical analysis have been drawn from the period 1948-1962. While there were of course numerous proximate shifts in the international setting during these years, the period exhibited both a fundamental contextual unity and the characteristics mentioned above as delimiting the boundaries of relevance for the hypotheses of this study.

In retrospect, the termination of the Second World War appears to mark a sharp break in the international system apropos of the physical resources available for use in international politics, the basic axes of international contention and patterns of political alignment, and the operative arrangements for regulating power in the international system.[4] To

[4] See Oran R. Young, "On the Nuclearization of International Politics," pp. 101-145 in Richard A. Falk, Robert C. Tucker, and Oran R. Young, *On Minimizing the Use of Nuclear Weapons*, Center of International Studies, Princeton University, Research Monograph No. 23, 1966.

begin with, the postwar period witnessed an interrelated sequence of remarkable changes in military technology leading to qualitative alterations in the fundamental characteristics of power in international politics. The overall impact of these changes was sharply accentuated by the conjunction of major developments in at least four areas: the perfection of new explosives, particularly nuclear and thermonuclear; the arrival of long-range delivery capabilities, especially ballistic-missile systems; the speed of delivery associated with new technologies which led to a telescoping of time with regard to potential military exchanges among major powers; and the increased mobility with which powers were able to deploy and utilize personnel and resources for military purposes. Fundamentally, these changes radically enlarged the scope of man's freedom of will to use force in international politics by sharply reducing the physical limitations on his ability to employ high levels of force throughout the world on a simultaneous and coordinated basis. As a result, intrinsically political restraints have become increasingly crucial to the regulation and management of power in international politics. And in fact, the very reduction of the physical limitations on man's freedom of action, dangerous though it may seem from many perspectives, has generated a variety of political restraints that play a major role in the management of force in the international system.

These technological developments quickly produced several important shifts in the setting of international politics. First, they led to a drastic increase in the technological imbalances favoring offensive over defensive weapons. In the 1948-1962 period, this offense-defense imbalance produced a number of the major dangers to international stability which lay relatively near the surface of international politics. Problems such as preventive war, preemption, surprise attack, accidents, miscalculations, and catalytic warfare, for example, were all severely heightened by the combination of an offense-defense asymmetry with a general revolution in military technology.[5]

[5] Exploration of the relationships between these problems and changes in military technology constitutes one of the most significant contribu-

Second, the impossibility of achieving a successful defense in this setting in turn led to the development of overriding deterrent strategies emphasizing contingent threats of "punishment" in place of defensive strategies based on the possibilities of physical "denial."[6] While deterrent postures may under some circumstances produce political relationships that are quite stable, deterrence nevertheless presents certain fundamental difficulties both from the perspective of the individual state and from the perspective of the overall system. In essence, the fact that each actor in the system must ultimately accept the exposure of its core values as hostages for the system's stability creates a situation in which every actor is dependent upon the "reasonableness" of one or more of the others for its survival. Since deterrence is essentially a psychological relationship involving interdependent actors, it also produces difficulties concerning such matters as credibility, resolve, and political will, and requires maintenance and periodic readjustment in the wake of both technological and political changes. Third, the impact of technological changes after the Second World War accentuated the qualitative superiority of the superpowers over all other states in international politics. While this distinction has become blurred in recent years, it was one of the most salient characteristics of international politics during 1948-1962. This qualitative superiority of the superpowers cut several ways politically, however, since it made their fundamental "responsibility" for the stability of the international system increasingly obvious besides placing them in positions of dominance in many specific political interactions within the international arena.

Under the circumstances, the changing nature of the "strategic balance" between the superpowers emerged as a critical determinant of the course of international politics in the postwar world.[7] This development, however, led to a number of

---

tions of Thomas Schelling's book, *The Strategy of Conflict* (Cambridge: Harvard University Press, 1960).

[6] For an analytic discussion of these concepts, see Glenn Snyder, *Deterrence and Defense* (Princeton: Princeton University Press, 1961), Chap. 1.

[7] The term balance here refers to the distribution of effective military power between the two superpowers. For a discussion of the various

characteristic problems since a strategic balance is both intrinsically volatile and easily subject to misperception. It is extremely difficult to calculate with certainty the state of the balance at any given point in time since the weapons systems deployed by the superpowers are not identical either in numbers or types and since the doctrines governing their use tend to diverge considerably. In addition, the strategic balance is constantly evolving as changes occur in both military technologies and prevailing doctrines, thus necessitating continual processes of balance renewal and adaptation. Furthermore, there are always possibilities for individual states to manipulate the strategic balance, at least perceptually, as a way to achieve political objectives.

A strategic balance of this kind is an important feature of international politics, with significant implications for international bargaining, especially under conditions of crisis. The volatility and ambiguities of the balance produce a variety of problems concerning: shifts, lags, perceived gaps, asymmetrical advantages, and overreactions. Under the circumstances, confusions and miscalculations about the existing state of the strategic balance have operated as factors of causal significance in the development of a number of the severe crises of the postwar period.[8] In addition, one of the critical axes of great-power politics during this period has been composed of efforts to induce significant shifts in the strategic balance through politico-military actions short of open warfare. As a result, crises have frequently ensued when such activities by one party in the system have exceeded the toleration of one or more of the other actors with a major interest in the state of the strategic balance.[9]

A further element of contextual unity in the 1948-1962 period arises from the fact that it spans the period of marked

---

meanings attached to the term balance in analyses of international politics, see Martin Wight, "The Balance of Power," in Herbert Butterfield and Martin Wight, eds., *Diplomatic Investigations* (London: George Allen and Unwin, 1966), pp. 149-175.

[8] In the development of the Taiwan Strait crisis of 1958, for example. The critical ambiguities in this case were those associated with the Soviet technological gains becoming evident during 1957.

[9] The Soviet initiatives leading to the Cuban crisis of 1962, for example.

for the political allegiance of the nonaligned states, these states frequently could achieve some degree of effective political influence in their own right as well as room for maneuver in avoiding control by the superpowers. This safety valve for the activities of the lesser states became particularly important in the period under discussion as the wholesale dismemberment of the former colonial empires led rapidly to the entrance into the international system of large numbers of newly independent but frequently weak and internally unstable states.

As has been noted, the stability of the overall system during this period of bipolarity largely depended upon the relationship between the superpowers. So long as they did not become involved in a direct confrontation of major proportions, the system demonstrated a striking degree of violence tolerance. The period following the Second World War was in fact characterized by both intense and extensive violence in many parts of the international system, especially in connection with the decline of colonial arrangements and the emergence of the "new states."[16] For the most part, however, fundamental challenges to the stability of the system could arise only from two sources: direct clashes between the two superpowers; and the expansion or explosion, through escalation, of lower levels of conflict into direct superpower confrontations.[17]

Several important aspects of the relationship between the superpowers, nevertheless, cast doubt on the viability of an international system so heavily dependent upon the stability of a single axis of contention. The situation created by the volatility and ambiguities of the strategic balance was further unsettled by the nature of the prevailing military technology. At the same time, the superpowers during this period

[16] In addition, the "new states" themselves, after attaining independence, have often become important sources of the contemporary upsurge in cases of extended civil strife and internal war, with international implications.

[17] For a discussion of escalation in terms of the concepts of expansion and explosion into superpower conflict, see Morton Halperin, *Limited War in the Nuclear Age* (New York: John Wiley, 1963), Chap. 1.

increasingly pursued divergent and competing world views.[18] As a result, the degree to which the superpowers would act moderately in international politics was cast into doubt in a system whose very existence increasingly depended on political moderation in place of physical limitations. In this regard, it should be emphasized that the most dangerous international crises of the period, even though frequently catalyzed by more proximate military asymmetries or political difficulties, grew out of this development of deep-seated political antagonisms.[19]

The period of bipolarity, however, did witness a number of stabilizing developments in international politics. The simplicity and relative clarity of the system has already been mentioned. The ultimate "responsibility" of the superpowers to maintain stability became obvious and inescapable. And in fact these powers reacted with striking caution in the presence of ongoing or impending hostilities, especially when the prior and preponderant involvement of the opposing superpower was evident. Moreover, the two superpowers over the course of time demonstrated a tacit propensity to elaborate at least minimal *procedural* rules to regulate the most serious dangers to the international system arising from their continuing competition. In addition, the process of adapting to the "nuclearization" of international politics, as well as developments in military technology, gradually began to foster perceptions that the strategic balance was for all practical purposes becoming a stalemate. There were, of course, important proximate fluctuations in this area. But the shift toward increasing concentration on achieving strategic invulnerability and guaranteed second-strike capabilities in the mid-fifties marked an important turning point in thinking about the strategic balance. Given this perceptual background, uncertainty

[18] Conflict of this type involves incompatible views about the proper distribution of values in the world and the appropriate mechanisms for accomplishing political aims. In the 1948-1962 period, as the United States shifted from relative isolation to extensive involvement in world politics and as the Soviet Union became an increasingly powerful actor in the international system, conflict of this kind gained in importance.

[19] The various Berlin crises of the 1948-1962 period are obvious illustrations of this.

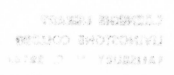

about the strategic balance more and more began to shift from its earlier destabilizing role to being a source of stability in relations between the superpowers.[20]

The contextual unity of the 1948-1962 period is further emphasized by the fact that several major changes in the underpinnings of international politics have become conspicuous since 1962. Taken together, these developments have elicited a distinct shift away from the preceding pattern of bipolarity both in terms of the fundamental power structure of the international system and in terms of the principal axes of contention around which political activities coalesce in the system.

The power structure of the system has been changing under the impact of a gradual but significant redistribution of effective power throughout the international system.[21] A number of interrelated factors account for this trend including: the development of greater stability in the strategic balance between the superpowers; the tendency of the superpowers to offset each other in many situations, thereby reducing the freedom of action of both; the significant, though not rampant, proliferation of nuclear capabilities in the system; the growing conservatism of the superpowers in their international activities; the dilution of ideological politics with concerns about international stability and material welfare; the assertion or reassertion of considerable national autonomy on the part of many lesser powers in the system; the reemergence of several additional great powers which, though not nearly as mighty as the superpowers, act as focal points of political activity and influence in the system; and the coalescence of new political groupings on bases other than the East-West axis of contention.

[20] Uncertainty over the motives or activities of an opponent becomes an incentive to launch a first strike in a situation in which the achievement of such a move is critically important (and the dangers of surprise attack and preemption therefore very salient). In a situation characterized by increasing emphasis on strategic invulnerability and guaranteed second-strike capacities, on the other hand, uncertainty is more likely to act as a deterrent to the launching of a first strike.

[21] See Oran R. Young, *The Intermediaries: Third Parties in International Crises* (Princeton: Princeton University Press, 1967), Chap. 9.

53

The period since 1962 has witnessed a remarkable rise in the importance of new axes of contention in international politics, owing to both the growing numbers of autonomous actors and the increasing salience of additional power centers. Patterns of international contention based on North-South divergences, problems of nationalism and local autonomy, disputes mainly relevant to specific regions or subsystems, and situations of internal war have clearly worked to alter the highly polarized pattern of international contention characteristic of the bipolar period. The result has been to make the international system more complex politically, though it is doubtful whether the system as a whole has become any more stable.

More specifically, the changes that have become manifest since 1962 have altered what were distinguishing features of international politics in the preceding period. The networks of security alliances serving to hold the Eastern and Western blocs together have begun to deteriorate as a result of centrifugal pressures arising from both political and technological changes.[22] Also, the two superpowers have begun to react to the emergence of common and overlapping interests between themselves, a development stimulated by the changing patterns of political contention in the system. They have thus begun to formulate policies involving mutual coordination in contrast to those stressing alliance cohesion and global competition, at least on some important issues.[23] In addition, the emergence of power centers and axes of international contention outside the earlier bipolar setting is leading, in turn, to the development of new power balances and arrangements for the management of power in various parts of the international system. And at least some of these new arenas are sufficiently discontinuous in political terms that the superpowers, concerned with all of them, are increasingly faced with patterns of competitive and cooperative interests

[22] On this subject, see *loc.cit.*; and Klaus Knorr, *On the Uses of Military Power in the Nuclear Age* (Princeton: Princeton University Press, 1966), pp. 152-163.

[23] Consider the important and in some ways startling history of the debate over nuclear nonproliferation since 1963.

between themselves which vary substantially from one arena to another.[24]

The Selection of Specific Cases for Analysis

In general, therefore, the 1948-1962 period has important advantages as a focus for empirical analysis concerning bargaining under conditions of crisis. It exhibits sufficient contextual unity to keep within manageable proportions the problems of time scale and fundamental commensurability, thus making it possible at least to think in terms of the substantiation of hypotheses applicable to cases of crisis within this period. Also, the links between crises on the one hand, and the problems of international stability and the use of force in international politics on the other, as outlined in the Introduction, are particularly interesting within the framework of this period.

The preliminary set of cases for the empirical portions of this study, therefore, was composed of all crises involving the superpowers which occurred during 1948-1962. Within this set, the selection of specific cases of crisis for extended analysis and systematic comparison was based on: the definitional concepts set forth in Chapter One; the criteria concerning the orientation of hypotheses outlined earlier in this chapter; and the intrinsic interest of individual cases in relation to the underlying substantive concerns of the study. The Korean conflict, for example, was set aside since it was actually a relatively protracted war rather than a crisis. The clash at Suez in 1956, while obviously a significant crisis from some points of view, was also not included because it was characterized by effective, though tacit, Soviet-American coordination to guarantee the stability of the international system. It was therefore essentially a case of superpower coordination rather than opposition. Other crises such as the clash in the Taiwan Strait in 1954-1955, the Middle East crisis of 1958, and the Berlin crisis of 1958-1959 were ultimately excluded as having less intrinsic interest in the context of this study. This process

[24] For a discussion of the complexities introduced by this set of developments, see Oran R. Young, "Political Discontinuities in the International System," *World Politics*, XX, No. 3 (April 1968), 369-392.

of elimination led to the choice of four specific cases of crisis for extended comparative analysis: the Berlin crisis of 1948-1949; the Taiwan Strait crisis of 1958; the Berlin crisis of 1961; and the Cuban missile crisis of 1962.

The first Berlin crisis was one of the most prolonged crises of the postwar period. The period of buildup to this crisis can be traced at least to the breakdown of the Allied Control Commission for Germany in March 1948. Subsequently, the crisis evolved into a full-blown confrontation during the last ten days of June in the aftermath of the Western currency reform of June 18 and the ensuing imposition of a full land blockade of the Western sectors of Berlin by the Soviet Union. Outwardly, the opposing positions assumed in June 1948 remained in the balance until May 1949 since the blockade was not actually lifted until that time. Many aspects of the confrontation over Berlin became increasingly routinized as time passed, however, so that by the early part of 1949 much of the atmosphere of acute crisis had disappeared. In addition, the directness and clarity of the fundamental lines of conflict underlying this clash made the Berlin crisis of 1948-1949 a relatively simple one analytically. Problems of alliance coordination on both sides were quite circumscribed during this crisis, so complications arising from discontinuous interests and confusion among allies were at a minimum. And since Germany was still largely devoid of independent political will in 1948, the crisis became largely a straightforward confrontation among outside powers concerning the political future of Germany.

August 23, 1958, the date on which the Chinese People's Republic sharply intensified its shelling of the offshore islands under the control of the Chinese Nationalists, provides a comparatively clearcut beginning for the 1958 crisis in the Taiwan Strait. Some prior developments such as the Mao-Khrushchev meeting in Peking (July 31–August 3) were plainly important in shaping the proximate decision to initiate this crisis, but the 1958 case is one in which the inception of the crisis as a major international event is obvious. Nevertheless, the resultant crisis became a rather complex one since the confrontation ultimately involved several levels of conflict and diverging interests. The alliance relationships between each Chinese participant and its superpower ally were far from monolithic so that the crisis never became a direct contest between two well-coordinated adversaries. Moreover, as the crisis unfolded, new ambiguities arose owing to the development of a triangular pattern of interaction involving the Chinese Nationalists, the Chinese People's Republic, and the United States, a pattern superimposed on the continuing bilateral aspects of the confrontation. The critical phases of confrontation and the ultimate disengagement process associated with this crisis assumed proportions much less clear cut analytically than the initiation sequence referred to above.

The conflict focusing on Berlin constantly simmered near the verge of crisis following the denouement of the Soviet ultimatum of November 1958, which occurred during the early months of 1959. During 1961, however, Berlin became the center of an extraordinarily complex crisis involving several intricate axes of contention. From the beginning of the year, a series of major disturbances within the German Democratic Republic began to grow toward crisis proportions. In addition, at the Kennedy-Khrushchev meeting in Vienna, on June 3-4 the Soviets chose to reactivate the direct East-West aspects of the Berlin conflict. These two developments soon began to interact with each other, ultimately touching off the dual crisis over Berlin that moved rapidly into a phase of direct confrontation in August 1961. Interestingly, the long-festering crisis within the German Democratic Republic was terminated quickly and decisively in the aftermath of the closure of the sector boundary in Berlin on August 13. The East-West aspects of the confrontation, on the other hand, were sharply affected by the development of the local crisis and ultimately continued on an indeterminate basis into the fall of 1961.

The Cuban crisis of 1962 assumed urgent proportions at slightly different points in time as far as the major participants were concerned. From the point of view of the United States, the crisis clearly began on October 15, the day on which "hard" information about the work on installations for Soviet offensive missiles in Cuba became available. From the

Soviet point of view, on the other hand, the situation became compelling only in the wake of the Kennedy speech on October 22, though in their planning operations the Soviets surely considered the possibility that their actions in Cuba would spark a major crisis.[25] Despite the great intensity of the ensuing crisis, however, several characteristics make it somewhat less complex analytically than several of the other cases under consideration. For one thing, the actual confrontation became almost immediately a direct Soviet-American clash. Alliance considerations were sharply deemphasized and, above all, the two major participants coordinated in adopting a *de facto* but highly effective policy of reducing the influence of the Cuban government during the crisis. In addition, the fact that the crisis covered only a brief span of time minimized the importance of a number of confusing factors and ambiguities that usually become significant when a crisis is prolonged.

[25] It is increasingly evident that the Soviets seriously miscalculated the *probability* of a decisive American reaction to their initiatives in Cuba during 1962. But it is highly unlikely they had not considered the *possibility* of such a reaction.

PART II
CONTEXTUAL FACTORS

Introduction

The chapters of Part II deal with those aspects of the political context of crises which tend to condition the processes and prospects of international bargaining. The concept of political context here is different from that of the interaction process formulated in the opening section of Chapter Two. Context does not refer directly, for example, to the problems of scope, domain, and mode. Instead, the concept of context refers to the political, attitudinal, and perceptual factors that set a crisis apart from the ordinary flow of international politics.

By definition, a crisis constitutes a break in the pattern of interactions characteristic of the preceding flow of international politics. This quality of crises stems both from fundamentally physical factors and from more intangible factors related to perceptual and attitudinal phenomena. Crises typically involve a different time scale than the ordinary flow of international politics, and they tend to produce, simultaneously, a hiatus in many ordinary patterns of interaction *and* an intensification of interactions relating to the issues pertinent to the crisis. At the same time, conditions of crisis are apt to lead to substantial shifts in attitudes and expectations with regard to a variety of subjects including control problems, risk-taking, the motives of other participants, and so forth. Stressing the breaks in existing patterns of interaction caused by crises, however, should not make one lose sight of the ultimate connections of crises to past and future aspects of the broader international political setting. While a crisis is likely to acquire a certain dynamic of its own, the course of international politics prior to the crisis will be a major determinant of its basic dimensions and the fundamental political realities governing behavior during the course of the crisis. Equally important is the tendency of crises, once ended, to influence greatly the subsequent course of international politics. In this connection crises can become political watersheds in which previously independent trends in international politics are brought together and in which political relationships are sufficiently fluid so that their direction can be altered significantly.

It will be useful in this book to distinguish and analyze independently some of the contextual features of crises. From the perspective of individual actors, severe crises often attain a certain momentum that makes them somewhat unpredictable and that emphasizes important uncertainties underlying the bargaining process. At the same time, conditions of crisis are apt to affect communications processes in ways that necessitate putting greater reliance on actions rather than words to achieve genuine understanding. Furthermore, crisis interactions often produce sharper distinctions with regard to participants than non-crisis situations. During crises, as during wars, it becomes somewhat more difficult to occupy the middle ground, and states therefore tend to become categorized in terms of their interests and allegiances. In short, it is not only a tendency to produce breaks in preceding patterns of international politics that makes crises interesting from the point of view of bargaining; the distinctive features of the political context of crises are important determinants of bargaining in their own right.

4. Political Fluidity

HYPOTHESIS. Periods of crisis tend to be politically fluid in two distinct senses:

  1. Crises take place when the existing setting of international politics is significantly disturbed, and

  2. Crises themselves generate pressures and prospects for important shifts and realignments of political forces in the international system.

Not only do crises typically constitute noticeable breaks with the preceding flow of international interactions, they also tend to occur during periods when at least some of the established patterns of influence, axes of contention, and informal rules of the game governing the course of international relations are being questioned by important actors and made ambiguous by an increase in probing actions and testing behavior. Under such conditions the flow of international politics is apt to be disturbed by: heightened anxieties on the part of decision-makers about potential disadvantages for their own country stemming from foreseeable political shifts; growing uncertainties based on the declining efficacy of previous world views and assumptions; increasing incentives for individual states to take initiatives to ward off the potential negative consequences of change; and rising dangers of miscalculations in an atmosphere rife with such fears and uncertainties. Unsettled periods of this kind frequently evoke an air of political expectancy which creates in decision-makers a psychological receptivity to the possibility of sharp breaks with the past. In this context crises often appear as short but intense confrontations growing out of a merging in space and time of the disturbances just outlined.

As has been noted, crises themselves, though rather short in duration, are apt to be important *sources* of change in the political setting of international relations.[1] The demands of

---

[1] This notion is plain in conceptual terms, but the consequentiality of crises is not so easily dealt with operationally, especially for comparative analysis. The attempt to treat this problem later in the chapter is based on systematic qualitative assessments rather than quantitative indicators.

crisis interaction usually make it difficult for parties to avoid taking a relatively clear stand of some kind. Though the result may occasionally be a reaffirmation of old patterns of international politics, when the international setting is already fluid it is more often likely to amount to a *de facto* push toward significant realignments of political forces in the international system. To begin with, the pressures of crisis interactions tend to bring the underlying tensions and conflicts of previous alignments to a head. Also, conditions of crisis in fact often facilitate political shifts since it is generally easier to make changes when many diverse and demanding events are occurring simultaneously and under the pretext of tactical necessity. This is not to say that critical changes are likely to be fully consummated during short periods of crisis. On the contrary, changes catalyzed by crises affecting the substantive directions of new patterns and alignments are usually more important in the long run. It is for this reason that major crises are frequently remembered and emphasized as benchmarks in the development of new relationships in international politics.

These qualities of political fluidity substantially increase the importance of bargaining during an international crisis by making it something more than just another round in an ongoing but somewhat repetitious and ineffectual clash over the allocation of political values. Although major political shifts may either be brought to fruition or be clearly set in motion for the future during crises, the fluidity of such periods also raises the perceived dangers of negative outcomes for individual participants. As a result, crises are likely to produce ambivalence from an awareness of increased scope to influence the future course of international politics and from concern over the uncertainties and indeterminate quality of the interaction. In short, bargaining during crises is a very serious matter because crises represent periods of both potential danger and opportunity.

Berlin, 1948-1949

The Berlin blockade of 1948-1949 occurred in a remarkably fluid European political setting. Most of the European states had not yet fully recovered their political and economic viability following the disruption of the war. At the same time, the solidification of Soviet influence in Eastern Europe had begun to create a kind of political vacuum in the heart of the Continent. As a result, the German situation was clearly emerging as the key to the future power balance of Europe. But Germany itself lay helpless as a defeated and occupied country governed, in theory, by a four-power Control Commission that was, in fact, unable to function because of internal disagreements.[2] A sense of the resultant fluidity appears, for example, in General Lucius Clay's statement of April 10, 1948: "We have lost Czechoslovakia. Norway is threatened. We retreat from Berlin. When Berlin falls, western Germany will be next. If we mean . . . to hold Europe against Communism, we must not budge. We can take humiliation and pressure short of war in Berlin without losing face. If we withdraw, our position in Europe is threatened."[3] Berlin was increasingly becoming a symbol of the general struggle for political predominance in Europe.

This struggle for influence in central Europe came to a head in the broader context of international problems. Some of these difficulties were traceable to the legacy of the Second World War, as in the upheavals in Indochina and the Dutch East Indies. Others had deeper roots. The problem of Palestine, for example, was a major focus of international concern throughout 1948. Israel declared its independence on May 14, 1948, and in Palestine there ensued a period of intermittent hostilities lasting into the early months of 1949.[4] This problem, in particular, drew the attention of the great powers away from the European stage from time to time.

The year 1948 witnessed the culmination of the immediate postwar efforts by the Soviet Union to solidify its influence in Europe. The Czech coup occurred at the end of February.

---

[2] See Lucius D. Clay, *Decision in Germany* (Garden City, N.Y.: Doubleday, 1950), pp. 343-357.

[3] *Ibid.*, p. 361.

[4] During the summer of 1948, a cease-fire in this area was negotiated, broken, and renegotiated. Nevertheless, hostilities continued intermittently until the signing of individual armistice agreements between Israel and the various Arab states during the early months of 1949.

Then the Soviet Union began to pressure Finland and even Norway in the interests of extending its influence, though not its direct control, over these countries. The spring of 1948 also saw the height of indigenous Communist strength in Italy and France—and the problem of Germany loomed ever larger. Discussions on Germany by the four powers broke down completely at the meeting of the Council of Foreign Ministers in London in November and December 1947.[5] And the decline of the Allied Control Council for Germany inevitably followed this breakdown during the early months of 1948.[6] The Soviet push in Europe during the early months of 1948 was not without its setbacks however. The Italian elections of April 18 delivered a severe blow to the Communist movement in that country. The dispute with Yugoslavia, on the upswing since March, culminated in an open break within the Cominform at the end of June.[7] The Finnish elections of July 1 and 2 were a defeat for the Communists in that country. And above all, indications began to emerge during the first half of 1948 that the West was preparing to go ahead with plans for the separate reorganization of western Germany regardless of Soviet protests.

All this leads to two diverging explanations for the crisis that developed over Germany in the middle of 1948. On the one hand, looking at the whole sweep of postwar developments, it is possible to argue that the Soviets were riding the crest of a wave of expanding political influence in Europe and making the most of it while it lasted. Thus, Germany was clearly the crucial point for further expansion. And in 1948 the Soviets possibly viewed the obvious preoccupation of the United States with its first really contentious presidential election in some years as one factor making it safer to push in Eu-

[5] For details in the treatment of the German problem at these meetings in London, see Clay, *op.cit.*, pp. 161-162, 343-348; and Jean Edward Smith, *The Defense of Berlin* (Baltimore: The Johns Hopkins Press, 1963), pp. 99-100.

[6] For a discussion of the sequence of events, consult Manuel Gottlieb, *The German Peace Settlement and the Berlin Crisis* (New York: Paine-Whitman, 1950), pp. 182-183.

[7] The actual public announcement of an open break within the Cominform occurred on June 28. For details see the *New York Times*, June 29, 1948, p. 1.

rope.[8] On the other hand, the Soviets, stung by several recent setbacks and aware of the beginnings of an effective Western program for the reorganization of Europe, may have felt the need for a dazzling success at this juncture which would also have the advantage of securing the western boundaries of the emerging Soviet bloc.

The fact that Western activities aimed at resuscitating the political and economic viability of Western Europe were reaching serious proportions during the spring of 1948 supports the second of these theses.[9] The European Recovery Act (Marshall Plan) was signed on April 3 and implementation began almost immediately with the establishment of the Organization for European Economic Cooperation (OEEC) on April 16. Even before this, however, the creation of the Western European Union (WEU) by the Brussels treaty of March 17 marked the start of serious efforts to improve the security arrangements of Western Europe. At the same time, American interest in the problems of European security began to rekindle with the beginning of rearmament in the United States during the spring of 1948[10] and with the passage of the "Vandenburg Resolution" on June 11.[11] Above all, however, Western activities began to impinge directly on Soviet interests with the development of an agreed plan for the reorganization of the western zones of Germany. Though Bizonia had been created as early as 1946, the real move toward the reorganization of western Germany began only after the unsuccessful foreign ministers conference of December

[8] This hypothesis is formulated and discussed in John Foster Dulles, *War or Peace* (New York: Macmillan, 1953), p. 130.

[9] A particularly interesting case that Soviet actions during 1948 in both Czechoslovakia and Berlin were essentially defensive is given in George Kennan, *Memoirs, 1925-1950* (Boston: Little, Brown, 1967), pp. 401-402 and 419-421.

[10] For an inside account of the highly complex debate over rearmament in the United States during the spring of 1948, see Walter Millis, ed., *The Forrestal Diaries* (New York: Viking, 1951), pp. 422-450.

[11] The Vandenburg Resolution opened the way for American participation in external alliances dealing with problems of security. Formally speaking, the resolution is Senate Resolution 239, 80th Congress, 2nd Session, June 11, 1948. The text can be found conveniently in Ruhl Bartlett, ed., *The Record of American Diplomacy* (New York: Knopf, 1959), pp. 727-728.

1947. The focus of developments in this area during the winter and spring of 1948 was the London Conference (meeting on several separate occasions) on German problems attended by the United States, Britain, France, and the Benelux countries. The significance of these meetings became clear with the announcement on June 7 of recommendations for currency reform and political reorganization in the western zones of Germany alone.[12] Announcement of this plan evidently led the Soviets to conclude that time was rapidly running out for further efforts to consolidate their political position in central Europe.

The crisis over Berlin, then, as a symbol of the general contest for influence in central Europe, had a number of profound political consequences. At the most general level, it was a major factor in solidifying the West politically and in fixing boundaries in the so-called cold war that have remained important ever since.[13] While the cold war had been evolving for some time prior to the crisis, Berlin more than anything else crystallized the issues between the superpowers and made the concept of cold war a commonplace in political discussions. Developments of this general nature are largely responsible for subsequent descriptions of the Berlin crisis as "a historic watershed" in the postwar era.[14] And it is evidently in this connection that Willy Brandt speaks of 1948 as "a turning point in the history of Berlin, of Germany, and of Europe."[15]

The more immediate effects of the crisis in Germany itself were particularly outstanding. Political leaders in western Germany had mixed reactions to the June 7 announcement in London.[16] Though they desired political autonomy, they

[12] For the texts of both the general communique and the substantive recommendations released on June 7, see Raymond Dennett and Robert K. Turner, eds., Documents on American Foreign Relations, Vol. X; January 1–December 31, 1948 (Princeton: Princeton University Press [for the World Peace Foundation], 1950), 109-114.

[13] See W. Phillips Davison, The Berlin Blockade: A Study in Cold War Politics (Princeton: Princeton University Press, 1958), pp. 281-300.

[14] See, for example, Gottlieb, op.cit., p. 211.

[15] Willy Brandt (as told to Leo Lania), My Road to Berlin (Garden City, N.Y.: Doubleday, 1960), p. 187.

[16] See Smith, op.cit., p. 133.

were extremely hesitant to act in a manner that would reduce the prospects for German reunification. The crisis in Berlin, however, had a profound effect in changing political attitudes, and "from the middle of June onward they [the West
German leaders] were far more receptive to the idea of the
West German State than they were when the recommendations of the London meeting were first announced."[17] In addition, movement toward the establishment of a West German
State progressed during the crisis first in the so-called Parliamentary Council, which met on September 1, and then
in a German constitutional convention which convened in the
spring of 1949. The political and economic split of Germany
was finalized, therefore, in the course of the crisis. Shortly
after the termination of the blockade the Federal Republic
of Germany (FRG) was formally established, followed within a few months by the German Democratic Republic (GDR)
in eastern Germany.[18] The Berlin crisis was similarly influential in determining the subsequent political orientation of
West Germany: it made a Western state out of the country
and led to the gradual incorporation of West Germany into
the economic and security arrangements being developed for
Western Europe. In so doing, the crisis spawned a durable
counterweight to the Soviet bloc in central Europe, but it
also helped to perpetuate the underlying German problem,
which still remains an important source of tension in international politics.

The Berlin crisis was also a critical factor in shaping the
course of political developments in Europe in general. As indicated above, it was paramount in replacing a political
vacuum in central Europe with a sharply delineated confrontation of major political forces. Though this confrontation has
had its dangers, it has provided the basis of the European
balance of power during the years since.[19] The first discus-

[17] Drew Middleton, *The Struggle for Germany* (Indianapolis: Bobbs-
Merrill, 1949), p. 152. For further discussion of this point, consult Philip
Windsor, *City on Leave* (New York: Praeger, 1963), p. 127.
[18] The Basic Law of the FRG was formally proclaimed on May 23,
1949. The GDR was established on October 7, 1949.
[19] For a provocative discussion of this point, see *The Economist*, June
10, 1948, p. 1,055.

sions about a North Atlantic Treaty, which was finally signed on April 4, 1949, were held in July 1948, and the Berlin crisis clearly spurred their development.[20] West Germany was put on the road toward autonomous political viability. The Marshall Plan began to be effective by the end of 1948. Moreover, the crisis dealt a severe blow to the indigenous Communist movements in France and Italy besides being a successful confrontation with direct Soviet power. In short, "The Berlin crisis had a tonic effect not only in Germany. It was consolidating the whole of Western Europe under American leadership and inducing closer forms of association and common defense arrangements."[21]

Finally, the Berlin crisis of 1948-1949 was at least partially responsible for several important shifts in American attitudes toward the outside world. To begin with, the spectacular unfolding of the potentialities of air transport during the crisis drew the United States perceptually closer to Europe.[22] This development was an important precursor to the expanded American commitment to European defense under NATO in the early fifties. In addition, the Berlin crisis gave impetus to the American rearmament movement just beginning to get under way during the spring of 1948. In the longer view, this American movement toward rearmament, which was further accelerated during the Korean conflict, has had vast consequences for the course of international politics.

Taiwan Strait, 1958

The 1958 crisis in the Taiwan Strait erupted rather abruptly on August 23 with a sudden intensification by the Chinese Communists of artillery bombardment, aimed primarily at the Quemoy island group.[23] This eruption was not, however, with-

[20] See Frank Howley, *Berlin Command* (New York: G. P. Putnam's Sons, 1950), pp. 272-274; see also the useful discussion in Gottlieb, *op.cit.*, p. 209.

[21] *Ibid.*

[22] See Clay, *op.cit.*, p. 386. For an elaboration of the technical details, see also Charles J.V. Murphy, "Berlin Air Lift," *Fortune*, November 1958, pp. 89-93, 218-229.

[23] This group, located in the mouth of Amoy harbor, includes a number of individual islands ranging in size from Big Quemoy to various small projections of rock.

out advance warnings.[24] Also, the initiation of the crisis occurred in a context of considerable political fluidity that did much to create an environment conducive to a crisis of substantial proportions. The political fluidity in this instance arose from a combination of local problems in East Asia and several aspects of the global balance of power.

In the first instance, the uneasy and unstable stalemate in the Taiwan Strait provided a backdrop of constant tension and uncertainty in the local arena. Neither the Chinese People's Republic (CPR) nor the Republic of China on Taiwan was prepared to accept a settlement of the Taiwan issue that would formally recognize the existence of the other. During 1958 the situation worsened. In Fukien province the Chinese Communists completed a number of military airfields and transportation links, begun in the aftermath of the 1954-1955 crisis, and promptly undertook a substantial military buildup in the area.[25] In addition, CPR dealings with the Soviet Union in the period following the Moscow meeting of October 1957 gave rise to a fear among the Nationalists that the CPR might soon have a nuclear capability sufficient to make the Nationalist position untenable.[26] Harold Hinton catches the resultant uneasiness well: "The situation was especially disturbing because it was known that the CPR was trying to develop nuclear weapons, which when acquired would make a Nationalist landing virtually impossible, but that it had not yet developed them. During this transitional period, the Nationalists' incentive to attack would be at a maximum. It began to look in 1958 as though the Nationalists, perhaps as a result of pressures exerted on the United

[24] On this point see Charles A. McClelland, Daniel Harrison, Wayne Martin, Warren Phillips, and Robert Young, *The Communist Chinese Performance in Crisis and Non-Crisis: Quantitative Studies of the Taiwan Strait Confrontation, 1950-1964*, Report to the Naval Ordnance Test Station (China Lake), December 14, 1965, pp. 43-44; and *The Economist*, August 16, 1958, p. 522.

[25] See Robert W. Barnett, "Quemoy: The Use and Consequence of Nuclear Deterrence," Harvard Center for International Affairs, March 1960, pp. 7-8; Donald Zagoria, *The Sino-Soviet Conflict 1956-1961* (New York: Atheneum, 1964), p. 201; and *The Economist*, August 23, 1958, p. 582.

[26] In fact, it is now known that the Soviet Union and the CPR signed an agreement on advanced technology for defense during October 1957.

States the previous year, were acquiring for the first time the ability to invade the mainland in force."[27]

This fluidity in the Taiwan Strait was heightened substantially during most of 1958 by a rather high level of political turmoil and uncertainty within the CPR. The conjunction of two sets of developments produced this condition. First, the regime had reacted negatively to the consequences of the liberalization campaign of 1957 and had instituted a fairly severe crackdown at the beginning of 1958.[28] Second, the "great leap forward" began to get under way on a large scale in the middle of 1958. The first formal order to organize people's communes, for example, was issued on August 29,[29] a date that makes this development virtually simultaneous with the inception of the 1958 crisis in the Taiwan Strait. Several aspects of this internal turmoil appear to be closely tied to the increasing tension in the confrontation in the Strait. To begin with, the signs of disturbance inside the CPR evidently made the Nationalists hopeful that the time for an attempt to return to the mainland had at last arrived. In addition, both the military buildup in Fukien province and the "liberate Taiwan" campaign launched by the CPR during July 1958[30] seem to have been related at least partially to the goals of deterring the Nationalists and reducing internal tension within the CPR by providing an external distraction.

These elements of local fluidity dovetailed with other patterns of international change to create an atmosphere of acute uncertainty by the middle of 1958. Above all, several outstanding advances in Soviet military technology, beginning

[27] Hinton, *Communist China in World Politics* (Boston: Houghton Mifflin, 1966), p. 265. The final point in this statement, dealing with the growth of Nationalist forces, is clearly too strong. In fact, one of the things that the crisis itself demonstrated was the existence of some highly significant weaknesses in the military establishment of the Nationalists.

[28] See Richard Stebbins, *The United States in World Affairs 1958* (New York: Harper and Row [for the Council on Foreign Relations], 1959), p. 304; and Barnett, *op.cit.*, p. 16.

[29] Stebbins, *op.cit.*, p. 310.

[30] For a discussion of the cessation of the "liberate Taiwan" campaign during August and some general comments on the links between the internal and external propaganda needs of the CPR during this period, see *infra*, Chap. Sixteen.

in 1957, had generated perceptions that the overall East-West strategic balance might be shifting markedly.[31] The Chinese especially appear to have felt that these changes were of far-reaching significance and should be put to good advantage as extensively as possible in political relations with the West. Particularly, the Chinese (unlike the more circumspect Russians) apparently calculated that the shifting strategic balance would make the West increasingly cautious in more and more areas, thus providing an effective umbrella under which a variety of probes could be successfully carried out.[32] The probe in the Taiwan Strait was to serve as a primary test of this theory.

In this context the Middle Eastern crisis which flared up on July 14[33] became a major cause of international fluidity underlying the subsequent crisis in the Taiwan Strait and a source of severe disappointment to the Chinese. The previously somewhat abstract Sino-Soviet disagreement about the significance of the shifting strategic balance was concretized in this crisis.[34] The Chinese appear to have insisted that a "get tough" policy vis-à-vis the West was necessary at this juncture[35] and that Khrushchev's evident prudence during the Middle Eastern crisis, even at the diplomatic level, was based on serious miscalculations. More specifically, the Middle Eastern crisis seems to have had at least two direct effects on the subsequent crisis in the Taiwan Strait. The Chinese came away from it highly disappointed and perhaps half-determined to find an opportunity to demonstrate the validity of their own view. Also, the hope that the West would continue to be substantially preoccupied with the Middle East

[31] In particular, the year 1957 witnessed the testing of the first Soviet ICBM and the launching of the first satellite into space (Sputnik I).

[32] There is no doubt about the existence of a Sino-Soviet disagreement in this area. For a discussion concerning the significance of this disagreement, consult the alternative formulations in Zagoria, *op.cit.*, Chap. 7; and in Morton Halperin and Tang Tsou, "The 1958 Quemoy Crisis," in Morton Halperin, ed., *Sino-Soviet Relations and Arms Control* (Cambridge: M.I.T. Press, 1967), Chap. 10.

[33] The *coup d'état* in Iraq occurred on July 14 and the expeditious landing of American marines in Lebanon followed during the early hours of July 15.

[34] On this subject see Zagoria, *op.cit.*, pp. 195-196.

[35] *Ibid.*, p. 198.

evidently influenced Chinese thinking about the prospects for success with a probe in the Strait and about the auspicious occasion to initiate such a probe.[36]

Finally, the middle of 1958 was an uncertain period in Sino-American relations. The ambassadorial talks between the two countries, begun in Geneva in 1955, had terminated with the meeting on December 13, 1957.[37] There followed during the first half of 1958 a series of exchanges about the continuation of the meetings that in fact resulted only in acrimonious disagreements.[38] Simultaneously, the CPR more and more emphasized its notion that the time was ripe for a "get tough" policy vis-à-vis the United States. The United States only added fuel to the fire with the publication on August 11 of a new and rather unyielding statement of American policy toward China.[39] Therefore, an atmosphere of increasing uncertainty in this area also coincided with the tension and disturbances emanating from East Asia.

Interestingly, the eruption of the crisis in the Taiwan Strait in August did not have an immediate disruptive effect on the more general course of East-West relations. In fact, there occurred a relatively sharp compartmentalization of the crisis from several other aspects of East-West relations. This development was particularly evident with regard to the handling of the Middle Eastern crisis and the course of the disarmament dialogue during the second half of 1958.

Following the "good neighbor" resolution of August 21 in the General Assembly of the United Nations,[40] the Middle

[36] *Ibid.*, p. 206.

[37] The proximate cause of this termination was the reassignment of the American ambassador to Switzerland (U. Alexis Johnson) to the Far East together with the unwillingness of the CPR to accept alternate arrangements proposed by the United States.

[38] For the details of these exchanges, see Chalmers Roberts, "Caught in a Trap of Our Own Making," *The Reporter*, Vol. 19, No. 5 (October 2, 1958), 11-13.

[39] See the text of this statement, dated August 11, 1958, in *Department of State Bulletin* (hereafter cited as *DOSB*), XXXIX, No. 1002 (September 8, 1958), 385-390.

[40] For a general discussion of the Assembly's handling of the Middle Eastern crisis in 1958, consult Richard I. Miller, *Dag Hammarskjold and Crisis Diplomacy* (New York: Oceana, 1961), Chap. VII.

Eastern crisis gradually began to subside. Despite their failure to agree on a summit conference to deal with the Middle East, the United States and the Soviet Union tacitly proceeded to bring a nondisruptive end to the crisis. In this milieu, United Nations presences were able to work in the Middle East, and the Secretary-General could operate in the area with considerable success.[41] As a result, by late October the United States felt able to withdraw its marines from Lebanon, and the acute phases of the crisis were over despite the continuation of various low-level disturbances.

The coincidence of favorable developments in the field of disarmament with the unfolding of the Taiwan Strait crisis is perhaps even more remarkable. At the end of August, the Geneva conference of experts concluded deliberations for the control of nuclear testing on an optimistic note.[42] Then between August 29 and October 10 the United States and the Soviet Union negotiated arrangements for another conference on nuclear testing, which opened in Geneva on October 31,[43] and for a conference on the specific problem of surprise attack, which opened in Geneva on November 10.[44] Moreover, the United States, the Soviet Union, and Britain agreed to impose a tacit moratorium on nuclear testing on October 31, despite the fact that they all conducted extensive nuclear tests during September and October. Finally, the first tentative signs of interest in coordinating, at least to some extent, on the peaceful uses of outer space appeared at the United Nations during the fall of 1958.

The outcome of the Taiwan Strait crisis of 1958 was, of course, indeterminate with regard to the specific objects of the contest. While the Nationalists retained physical control of the offshore islands, the CPR retained the ability to reacti-

[41] See Joseph P. Lash, *Dag Hammarskjold: Custodian of the Brush-Fire Peace* (Garden City, N.Y.: Doubleday, 1961), Chap. 9.

[42] For the relevant documents on the deliberations of the Geneva conference, see *DOSB*, XXXIX, No. 1004 (September 22, 1958), 452-462.

[43] The critical documents in this connection were the Soviet note of August 29, 1958, and the American reply of September 10, 1958.

[44] The exchange on this question followed the same pattern as the exchange on nuclear testing. The critical documents were the Soviet note of September 15, 1958, and the American reply of October 10, 1958.

vate the physical confrontation at any time of its own choosing. Despite this indecisiveness on the proximate issues, however, the crisis affected a number of more general issues of international significance.

In the first instance, the crisis had important consequences for Chinese Communist hopes about the Taiwan issue itself and the more general issue of the CPR's position in international politics. With regard to short-term and proximate effects, the outcome was largely negative. The CPR failed to take any of the offshore islands or to undermine the morale of the Nationalist regime on Taiwan. Moreover, it suffered a public demonstration of its military inferiority,[45] and its reputation among the nonaligned countries seems to have been somewhat damaged, at least temporarily.[46] At the same time, the crisis produced some general and intangible benefits for the CPR. In particular, it appears to have buttressed the CPR's political campaign to be recognized as a great power. As Harry Schwartz put it in October 1958, "the crisis they [the Chinese Communists] began last August has put their country at the center of the world stage."[47] In this respect, the crisis served to highlight the changing power structure in East Asia and the impossibility of ignoring the CPR as a major force in the area.

Also, the crisis lent a note of urgency to the annual debate on the China issue at the thirteenth session of the General Assembly, which began in New York on September 16. The day-to-day events of the crisis were followed closely by diplomats in New York, and the situation figured prominently in the Assembly's general debate. Nevertheless, the crisis failed to alter significantly voting alignments on the Chinese membership question. Despite some small shifts in the voting, this

[45] For an interesting discussion of this result, see Tang Tsou, "Mao's Limited War in the Taiwan Strait," *Orbis*, III, No. 3 (Fall 1959), 346-347.

[46] On this point consult R. F. Wall, "Formosa and the Chinese Offshore Islands," in G. Barraclough, *Survey of International Affairs, 1956-1958* (London: Oxford, 1962), p. 574.

[47] In the *New York Times*, October 12, 1958, Sect. IV, p. 5.

question was disposed of in a fashion essentially conforming to the pattern of previous sessions of the Assembly.[48]

The effects of the crisis were much more notable on the Sino-Soviet relationship. It is difficult to judge accurately whether events in the crisis itself played an important part in the genesis of the Sino-Soviet rift. Several widely divergent interpretations of the crisis from this perspective exist.[49] It is nevertheless possible to draw several conclusions in this area. First, though the evidence provided by the crisis was by no means definitive, the outcome clearly favored Khrushchev's position in the debate over the shifting strategic balance.[50] Second, the "1958 Taiwan crisis . . . confirmed the impossibility of China's achieving even local objectives in the face of United States opposition without overt Soviet backing."[51] Despite the CPR's rising political status, its military weakness still sharply curtailed its freedom of action, even in the Taiwan Strait. Third, the crisis (particularly in its later stages) appears to have led to a noticeable decline in the political value attached to the Sino-Soviet defense treaty by the Chinese.[52]

The 1958 crisis had further important consequences for the international position of the Chinese Nationalists and their future relationship with the United States. Above all, the crisis led to a clarification, and therefore an implicit reduction, of the American commitment to the Nationalists. This

[48] For a summary of the treatment of the Chinese representation issue by the General Assembly in 1958 as well as the details of the voting, consult *Yearbook of the United Nations 1958* (New York: United Nations Office of Information, 1959), pp. 89-91.

[49] Cf. the arguments of Zagoria, *op.cit.*, Chap. 7, and John Thomas, "Soviet Behavior in the Quemoy Crisis of 1958," *Orbis*, VI, No. 1 (Spring 1962), 38-64, on one side; and the arguments of Halperin and Tsou, *op.cit.*, on the other.

[50] For an exposition of this argument, see Alice Hsieh, *Communist China's Strategy in the Nuclear Era* (Englewood Cliffs, N.J.: Prentice-Hall, 1962), p. 129.

[51] *Ibid.*, p. 130.

[52] During the crisis, the Soviets began noticeably to confine their treaty obligations to the commitment to defend the CPR against a direct *American* attack on the mainland in force. Under the circumstances, the treaty retained little value in terms of many of the CPR's most important foreign policy interests. On this subject see also Thomas, *op.cit.*, p. 41.

77

shift manifested itself most strikingly in American insistence during October that Chiang Kai-shek publicly renounce the use of overt force as a means of returning to the mainland.[53] Though the American relationship to the Nationalist regime remained ambiguous on certain points in the aftermath of the crisis,[54] it is difficult to dispute the fact that the 1958 crisis had the effect of deemphasizing the military value of the off-shore islands, of obscuring the residual myth of a Nationalist return to the mainland in the foreseeable future, and, in general of tarnishing Chiang's claim to be the real representative of China.[55] Despite these important shifts, the United States was rebuked in the aftermath of the crisis for not forcing even greater alterations in the situation in the Taiwan Strait itself. Criticism centered primarily on American failure to force upon Chiang an arrangement for the offshore islands that would remove them effectively from local contention[56] and the consequent American failure to move decisively at this point toward a formal enunciation of a "two-Chinas" policy.

Finally, the crisis was an important determinant of the political setting of several subsequent developments. Above all, it contributed to the general uncertainty about international relations that pervaded the second half of 1958 as crises in the Middle East, the Far East, and Europe unfolded in succession.[57] More specifically, the firmness of the United States in the Taiwan Strait was probably a significant asset for the

[53] American pressure in this area showed itself especially in the American-Nationalist joint communiqué of October 23, 1958. For the text of the communiqué, see *DOSB*, XXXIX, No. 1011 (November 10, 1958), 721-722.

[54] In particular, the Nationalists subsequently sought to explain away their renunciation of the use of force to return to the mainland. For example, they raised the possibility of uprisings within the CPR and began to argue, in this connection, that renunciation of the use of force applied only to the *initiation* of violent actions.

[55] For a good discussion of these points, see O. Edmund Clubb, "Chiang's Shadow over Warsaw," *The Reporter*, Vol. 19, No. 5 (October 2, 1958), 16-17.

[56] Not only did the United States fail to exert decisive pressure for some form of internationalization of the offshore islands, the United States ultimately refused even to pressure the Nationalists into making token reductions of their garrisons on the islands.

[57] See Stebbins, *op.cit.*, p. 75.

West in the renewed Soviet-American confrontation over Berlin initiated by the Soviets in November 1958.[58] Beyond this, effects of the crisis on subsequent events remain somewhat nebulous.[59] The American reputation among the nonaligned states apparently suffered to some extent as a result of the firm stand of the United States during the crisis.[60] On the other hand, it is extremely difficult to discover any clearcut connections between the actions of the United States during the crisis and the substantial Republican losses in the American Congressional elections of November 1958.

Berlin, 1961

The crisis centering upon Berlin during 1961 arose from two clearly distinguishable sources. The controversy over Berlin was reactivated as a focal point of general East-West tension at the Vienna meeting between Kennedy and Khrushchev on June 3-4, 1961. In the meantime, an extremely serious internal crisis within the German Democratic Republic (GDR) had been building up rapidly since the early months of 1961. These two levels of crisis began to interact during the summer of 1961, thus producing many of the peculiar ambiguities and complexities of the 1961 Berlin crisis.

The political environment in which these events began to unfold was substantially fluid at several distinct levels. At the global level, there were in 1961 widespread feelings that the strategic balance was becoming more favorable to the Soviet Union.[61] The Soviet military advances of the late fifties were now buttressed by the highly politicized American concern with the "missile gap" and by the extensively advertised space exploits of the Soviet Union.[62] Though the

[58] For an interesting argument along this line, see William H. Chamberlain, "The Lesson of Quemoy," *The New Leader*, XLI, No. 46 (December 15, 1958), 21.

[59] A number of points concerning the impact of the crisis on the internal politics of the CPR are discussed in Chapter Sixteen *infra*.

[60] On this point see Wall, *op.cit.*, p. 574.

[61] For a discussion of changing perceptions about the nature of the strategic balance during this period, see Smith, *op.cit.*, p. 256.

[62] On August 7, 1961, for example, the *New York Times* ran a long and interesting account of Soviet efforts to advertise their space exploits for political purposes.

United States in fact retained its operational superiority at the strategic level, an increasingly important factor as the 1961 crisis wore on, perceptions of a shifting strategic balance were widespread in 1961 and appear to have been a consideration in the timing of the Soviet decision to rekindle the Berlin crisis.[63]

At the same time, a number of developments stemming primarily from American foreign policy reinforced this sense of flux.[64] There was a new and largely untested American Administration; some of Kennedy's actions suggested irresolution in foreign policy, and the Soviets evidently sensed—especially after Vienna—a slackening of American will and resolve in international problems. Other, more tangible, developments seemed to support the same conclusion. The American position on the Laotian situation was increasingly conciliatory, and the debate within the United States concerning military doctrines and postures suggested both confusion and dissension about existing arrangements. But, above all, the Administration had been genuinely shocked by the Cuban Bay of Pigs disaster in April and was still struggling to regain confidence as the summer of 1961 began. For these reasons, the East-West relationship seemed particularly fluid at this time. For the Soviets, faced with the growing militancy of the Chinese within the Communist bloc and the desirability of achieving a significant success for presentation to the Twenty-Second Party Congress in October, the situation appeared to be highly favorable.[65]

At a somewhat lower level, there were in central Europe during the early months of 1961 growing elements of political fluidity which clearly shaped both the point of actual confrontation and the basic nature of the 1961 crisis. The conflict over Berlin, which the Soviets had earlier brought to a boil in

[63] For a discussion of the impact of this factor on Soviet decision-making, consult Hans Speier, *Divided Berlin* (New York: Praeger, 1961), pp. 140-141.

[64] See Smith, *op.cit.*, p. 231.

[65] The Twenty-Second Congress of the Communist Party of the Soviet Union was expected, from the beginning of 1961, to be an important event both in terms of the Sino-Soviet disagreements on foreign operations and for domestic economic programs in the allocation of available resources. For discussion of these points, see Speier, *op.cit.*, p. 139.

November 1958, had been left unresolved and with no amelioration of the Soviet anxiety to achieve international acceptance of the permanence of the division of Germany. For this reason and because of the peculiar geographical location of Berlin, the possibility of the Berlin controversy's being reactivated was always present. By 1961, there were growing doubts in Europe about American determination to hold the line in Berlin.[66] Disagreements among the major NATO powers concerning defense policies were mounting rapidly. Moreover, problems of this kind were becoming more influential in the light of the declining viability of a straightforward strategy of nuclear deterrence for the defense of Europe in the wake of Soviet technological advances.[67] In the spring of 1961, the Kennedy Administration raised these issues squarely in the debate over the concepts of flexibility and graduated response. By early summer, however, these problems were far from an accepted resolution. On the contrary, the issues had become a major source of controversy within the NATO alliance, existing defense arrangements had been cast into doubt, and alternatives had not yet been implemented.

The most spectacular elements of political fluidity in Europe during the early months of 1961, however, arose from the internal crisis within the GDR.[68] This crisis developed from a number of sources. A strong push toward agricultural collectivization in the early months of 1961 had met with widespread popular resistance. For this reason and because of poor planning there were serious agricultural failures, and therefore food shortages, within the GDR during 1961. At the same time, industrial production quotas were less and less being met, and consumers' goods became even more

[66] See Smith, op.cit., p. 240.

[67] For a provocative discussion relating these developments to the buildup of the Berlin crisis of 1961, see Windsor, op.cit., p. 231. A more general discussion of American strategic thinking during the first year of the Kennedy Administration may be found in William Kaufmann, *The McNamara Strategy* (New York: Harper and Row, 1964), especially Chaps. 2 and 3.

[68] For a good discussion of the component elements and development of the internal crisis within the GDR, see Windsor, op.cit., pp. 236-237.

scarce than usual. All these problems were partially caused by, and certainly exacerbated by, the effects of the refugee flow through Berlin. The GDR was sustaining a significant loss of critical manpower through the exodus of refugees. Moreover, the possibility of flight for those remaining reduced the ability of the Ulbricht regime to implement its economic policies by means of coercion. The political situation within the GDR began to deteriorate rapidly. "By June of 1961, in fact, the Ulbricht regime was near collapse. If something were not done, and done quickly, a new 17th of June [1953] would be at hand."[69]

Under the circumstances, one of the Soviet motives in reactivating the global features of the Berlin controversy in June 1961 was doubtless the tactical one of relieving internal pressure on the regime of the GDR. The immediate results of Soviet initiatives at Vienna and afterward, however, were only to aggravate the crisis within the GDR.[70] The flow of refugees began to rise sharply as fear that the sector boundary in Berlin would be closed spread in East Germany. This heightened the crisis within the GDR, which in turn influenced the overall East-West conflict.

The 1961 Berlin crisis therefore emerged from a background of substantial political fluidity. In addition, it was played out during the second half of the year against a backdrop of concomitant international disturbances. During June and July the Iraqi-Kuwait dispute came to a head. This dispute acquired important international implications following the military intervention of Great Britain on June 25. Then on July 19, the Bizerte crisis between France and Tunisia erupted. This crisis ultimately generated considerable violence and became the subject of an emergency session of the United Nations General Assembly during August. The later months of 1961 also witnessed some of the tensest moments of the Congo crisis, especially in connection with the attempted secession of Katanga. Severe fighting occurred during September and December; Hammarskjold was killed in a

[69] Smith, *op.cit.*, p. 256.
[70] For a discussion of this paradoxical aggravation, see *ibid.*, pp. 256-257.

plane crash during September while attempting to bring the crisis under control, and partly as a result the United Nations itself was thrown into a state of severe internal confusion. The forcible Indian seizure of Goa at the end of the year added yet another disturbance to the international setting. And throughout these months, difficulties surrounding the Geneva negotiations on Laos, and efforts to achieve an arms control agreement concerning nuclear testing created additional problems in East-West relations. These two sets of negotiations became significantly involved in the Berlin crisis because they offered indirect channels for exercising pressure aimed ultimately at the Berlin confrontation. The dramatic announcement by the Soviet Union on August 30 stating its decision to resume nuclear testing, for example, was at least partially designed to exert pressure on the Western powers to negotiate on the issues of the Berlin crisis on terms favorable to the Soviet Union.

It remains to inquire whether the Berlin crisis itself was influential in bringing about or catalyzing political change. Most specifically, the crisis clearly altered several aspects of the situation of the city of Berlin. The closing of the sector boundary halted the flow of refugees. The crisis led to a final administrative division of the city, the termination of free movement between the eastern and western sectors of the city, and a definitive disruption of the four-power political regime in Berlin. Moreover, Berlin lost a good deal of its quality as a Western showplace and source of demonstration effects within the GDR as a result of the 1961 crisis. And the symbolic value of the city in West German eyes as a sign of hope for the eventual reunification of the country was diminished. At the same time, it is important to emphasize that the crisis did not destroy the political autonomy of West Berlin or lead to any significant curtailment of access to the city from the West.

The outcome of the 1961 crisis was of critical importance in stabilizing the internal situation within the GDR. The closing of the sector boundary successfully terminated the large-scale and critical manpower drain caused by the refugee flow. And this was accomplished without serious internal uprisings, let alone disturbances in any way reminiscent of those of June 1953. In the upshot, the Ulbricht regime was able both to stabilize its proximate situation and to increase its longer-term control over the East German population by destroying the option of flight.[71] In the immediate aftermath of the crisis, the regime engaged in a successful, though highly coercive, crackdown aimed at eliminating the sources of the 1961 disturbances. But in terms of longer-run effects, the added control acquired by the Ulbricht regime as a result of the 1961 crisis has been a major factor allowing it to engage in an increasingly successful program of industrialization in East Germany.

Though less striking, the effects of the crisis in the Federal Republic of Germany were also significant. Most immediately, the crisis had a major impact on the nationwide elections of September 17 and was a key factor in the Christian Democratic Union's (CDU) loss of its parliamentary majority.[72] Thus, West Germany was in the hands of a caretaker government for a number of weeks following the election while the crisis was still going on. Moreover, the relative defeat of the CDU in this election effectively marked the beginning of the end of Konrad Adenauer's reign as Chancellor, making the 1961 election an important turning point in postwar German politics. At the same time, the 1961 crisis became a factor in altering the relationship between the Federal Republic and its NATO allies.[73] The crisis not only emphasized certain important divergences of interest between the FRG and the United States, it also led to an increasing interest in the possibilities of a Franco-German axis on the Continent. In this connection, the 1961 crisis was an important link in the chain of developments culminating in the treaty between France and the FRG in January 1963.

[71] For an interesting discussion of the extent to which the destruction of the option of flight forced East Germans to think more in terms of working within the existing system, see Geoffrey McDermott, *Berlin: Success of a Mission?* (New York: Harper and Row, 1963), p. 42.

[72] On the impact of the crisis on the elections of September 17 in the FRG, see John W. Keller, *Germany, the Wall and Berlin* (New York: Vantage Press, 1964), pp. 96-111.

[73] See John R. Dornberg, "Berlin: Consequences of Crisis," *The Nation,* Vol. 193, No. 6 (September 2, 1961), 111-113.

of other countries in the area. During the earlier months of 1962, for example, the Organization of American States (OAS) had begun to move toward a policy of sanctioning Cuba in an effort to bring a halt to these developments.[77] At the same time, the United States was becoming steadily more concerned about the potential of Cuba as a source of Communist-oriented, subversive activities in Latin America. This led, among other things, to a further deterioration of relations between the United States and Cuba, to the point where hostilities did not seem wholly implausible. As a result, the Cuban government, already subject to considerable influence from Moscow, evidently felt impelled to encourage actively a sharp increase in shipments of Soviet military matériel to the island. The Caribbean in the later months of 1962, then, was a highly unstable arena.

Developments involving the global interests of the United States and the Soviet Union provided the additional elements of fluidity for a major confrontation in the Caribbean. As indicated in the preceding section, the inconclusive outcome of the Berlin crisis of 1961 had left an atmosphere of great uncertainty with regard to the state of both the strategic balance and the political postures of the United States and the Soviet Union. In the United States, moreover, public opinion concerning Cuba had become steadily more agitated in the aftermath of the fiasco at the Bay of Pigs in April 1961. Under these circumstances, the juxtaposition of the Soviet arms buildup in Cuba during the summer and the upcoming 1962 Congressional election within the United States further heightened American sensitivities about Cuba. The opposition Republicans found it impossible to leave an attractive issue alone, and the defensiveness of the Kennedy Administration on the issue stimulated additional attacks. The problem for the Soviets, on the other hand, was different. The true proportions of the "reverse missile gap" were by this time becoming

[77] See, for example, the second and sixth resolutions of the Punta del Este Conference of January 1962. The texts of these resolutions can be found conveniently in David L. Larson, ed., *The "Cuban Crisis" of 1962: Selected Documents and Chronology* (Boston: Houghton Mifflin, 1963), pp. 216-220.

increasingly evident and embarrassing to the Soviets,[78] who were apparently quite genuinely disturbed by the counter-force posture and first-strike implications they saw in the un-folding "McNamara strategy."[79] Under the influence of these perceptions, the Soviet Union appears to have become in-creasingly interested in projects aimed at diversifying its stra-tegic arrangements, at least temporarily, while also consider-ing ways to augment its overall strategic strength. For these reasons, Cuba had the misfortune to become simultaneously an object of extreme American sensitivity and of Soviet inter-est in affecting, at least politically, the strategic balance.[80] Coupled with the concurrent problems of local instability in the Caribbean, these broader elements of fluidity set the stage for a serious confrontation in the area.

The actual crisis in 1962 lasted such a short time that intra-crisis political fluidity was, on the whole, of only secondary importance. The one real exception to this conclusion lies in the explosive situation presented by the "offensive" Soviet mis-siles in Cuba. There were important uncertainties about these missiles since it was unclear when they would begin to be-come fully operational. Though the subject is controversial, there is no doubt that if some of the Soviet missiles had be-come operational before the end of the crisis, this develop-ment in itself would have had important effects on key bar-gaining equations.[81] In addition, the very presence of these missiles in Cuba had an important impact on political per-spectives and expectations which played a role in determin-ing the outcome of the crisis. Though one result was a sense of heightened danger, the presence of Soviet offensive mis-

[78] For an interesting exploration of the implications of this develop-ment, consult Arnold L. Horelick and Myron Rush, *Strategic Power and Soviet Foreign Policy* (Chicago: University of Chicago Press, 1966), especially pp. 83-103.

[79] See Kaufmann, *op.cit.*, especially Chap. 2, for a general formulation of the principal elements of the so-called McNamara Strategy.

[80] On this conjunction of developments, see Arnold Horelick, "The Cuban Missile Crisis: An Analysis of Soviet Calculations and Behavior," *World Politics*, XVI, No. 3 (April 1964), 363-389.

[81] See *ibid.* for what is perhaps the most balanced discussion of this point.

a spur to the disarmament and test-ban talks."[91] Also, the Eighteen Nation Disarmament Conference resumed its meetings in Geneva on November 26. And 1963 was the year of the "hot line," the partial test-ban treaty, and the space resolution at the United Nations.

The crisis had at the same time a marked impact on developments *within* the two major blocs. Though the effect of the crisis in this regard was essentially to boost ongoing changes, the net consequences were significant. Interestingly, the overall result of the 1962 crisis for the NATO alliance seems to be that it augmented the already present sense of disarray. It is of course true that the United States demonstrated its willingness to act in the Cuban crisis. But the secrecy surrounding the American decision-making process was a difficult pill to swallow for those NATO members already resentful of American control within the alliance. Moreover, the fact that the crisis took place in the western hemisphere sharply stressed the lack of congruence between the global interests of the United States and the more Europe-centered interests of the other allies. Finally, the temporal juxtaposition of the Cuban crisis and the Nassau Conference with its public disclosure of the Skybolt decision (in December) heightened the impact of both of these reactions.

The principal effect of the crisis on the Soviet bloc, on the other hand, arose from its influence in widening the Sino-Soviet rift. As *The Economist* put it in November, "That the Cuban crisis has divided the Communist world, and will continue to do so, is obvious enough. The events of October in the Caribbean have brought out with the greatest possible drama all the crucial points of division that have marked the Communist world during the last three years."[92] The Soviet failure in Cuba subsequently became a major source of ammunition for the Chinese during the 1963 polemics. The Chinese were able to strike close to home with their charges of Soviet "adventurism" and "capitulationism" arising out of

[91] Izakov, *op.cit.*, p. 11.
[92] *The Economist*, November 10, 1962, p. 547.

the Cuban crisis.[93] In general, the obvious demonstration of Soviet fallibility in the Cuban crisis has stimulated the growing trend of recent years in the Communist world away from unquestioning acceptance of the leadership position of the Soviet Union.

Finally, the 1962 crisis produced two highly significant side effects, though these were essentially temporary in their international relevance. It gave the Kennedy Administration a "new sense of confidence"[94] and operated to dispel doubts about American willingness to take a firm stand, previously resulting from the Administration's handling of problems, involving the Bay of Pigs, the Vienna meeting, Berlin, and Laos. In this respect, the crisis may well have had a salutary international effect, broadly speaking, by bringing the perspectives of both Kennedy and Khrushchev more into line with reality. In addition, the outcome of the Cuban crisis clearly stifled any Soviet plans for initiatives with regard to Europe. Although it is quite likely that the Soviets initially hoped to reap some advantages on the Berlin question from their activities in Cuba,[95] the actual outcome of the crisis appears to have worked to the opposite end.

Conclusion

The preceding analysis confirms, on the whole, both major elements of the hypothesis that periods of crisis tend to be politically fluid. At the same time, it raises other general points about the political context characteristic of periods of crisis. One of the things that makes individual crises particularly interesting as objects of study is the extent to which they emphasize the connections and interactions between local and global aspects of international politics. In the first instance,

[93] For a discussion of the treatment of the 1962 crisis during the Sino-Soviet polemics of 1963, see William Griffith, *The Sino-Soviet Rift* (Cambridge: M.I.T. Press, 1964), especially pp. 60-66.

[94] See I. F. Stone, "The Brink" (a review of *The Missile Crisis* by Elie Abel), *The New York Review of Books*, VI, No. 6 (April 14, 1966), 12-16.

[95] For a discussion of the links between Berlin and Cuba in Soviet thinking, see Z. B. Brzezinski, "Cuba in Soviet Strategy," *The New Republic*, Vol. 147, No. 18 (November 3, 1962), 7-8.

major crises generally offer a microcosm of ongoing changes in international politics, and, as they develop, they tend to concentrate these dynamic elements around a single point of confrontation that is both clearly demarcated geographically and very intensive in terms of the interplay of contending forces. On the other hand, the consequences of these well-defined confrontations generally affect a wide range of relationships in the overall international arena. Though crises frequently do not cause drastic and immediate breaks with the past, in international relationships they often mark turning points of broader significance than developments in the specific locale of their occurrence. Beyond this, there is apparently a great tendency for individual crises to become interconnected with each other. There were, for example, some very evident connections among the major crises of 1958 in the Middle East, the Far East, and Europe. And it is now becoming increasingly clear that there were important political and psychological links connecting the Cuban crisis of 1961, the incessant Berlin situation, and the Cuban missile crisis of 1962. It is, in fact, not so easy to catalyze a major confrontation in an atmosphere of international calm. But once a major crisis occurs, unless it somehow clears the air decisively as was the case with the Cuban crisis of 1962, it would appear that the probabilities of further crises are enhanced.

More specifically, the cases examined in this chapter offer interesting examples of the problems concerning background fluidity raised in the introduction. Fears arising from disadvantageous trends in various broader patterns of international politics were important factors behind the initiation of the Berlin crisis of 1948-1949 and the Cuban crisis of 1962. Perceptions that shifting relationships and emerging patterns of international fluidity were creating a favorable atmosphere for new initiatives, on the other hand, appear to have been important motives behind the Taiwan Strait crisis of 1958 and the 1961 phase of the confrontation over Berlin. Moreover, the Taiwan Strait case and the 1962 Cuban crisis offer clear examples of miscalculations on the part of the initiating parties concerning changing relationships of commitment and strength. In the light of analysis, various aspects of all of these crises emerge as probing actions or testing behavior designed to clarify the limits of acceptable maneuverability in an arena of clearly changing but ambiguous patterns. In short, therefore, the relationships between various types of background fluidity and the initiation of specific crises are marked.

The cases are also impressive with regard to the effects of major crises in altering international political relationships. In this area, however, there are several clarifying points that arise from an examination of specific cases. Above all, it would be a mistake to assume decisive breaks in the *immediate* aftermath of a crisis. International relationships are generally too diffuse and amorphous to allow for such about-faces. Crises do, nevertheless, tend to have important catalytic effects in crystallizing and setting in motion forces of change that are only fully consummated over a longer period of time. In this sense, the impact of crises on relevant attitudes, perspectives, and expectations can be far greater and more influential than their palpable impact. Crises have a certain shock effect in these intangible terms. While major actors generally do not immediately proceed to an alteration of their concrete patterns of commitment and alignment in the aftermath of crises, critical perceptions upon which specific policy calculations are based are likely to reflect markedly the impact of severe crises.

Significant consequences of international crises are frequently unintended and may even be unrecognized in the immediate aftermath of a confrontation. The effects of a crisis echo through the international political system far beyond both the local arena in which the actual confrontation occurs and the specific issues which initiated it. Given the semi-iterative quality of international politics, specific events are apt to take on great symbolic significance in the subsequent flow of international interactions. This is particularly the case in a world increasingly interdependent in the sense that there are growing links between developments in various subsystems (or patterns of relationships) of the overall arena. The fact that crises usually occur in times of substantial background fluidity only increases the scope for these ramifying effects. Under such circumstances, efforts to assess the political results of any given crisis and its unfolding aftermath must necessarily include material on a variety of unintended and unrecognized consequences.

5. The Force of Events

HYPOTHESIS. Under conditions of crisis, "force-of-events" considerations increase in prominence, a development stemming from:

1. Increases in the physical interdependence of the principal participants, and

2. Perceptions on the part of decision-makers that their ability to control the course of events is declining.

The notion of a force-of-events is somewhat difficult to pin down with any precision. There are, in fact, several distinguishable components of the phenomenon that are of interest in analyzing bargaining under conditions of crisis. In concrete terms, the direct confrontation produced by a crisis tends to lock the participants into sharply defined commitments that emphasize their physical interdependence and that consequently reduce their ability to control the course of the interaction independently. Under ordinary conditions, states frequently handle conflict through tacit agreements to avert direct confrontations. Avoidance is often practiced by abstaining from sharp initiatives or large-scale operations in the same geographical area simultaneously. Moreover, the diffusion generated by the contemporaneous pursuit of multiple international interests generally softens the intensity of conflict in any specific locality. The concept of "peaceful coexistence" coupled with a continuation of conflict by various indirect means, for example, embodies the view that conflict is important but direct and clearly demarcated clashes are unacceptably dangerous in the contemporary world. The direct confrontation of a major crisis, however, reduces the scope for ameliorating conflict, thus increasing the interdependence of the principals. Under conditions of crisis, therefore, each participant is apt to experience a reduction in its ability to control the consequences of the confrontation for itself.

At the same time, conditions of crisis tend to generate *perceptions* among decision-makers that their ability to exercise a conscious influence on the course of events is declining. This declining sense of efficacy is generally related to feelings that important local actors are beginning to get out of control or that the events of the crisis are beginning to acquire a momentum of their own. Impressions of this kind undoubtedly stem both from the actual increases in physical interdependence mentioned above, and from the sensations of an acceleration in the pace of events and a decrease in the adequacy of information that often accompany conditions of crisis. This is not to say, however, that reality will necessarily correspond with such perceptions. Conscious control may in fact sometimes increase during crises since decisionmakers under such conditions frequently institute extraordinary procedures aimed at insuring control and since crisis conditions often stimulate creative and imaginative thinking about ways to conduct and terminate them. There are important possibilities for inverse relationships in this area, therefore, since the very perception that control is declining usually stimulates efforts to maintain or increase control.

Berlin, 1948-1949

On the whole, the Berlin crisis of 1948-1949 was characterized by conscious and sustained efforts on both sides to control the course of events. Nevertheless, a number of control problems arose during the crisis from the clear-cut confrontation of military forces in and around Berlin. Although this crisis occurred before *concepts* concerning escalation and inadvertent war had become "fashionable," the physical juxtaposition and interdependence of the two sides made dangers of this kind very real. As Drew Middleton put it on June 27, 1948, "Where troops of two antagonistic powers are in close contact as they are in Berlin, the possibility of the type of 'incidents' which lead to war is always present."[1]

Three types of control problem arising from the physical interdependence associated with this Berlin crisis are discernible. First, it was always possible that any one of several types of incident in the air corridors would expand from an isolated case of harassment or violence to widespread hostilities.[2]

[1] Drew Middleton, in the *New York Times*, June 27, 1948, Sect. IV, p. 3.
[2] For further discussion of the dangers of incidents in the air corridors to Berlin, see *infra* Chap. Thirteen.

Second, confrontations between armed units along the rail lines or autobahn might have provoked unmanageable escalation. After the full Soviet blockade of Berlin was imposed in late June, this danger was effectively confined to possible retaliatory measures should the West have attempted to break the blockade with armed convoys. No such effort was ever made during the crisis precisely because of fears that the resultant clash might get out of hand.[3] Third, civilian demonstrations and riots in the city itself,[4] which on several occasions were controlled only through the intervention of armed police, created situations that could easily have instigated sharp clashes between Soviet and Western troops. The mass meeting on September 9 around the old Reichstag building at the sector boundary, for example, was particularly dangerous in this respect.[5] Each of these types of control problem was complicated by the fact that local commanders on both sides could make significant decisions about such matters on their own authority.[6]

The 1948-1949 crisis produced few indications of any generalized perceptions on the part of decision-makers that the whole situation was or might become uncontrollable. There were, however, clear signs that decision-makers in the national capitals were seriously concerned about the possible consequences of specific incidents. Referring to the air disaster over Berlin on April 5, 1948, *The Economist* cautioned that "The tragedy at Gatow, where an irresponsible Soviet

[3] A single armed train set out for Berlin from Helmstedt on June 21, but no attempt was made to force the train through when it ran into opposition in the Soviet zone of Germany. Moreover, no further efforts were made to break the blockade following its imposition on a full-scale basis on June 24. For material on the sending of the armed train, see Philip Jessup, "Review of Allied Action on Berlin Blockade" (statement in the United Nations Security Council, October 19, 1948). The text of this statement is in *DOSB*, XIX, No. 487 (October 31, 1948), 541-543.

[4] For detailed treatment of the civilian demonstrations and riots in Berlin during this period, consult W. Phillips Davison, *The Berlin Blockade: A Study in Cold War Politics* (Princeton: Princeton University Press, 1958), Chaps. 4 and 5.

[5] This episode is discussed in detail in *ibid.*, pp. 187-190.

[6] For example, the actual decision to *initiate* an airlift to Berlin was taken by General Lucius D. Clay in Germany rather than by higher officials in Washington.

pilot, 'frolicking' an incoming British plane, cannoned both himself and the other aircraft to destruction, is a bitter and urgent warning to those who paddle in the shallows of violence that they may find themselves sucked out into the main torrent."[7] This concern over the dangers of such incidents was echoed repeatedly during the critical phases of the crisis in the summer of 1948. President Truman worried about the "risk that a trigger-happy Russian pilot or hotheaded Communist tank commander might create an incident that could ignite the powder keg."[8] And it is evident from their statements that the Soviet were plagued by similar anxieties.

As a result, both sides were for the most part meticulous in their efforts to avoid overt violence throughout the 1948-1949 crisis. There is no evidence that decision-makers in the capitals ever lost control during the crisis. Moreover, the fact that the only military casualties of the crisis were the men lost in the April 5 incident and in airlift accidents makes it clear that concern over the dangers of confrontation was also operative at local command levels around Berlin.[9] Nevertheless, the dangers arising from physical interdependence in this crisis were genuine. While the safety record compiled during the 1948-1949 crisis was in fact an excellent one, it certainly does not stand as evidence that fears concerning control problems were not solidly grounded.

Taiwan Strait, 1958

The 1958 crisis in the Taiwan Strait produced a high level of awareness concerning the existence and dangers of force-of-events considerations. Problems of this kind arose from several separate sources during this crisis. In the first instance, the clarity of the actual points of contact increased the salience of the elements of conflict in the situation and reduced the opportunities for mutual disengagement without evident losses of prestige. Above all, however, the presence of signifi-

[7] *The Economist*, April 10, 1948, p. 576.

[8] Harry Truman, *Years of Trial and Hope* (Garden City, N.Y.: Doubleday, 1956), p. 124.

[9] For a discussion lending considerable weight to this conclusion, see Lucius D. Clay, *Decision in Germany* (Garden City, N.Y.: Doubleday, 1950), p. 374.

cant, though obviously restrained, violence created serious control problems during this crisis. In general, violent interactions acquire a momentum of their own, making initial restraints difficult to maintain. The proximity of the confrontation and the presence of significant violence during the 1958 crisis necessitated some delegation of effective responsibility for decisions affecting matters of control to local officers. Though this necessity for delegation of authority was a topic of considerable concern during the 1958 crisis, it could not be avoided altogether.[10]

The force-of-events problems of this crisis fall into several categories. First of all, the danger existed that genuinely inadvertent incidents might touch off an expansion of violence that would be extremely difficult to control. Though there was some danger of developments along these lines between Nationalist and Communist Chinese forces, the most salient fears of inadvertent actions hinged on the possibility of violent clashes between Chinese Communist and American forces. The crucial issue here arose from the use of American forces to break the artillery blockade of Quemoy. Though American escort vessels did not go all the way in to the beaches of Quemoy, they did go inside the range of Communist Chinese coastal artillery, thereby creating the danger that one or more American vessels might be accidentally hit and thus provoke a direct Chinese-American encounter.[11] There was also the possibility of accidental contact between American escort vessels and Chinese forces during convoy operations in the Strait itself. It was obviously important to the Chinese People's Republic (CPR) to disrupt efforts to resupply Quemoy. As the artillery blockade around Quemoy itself began to fail, Chinese incentives to utilize torpedo boats or aerial strafing against Nationalist convoys mounted despite the danger of accidental contact with American escort forces. Throughout September, the danger of violent contacts around Quemoy it-

[10] For an interesting account of this problem from the point of view of decision-makers in Washington, see Dwight Eisenhower, *Waging Peace 1956-1961* (Garden City, N.Y.: Doubleday, 1965), p. 299.

[11] See Dulles' news conference of September 9, 1958. The complete transcript is in *DOSB*, XXXIX, No. 1005 (September 29, 1958), 485-493. On the question of escorts, see especially p. 485.

self and in the Taiwan Strait was heightened by the fact that American forces were under orders to respond with overt force if fired upon by Chinese forces.[12]

A second set of force-of-events problems in the 1958 crisis arose from the danger that *ongoing* patterns of violence between the CPR and the Nationalists might begin to escalate beyond control. In view of the great tactical significance of maintaining control of the air over the Strait and the bargaining implications of the aerial contest, the possibilities that Communist-Nationalist air battles might broaden were very real.[13] The narrowness of the air space over the Strait and the willingness of the United States to supply advanced weapons such as the Sidewinder missile to the Nationalists[14] intensified the threat of unmanageable escalation along these lines. The surface contest focusing on the artillery blockade of Quemoy at the same time produced possibilities for escalation.[15] As it was, the blockade, as initially laid down, could be broken without an upswing in the level of violence on the part of the Nationalists, and the CPR refrained from utilizing available countermeasures as the blockade began to give way, preventing the situation from escalating to dangerous proportions. The cautiousness of the CPR at this critical juncture was apparently due to the credibility of both actual and contingent American responses.[16]

Third, from the perspective of the United States and the Soviet Union some of the most serious force-of-events problems of the 1958 crisis arose from possible catalytic actions

[12] On this point consult Eisenhower, *op.cit.*, pp. 295-299; and Donald Zagoria, *The Sino-Soviet Conflict 1956-1961* (New York: Atheneum, 1964), p. 215.

[13] On the importance of the aerial contest over the Strait, see Tang Tsou, "Mao's Limited War in the Taiwan Strait," *Orbis*, III, No. 3 (Fall 1959), 345.

[14] In fact, the introduction of Sidewinder missiles in the air battle of September 24 tipped the balance decisively in favor of the Nationalist air force, which had been gradually demonstrating its superiority in any case. At the time, however, the possibility that introduction of qualitatively new weapons by one side might lead to a similar response by the other side did not seem wholly implausible.

[15] See the *New York Times*, September 7, 1958, Sect. IV, p. 1.

[16] For further comments on this subject see *infra* Chap. Thirteen; and John Thomas, "Soviet Behavior in the Quemoy Crisis of 1958," *Orbis*, VI, No. 1 (Spring 1962), 46.

by their Chinese "clients." Neither superpower was in a position to control fully its Chinese ally, and both the CPR and the Nationalist Chinese had plausible motives for such conduct at certain points during the crisis. Toward the end of September, C. L. Sulzberger summarized this relationship well in his statement that "neither Washington nor Moscow is a completely free agent. Each is subjected to strong influences from client states who are prepared to be more bellicose than their patrons."[17]

With regard to American-Nationalist relations, these problems stemmed from certain Nationalist interests that might profit from an expansion of the violent exchanges. Generally, there is some reason to suppose that Chiang Kai-shek hoped "his oft-proclaimed determination to return to the mainland would become a reality if the United States could be embroiled in a war with Communist China."[18] More specifically, the Nationalists, throughout the 1958 crisis, periodically attempted to extract American acquiescence to a program of Nationalist bombing raids against the mainland. The proximate issue in this connection was the Nationalists' desire to bomb the coastal batteries opposite Quemoy, arising from distrust and impatience with the nonviolent means supported by the Americans to break the artillery blockade of Quemoy. Throughout the crisis the United States made extensive use of political and physical restraints[19] to prevent the Nationalists from extending the pattern of violent exchanges to the mainland, thereby touching off a considerable expansion of the military confrontation. As it happened, the United States succeeded in this endeavor in the 1958 crisis; but it became perfectly clear that the United States could not exercise *absolute* control over the Chinese Nationalists or

[17] C. L. Sulzberger, the *New York Times*, September 29, 1958, p. 26.

[18] For the quotation and additional comments, see Tang Tsou, "The Quemoy Imbroglio: Chiang Kai-shek and the United States," *Western Political Quarterly*, XXII, No. 4 (December 1959), 1,077.

[19] Physical restraints included American efforts to restrict such things as the supply of jet fuel available to the Nationalists. In the crisis, however, political restraints, though far less tangible, were ultimately of greater importance.

102

prevent actions by them which might have led to direct American involvement in major hostilities.[20]

The Soviet problem with the Chinese Communists was somewhat more ambiguous since both parties were generally agreed on the need for great caution in the use of overt force during the crisis. Nevertheless, at several specific junctures the CPR exhibited less fear than the Soviet Union about the possible consequences of its actions, and in general it is quite clear that the CPR had greater incentives to take risks during the crisis than the Soviet Union.[21] Evident Soviet concern about the consequences of catalytic actions by the CPR was exacerbated by a general Soviet fear of escalating from localized violence in the Taiwan Strait to "world war."[22] Several aspects of the Soviet attitude are worth noting. First, Soviet strategic doctrine at the time placed considerable emphasis on the danger of unmanageable escalation arising from local hostilities.[23] Second, the Soviets apparently feared that a general war would result in direct physical damage to the Soviet Union rather than China. Third, the Soviet view of the strategic balance, in contrast to the Chinese, indicated that 1958 was not yet the time to challenge American superiority in matters affected by the overall strategic balance. At least partially as a result of these calculations, the Soviets began to stress in September that their role in the crisis was limited almost entirely to a deterrent function and that

[20] This was the case despite the relatively restrictive formal language of the American-Nationalist treaty of 1954. On the exact meaning of the treaty language, see the text of the Dulles-Yeh exchange clarifying the terms of the treaty in DOSB, XXXII, No. 813 (January 24, 1955), 152. For some interesting, though rather alarmist, points concerning the question of American control over Nationalist actions, see the speech by Dean Acheson reported in the New York Times, September 7, 1958, p. 2.

[21] This was true particularly of the air battles over the Strait and the possibilities of testing the limits of the American system for escorting Nationalist supply vessels.

[22] For comments on the general perspectives of the Soviets and their assessment of the specific dangers of the 1958 crisis, see Zagoria, op.cit., p. 217; and Thomas, op.cit., p. 61.

[23] For a full discussion of the Soviet concern about escalation, consult V. D. Sokolovsky, ed., Military Strategy: Soviet Doctrine and Concepts, intro. by Raymond Garthoff (New York: Praeger, 1963), Chap. IV.

they had no intention of becoming involved in the civil war aspects of the East Asian confrontation.[24] As it turned out, the CPR itself reacted cautiously at critical stages in the crisis and did not actively attempt to embroil the Soviets deeper. Here too, however, the 1958 crisis pointed up the CPR's capacity to undertake, without full Soviet consent, actions which might force the Soviet Union into overt and major hostilities.[25]

Berlin, 1961

The 1961 Berlin crisis produced several distinctive and highly significant types of force-of-events considerations. Available evidence suggests that in 1961 potential dangers along these lines were genuine and that perceptions of them, at least on the part of the principals in the crisis, were relatively realistic. At a number of key points during the crisis, these parties made clear and substantial efforts to insure that the control problems of the confrontation did not get out of hand. This heightened concern with controlling the force of events did not, however, remain constant throughout the crisis. The Soviets in particular made several attempts to manipulate the control problems of the crisis for bargaining leverage. Their most serious activities to this end came in a series of verbal initiatives, prior to the closing of the sector boundary in the city by the German Democratic Republic (GDR) on August 13, to raise Western fears of war breaking out over the Berlin question.

The control problems arising during this crisis can be divided into several rather distinct categories. There were, to

[24] The shift in the Soviet posture on this question culminated in Khrushchev's statement of October 5 in which he made it clear that "we [the Soviets] have not interfered and do not intend to interfere in the civil war which the Chinese people are waging against the Chiang Kai-shekite clique." This statement appeared originally in *Pravda*, October 6, 1958. The text can be found conveniently in the *Current Digest of the Soviet Press* (hereafter cited as *CDSP*), X, No. 40 (November 12, 1958), 18.

[25] This, in fact, is the point at which the 1958 crisis seems to have become a source of Sino-Soviet disagreements. In other words, problems arising from the actual conduct of the crisis seem to have made a greater impression on the Soviets than problems associated with the planning for the probe in the Strait during July and August.

begin with, two important types of problem associated with the internal crisis of the GDR during the period before the closure of the sector boundary. In the first instance, the internal situation of the GDR was sufficiently serious to arouse genuine concern about the dangers of internal collapse, major uprisings, or severe riots.[26] This was especially true in the United States during this period. As the *New York Times* put it on August 10: "President Kennedy and his aides are reported to be worried that restive East Germans may stage another uprising against Communist rule. The Administration considers this to be the most dangerous aspect of the current East-West controversy over Germany and Berlin."[27] As a result, much emphasis was placed on the point that the West should not do anything to aggravate the situation by acting in such a way as to raise false hopes within the GDR of the kind that played a role in Hungary in 1956. And the fear was expressed that serious uprisings in East Germany might lead to hasty military intervention by West Germany, the United States, or the Soviet Union, thereby triggering substantial and overt hostilities.[28]

The stream of refugees out of East Berlin also generated force-of-events considerations during this period. In a sense, the refugee flow was a dynamic force during the upswing phase of the 1961 crisis. Growing in any case as a result of the internal GDR crisis, the flow of refugees became a flood in the wake of Soviet actions, beginning at Vienna in early June, to reactivate East-West tension over the Berlin question. The result was a kind of positive feedback process producing both rising tension among the major parties to the crisis and ever increasing numbers of refugees arriving daily at the reception centers in West Berlin. By early August the refugee flow was threatening to become unmanageable.[29] Under these circumstances, Western as well as Eastern misgivings

[26] On the problems arising from the internal situation of the GDR, see Philip Windsor, *City on Leave* (New York: Praeger, 1963), p. 236; and Richard Stebbins, *The United States in World Affairs 1961* (New York: Harper and Row [for the Council on Foreign Relations], 1962), p. 85.

[27] *New York Times*, August 10, 1961, p. 1.

[28] See Jean Edward Smith, *The Defense of Berlin* (Baltimore: The Johns Hopkins Press, 1963), p. 263.

[29] Windsor, *op.cit.*, p. 237.

105

about the refugee flow began to soar.[30] The Western "sigh-of-relief" reaction immediately following the August 13 boundary closure was certainly genuine in the context of these control problems.[31]

The closing of the sector boundary by the GDR, however, brought with it a new set of control problems and force-of-events considerations. In the first instance, there was the serious danger of frustrated uprisings in the East as well as popular demonstrations or incidents on both sides of the sector boundary in Berlin which might well get out of control. Clearly aware of these problems and obviously concerned about a Budapest-type uprising,[32] "the authorities on both sides of the border were determined to prevent the situation getting out of hand."[33] East Berlin was, for all practical purposes, occupied by armed police and military contingents whose primary function was to prevent serious uprisings and incidents. For their part, Western authorities went to considerable lengths to appeal for calm. And the police forces (as well as military contingents in the East) of both sides assigned to duty along the sector boundary itself made every effort to maintain order, a *de facto* program of complementary rather than opposing action. Despite these coordinated efforts, Berlin witnessed some striking examples of crowd behavior producing relatively severe incidents in the days immediately following the closure of the sector boundary. Both sides, as a result, seriously began to doubt the manageability of the local situation in Berlin.

The closing of the sector boundary engendered additional control problems in the city by sharply and unmistakably de-

[30] For an interesting discussion of the development of Western misgivings, see Smith, *op.cit.*, p. 262.

[31] The "sigh of relief" notion was originally applied to Dean Rusk's statement of August 13 in which he pointed out the illegality of the closing of the sector boundary in Berlin, but indicated by his silence on other issues American relief that the Eastern initiative had not been more far-reaching. For some interesting comments on this reaction, see Theodore Sorensen, *Kennedy* (New York: Harper and Row, 1965), p. 593.

[32] On the use of the analogy to the Budapest uprising of 1956, see Deane and David Heller, *The Berlin Wall* (New York: Walker, 1962), p. 36.

[33] *The Economist*, August 19, 1961, p. 711.

marcating the flashpoint of the crisis. The dangers arising from this development were immediate and prolonged. Some control problems hinged on the possibility of Western attempts to interfere physically with the closing of the boundary, a subject that has remained controversial since the crisis.[34] The West chose to make no physical response to the Eastern initiative, thereby alleviating the immediate control problem but also acknowledging its fear of the consequences of action under the circumstances.[35] The presence of opposing troops along the sector boundary in Berlin, however, kept control problems relevant for some months. The resultant danger was heightened in that the sector boundary figured prominently in the bargaining tactics employed by East and West in the remaining phases of the crisis: each side used provocative shows of force along the Wall on several occasions to demonstrate its determination in the bargaining.[36] Though both sides generally exercised marked caution in connection with these shows of force, a confrontation of heavy armor at point-blank range, for example, constitutes a highly interdependent situation in which neither side can fully control the outcome and in which the responsibility for making decisions that might touch off dangerous incidents devolves to a low level in the command structure.

Besides these problems emanating ultimately from the internal crisis of the GDR, other control problems also arose from broader East-West elements of the 1961 confrontation. In general, these are the factors Windsor is referring to in writing about "a localized threat to Berlin, which by the very fact of its local limitation immediately raised the threat of an

[34] The matter has been widely discussed in the West. For some particularly interesting comments, see Kurt L. Shell, "Berlin," in Walter Stahl, ed., *The Politics of Postwar Germany* (New York: Praeger, 1963), pp. 85-102 (especially p. 99).

[35] For further discussion concerning the consequences of this decision, see John Mander, *Berlin: Hostage for the West* (Harmondsworth, Middlesex: Penguin, 1962), p. 113; and Smith, *op.cit.*, p. 276.

[36] These shows of force were not, however, utilized without considerable trepidation. Referring to the confrontation on August 25, for example, Smith writes, "Following the movement of Allied troops to the sector boundary, Secretary Rusk became worried that a major conflict would be touched off in Berlin by 'some PFC on the border.'" See Smith, *op.cit.*, p. 301.

all-out nuclear war."[37] The point here is that a crisis involving the superpowers is likely to become increasingly difficult to control as the specific point of confrontation becomes more sharply defined and geographically delimited. This inverse relationship stems from a number of factors including: the directness of the confrontation; the declining significance of buffers or political "cushions"; the decreasing possibilities of conducting the conflict by indirect means; and the reduction of roles for intermediaries.[38]

To be more specific, fears concerning force-of-events considerations in direct relations between the Western allies and the Soviet Union during the 1961 crisis focused on the problem of access routes across the GDR to Berlin. The crucial political problem was the threat of a separate peace treaty between the Soviet Union and the GDR and the inference that all questions relating to Western access would subsequently come under the control of the East Germans.[39] Fear of this outcome was clearly a powerful influence on the Western allies during the crisis. But in the final analysis, it was the Soviets who were in a position to decide on the *de facto* arrangements governing Western access; that they were ultimately willing to incur significant political costs by foregoing the threat of a separate peace treaty is a clear indication that they too feared the dangers that could arise if East Germany controlled this area. The overall tension and the bargaining requirements of the 1961 crisis also increased the possibilities of serious East-West flare-ups occurring along the access routes, thus igniting a sequence of hostile events extremely difficult to control. In this connection, Windsor is probably right in his contention that it would have been more difficult to control escalation following one or more severe incidents in the air corridors than following hostile

[37] Windsor, *op.cit.*, p. 236.

[38] Whereas many of the political, economic, and ideological processes through which the great powers compete for support in the international arena allow them to avoid the necessity of squaring off against each other directly, a physical confrontation makes direct contact inevitable, thereby increasing the problem of "face-saving."

[39] The logic here was that the treaty would grant full sovereignty to the GDR and that a sovereign state must necessarily have complete control over rights of transit across its territory.

108

clashes on the ground.[40] But the dangers of either happening were sufficient to give pause to both sides. Here two further points are relevant. Both sides coordinated their efforts to avoid serious incidents along the access routes during the tensest periods of the 1961 crisis. The Soviets, especially, were careful to make it clear at the time of the closure of the sector boundary in Berlin that there would be no concomitant moves against the Western position with regard to the access routes. In addition, probing actions involving the access routes during other phases of the crisis were never pushed beyond the level of mutual tolerance. This again meant that the Soviets in particular, as the party on the tactical offensive during most of the crisis, had clearly to restrain their actions out of respect for the general control problems of the crisis which neither side could cope with alone, regardless of its desires or intentions.

Cuba, 1962

The close juxtaposition of antagonistic forces and the psychological intensity that characterized the Cuban confrontation of 1962 generated sharp and pervasive force-of-events considerations. This crisis, like those which had preceded it, held the serious potential danger of incidents that could have led to inadvertent hostilities and unmanageable escalation. In 1962 the danger could be further separated into several distinguishable categories. First, the American naval blockade and the resultant possibility of clashes between Soviet and American ships at sea created a tense and delicate situation. If the Soviet ships had chosen to ignore American warnings, it might well have been impossible to halt them without firing at least some shots.[41] Also, the physical setting of the confrontation at sea made it inevitable that individual captains would have a large degree of operational control over specific points of contact. As Pachter puts it, "If any sea captain had a loose hand on the trigger, naval war might break out."[42] Second, the extensive American reliance on both

---

[40] For his own formulation, see Windsor, op.cit., p. 253.
[41] See infra Chap. Fourteen for further discussion of this point.
[42] Henry Pachter, Collision Course (New York: Praeger, 1963), p. 42.

high- and-low-level reconnaissance flights over Cuba was another potential source of danger for the possibility of serious incidents, especially in view of the presence of Soviet-manned surface-to-air (SAM) missiles on the island. An American U-2 was actually shot down over Cuba on the morning of October 27, at an extremely tense stage in the confrontation, which demonstrates the very real danger this threat posed. In this particular case, there was no direct American retaliation, but evidence indicates a forceful American response to a second similar incident would have been highly probable.[43] Third, there were various possibilities for incidents causally unrelated to the missile crisis to become serious in the context of the tense atmosphere of the crisis. The danger of this type of incident is illustrated by the straying of a U-2, on an air-sampling mission over the North Pole, into Soviet airspace over the Chukotsk Peninsula on October 27. As Khrushchev put it, "An intruding American plane could be easily taken for a nuclear bomber, which might push us to a fateful step."[44]

Besides the relatively concrete problem of incidents, the Cuban crisis caused some intangible but very pervasive concerns about the controllability of force in a tense action-reaction relationship. This problem concerned Walter Lippmann, for example, in his argument that "There is a line of intolerable provocation and humiliation beyond which popular and governmental reactions are likely to become uncontrollable."[45] Several other considerations of this kind came into focus during the Cuban crisis. There was, to begin with, a strong sense of urgency by decision-makers, who felt that time might somehow "run out" if a nonviolent end to the crisis was not quickly found.[46] In the early phases of the crisis, the Americans related this sensation to the problem of maintaining secrecy concerning their knowledge of the missiles

[43] See Henry Brandon, "An Untold Story of the Cuban Crisis," *Saturday Review*, March 9, 1963, p. 56.

[44] From Khrushchev's letter of October 28, 1962, to Kennedy. The relevant text can be found in Pachter, *op.cit.*, p. 225.

[45] Walter Lippmann, "Cuba and the Nuclear Risk," *Atlantic Monthly*, Vol. 211, No. 2 (February 1963), 57.

[46] For a discussion of perceptions along these lines, see Sorensen, *op.cit.*, p. 680.

and to the chance that precipitate actions might follow a Soviet discovery of the level of American knowledge about the missile installations. After the whole situation was made public by Kennedy on October 22, the time problem began to focus on the dangers that might ensue in the event some of the "offensive" Soviet missiles on Cuba actually became operational. A second aspect of this general problem of controllability sprang from a sense that initial actions in a related sequence exert pressure for decisions to move forward with the remaining elements in the sequence.[47] Once a course of action is set, a kind of built-in logic operates to give past actions in the sequence a strong influence on decisions about the future. Finally, there is the problem of momentum.[48] Action-reaction sequences sometimes acquire a certain momentum of their own resulting from delays in stopping or changing plans already in motion as well as from the tendency of decision-makers to resist new information relating to problems on which they have already reached a decision.

Whatever the actual danger along these lines may have been, decision-makers attached much importance to these force-of-events considerations during the 1962 Cuban crisis. There was a pervasive, though generalized, feeling during the crisis that forces beyond the control of the participants were at work. At times, "A morbid feeling of inevitability began to take hold of some of the participants,"[49] and, toward the end, many felt that the crisis "seemed inexorably approaching a cataclysmic climax."[50] Important participants appear to have felt they were holding the reins on powerful "engines of war" that were somehow straining to break free. In the American Executive Committee on October 27, for example, "there was doubt about how much longer the crisis

[47] For an interesting example of thinking along these lines, see the statement by Frank Aiken, foreign minister of Ireland, in the United Nations Security Council on October 24, 1962. The text of the relevant portion of the statement is in David L. Larson, ed., *The "Cuban Crisis" of 1962: Selected Documents and Chronology* (Boston: Houghton Mifflin, 1963), p. 120.

[48] On the problems of momentum in the 1962 crisis, see Sorensen, *op.cit.*, p. 708.

[49] Brandon, *op.cit.*, p. 56.

[50] *Loc.cit.*

could be carefully controlled."[51] Kennedy himself drew parallels between the Cuban crisis and the atmosphere during the summer of 1914 described by Barbara Tuchman in *The Guns of August*.[52] And Khrushchev subsequently spoke of "the fuse of war which had already been lighted."[53] In short, there was a widespread sensation among leaders of being on the brink of disaster and facing a situation in which their ability to control the course of events, despite their best intentions, was very limited.

Nevertheless, both sides made substantial and relatively effective efforts to maintain control over events during this crisis.[54] Largely because of their fears concerning force-of-events considerations, leaders on both sides were extremely careful to avoid the consequences of these dangers. It is clear Kennedy thought explicitly in these terms,[55] and the extreme caution of the Soviets during the week of October 22 makes it evident that they, too, were cognizant of these dangers. This awareness was of great importance in controlling both the naval confrontation and the problem of overflight. At sea, the United States pulled back its blockade to maximize Soviet decision time and then proceeded with extreme caution in stopping Soviet ships. The Soviets, on the other hand, turned all "objectionable" vessels back before contact and were cooperative in submitting the remaining ships to search procedures. In the air, as noted earlier, several incidents occurred to prove the existence of very real dangers for control. But the marked restraint exercised in these cases also provides excellent evidence of the high priority both sides attached to maintaining control over their forces.

[51] This statement appears in "The Cuban Crisis: A Step by Step Review," printed in the *New York Times*, November 3, 1962, pp. 1, 6-7. The text can be found conveniently in Larsen, ed., *op.cit.*, p. 242.

[52] The Tuchman book was at the time popular reading among officials in Washington. On this point see Arthur Schlesinger, Jr., *A Thousand Days* (Boston: Houghton Mifflin, 1965), p. 832.

[53] This statement appears in Khrushchev's speech to the Supreme Soviet on December 12, 1962. The relevant portion of the text can be found in Pachter, *op.cit.*, p. 246.

[54] See Albert and Roberta Wohlstetter, "Controlling the Risks in Cuba," *Adelphi Paper No. 17* (London: The Institute of Strategic Studies, April 1965), pp. 17-18.

[55] For confirmation see Sorensen, *op.cit.*, p. 708.

Conclusion

An analysis of the case materials in this chapter shows that force-of-events problems of major international crises are very real but also tend to evoke high levels of concern and attention on the part of decision-makers. The seriousness of the potential danger appears to be especially evident with regard to the possibilities of specific incidents touching off escalation sequences difficult to manage. In particular, it is clear that conditions of crisis, regardless of intentions, can necessitate *de facto* devolutions of decision-making, thus giving local commanders the ability to undertake actions considerably affecting these force-of-events considerations. The 1958 crisis in the Taiwan Strait was cited as an example in which devolution of this kind occurred on the American side despite explicit efforts to centralize control.

The cases also offered impressive evidence of efforts by decision-makers to take these problems into account and to maintain control over the action-reaction processes of major crises. Considerations of this kind have regularly produced important attempts at coordination between antagonists especially (even though this is paradoxical) during the most critical phases of crises. Though these efforts are of great importance, however, one must not conclude that force-of-events problems of major crises are ultimately not serious. The various distinguishable problems in this area differ markedly in fact, in terms of their susceptibility to conscious control. It is possible to centralize command relationships to some extent, but not to prevent effective devolutions of decision-making entirely. Moreover, it is less difficult to reduce the dangers of escalation following a catalytic event or a genuine accident in a straightforward bilateral confrontation than to control the dangers attendant upon such developments in a more complex relationship.

In general, this distinction between straightforward bilateral or single-axis crises on the one hand and more complex situations on the other is an important one in analyzing force-of-events considerations. The participation of additional actors, especially when they are of divergent types and capacities, is apt to introduce a variety of new force-of-events problems. Not only is the conceptual symmetry of the bilateral confrontation broken, the addition of more participants is likely to produce new axes of contention, greater scope for confusion, larger divergences in motives even among nominal allies, and serious dangers of catalytic actions affecting the stability of the whole confrontation. An especially interesting feature of these more complex relationships is the extent to which they frequently improve the bargaining position of states that are intrinsically weak or ordinarily very much under the influence of the great powers. Above all, such situations may give the lesser states a catalytic influence in the sense that they can credibly threaten to involve the great powers against their will in overt hostilities, even though these lesser states do not generally have the strength to determine the outcomes of such hostilities in their own right.[56] Considerations of this kind are important in explaining the relationship between the German Democratic Republic and the Soviet Union during the 1961 crisis as well as in reconstructing the relationship between each of the superpowers and its Chinese "client" during the course of the Taiwan Strait crisis of 1958. In situations of this kind, an attractive opportunity for manipulative bargaining for the lesser powers may become a source of difficult control problems for the great powers.

More generally, however, the presence of force-of-events considerations in major crises sets up a tension between pressures for prudent responses and incentives to take advantage of such considerations for purposes of bargaining.[57] In this connection, it is of considerable interest to note that fears

[56] This is obviously a much lower-level conception of catalytic action than the ideas along these lines sometimes discussed by the nuclear strategists. Catalytic actions, and especially threats concerning such actions, actually occur with some regularity at these lower levels, however. It is in this context that actions of this kind really do have a serious impact on international politics.

[57] In highly interdependent bargaining relationships, the ability to manipulate the risks associated with a given situation can be very valuable for any individual actor precisely because of the dangers involved. The most systematic treatment of problems of this kind appears in Thomas Schelling, *Arms and Influence* (New Haven: Yale University Press, 1966), Chap. 3.

114

and cautious responses usually predominated at critical junctures in the cases discussed above. Several brief points about this relationship can be made. First, the statements of decision-makers involved in these confrontations make it plain that heightened fears concerning the destructiveness of war and the uncontrollability of escalation in the nuclear context are important determinants of this predominance of cautious responses. Next, the evidence strongly suggests that in complex crises the great powers are apt to be more apprehensive about the dangers of serious inadvertent clashes and therefore more prepared to forego the gains to be had from manipulating risks than the participating lesser powers which, in any case, can always argue that the ultimate responsibility in these areas lies with the big powers. Third, even among the great powers the relationship between prudent responses and manipulative bargaining with regard to force-of-events problems tends to vary over the different phases of any given crisis. Though the relationship is a paradoxical one,[58] there is an apparent tendency for these powers to attempt to make gains through the manipulation of perceived risks *before* and *after* the most critical phases of a confrontation but to assume a stance of cautious coordination when tension rises to peak levels.

[58] The paradox arises from the fact that an opponent's greatest receptivity to fears and therefore to risk-manipulation usually corresponds with the tensest points of a crisis confrontation. It would therefore seem desirable to push along this channel of bargaining during periods of maximum tension. At the same time, however, such periods of tension are apt to raise the fears of the first party also, thereby making it increasingly hesitant to employ such dangerous techniques to acquire influence. Under the circumstances, both sides are likely to refrain from utilizing the techniques of risk-manipulation during periods of maximum tension unless there are vast asymmetries in their perceptions of the dangers associated with the situation.

6. Problems of Communication

HYPOTHESIS. As a crisis becomes more intense, "effective" communication among the protagonists concerning such matters as attitudes, expectations, intentions, and resolve will be based increasingly on physical actions in contrast to verbalized statements through diplomatic channels.

Analysts of international politics have argued from time to time on a general basis that the volume of communication among the protagonists is apt to decline sharply during periods of crisis. Unless communication is defined very narrowly, however, this generalization does not appear to stand up well, at least with respect to confrontations short of all-out warfare. What does tend to happen under conditions of crisis is that the prevailing *modes* of communication begin to shift from direct verbalized efforts to more indirect or even tacit procedures.

It is important to distinguish, in this connection, between the sheer intake of information and the effectiveness of verbalized communications. Problems of accuracy, levels of "fidelity," and processing speed, for example, can reduce the effectiveness of communication without any drop in the overall volume of verbalized communications. Or on matters involving efforts to demonstrate determination, diplomatic statements may become more and more inadequate even though they are formulated in firm language and reiterated frequently. In communicating through diplomatic channels, typical difficulties that may become increasingly influential during periods of high tension include: degradation of physical facilities; overloading; rising noise levels and confusion; ambiguous, contradictory, or inconsistent signals; and mistrust concerning the authenticity or credibility of diplomatic communications. During open hostilities, there is generally some danger of communications facilities being physically disrupted or degraded. Under conditions of crisis short of major hostilities, however, the problems of confusion, contrary or inconsistent signals, and mistrust are likely to be more relevant

116

and influential. Under these circumstances, the difficulties of communicating effectively through diplomatic channels may lead to a situation in which actions increasingly take on the role of effective conveyors of information regardless of the conscious intentions of the parties.

In analyzing problems of communication, it is also important to distinguish between the existence of genuine *understanding* concerning the fundamental dimensions of the situation on the part of the protagonists and the presence of various proximate communications activities. Under conditions of crisis, serious misunderstandings may arise whether or not channels of communication remain open. In the first instance, the disturbances of the international setting that characterize periods of crisis frequently unsettle previous understandings and open up new possibilities for misinterpretations and miscalculations. The specific confrontation point of a crisis, moreover, generally forms around some concrete issue or set of issues that has been a source of disturbance in international politics for some time. As a result, the various parties often enter a crisis with a strong set of diverging predispositions, perspectives, and attitudes about the issues involved which have grown up over a period of time. Both the gradualness with which such positions develop and the fact that they frequently produce incompatible assumptions and patterns of perception among the parties to a crisis concerning new developments may well make mutual understanding on the major issues extraordinarily difficult regardless of the level of proximate communication.

Nevertheless, shifts in the prevailing modes of communication under conditions of crisis, especially in the direction of more indirect and tacit forms of communication, will tend to have a substantial impact on bargaining processes. Under such conditions, it is important to formulate positions simply and unambiguously in order to achieve even superficial understanding. Only distinctions and "proposals" that are relatively simple and unambiguous can be made to apply with certainty. The existence of incentives to manipulate diplomatic contacts for purposes of "strategic bargaining" under conditions of crisis[1] also places a growing emphasis on the importance of physical actions as a means of authenticating verbalized statements as well as to demonstrate seriousness or resolve. Moreover, actual *or* perceived urgency in communicating with other parties may increase during crises, especially if overt hostilities are seen by decision-makers as an imminent danger. As a result, efforts to communicate will sometimes be infused with a "one-shot" quality in the sense that a failure on the first try will be seen as reducing the probability that a second will be successful.

Berlin, 1948-1949

The onset of the Berlin crisis of 1948-1949 did not terminate direct verbalized communication between the two sides for the duration of the crisis. In fact, communication of this kind continued on two distinct levels. One was high-level exchanges emanating from the capitals of the principal protagonists.[2] An exchange of formal notes occurred in July with the West initiating the exchange on July 6 and the Soviets responding on July 14. Then, on July 30, the Western ambassadors in Moscow presented an *aide-memoire* to the Soviet foreign office together with a request for discussions which led to the Moscow negotiations of August 1948.[3] These negotiations included direct meetings with Stalin on August 2 and 23 as well as a series of drafting sessions with Molotov on August 6, 9, 12, 16, and 27. The upshot of these meetings was the four-power directive of August 30 to the military governors in Berlin. An additional series of high-level exchanges followed the collapse of discussions in Berlin aimed at implementing this directive. This September sequence included

[1] The fact that one or more of the participants may desire, for purposes of bargaining, to dissimulate or consciously to cloud various issues during any given phase of a crisis complicates this problem of understanding.

[2] The texts of all the diplomatic notes can be located easily in *DOSB*, the *New York Times*, and Raymond Dennet and Robert K. Turner, eds., *Documents on American Foreign Relations*, Vol. X: *January 1–December 31, 1948* (Princeton: Princeton University Press [for the World Peace Foundation], 1950).

[3] For a good account of the Moscow negotiations of August 1948, see Walter Bedell Smith, *My Three Years in Moscow* (Philadelphia: Lippincott, 1950), pp. 230-260.

aide-memoires or notes from the Western powers on September 14, 22, and 26 (27)[4] and from the Soviet Union on September 18, 25, and October 3. The sequence was effectively terminated by the formal Western request of September 29 for a Security Council debate on the Berlin situation. The two sides thereupon proceeded to confront each other verbally at the United Nations throughout October and into November. These contacts, however, ultimately emerged as the last opportunity for direct high-level communication prior to the final announcement of an agreement to end the blockade and counterblockade on May 4, 1949.

During this period, direct communication also continued in the local arena of the crisis among the military governors for Germany and among the commandants for Berlin. An ineffective four-power meeting of financial representatives was held on June 22,[5] two days before the full blockade was imposed. The four military governors themselves held a brief and fruitless meeting at Potsdam on July 3. And during the whole period following the June 24 actions, there were periodic exchanges of letters on a local basis, especially between Robertson and Sokolovsky and Clay and Sokolovsky. Later on, during the first week of September, the four military governors held a number of additional meetings in an unsuccessful attempt to agree on concrete terms for the implementation of the August 30 directive. Finally, it is worth noting that a limited amount of personal and often informal contact involving Western and Soviet occupation personnel continued throughout the period of crisis.[6] These contacts never acquired any particular significance in determining the course of the crisis.

Despite this continuation of direct communication, however, the crisis produced a marked shift toward actions as a substitute for words. All normal channels of East-West com-

[4] Two dates appear here because the Western powers did not present their notes simultaneously in this exchange.

[5] The June 22 meeting was called to discuss the currency situation in Germany. It followed the Western announcement on currency reform on June 18 and was, in turn, immediately followed by the Soviet currency reform for eastern Germany and Berlin.

[6] See Frank Howley, *Berlin Command* (New York: G. P. Putnam's Sons, 1950), pp. 239-244; and Lucius D. Clay, *Decision in Germany* (Garden City, N.Y.: Doubleday, 1950), p. 373.

munication on German questions began to break down as the Berlin crisis built up. The hopelessly divided meeting of the Council of Foreign Ministers in London during November and December 1947 was the last meeting of this kind until May 1949. The Allied Control Commission for Germany ceased to function with the breakup of the meeting on March 20, 1948, and finally, the Berlin Kommandatura also passed into limbo after the meeting on June 16. From this point on direct communication remained on the level of makeshift contacts. As a result, major gaps in direct communication occurred during the most critical phases of the crisis. The military governors held only one halfhearted meeting (on July 3) between March 20 and September 1, and the Kommandatura did not meet at all. No formal communication about the crisis on a high level occurred until the Western note of July 6,[7] which was followed by a hiatus of eight days before the Soviets responded and a further gap of fourteen days before the West took steps to initiate real negotiations. The principal efforts at direct communication during this period, therefore, were sporadic and *ad hoc* at best.

Effective communication during the crisis thus became increasingly "symbolic." Communication by unilateral actions assumed a crucial role, especially in the local arena where the confrontation was. The gradual imposition of the blockade itself during the spring of 1948 started this sequence since "The Russians made it clear, by one piece of obstruction after another, that they were ready to hinder, reduce or stop all traffic coming into Berlin from the West by road, rail, canal and even air."[8] The point was clear to the Western powers, and the battle of unilateral actions was on. Outstanding among the subsequent actions affecting the communications process during the crisis were: the development and

[7] American, and therefore Western, thinking about the crisis on an official level developed rather slowly. Among other things, Truman was away from Washington during much of June, and the Presidential campaign of 1948 was beginning in earnest at this time. For an interesting discussion of this subject, see the article by Jack Raymond, *New York Times*, June 25, 1958, pp. 1, 18.

[8] *The Economist*, July 3, 1948, p. 1. While this statement contains an exaggeration concerning the issue of air traffic, its basic point is an important one.

ultimately successful maintenance of the Western airlift; the various actions and counteractions within Berlin itself aimed primarily at affecting the morale of the population;[9] and the clear-cut promotion of Western plans for an autonomous West German state and for the development of integrated Western security arrangements. One of the most interesting aspects of this form of communication is that actions tend simultaneously to alter both the substantive context of a crisis and the basic evaluations of the participants in ways that words cannot. This was certainly the case during the Berlin crisis of 1948-1949.

This shift toward symbolic communication produced several additional consequences. First, the continuing high-level diplomatic contacts quickly degenerated into futile haggling and became little more than a cover for the truly important, and typically nonverbal, interactions of the crisis.[10] At some point during the August negotiations, the Soviets evidently concluded that high-level contacts were not likely to produce any interesting results from their point of view. By the time of the September exchanges, both sides were stating their positions in a repetitious and generally fruitless manner, though they clearly felt the necessity of maintaining the external facade of diplomatic interaction. Second, the combination of an unfolding sequence of important actions and the degeneration of formal diplomatic exchanges ultimately created a setting for several developments in informal communications. Phenomena of this kind became increasingly important toward the end of the crisis. Stalin's tentative "peace feelers,"[11] for example, were first released through such media as his answers to the questions of an American newspaperman, Kingsbury Smith, which appeared at the end of

[9] For an interesting account of these activities, see W. Phillips Davison, *The Berlin Blockade: A Study in Cold War Politics* (Princeton: Princeton University Press, 1958), Chap. 8.

[10] In this connection, Gottlieb is quite correct in arguing that each side attempted, at first, to use the negotiations to intimidate the other. But, as he also observes, "neither side was really intimidated." As this outcome became clear, therefore, serious interest in direct negotiations began to plummet. See Manuel Gottlieb, *The German Peace Settlement and the Berlin Crisis* (New York: Paine-Whitman, 1950), p. 202.

[11] On this subject see *The Economist*, February 5, 1949, p. 225.

January 1949. American "responses" were formulated informally by high officials such as Dean Acheson in superficially light-hearted but intrinsically significant terms. Subsequently, the process of indirect communication shifted to the United Nations. In February, the famous informal contact between Jessup and Malik took place. During March and April, the Soviet Union and the United States discreetly sounded each other's attitudes on the Berlin confrontation through informal contacts involving middle-level representatives at the United Nations.[12] As a result, "arrangements for the ending of the blockade of Berlin were agreed to without [formal] meetings at any level."[13]

Beyond the question of communication in the narrower sense, however, the Berlin blockade also raised serious problems concerning genuine understanding among the principal participants. For several reasons, the protagonists found it difficult to grasp fully the fundamental bases of opposing positions during this crisis. The underlying issues of the conflict had been building up ever since the establishment of the joint occupation regime for Germany in 1945. The origins of the Berlin crisis of 1948-1949 can therefore be traced back through a long series of actions and reactions over several years. The constant emphasis of both sides on efforts to apportion the blame for the crisis itself was hence bound to be vain and inconclusive.[14] Each side had accumulated a web of interpretations and attitudes allowing for a consistent explanation of each new event in its own terms, but that made it almost impossible to appreciate the basis of the opponent's position.[15] Moreover, the conflict symbolized by the specific

[12] These contacts occurred in the arena provided by the existence of the United Nations but did not involve any formal United Nations activities. Moreover, it is notable that when both sides desired to communicate, they were able to do so effectively without contacts between high-level representatives.

[13] Dean Acheson, "On Dealing with Russia: An Inside View," *New York Times Magazine*, April 12, 1959, p. 27.

[14] The desire to transfer the blame for the 1948-1949 crisis is especially evident in the texts of the notes and *aide-memoires* exchanged during September 1948.

[15] The Berlin crisis is hardly recognizable as the same clash from reading the exegetic material promulgated by the two sides.

crisis over Berlin was both sharply delineated in physical terms and laden with political significance. The situation had critical implications for the political future of Germany as well as for the balance of power in all of Europe. Problems of political understanding went much deeper than failures of communication in the narrow sense of specific factual misunderstandings. In the context of the Berlin crisis of 1948-1949, these problems acquired some of the qualities of a genuine dilemma.

Taiwan Strait, 1958

Though the 1958 crisis in the Taiwan Strait grew out of several major misunderstandings, much of the interaction during the actual period of crisis was characterized by relatively distinct and, for the most part, successful efforts at clarification.[16] In this connection, the critical focus of communication during the crisis was the relationship between the United States and the People's Republic of China (CPR). Given the history of hostility between these two states and especially the rigidities of their postures toward each other in 1958, the communications successes achieved in the absence of normal channels of direct communication during the actual period of crisis are striking.

Direct contacts among the principal opposing parties in the 1958 crisis, though not entirely lacking, never became a critical determinant of the course of the confrontation in any of its phases. Contacts of this type did not occur at all until a relatively late stage and did not become significantly numerous even after their initiation. There were, however, several channels in which direct contacts relevant to the crisis did take place.

Direct contacts between the United States and the CPR began only with the resumption of ambassadorial talks in Warsaw on September 15.[17] These talks grew out of Chou En-

[16] Discussions of the communications problems of this crisis frequently contain confusing discrepancies because of the relatively great differences in local time between, say, Washington and Peking. There is no solution for the difficulty except to keep it in mind in considering questions for which small variations in time make a difference.

[17] For an analysis of the circumstances of the Warsaw meetings, see

123

lai's statement of September 6[18] and an immediately favorable response from the United States, but the first meeting occurred only after a substantial delay that spanned a critical period in the course of the crisis. The talks in Warsaw[19] ultimately played no effective communications role because neither side was prepared to discuss the fundamental bases of its own position seriously and because, in the later meetings, the CPR was uninterested in utilizing the talks as a device to disengage itself from the crisis. Though this was the extent of direct contact between the United States and the CPR, several channels of direct Soviet-American contact also materialized in the course of the crisis. An exchange of letters between Khrushchev and Eisenhower, initiated by the former, on September 7 and 12,[20] was followed by a second Khrushchev letter on September 19,[21] which Eisenhower returned unanswered. It is important to note that these contacts occurred only after the termination of the first major phase of the crisis[22] and appear to have stemmed primarily from a Soviet desire to deter any possible American actions involving violence directed against the Chinese mainland. In this connection the Khrushchev letters were not entirely irrelevant,[23] though they were not of critical importance since the United States was, in any case, carefully avoiding actions that might lead to attacks on the mainland and since both letters appear to have been at least partially misinterpreted by their

Chalmers Roberts, "Caught in a Trap of Our Own Making," *The Reporter*, Vol. 19, No. 5 (October 2, 1958), 11-13.

[18] For the text of the September 6 statement, see Paul Zinner, ed., *Documents on American Foreign Relations 1958* (New York: Harper and Row [for the Council on Foreign Relations], 1959), pp. 440-442.

[19] The Warsaw meetings continued through the remainder of the crisis but at infrequent intervals.

[20] For the texts of the two letters, see DOSB, XXXIX, No. 1005 (September 29, 1958), 498-503.

[21] The full text of this letter appeared in the *New York Times*, September 20, 1958, p. 2.

[22] For a discussion of the exact timing of the various phases of the 1958 crisis, see *infra* Chap. Eight.

[23] On the deterrent function of Khrushchev's statements, see John Thomas, "Soviet Behavior in the Quemoy Crisis of 1958," *Orbis*, VI, No. 1 (Spring 1962), 62.

American recipients.[24] Beyond this, there was a certain amount of direct, though informal, Soviet-American contact at the United Nations. The absence of the CPR made these contacts somewhat peripheral to the mainstream of the crisis. But it is worth noting that communication along these lines did reach the level of direct contact between Dulles and Gromyko.[25]

One of the critical channels of communication during the 1958 crisis was a somewhat peculiar form of indirect contact. This contact did not involve unusual or unorthodox message bearers as has been the case in several other crises; rather, it stemmed from efforts by the principal participants to interpret each other's statements made in clearly internal arenas but with an obvious eye to the possibility of external consumption. Here there is ample evidence of each major participant's closely following the principal news media of the others, though it is also clear their interpretations sometimes greatly erred in political understanding. In this somewhat peculiar game of indirect communication, there was a tendency on all sides to focus especially on a small number of highly salient or "indicative" statements promulgated by the opponent.

The Soviets and the Chinese typically divided American statements concerning the crisis into those by administration officials and those by domestic opponents of official American policy. Eisenhower and, above all, Dulles were taken as the relevant spokesmen in the American Administration. Dulles' statements of September 4, 9, 18, 30, and October 14, as well as Eisenhower's statements of September 11 and October 1, therefore received particular attention in Soviet and Chinese

[24] The bellicosity of Khrushchev's language, especially in his letter of September 19, appears to have stemmed from the Soviet desire to maximize deterrence against the perceived danger of an American move to reverse the crisis by striking against the Chinese mainland. The Americans, however, were evidently inclined to read the letters in the light of a concern about the dangers of a Soviet involvement in the actual physical confrontation engendered by the crisis.

[25] In fact, a Dulles, Gromyko, Hammarskjold dinner took place in New York during this period. Whether or not anything of importance was said at this meeting, it is clear the United Nations assisted in providing an arena for informal Soviet-American contact.

interpretations.[26] At the same time, both Soviet and Chinese analyses, usually quoting various American newspapers, laid great stress on the significance of domestic American opposition to the Administration's posture during the crisis, a procedure which appears to have contributed to several important misunderstandings during the course of the confrontation.

Interest in CPR statements on the part of the American and the Chinese Nationalists can be divided into categories on the basis of timing. In the period immediately following August 23, much attention was given to interpreting CPR radio broadcasts, beamed directly to Quemoy and Taiwan, threatening an "imminent" invasion of the offshore islands.[27] Then in early September, interest focused strongly on the various aspects of Chou En-lai's statement of September 6 because of the clear divergences between this and preceding CPR statements. And toward the end of the crisis there was great interest in the statements issued by Marshal Peng Teh-huai on October 6, 13, and 25,[28] both because they were indicators of CPR thinking on the problems of disengaging from the crisis and because they were the key statements in the Chinese Communist effort to generate tension between the Americans and the Nationalists during this final phase of the crisis.[29] With regard to Soviet statements, on the other hand, the situation was considerably more ambiguous. The early phases of the crisis were marked by a noticeable absence of explicit Soviet statements about it.[30] Then, following

[26] The full texts of all these statements can be conveniently located in *DOSB*.

[27] See Donald Zagoria, *The Sino-Soviet Conflict 1956-1961* (New York: Atheneum, 1964), pp. 210-211.

[28] The critical portions of the texts of the three statements can be found in Zinner, ed., *op.cit.*, pp. 474-477.

[29] See Richard Stebbins, *The United States in World Affairs 1958* (New York: Harper and Row [for the Council on Foreign Relations], 1959), pp. 327-328. For further discussion of the CPR's ideas of driving a wedge between the Nationalists and the Americans during this period, see *infra* Chap. Fifteen.

[30] On this subject see Thomas, *op.cit.*, p. 42. It now seems likely, however, that this Soviet tendency to play down the crisis during its early phases was quite compatible with the desires of the CPR. For a thorough discussion of the motives of the Soviet Union and the CPR in this con-

Khrushchev's formal letter of September 7, the most salient Soviet statements on the crisis were those emphasizing the civil-war aspects of the situation and the limitations on Soviet commitments to the defense of the CPR. This drift in Soviet statements was climaxed by Khrushchev's statement of October 5,[31] which was especially significant because of its temporal juxtaposition with Peng's first cease-fire statement on October 6.

Another channel of indirect contact during the 1958 crisis originated from activities carried out within the United Nations. There are, for example, indications that V. K. Krishna Menon of India and Halvard Lange of Norway attempted in late September to serve as intermediaries between the United States and the CPR.[32] It is possible that some of the new formulations that emerged at Dulles' press conference of September 30 were a response to indications conveyed along this channel of shifts in Chinese thinking.[33] The subsequent course of events, nevertheless, makes it clear that these indirect efforts did not ultimately play a crucial role in shaping the fundamental course of the crisis.

These indirect forms of communication were critically supplemented, however, by physical actions that, either by design or on a *de facto* basis, helped to clarify the positions of the principals. This communications function of actions became particularly important during the 1958 crisis in the absence of

---

nection, consult Morton Halperin and Tang Tsou, "The 1958 Quemoy Crisis," Chap. 10 in Morton Halperin, ed., *Sino-Soviet Relations and Arms Control* (Cambridge: M.I.T. Press, 1967).

[31] For the text of the October 5 statement, which appeared originally in the October 6 issue of *Pravda*, see *CDSP*, X, No. 40 (November 12, 1958), 18.

[32] By this time, it was already becoming clear the Warsaw talks were unlikely to produce major results. For information on these indirect communications activities in the United Nations framework, consult the *New York Times*, October 10, 1958, pp. 1 and 4, and October 11, 1958, p. 1. Unfortunately, the exact dimensions of Menon's and Lange's activities during this period are still somewhat obscure.

[33] See Stebbins, *op.cit.*, pp. 325-327. The interpretation has been offered by several writers that, at this stage in the crisis, the United States and the CPR were actually engaging in indirect negotiations concerning the possibilities of a compromise that would allow for a formal renegotiation of the status of the offshore islands. For a discussion of several weaknesses in this interpretation, see *infra* Chap. Twelve.

127

many direct forms of communication. Also, various prepara-
tory activities did much to communicate the credibility of contingent actions whose credibility could not, because of their
nature, be satisfactorily conveyed by diplomatic procedures
alone.[34] In this connection, the contrast between American
actions and Communist Chinese actions was particularly striking and influential.

Though the Chinese initiated the 1958 crisis with a series
of sharp and intense actions, their actions during the course
of the confrontation became steadily more cautious. They
made no serious effort to gather an invasion fleet opposite
Quemoy.[35] They did not utilize available means to intensify
the blockade of Quemoy after the introduction of substantial
American assistance to the Nationalists aimed at breaking it.
And they ultimately allowed their artillery barrage against
the offshore islands to decline to relative insignificance. In
conjunction with these points, note that during the crisis the
Soviets neither alerted nor built up their military forces in
Asia. Nor did they undertake any other discernible preparations relevant to a possible decision to come to the aid of the
CPR physically. The United States, on the other hand, not
only responded rapidly and vigorously to the initiation of
the crisis in terms of actions but also continued to augment
its military capabilities in the Western Pacific with a series
of impressive moves right up to the end of the crisis. In this
regard, the United States: (1) reacted quickly with a decision to augment its Seventh Fleet in the Taiwan Strait during the opening phase of the crisis, (2) demonstrated a willingness to apply considerable force in the effort to break the
blockade of Quemoy, (3) showed itself ready to supply the
Nationalists with the equipment required to achieve air su-

[34] For example, the actual physical reality of the American buildup in
the Taiwan Strait constituted the most persuasive testimony to American
resoluteness in the confrontation. Even more concretely, the willingness
of the United States to place escort vessels within the effective range of
CPR artillery provided more telling evidence concerning the American
position on the contingent use of force than any verbal threats.

[35] On this point see Harold Hinton, *Communist China in World Politics*
(Boston, Houghton Mifflin, 1966), p. 266; and Zagoria, *op.cit.*, p. 208.

periority over the Taiwan Strait, and (4) proceeded with what amounted to a massive buildup of air, naval, and anti-aircraft capabilities in the Strait and on Taiwan itself even during the later phases of the confrontation. In the final analysis, it was the congruence between these American actions and the firm diplomatic posture of the United States that evidently impressed the CPR and the Soviet Union.

From a more general perspective on the problems of communication, the 1958 crisis appears finally as a pattern of significant initial misunderstandings coupled with relatively successful corrective efforts. The Chinese decisions both to initiate the crisis on August 23 and to keep it going during September were based on serious misunderstandings and miscalculations about the probable responses of the Nationalists and the Americans.[36] Nationalist and, especially, American reactions during the crisis, however, were of considerable importance in correcting CPR misimpressions. Given the critical importance of the initial misunderstandings, the success of these subsequent efforts at communication constitutes a striking feature of the 1958 crisis: a combination of cautiousness on the part of the CPR and the ability of the Americans and the Nationalists to respond credibly to the CPR's initiatives without overreacting[37] appears to have been the key to important communications successes. Finally, it is worth noting that the ultimate termination of the crisis occurred through a process of tacit coordination.[38] In terminating the crisis, the formal sessions at Warsaw proved entirely irrelevant. Instead, the antagonists proceeded to disengage from the confrontation by operationalizing certain increasingly evident overlapping interests on a completely tacit

[36] For further discussion of these misunderstandings, see *infra* Chap. Eight.

[37] In this connection, American decision-makers deserve a certain amount of credit not only for organizing workable control procedures for their own forces but also for providing an effective check on Nationalist pressures to raise the level of force being utilized.

[38] On this point see Charles McClelland, Daniel Harrison, Wayne Martin, Warren Phillips, and Robert Young, *The Communist Chinese Performance in Crisis and Non-Crisis: Quantitative Studies of the Taiwan Straits Confrontation, 1950-1964*, Report to Naval Ordnance Test Station (China Lake), December 14, 1965, p. 44.

basis.[39] The result was a termination of the crisis without a settlement of the underlying issue.

Berlin, 1961

Though formal contacts among the major participants were not lacking during the 1961 Berlin crisis, they were neither remarkable for their volume nor distinguished by a high degree of effectiveness. The formal Soviet *aide-mémoire* of June 4 marked the point of reactivation of the East-West controversy over Berlin and set forth the principal threats to be employed by the East in 1961.[40] There followed during the summer a series of high-level notes, with those of the West appearing on July 17, August 3, 17, and 26, and September 8 and 26, and those of the Soviet Union on August 16, 18, and 23, and September 3 and 17.[41] There was, in addition, a limited amount of formal contact at lower levels. Such contacts occurred primarily among the ambassadors of the United States, Britain, and France to West Germany and of the Soviet Union to both Germanys,[42] and among the commandants of the forces of the four occupation powers in Berlin.[43] Several characteristics of these formal contacts are significant. Though the June 4 *aide-mémoire* was of some importance, this general form of communication remained sluggish and rather ineffectual throughout the crisis. Both the timing and the content of these communications were, for the most part, strongly conditioned by the bureaucratic rigidities of foreign office protocol.[44] Thus, the notes were essentially formal protests or

[39] For further discussion of this extraordinarily interesting case of effective coordination among adversaries, see *infra* Chap. Twelve.

[40] For the full text of the June 4 *aide-mémoire*, see *DOSB*, XLV, No. 1154 (August 7, 1961), 231-233.

[41] The full texts of all of these notes can be located conveniently in *DOSB*.

[42] Since the Soviet Union had officially recognized both the GDR and the FRG by 1961, it had ambassadors both in Bonn and in Pankow. The Western powers, on the other hand, had ambassadors only in Bonn. As a result, relations between the Western ambassadors and the two Soviet ambassadors were somewhat irregular.

[43] With regard to contacts among the commandants of the occupation forces, see Geoffrey McDermott, *Berlin: Success of a Mission?* (New York: Harper and Row, 1963), p. 48.

[44] For an interesting and important example, consult Theodore Soren-

counterprotests lacking in genuine efforts to communicate useful information. They served more "to imprison each side a degree more tightly in its own web of argument"[45] than to facilitate effective understanding.

On the whole, the 1961 Berlin crisis produced remarkably little face-to-face diplomatic contact. Moreover, such contacts as did occur along these lines commenced only at a very late stage in the crisis. The first formal face-to-face contact did not occur until Gromyko's trip to New York during September for the opening of the 16th session of the United Nations General Assembly.[46] On this trip Gromyko met successively with Rusk and with Home in New York on September 21 and the following days, with Kennedy and Rusk in Washington on October 6, and with Macmillan and Home in London on his way back to Moscow. During this period, Western leaders apparently entertained hopes for the initiation of talks somewhat analogous to those growing out of the Jessup-Malik contact at the United Nations in 1949. Such hopes, however, failed to take into account the differences between the phases of the first Berlin crisis during February and March 1949 and the renewed Berlin crisis during September 1961.[47] There followed in November 1961 the formal interview which Kennedy accorded to Adzhubei in which Berlin was discussed as one of a number of subjects.[48] Then, in November 1961 and during the winter of 1962 Llewellyn Thompson, the American ambassador to the Soviet Union, conducted a series of semi-

---

sen's discussion of the difficulties associated with the drafting of the Western note of July 17, in *Kennedy* (New York: Harper and Row, 1965), p. 587.

[45] *The Economist*, July 22, 1961, p. 322.

[46] On Gromyko's activities in New York, see the *New York Times*, September 24, 1961, Sect. IV, p. 1.

[47] By February 1949, the airlift was a manifest success, Western countermeasures were beginning to achieve a significant impact, and an ineffectual continuation of the blockade by the Soviet Union hardly looked attractive in propaganda terms. In September 1961, on the other hand, the Berlin confrontation had become very fluid, and critical changes in the bargaining positions on both sides were in the offing.

[48] For the text of Kennedy's interview with Adzhubei, which took place at Hyannis Port on November 25, see Richard Stebbins, ed., *Documents on American Foreign Relations, 1961* (New York: Harper and Row [for the Council on Foreign Relations], 1962), pp. 231-246.

formal talks at the Soviet foreign ministry to explore the possibilities of initiating East-West negotiations to rationalize the position of Berlin.[49] Finally, the same objective was pursued in a series of meetings between Rusk and Gromyko in Geneva during March 1962,[50] and between Rusk and Dobrynin, the Soviet ambassador to the United States, in Washington during April.

Several characteristics of these face-to-face contacts are noteworthy. As mentioned above, communication of this type was remarkably restricted during the 1961 crisis considering the duration of the confrontation. There was a total failure to initiate full-blown negotiations concerning Berlin despite the proclaimed interest of both sides in negotiations and despite rather clear hints at the time of several of the contacts outlined above to the effect that formal negotiations would soon be initiated. Moreover, with the possible exception of the September 1961 meeting between Rusk and Gromyko,[51] the face-to-face contacts during this crisis occurred too late to affect the outcome of the actual crisis seriously. Though the possibility of renegotiating the status of Berlin was always present, the actual course of events in and around Berlin was beginning to determine the denouement of the 1961 crisis by sometime in October regardless of formal positions on the need for negotiations.

Informal and often rather indirect means of communication appear to have played a somewhat greater, though frequently ambiguous, role during the 1961 crisis. Some contacts of this kind were largely perfunctory and therefore relatively inconsequential. This seems to be the most reasonable assessment, for example, of the informal contacts among the comman-

[49] See, for example, Philip Windsor, *City on Leave* (New York: Praeger, 1963), p. 232.

[50] These meetings could be conducted both quietly and informally since the Secretary of State and the Foreign Minister were in Geneva in any case for the opening session of the Eighteen Nation Disarmament Conference.

[51] The developments underlying Khrushchev's statements on Berlin in his speech of October 17 were evidently at least hinted at during these meetings in September. On this subject see Rusk's statements at his press conference of October 18. The relevant text is in *DOSB*, XLV, No. 1167 (November 6, 1961), 746.

dants in Berlin[52] and of the September missions of Nehru and Nkrumah to Moscow and Sukarno and Keita to Washington.

A second category of informal communications activities covers efforts to manipulate the understanding or bargaining position of the opponent. Though both sides, of course, operated along these lines, the Soviets were particularly active in this area during the 1961 crisis. One objective of such activities was to instill fear in the opponent by indirect means. These efforts included: Khrushchev's "sabre-rattling" speeches during June and July; informal threats passed along to various Western diplomats in Moscow during the same period;[53] various informal letters dispatched by Khrushchev; Khrushchev's contact with John McCloy, whom he summoned to Sochi following Kennedy's speech of July 25; and the series of Kennedy speeches culminating with his address to the nation on July 25. Another objective of such contacts apparently was to hint informally at the possibilities of various deals in order to sow dissension among allies. Prime examples of this type of contact during the 1961 crisis were the Adenauer-Smirnov meeting in Bonn on August 16 and the conversation between Khrushchev and Kroll, the West German ambassador to the Soviet Union, in Moscow in October.[54]

A third category of informal contact encompasses genuine efforts to convey or to acquire information. The actual extent of such efforts during the 1961 crisis remains unclear. Soundings that were treated seriously, though their ultimate impact seems to have been relatively small, were made by Dobrynin in Washington during June and July on the strength of American resolve about Berlin and by Thompson in Moscow during September concerning the possible usefulness of formal East-West negotiations. Other informal contacts of this kind, though possibly more important, are obscure. There have been indications from time to time that informal East-West contacts occurred during late August in London and

[52] See McDermott, *op.cit.*, p. 48.

[53] Diplomats threatened in this way included the British and Greek ambassadors to the Soviet Union.

[54] Each of these meetings became a source of considerable displeasure and of various recriminations in the West. Such reactions did not reach criticial proportions in either case.

Bonn.[55] In addition, several references to an informal Kennedy-Khrushchev correspondence concerning Berlin have appeared. Sorensen, for example, has written that "Berlin was the principal topic of the Kennedy-Khrushchev letters. The initiation of the correspondence in September, 1961, helped cool off the crisis. . . ."[56] Despite the intriguing possibilities of such a correspondence, it now seems most likely that the extent of this contact was a message conveyed informally to Kennedy from Khrushchev through C. L. Sulzberger, who talked at some length with Khrushchev in Moscow in early September.[57] Although this message was apparently significant as an indication of change in Khrushchev's attitudes concerning the evolving bargaining positions of the United States and the Soviet Union, it can hardly be viewed as a major communications breakthrough.

A summary assessment of the informal contact during the 1961 crisis is difficult. As has been the case in other crises, the Soviets in particular demonstrated a penchant for utilizing various unusual forms of informal and indirect contact. The net results, however, seem to have been limited. The relative level of informal contact in this crisis was not notably high. On balance, the manipulative efforts seem to have had only limited influence in that they did not produce any radical alterations in the postures of either side. This leaves the area of genuine efforts to convey information on an informal basis. Though much evidence is still incomplete in this area, the best judgment at present is that such contacts were probably of some importance but not critical to the ultimate outcome of the crisis.

The restricted nature of all these verbalized forms of contact created a situation during the 1961 crisis in which there was considerable scope for communication by actions. Because the nature of the confrontation on the ground in and around Berlin put great pressure on both sides to take a variety of actions during the summer and fall, it was inevitable that

[55] On this subject see the *New York Times*, August 23, 1961, p. 4.

[56] Sorensen, *op.cit.*, p. 599.

[57] For an important effort to clarify this issue, see C. L. Sulzberger, the *New York Times*, November 6, 1966, p. 10.

the communications role of actions would increase. Here it seems useful to make at least a rough distinction between actions undertaken with the conscious intention of conveying information to other parties and actions in which the communications function was essentially a byproduct. The various moves of both sides to mobilize military forces during the crisis, though ultimately of doubtful success as communications devices, clearly had as one of their purposes a desire to demonstrate serious resolve to the opponent.[58] Similarly, the Soviet move to resume nuclear testing at the beginning of September was, at least partially, an action to pressure the West.

Perhaps the most successful communications efforts along these lines in 1961, however, were those of a less conscious nature. The outstanding example came in the period immediately following the closure of the sector boundary in Berlin on August 13, during which the remarkably cautious and proper behavior patterns of the two sides were a critical factor in the process of tacit coordination that occurred. Speaking of this situation, Jean Smith, for example, concludes that "formal consultation between East and West was at a minimum. But the signals exchanged were clear and unmistakable."[59] By the same token, the noticeable increase in the firmness of Western responses to new Eastern initiatives later in August played an important communications role in this crisis even though these responses did not stem, in the first instance, from a search on the part of Western decision-makers for communications devices. During this period, several impressive Western "shows of force" in response to new Eastern demands[60] provided eloquent testimony concerning the relative hardening of the Western position.

It would be a mistake, however, to assume that communica-

---

[58] For a good discussion of the various moves in this area, consult Arnold L. Horelick and Myron Rush, *Strategic Power and Soviet Foreign Policy* (Chicago: University of Chicago Press, 1966), p. 124.

[59] Jean Edward Smith, "Berlin Confrontation," *The Virginia Quarterly Review*, Vol. 42, No. 3 (Summer 1966), 364.

[60] A particularly important case from the bargaining standpoint arose from the firm Western response to the so-called "hundred meters" edict promulgated by the GDR in late August.

tion through actions completely took up the slack in communications left by the restricted use of other procedures during the 1961 crisis. In fact, the actions of the principals in the crisis were frequently ambiguous, contradictory or inconsistent over time. And there were several occasions on which actions were more nearly a source of confusion than a procedure for improving understanding. Despite the very striking communications success in coordinating actions in the aftermath of the actual closing of the sector boundary in Berlin, therefore, the 1961 crisis as a whole was characterized by a number of communications failures between East and West. As a result, there were serious deficiencies of understanding between the parties at a number of points in the crisis, a factor leading to several dangerous developments.

To begin with, the genesis of the crisis was closely linked to a decline in the clarity of the basic East-West relationship during 1961. Problems of understanding arose in this connection from a combination of new elements of fluidity in the underlying political setting of East-West relationships, serious ambiguities in the posture of the United States during the early months of 1961, and substantial misinterpretations by the Soviet Union of both the nature of emerging political realities and the strength of American resolve. Indeed, these deficiencies of mutual understanding embedded in the crisis from its inception were not really cleared up until sometime during the fall of 1961. From July until October, there were serious failures of understanding about the objectives of and constraints on the major participants in the crisis. This confusion was particularly apparent in the Western failure to appreciate fully the underlying dimensions of the Soviet position until a very late stage in the crisis. This failure is by no means entirely attributable to Western misperceptions. In fact, it now seems clear that the Soviets purposefully maintained ambiguous and fluid objectives during this period in order to be able later to opt for the maximum goals the unfolding situation would support and that the Soviets dissimulated, for tactical reasons, about the constraints on their position[61] so that many decision-makers in the West

[61] A particularly influential case of such dissimulation arose from the

were confused until late in the confrontation. Finally, the efforts of both sides during the summer of 1961 to demonstrate the credibility of their resolve with regard to Berlin led to further confusion and failures of mutual understanding. The basic bargaining situation was extremely delicate since *both* sides obviously feared the possible consequences of large-scale hostilities while *each* side desired to maneuver in such a way as to suggest that the other party was more afraid of these dangers at any given moment in time. In the course of this constant jockeying for bargaining advantages, problems arose both from ambiguities in the impressions conveyed by the specific actions of each side and from occasional misinterpretations of new developments by one or more parties. Given the sharpness of the physical confrontation in and around Berlin during the summer and fall of 1961, these deficiencies of mutual understanding produced dangerous control problems. And difficulties of this kind were undoubtedly a significant factor in determining the tortuous course of the negotiations question during the 1961 crisis.

Cuba, 1962

In analyzing problems of communication during the Cuban missile crisis, it is important to note at the outset that the level of relevant communication between the Soviet Union and the United States in the pre-crisis period was relatively low. There were several diplomatic exchanges during September but they were primarily for purposes of formal emphasis. The Soviets stressed repeatedly their lack of interest in installing "offensive" weapons in Cuba[62] while the Americans made some rather general threats concerning the steps that would be taken if the Soviets did, in fact, install such weapons.[63] And in the early days of October communication

---

Soviet effort to gain bargaining advantages by threatening to sign a separate peace treaty with the GDR. For further discussion of this subject, see *infra* Chap. Fifteen.

[62] See, for example, the language of the TASS communiqué of September 11, 1962. The text of this communiqué can be found in David L. Larson, ed., *The "Cuban Crisis" of 1962: Selected Documents and Chronology* (Boston: Houghton Mifflin, 1963), pp. 7-17.

[63] For examples see Kennedy's statements of September 4 and 13, 1962. The texts appear in *ibid.*, pp. 3-4 and 17-18.

declined still further as the veil of official silence concerning activities in Cuba became more impenetrable.

Moreover, this somewhat ominous silence continued throughout the week of October 15, while American decision-makers were debating alternative responses, with the exception of several Soviet efforts to divert attention from unusual actions in Cuba. On October 16, for example, Khrushchev had a lengthy conversation with Ambassador Kohler in Moscow during which he made a number of reassuring statements concerning Cuba. And on October 18, there occurred the well-known Kennedy-Gromyko meeting in Washington during which *Berlin* was the primary focus of attention.[64]

During the period of direct confrontation, which followed Kennedy's speech of October 22, there was a distinct increase of diplomatic contact. Perhaps most important was the exchange of messages between Kennedy and Khrushchev. These exchanges began with Kennedy's letter of October 22 and Khrushchev's reply of October 23. By the time a termination arrangement for the crisis was agreed upon on October 28, "the two men had exchanged ten letters—five each way—in seven days."[65] These letters varied considerably in terms of format and mode of transmission. And there were, on several occasions, problems with time lags.[66] But it is generally agreed that these exchanges had a major impact on the course of the crisis, especially from October 26 onward.[67] Direct communication of a rather formal sort also increased during the week of October 22 on a person-to-person basis in the cap-

[64] A summary of Kennedy's interview with Gromyko on October 18 is printed in Henry Pachter, *Collision Course* (New York: Praeger, 1963), pp. 188-192.

[65] This statement appears in "Cuban Crisis: A Step by Step Review," *New York Times*, November 3, 1962, pp. 1, 6-7. The text can be located conveniently in Larson, ed., *op.cit.*, p. 242.

[66] Available records indicate that, during this crisis, it took at least four hours for the transmission and translation of letters between Washington and Moscow. In addition, the fact that the letters did not have a standard format caused problems. It is still not clear, for example, whether the Soviet letter received in Washington on October 26 or the one received on October 27 was actually composed first in Moscow.

[67] For some interesting points on this subject, see Rusk's statements in his interview with David Schoenbrun on November 28, 1962. The text appears in *ibid.*, p. 269.

itals. Several meetings of some significance occurred in Washington between Robert Kennedy and the Soviet Ambassador to the United States (Dobrynin). In addition, Kohler and Gromyko appear to have met directly at least once in Moscow. These meetings, nevertheless, appear to have been of far less importance than the Kennedy-Khrushchev exchange of letters.

The United Nations provided a further point of direct contact between the protagonists during the overt phase of the 1962 crisis. Although the Security Council meetings offered the most obvious point of contact between representatives of the two sides, these formal meetings were almost entirely given over to rhetorical debate and did not, for the most part, facilitate effective communication. On the other hand, the headquarters setting in New York furnished a useful context for less formal contacts between Stevenson and Zorin as well as among various members of their staffs.[68] In addition, the Secretary-General was on several occasions able to act as intermediary, thus facilitating a kind of two-step process of communication between the principals. As Pachter has put it, "Every time the U.S. and the U.S.S.R. were not talking to each other, they could talk separately to the Secretary-General."[69]

The Cuban missile crisis also produced an increase in indirect and unusual modes of communication. Activities of this kind, which fall somewhere between direct diplomatic contact and communication through actions, have appeared with some regularity in East-West crises, but they were particularly evident during the Cuban crisis. On October 23, for example, Khrushchev called on the American opera singer, Jerome Hines, after a performance in Moscow, an act that was interpreted by a number of American officials as a sign the Soviet premier desired to avoid open hostilities over Cuba.[70]

[68] John McCloy, for example, was attached to the American delegation to the United Nations during the crisis. Moreover, toward the end of the confrontation, Khrushchev's announcement of his decision to send Vasily Kuznetsov to New York was widely interpreted as an indication of genuine desire by the Soviets to terminate the crisis.

[69] Pachter, *op.cit.*, p. 96.

[70] This episode is discussed in Arthur Schlesinger Jr., *A Thousand Days* (Boston: Houghton Mifflin, 1965), p. 821.

Then on October 24 Khrushchev unexpectedly called in the American industrialist William Knox, who was in Moscow for other reasons, for a three-hour conversation.[71] Khrushchev appeared to Knox to be in a blustery mood, but his very desire to utilize this channel of communication was deemed significant in Washington. Also, on October 24, the Soviet premier sent a telegram to Lord Russell in which he appeared to show an interest in finding a nonviolent way out of the crisis.[72] Finally, in the period between October 26 and 28, the so-called Fomin-Scali meetings took place.[73] These informal meetings occurred on the initiative of an officer in the Soviet embassy in Washington and evidently constituted an attempt to probe, informally, probable American reactions to several specific ideas concerning terms for terminating the crisis.

Several general characteristics of these indirect efforts at communication are worth noting. They were initiated for the most part by the Soviets. In general, this is compatible with earlier indications of Soviet interest in indirect and often semi-symbolic modes of communication. Most of the indirect contacts during this crisis also indicated a Soviet desire to work out acceptable terms for ending the crisis. This suggests that indirect contacts are an interesting alternative in handling at least some of the bargaining impediments arising during major crises.

It is also important to stress that the role of concrete actions in the communications process increased greatly during the Cuban missile crisis. The distinction between American and Soviet actions, in this connection, is revealing. The concrete actions of the United States were extremely important in conveying the strength of American determination during this crisis: the naval blockade was rapidly implemented; the American mobilization of armed forces was obviously serious;

[71] On this line of communication see Roger Hilsman, "The Cuban Crisis: How Close We Were to War," *Look*, Vol. 28, No. 17 (August 25, 1964), 19.

[72] The text of the telegram is printed in Pachter, *op.cit.*, p. 209.

[73] Fomin was widely believed to be the head of Soviet intelligence operations in the United States and therefore a person of some significance. John Scali was a relatively well-known Washington correspondent for the ABC television network. For a good account of the Fomin-Scali meetings, see Hilsman, *op.cit.*, pp. 20-21.

moreover, the United States was able to make credible its conditional willingness to use overt force at specific contact points in and around Cuba. The idea of applying "enough military pressure to make our will clear"[74] came through strongly. This posture was driven home with particular force toward the end of the week of open confrontation by mounting evidence of American preparations for an armed attack on Cuba within a few days.

Soviet actions, on the other hand, belied the verbal threats of the Soviet Union by indicating, for the most part, a desire to avoid violence. The Soviet Union did not mobilize its armed forces as thoroughly as the United States did. Soviet ships with objectionable cargoes turned back before reaching the American blockade. And the remaining ships were careful to submit to all the requests of American naval officers. In short, throughout the period of confrontation, the Soviets acted with extreme caution whenever there was any danger of violent contact.

The level of mutual understanding between the two sides during the course of the 1962 crisis was, on the whole, rather high. It is both accurate and important to emphasize that the crisis *arose* in the context of serious misunderstandings and miscalculations involving both of the key protagonists.[75] During the period of actual confrontation, however, the two sides proved able to utilize a number of modes of communication in order to clarify their positions and to reach agreement on terminating the crisis without resorting to violence. George Ball gives a good indication of the resultant mixture of several modes of communication in the statement that "lines of communication were opened directly between Washington and Moscow and through the United Nations to permit a political solution, albeit a political solution shaped by our willingness and ability to use force."[76] There is, therefore, an im-

[74] Sorensen, *op.cit.*, p. 694.

[75] At a minimum, the Soviets seriously miscalculated the probable American response to their initiatives in Cuba. On the other hand, American decision-makers failed, until a very late date, to understand the nature of Soviet political and strategic calculations focusing on Cuba.

[76] George Ball, "Lawyers and Diplomats" (address delivered on December 13, 1962). The text appears in *DOSB*, XLVII, No. 1227 (December 31, 1962), 990.

portant sense in which the Cuban crisis was a major communications success. As the Wohlstetters have put it, "The resolution of the missile crisis may be regarded as in the main a brilliant example of a successful communication of a precise and firm intention."[77] For this reason, it is interesting that the missile crisis subsequently became an important factor in generating widespread popular concern about the dangers of communications failures during crises as well as influential political pressures to improve the situation by the acceptance of devices such as the so-called "hot line" between Washington and Moscow.[78]

Conclusion

An analysis of these case materials indicates that changes in the prevailing modes of communication under conditions of crisis tend to occur in relative rather than absolute patterns. Diplomatic contacts do not necessarily decline in volume during crises but: formal diplomatic communication is frequently sluggish relative to the needs of the situation; diplomatic contacts often degenerate into ineffectual haggling; and the bargaining context tends to increase the importance of supporting diplomatic statements with actions or incisive contingent preparations to achieve credibility. Under these circumstances, efforts to communicate by actions will rise sharply in importance in comparison with diplomatic contacts. Several additional distinctions, however, are worth making. There are generally powerful international pressures during crises to maintain at least the facade of diplomatic contacts or negotiations even when such modes of communication have become fruitless. Next, there is an important difference between actions undertaken primarily as conscious attempts to communicate and actions based on other considerations which nevertheless have *de facto* results in the area of communication.

[77] Albert and Roberta Wohlstetter, "Controlling the Risks in Cuba," *Adelphi Paper No. 17* (London: Institute of Strategic Studies, April 1965), p. 20.

[78] The so-called "hot line" agreement, providing for a direct telecommunications link between Washington and Moscow, was signed in Geneva on June 20, 1963. For the text see *Documents on Disarmament 1963* (Washington: United States Government Printing Office, 1964), p. 236.

Furthermore, it should not be assumed actions will always operate to clear up ambiguities left by other modes of communication. In fact, actions may generate confusions when they are inconsistent, contradictory or deliberately designed to obscure realities. In addition, actions, far more than diplomatic contacts, often change the basic circumstances or context of a crisis as well as communicate information to other participants. Such effects may occur along a number of different channels, from actions affecting the physical maneuverability of various parties to actions altering perceptions concerning risks and fears of destructive outcomes.

The cases also emphasize the relative importance of irregular or unusual modes of communication during periods of crisis. Activities of this kind usually occupy a middle position between the relatively formal procedures involved in diplomatic contacts and the more *de facto* or indirect quality of communication by means of actions. Though some informal contacts of this kind do, in fact, occur all the time on a relatively routine basis, the bargaining impediments and communications problems of crises are apt to raise the importance of these informal modes of communication during such periods. In the postwar period, the Soviets have shown far and away the most clearcut interest in exploring the possibilities of circumventing the more normal channels of communication by means of such devices. In the two Berlin crises and in the Cuban missile crisis, the relative clarity and extensiveness of Soviet interests in informal procedures of this kind was remarkable.

At the same time, it is important to emphasize the extent to which communications activities are likely to become an attractive focus of manipulation for purposes of strategic bargaining under conditions of crisis. The confrontations over Berlin in 1948-1949 and in 1961, in particular, produced examples of several distinguishable types of manipulation relating to communications activities. It is sometimes possible to dissimulate overtly in order to alter the effective distribution of perceptions concerning risks and fears emanating from a crisis. Again, threats to refuse or to terminate negotiations during a confrontation can be of considerable value against a government under powerful domestic or international pressures to negotiate. Moreover, selective communication designed to discriminate among opposing allies is sometimes a useful device in reducing the effective cohesion among opponents whose interests are not entirely congruent. The evidence suggests that, from the point of view of individual participants, manipulative possibilities of this kind will often seem attractive. From a more general interaction perspective, however, it is evident that activities of this kind tend to exacerbate rather sharply the dangers of serious *misunderstandings* during crises.

The Berlin crisis of 1961 and the Taiwan Strait crisis of 1958 make it clear that there is no necessary correlation or causal connection between sheer communication and genuine understanding. In fact, important misunderstandings may arise from a number of sources during crises regardless of the level of communication. These sources of misunderstanding include: the building up over time of diverging interpretations, as occurred with the first Berlin crisis; prior predispositions about changing international realities, as in the case of Chinese (CPR) attitudes underlying the Taiwan Strait crisis of 1958; initial miscalculations concerning one or more opponents, as happened with the Soviet initiative in the Cuban crisis of 1962; and manipulative moves that temporarily obscure true relations of strength, as in the 1961 Berlin crisis. From the point of view of the stability of the international system, genuine understanding during crises, though frequently difficult to achieve, is clearly more important than the sheer maintenance of communication in some proximate or technical sense. But if it is present during a major crisis in the current nuclear environment, the prospects of maintaining minimal control during the course of the confrontation are much better, regardless of the level of more specific communications activities. In this connection, it is also worth emphasizing that the case materials suggest real possibilities of improving basic understanding during crises even when it is not present at the outset. The Berlin crisis of 1948-1949, the Taiwan Strait crisis of 1958, and the Cuban missile crisis make it clear that communication by means of physical actions, in particular, can play a critical role in improving understanding in situations of this kind. Also, crises in which basic understanding is obscured during the tensest phases of confrontation are apt to be extremely dangerous from the point of view of control even if formal channels of communication remain open. The serious dangers in this area that characterized the 1961 Berlin crisis arose, to a substantial degree, out of these problems of mutual understanding.

7. Peripheral Actors

> HYPOTHESIS. The role of peripheral actors such as international organizations, nonaligned states, and nonengaged allies or partners will generally be minimal during the upswing phase of a crisis; the influence of such actors, however, will increase once a crisis confrontation becomes full-blown in physical terms.

The critical point of the above hypothesis involves the distinction between the upswing phase and the full confrontation phase of a crisis. Though the point of separation between phases is sometimes difficult to pin down with precision in concrete cases, the underlying concepts concerned are relatively clear. The phase of full confrontation begins when physical forces of the principal participants are deployed within a circumscribed geographical area in interdependent patterns designed to influence the course of the crisis. In this connection, the relevant contrast is with the predominantly diplomatic activities of the preceding phase. Thus, in rough terms, the imposition of a full blockade of Berlin during the last week of June 1948 and the initial buildup of American naval forces in the Taiwan Strait in the days following August 23, 1958, marked the onset of the confrontation phase of these crises.

The upswing phase of a crisis tends to be ambiguous or obscured. A *fait accompli* is sometimes accepted by the party on the tactical defensive, in which case a full-scale confrontation will never occur. On the other hand, when a decision is taken to respond to another party's initiatives, it will probably be made in private and at least partially on the basis of information fully available to only a limited number of decision-makers. Efforts to maintain secrecy are frequently important both to the party undertaking initiatives likely to touch off a crisis and to the respondent during the initial period in which it is still formulating its basic pattern of reaction. In addition, the fact that the respondent is often under considerable pressure to react to the initiatives of an adversary with dispatch can reduce the scope for action on the part of peripheral actors during the upswing phase of a crisis. For all these reasons, peripheral actors are likely to be poorly informed during this phase. In any case, they are apt to be unprepared to act with either the speed or the decisiveness necessary to affect significantly the processes by which the principals become locked into a full confrontation.

This relationship begins to change, however, once the protagonists move into the phase of full-blown confrontation. From this point onward, visible attempts to jockey for position and to utilize the tactics of "strategic bargaining" within a framework of physical interdependence will tend increasingly to become the dominant mode of interaction. Under these circumstances, the growth of various perceptual rigidities as well as more specific bargaining impediments may open up new roles for peripheral actors. At the same time, perceptions concerning force-of-events problems and overlapping interests in avoiding outcomes of mutual loss are likely to become more influential in the calculations of the protagonists as a crisis moves from an initial phase of fairly rapid buildup into the phase of full confrontation in which "contest-of-resolve" images become increasingly critical. The basic qualities of the confrontation phase of a crisis, therefore, are apt to generate more opportunities for action on the part of peripheral parties than is true of the upswing phase. It is important to emphasize, however, that this in no way guarantees that peripheral actors will be able to make use of these opportunities in any given crisis. In fact, bargaining processes during crises often fluctuate as the perceptions, expectations, and tactical maneuvers of the principal participants shift. In an environment of this kind, the actual influence of peripheral actors depends, among other things, on precision timing, the ability to act with dispatch, and skill in formulating specific initiatives. Thus, while the roles of peripheral actors are likely to be greater, generally, during the confrontation phase of a crisis than during the upswing phase, the actual dimensions of these roles in any given case are largely dependent on the characteristics and abilities of the peripheral actors in question.

147

Berlin, 1948-1949

During the relatively long upswing phase of the first Berlin crisis—the period lasting from March until the last week of June 1948—there was virtually no pertinent activity by peripheral actors. The various states on the Western side were either fully engaged as partners or ultimately without influence. The United States, Britain, and France consulted on all moves affecting Germany during 1948; in fact, considerable diplomatic effort was expended to overcome the reluctance of the French to accept policies pointing toward the creation of an autonomous government in western Germany alone.[1] The Benelux states were kept informed of relevant developments during this period though they were unable to exercise much influence of their own. Germany too was still unable to play an independent role of any significance in the councils of either side. Peripheral actors were also somewhat inconsequential on the Soviet side. In view of the Soviet role as final tactical initiator of this crisis, it might be expected that prior consultation would have occurred within the emerging Soviet bloc. This, however, was a period of unilateral Soviet dominance in which genuine collaboration along these lines was neither offered nor expected in most foreign policy matters. Even the simultaneous development of the rift with Yugoslavia does not appear to have swayed Soviet thinking about Berlin or Germany in general during 1948.[2]

During this upswing phase, the role of international and nonaligned actors also remained unimportant. No one made a serious move to refer the situation to the United Nations. The great powers, who with the exception of China[3] were all actively engaged in the crisis, indicated a clear-cut desire to

[1] French disinclination came to the surface particularly in the negotiations concerning the creation of Trizonia and in the London meetings during the early months of 1948.

[2] It would be plausible to suppose that the problems with Yugoslavia would have made the Soviets all the more eager for a success in Central Europe during this period, but it is difficult to discern connections of any kind between the two developments.

[3] Besides being a Far Eastern power, China was effectively removed from a position of international influence during this period by its own civil war.

148

keep the situation out of the United Nations. Steps were taken to discourage Trygve Lie from exercising his authority under Article 99 of the Charter to bring the crisis before the Security Council. Also, there were in 1958 no nonaligned powers capable of effectively interceding in the crisis. The Afro-Asian bloc was still in an embryonic form as a force in international politics, and the few individual states that could meaningfully be labeled nonaligned at this time were largely concerned with their own problems. Especially in the European arena itself, the relevant states were either directly engaged in the crisis or still insufficiently recovered from the war to exercise a significant independent influence.

Interestingly, no peripheral actor assumed an important role in the crisis in the period *immediately* following the development of the Berlin crisis into an intense confrontation during the last week of June. For reasons outlined above, the only relevant candidate in this crisis was the United Nations. The great powers, however, continued to argue during July and August that the United Nations was not an appropriate arena in which to discuss the crisis. The Soviet Union maintained the only acceptable forum was the Council of Foreign Ministers. The Western powers, on the other hand, preferred, in the first instance, to seek with the Soviet Union direct negotiations aimed at removing the blockade and *then* to initiate a discussion of the whole German problem in the Council of Foreign Ministers.[4] The proximate result was the negotiations in Moscow during August 1948. From the end of June until well into September,[5] therefore, no peripheral actor was able to exercise a significant influence of any kind on the ongoing confrontation over Berlin.

On September 26, however, the foreign ministers of the

[4] In particular, the Western powers maintained they would not negotiate on the substantive issues at stake under duress. With regard to the possibility of discussions following the removal of the blockade, however, the Western powers favored the forum offered by the Council of Foreign Ministers.

[5] The military governors for Germany, meeting in Berlin during the first week of September, were unable to come to terms with regard to the operational meaning of the Moscow negotiations of August. In the wake of this failure, a number of somewhat recriminatory high-level notes were exchanged among the four powers.

three major Western powers, meeting in Paris,[6] announced the Western intention of referring the Berlin situation to the United Nations, and on September 29 this step was formally taken in concurrent letters to the Secretary-General. Though it is evident this was primarily a tactical maneuver by the Western powers following the failure of direct negotiations both on a high level in Moscow and on a lower level in Berlin, it did, for the first time, offer the United Nations an opportunity to play a role in the crisis. In the upshot, a number of parties within the United Nations indefatigably sought to exercise a moderating and conciliatory influence on the confrontation.[7]

The most extensive efforts along these lines took place in the Security Council. Council debate on the Berlin situation opened on October 19. At first, the nonengaged and "nonaligned" states within the Council joined efforts to formulate a compromise solution,[8] but the resultant resolution was vetoed by the Soviet Union on October 25. Juan Bramuglia, the Argentine foreign minister who was president of the Council during October,[9] then took the lead for moderation. Among other things, his activities led to the establishment of a committee of experts, headed by Gunnar Myrdal,[10] on currency problems. This committee worked at considerable length to achieve a compromise solution for the Berlin currency dispute, but its efforts were ultimately overtaken and rendered irrelevant by the flow of events in Berlin itself.[11]

[6] The foreign ministers were in Paris for the opening of the third session of the United Nations General Assembly, which was held in Paris in 1948.

[7] For a good brief account of United Nations activities dealing with the Berlin crisis, consult John C. Campbell, *The United States in World Affairs 1948-1949* (New York: Harper and Row, 1949), pp. 452-64.

[8] These states included: Argentina, Belgium, Canada, China, Colombia, and Syria.

[9] Bramuglia became President of the Council when the United States, whose turn it was in the regular rotation, stepped aside because of its involvement in the principal issue being debated.

[10] At the time, Myrdal was the director of the United Nations Economic Commission for Europe and already a widely known figure among economists.

[11] Because of various difficulties, the committee did not make its final report until March 1949.

During the same period, other organs of the United Nations began to take steps relating to the Berlin crisis. The General Assembly passed a unanimous resolution on November 3 expressing its anxiety about the Berlin confrontation and calling for redoubled efforts on the part of the principals to negotiate a settlement. In addition, Herbert Evatt, the president of the assembly during the 1948 session, took an active part in behind-the-scenes diplomatic activity concerning the crisis. At the same time, the Secretary-General became interested in the problem and began to undertake diplomatic initiatives of his own aimed at a compromise settlement. On November 13, Lie and Evatt joined forces and circulated a note on the Berlin confrontation to the parties involved which evoked written responses from both the United States and the Soviet Union though it had little effect on their concrete actions. Lie, moreover, extensively engaged in an early version of what has subsequently been labeled "quiet diplomacy" in an ultimately unsuccessful effort to reduce the differences between the two sides through informal contact.[12]

Thus, in the later phases of the Berlin crisis, the United Nations became the scene of diversified efforts to put moderating pressures on the protagonists. On the whole, however, these efforts were relatively ineffective. A number of the critical issues of the crisis were not susceptible to *negotiated* compromise, and the United Nations was unable to bring any substantial coercive pressures to bear. The currency issue, on which the focus of United Nations activities had come to rest by the end of 1948, was in fact more nearly a symptom than an underlying cause of the crisis.[13] In the final analysis, a number of the developments that eventually brought about the end of the confrontation began, by the turn of the year, to overtake the slower pace of United Nations activities. These developments included: the success of the Western airlift during the fall and winter months; the maintenance of popular morale in the western sectors of Berlin; and the continued

[12] For information on Lie's activities during the crisis, see Trygve Lie, *In the Cause of Peace* (New York: Macmillan, 1954), Chap. 12.

[13] In addition, the currency problem became progressively difficult to handle as the *de facto* political division of the city of Berlin became more and more far-reaching.

movement toward agreement on arrangements for the establishment of an autonomous government in western Germany despite the blockade of Berlin.

Taiwan Strait, 1958

Throughout the 1958 crisis in the Taiwan Strait, the influence of peripheral actors remained sharply limited. For the most part, the prerogatives of control in this crisis were tightly maintained by Peking, Moscow, Taipei, and Washington.[14] This relationship was emphasized in 1958 by the contrast between the relatively extensive role of the United Nations in the Middle Eastern crisis[15] that erupted on July 15 and the restricted role in the Taiwan Strait crisis of all peripheral actors combined. Nevertheless, it is true there was a clear increase in efforts by peripheral actors to influence the course of the Taiwan Strait crisis during its later phases as compared with its upswing phase.

During the upswing phase of the 1958 crisis—the period leading up to August 23 and including the days immediately following the obvious tactical initiatives of the Chinese People's Republic (CPR)—there were virtually no relevant activities on the part of peripheral actors. Several explanatory factors seem to lie behind this quiescence. The decision to initiate a probe against the offshore islands at this time was a fairly well-kept secret between the CPR and the Soviet Union. Early indications of an ensuing crisis, in the form of Chinese Communist propaganda and of military activities in Fukien province, were not strikingly enough at variance with constant signs of tension in the area to divert attention from the ongoing Middle Eastern crisis.[16] In addition, the United Nations was not particularly active during the upswing phase. The General Assembly was not in session until September

[14] See Robert W. Barnett, "Quemoy: The Use and Consequence of Deterrence," Harvard Center for International Affairs, March 1960, p. 95.

[15] For a general discussion of the activities of the United Nations in connection with the Middle Eastern crisis of 1958, see Richard I. Miller, *Dag Hammarskjold and Crisis Diplomacy* (New York: Oceana, 1961), Chaps. VII and VIII.

[16] For some factual material on the nature of the Chinese buildup in Fukien province, see *The Economist*, August 16, 1958, p. 522, and August 23, 1958, pp. 582-584.

16, with the exception of a brief emergency session between August 8 and 21 which was entirely devoted to the Middle Eastern crisis and disregarded East Asian developments. And the Security Council remained frozen on all substantive issues concerning China as it had been for some years prior to 1958. Despite these explanations, this indifference shown by peripheral actors toward various indications of impending trouble in the Taiwan Strait during August 1958 remains striking.

During the later phases of the crisis, the confrontation over the offshore islands came to be of great interest to peripheral actors, though there was still a kind of delayed reaction before concern about the dangers of the confrontation began to catalyze actions.[17] The thirteenth session of the General Assembly opened on September 16, when the ultimate outcome of the crisis was still very much in doubt. There were, nevertheless, several major restrictions on the ability of the United Nations to influence the course of the crisis. The fact that the CPR was not a member of the Organization, coupled with the known views of the Chinese Communists that the United Nations had no right to deal with the issues of the crisis, made many logical diplomatic alternatives politically infeasible.[18] In addition, the United States did not care to have the issues underlying the crisis fully aired in the General Assembly on the grounds that resultant pressures of world opinion for compromise would probably be directed primarily toward the United States.[19] The United States was therefore

[17] This delayed reaction phenomenon is clearly explainable in terms of the time required for governments not directly involved in a crisis to acquire and assimilate information about the situation. Developments of this kind sometimes lead peripheral actors to advocate "solutions" for a conflict which are already obsolete in terms of the unfolding realities of the immediate crisis.

[18] The United States, moreover, explicitly accepted this position of the CPR and acted accordingly. On this subject see Dulles' statements at his press conference on September 9, 1958, which appear in *DOSB*, XXXIX, No. 1005 (September 29, 1958), 489.

[19] The point here is that the United States, because of its greater sensitivity to world opinion and because of the asymmetrical situation that would arise from the absence of the CPR, would create difficulties for itself by formally submitting the Taiwan Strait crisis to the United Nations.

careful to confine itself to statements reserving the right to
bring the crisis to the United Nations on a formal basis in the
event the ambassadorial talks in Warsaw failed to produce
any positive results.[20] Moreover, throughout September the
United Nations continued to be preoccupied to a considerable
extent with the Middle Eastern crisis. Hammarskjold especially was deeply engaged during September in efforts to implement the Assembly's resolution of August 21 on the Middle Eastern situation.[21]

Nevertheless, the events of the crisis had an extensive informal impact on the early meetings of the Assembly's thirteenth session. Although there was no formal item on the
agenda relating to the crisis, the confrontation in the Taiwan
Strait set the tone of the opening debates.[22] Both Dulles and
Gromyko discussed the issue in major addresses on September 18,[23] and Gromyko returned to the subject in another
formal speech on September 25. Moreover, at least until the
early days of October, the crisis was evidently the single most
important topic of informal discussion at the United Nations.
These informal contacts reached a high point on September
27 when Hammarskjold dined with Dulles and Gromyko.
The crisis also had a considerable effect on the Assembly's
treatment of the Chinese membership issue during the 1958
session. The *de facto* association of the two issues was guaranteed by the Soviet Union, which successfully demanded that
the Assembly take up the issue of Chinese membership immediately upon opening rather than postponing discussion of it
until the crisis in the Strait had subsided.[24] It seems clear in

[20] See Dulles' comments in his address to the General Assembly on
September 18, 1958. The text of these remarks appears in *DOSB*, XXXIX,
No. 1006 (October 6, 1958), 526. The key point here concerns the possi-
bility that the United States might have found itself in a position to use
this device to exonerate itself and place the blame for failure in the
Warsaw talks on the CPR.

[21] Among other things, Hammarskjold was away from New York on a
trip to the Middle East between August 25 and September 12.

[22] See the discussion in *The Economist*, September 20, 1958, p. 913.

[23] The text of Dulles' address appears in *DOSB*, XXXIX, No. 1006
(October 6, 1958), 525-530. For the text of Gromyko's speech, see the
New York Times, September 19, 1958, p. 4.

[24] For a discussion of Soviet activities with regard to this issue, see
John Thomas, "Soviet Behavior in the Quemoy Crisis of 1958," *Orbis*,
VI, No. 1 (Spring 1962), 46.

this regard that the existence of the crisis strengthened the position of those favoring membership for the CPR, who argued that admission would increase the ability of the United Nations to deal meaningfully with problems of peace and security in Asia. On September 23, nevertheless, the Assembly formally disposed of the Chinese membership issue for 1958 in a fashion that demonstrated the continuing dominance of the American position on this question. The influence of these activities at the United Nations on the course of the final phases of the crisis should not be underestimated. Still, in the last analysis, none of them can be regarded as critically important in shaping the ultimate outcome of the confrontation.

Also during the early days of September, there was a marked rise of interest in the crisis by nonaligned states and nonengaged allies.[25] This development took the form, for the most part, of a sharp increase in general calls for moderation, based primarily on fears the confrontation might erupt into open and large-scale warfare. Insofar as it can be determined, the majority of *public* efforts along these lines took the form of pressure on the American government not to resort to violence over an issue as "unworthy" as the offshore islands.[26] Nehru, for example, called for the acceptance of arrangements to allow for a peaceful transfer of the islands to Communist Chinese rule.[27] And there were numerous general suggestions for conferences among the principals in the crisis. Though expressions of concern along these lines jumped during September, the resultant activities were almost entirely exhortatory in nature, and this new-found concern among the peripheral actors did not produce anything concrete and constructive about possibilities for diplomacy in the 1958 crisis.

Simultaneously, however, some of the peripheral actors attempted to influence the situation at the level of private diplomacy by behind-the-scenes activities in the forum provided

[25] France constituted an important, though only partial, exception. During the summer and fall of 1958, France was still deeply absorbed in its own internal problems stemming from the fall of the Fourth Republic in May.

[26] For an interesting discussion of this argument, see *The Economist*, September 20, 1958, p. 914.

[27] For information on Nehru's position in the 1958 crisis, see the *New York Times*, September 8, 1958, p. 3.

by the thirteenth session of the General Assembly. Though not itself an actor in this context, the United Nations offered a focal point and meeting place for the practice of private diplomacy. The following examples indicate the range of these activities during the Taiwan Strait crisis of 1958: (1) on September 23, V.K. Krishna Menon offered Indian "good offices" to the participants in the crisis,[28] (2) during the last days of September, a number of nonaligned states worked on the idea of having the General Assembly formally call for a foreign ministers' conference to arrange a termination of the crisis,[29] (3) during the same period, there were hints of Russo-British discussions in New York pertaining to the crisis,[30] (4) also during late September, Krishna Menon and Halvard Lange of Norway apparently sought to establish an indirect communications link between the CPR and the United States involving the permanent mission of the United States to the United Nations in New York City,[31] (5) in the early days of October, informal discussion at the United Nations among a number of delegates focused on the possibilities of a role for Hammarskjold in terminating the crisis, and (6) at the same time, a number of discussions occurred among Asian delegates in an effort to formulate a face-saving formula for mutual disengagement from the crisis.[32] As it happened, none of these activities had a critical influence on the final phases or the ultimate outcome of the Taiwan Strait crisis. In fact, the principal participants were able to end the 1958 crisis through an interesting process of tacit coordination without outside assistance. Nevertheless, the efforts at private diplomacy outlined above were, for the most part, realistic

[28] This offer, however, was predictably unacceptable to the United States since the Indian government had previously identified itself with the view that the offshore islands should go to the CPR without any *quid pro quo.*

[29] See R. F. Wall, "Formosa and the Chinese Offshore Islands," pp. 566-574 in Geoffrey Barraclough, *Survey of International Affairs, 1956-1958* (London: Oxford, 1962), p. 572.

[30] See *The Economist,* September 27, 1958, p. 1,003.

[31] For information on these activities, which is fascinating but unfortunately incomplete, consult the *New York Times,* October 10, 1958, pp. 1 and 4, and October 11, 1958, p. 1.

[32] On this subject see *The Economist,* October 11, 1958, p. 116.

enough so that they might well have offered a plausible recourse had the protagonists encountered greater difficulty in terminating the crisis on a direct basis.

Berlin, 1961

The role of peripheral actors was extremely limited throughout the Berlin crisis of 1961. Two reservations to this general conclusion, however, must be made. It is doubtless true in a very general sense, as Dean Rusk suggested in September, that world opinion "makes itself felt on both sides in a situation of this sort in the direction of moderation and reasonableness."[33] Yet this factor is so amorphous and intangible that it relates more nearly to background conditions during a crisis than to definable roles for specified actors. In addition, though the role of peripheral actors remained small throughout the crisis, the relevance of these actors did increase noticeably during the later phases of the confrontation.

During the upswing phase of the crisis—the period from June 4 until the closure of the sector boundary in Berlin on August 13—peripheral actors made virtually no significant attempts to influence the course of the crisis. The nonaligned states in particular "seemed unconcerned with the Berlin crisis."[34] This lack of concern was especially evident in their almost complete indifference to American efforts to enlist support for the Western position in Berlin on the basis of legal rights emanating from the termination arrangements for World War II. At the same time, the Berlin situation did not come up at the United Nations during this phase. This inattentiveness was the result of several factors: (1) the United Nations was deeply involved in the protean Congo situation during July and August,[35] (2) the General Assembly was not in session during this phase, and (3) the Security Council was even more troubled than usual by Soviet-American dis-

[33] From an interview with Rusk on October 14, 1961. The text appears in *DOSB*, XLV, No. 1166 (October 30, 1961), 709.

[34] John W. Keller, *Germany, the Wall and Berlin* (New York: Vantage Press, 1964), p. 115.

[35] During the summer of 1961, the problems associated with the Katangese secession reached their high point, ultimately erupting into overt hostilities during September.

agreements during the summer of 1961.[36] There was some discussion outside the United Nations at this time about its possible participation in Berlin as part of a program aimed at creating an international status for the city.[37] Ideas along these lines never got beyond the stage of informal discussion, however, so that they did little to augment the actual role of the United Nations during the 1961 crisis.

In the aftermath of the August 13 boundary closure, the crisis quickly became the center of attention for a number of peripheral actors. Though their concrete influence remained for the most part limited, the interest of these actors was clearly engaged. In the first instance, a number of neutralist leaders began to speak out on Berlin. Nehru, for example, was especially vocal on the subject in the weeks immediately following August 13. Though the diplomatic calculations behind these activities are anything but clear,[38] the motives underlying them are not difficult to discern. The nonaligned states were concerned primarily with the danger of escalating hostilities involving the superpowers rather than with concrete arrangements for the future of Berlin or Germany. The principal thrust of their reaction to August 13, therefore, was to muster pressures on both sides for the initiation of negotiations and to adopt a somewhat undiscriminating posture in favor of terminating the crisis by compromise.[39] During the latter part of August, however, the actual influence of these activities on the course of the crisis was kept to a min-

[36] The conflict focusing on Dag Hammarskjold and the Office of the Secretary-General reached its climax during this period. Moreover, the Soviet Union and the United States had by this time assumed uncompromising positions with regard to the whole Congo operation.

[37] For indications of interest in the idea of a role for the United Nations in Berlin, see Philip Windsor, *City on Leave* (New York: Praeger, 1963), p. 238.

[38] In particular, Nehru appears to have been confused with regard to some of the technical details of the situation. In the final analysis, Nehru's position appears to have rested on the following: (1) both sides should do everything possible to minimize the dangers inherent in the situation, (2) the legal justification for the Western position in Berlin was rather shaky, and (3) the fundamental Western right of access to Berlin should, nevertheless, be guaranteed.

[39] For an interesting analysis of this reaction, see the *New York Times*, August 27, 1961, p. 1.

imum by the obvious inability of the neutralist leaders to formulate any concrete and precise diplomatic suggestions.

Thus, the opening of the previously scheduled Belgrade Conference of neutralist and nonaligned states on September 1 appeared to offer an excellent opportunity for these states to coordinate their influence with regard to the Berlin crisis. Hopes that the conference might produce useful initiatives on Berlin had indeed been voiced from the middle of August onward and had raised expectations along these lines. Given this background, the vagueness of the discussion of the Berlin crisis at the conference and the resultant failure to produce useful and influential diplomatic initiatives was a big disappointment to many.[40] The Belgrade Conference did produce a general suggestion for a summit conference on Berlin,[41] and it led to the peace missions of Nehru and Nkrumah to Moscow and of Sukarno and Keita to Washington. Many of the participants at Belgrade, however, had failed to grasp the fundamental nature of some of the critical aspects of the East-West bargaining process over Berlin, and the shock of the simultaneous Soviet decision to resume atmospheric nuclear testing had a distorting effect on the Belgrade deliberations which sharply reduced their relevance to the real problems of terminating the confrontation. In the end, therefore, the Belgrade Conference clearly demonstrated the new-found concern of the nonaligned states about the dangers of the Berlin crisis, but it also emphasized both the peripheral quality of their deliberations on the subject and the limitations on

[40] For analyses of the proceedings of the Belgrade Conference, see Paul Hofmann, the *New York Times*, September 3, 1961, Sect. IV, p. 4; and Harry Schwartz, the *New York Times*, September 10, 1961, Sect. IV, p. 3. For a general analysis of the Belgrade Conference, see Peter Lyon, *Neutralism* (Leicester, Eng.: Leicester University Press, 1963), Chap. VI.

[41] This suggestion came, however, at a somewhat inopportune moment, and as a result it made little impact diplomatically. In particular, such a conference would probably have favored the Eastern side at this time since the Western powers had not yet fully consolidated their remaining position in Western Berlin and since the Soviet threat to conclude a separate peace treaty with the GDR had not yet lost its credibility in the West. Moreover, bargaining relationships between the two sides were changing quite rapidly during this period, a fact that created uncertainties and made mutual acceptance of the suggestion for a summit conference all the more unlikely.

159

their abilities to influence the behavior of the great powers.

The aftermath of August 13 also led to mounting concern about the Berlin crisis at the United Nations. Various ideas for some form of United Nations "presence" in Berlin quickly acquired greater prominence. Interest in such a possibility was bolstered especially by discussion along these lines in the introduction to the annual report by the Secretary-General, released on August 24.[42] The death of Hammarskjold at Ndola on September 18 and the resultant internal crisis within the United Nations itself, however, effectively destroyed embryonic hopes for the development of a United Nations role of this kind during the 1961 crisis.

Nevertheless, the General Assembly played some part in the crisis during September and October, especially as a forum for informal communications and as a focal point for efforts by the protagonists in the crisis to win support for their policies. It is important not to overestimate the influence of these activities. Yet, the Berlin confrontation was a subject of great interest in the General Debate at the 1961 session, it became a major issue in the course of discussions in several of the committees of the Assembly, and it was one of the principal topics in major policy addresses by both President Kennedy[43] and Foreign Minister Gromyko. Perhaps the most significant role of the United Nations during these later phases of the 1961 crisis arose from the utilization of the Organization as an informal arena for the conduct of private East-West conversations. Though the resultant contacts during September between Rusk and Gromyko and between Home and Gromyko did not produce an arrangement for ending the crisis, they did mark the first high-level official contacts between East and West since the Berlin controversy was reactivated at Vienna in June.[44] In retrospect, these contacts appear to have played at least an instrumental role in the grow-

[42] The text of this report can be located conveniently in Wilder Foote, ed., *Dag Hammarskjold: Servant of Peace* (New York: Harper and Row, c. 1963), pp. 354-375.

[43] For the text of Kennedy's address to the General Assembly on September 25, 1961, see *DOSB*, XLV, No. 1164 (October 16, 1961), 619-25.

[44] There had, of course, been some very informal contacts in Washington, Moscow, London, Bonn, and Berlin itself during the summer.

ing realization on both sides that the scope for major shifts in bargaining strength in the 1961 crisis was narrowing rapidly by the beginning of October.

In contrast to the independent roles of peripheral actors, this crisis also produced efforts on the part of the protagonists to bargain by playing for the support of these actors. The United Nations figured in this process both in connection with efforts to propagate a role for the United Nations in Berlin which would favor the position of one of the protagonists and in connection with threats to air the whole issue in the United Nations as a means of mustering the support of world opinion for the side claiming to be the innocent victim of a contrived crisis. The first of these tactics came up primarily in Soviet ideas for a United Nations role as a guarantor under its plan to make West Berlin into a "free city." Both the June 4 *aide-mémoire*[45] and a number of subsequent Soviet statements contained suggestions along these lines. The United States, on the other hand, was the principal user of the second tactic in the 1961 crisis, suggesting on numerous occasions that the crisis would be brought to the attention of the United Nations on a formal basis if it reached the point of becoming a "serious" threat to world peace.[46] The apparent American objectives in using this tactic were to impress the nonaligned states favorably with American willingness to debate the issue in the United Nations if it should become really serious and to lay the groundwork for a possible American effort, in the General Assembly, to discredit the intentions of the Soviet Union in the Berlin crisis at some propitious moment.[47]

At the same time, the protagonists engaged in several more

[45] For the text of the Soviet *aide-mémoire*, see *DOSB*, XLV, No. 1154 (August 7, 1961), 231-233. Particularly interesting in this connection are such Soviet statements as, "The status of the free city could be duly registered by the United Nations and consolidated by the authority of that international organization." This statement appears on p. 232.

[46] As an example, consider Rusk's statement of July 23 that "if the crisis develops into a situation of very high tension, you can be certain it will come before the United Nations in some form." From an interview with Rusk reported in *DOSB*, XLV, No. 1155 (August 14, 1961), p. 285.

[47] For a discussion of this subject consult Hans Speier, *Divided Berlin* (New York: Praeger, 1961), p. 150.

direct efforts to enlist support among the nonaligned states for their positions on the Berlin issue. Such efforts were most evident during the upswing phase of the crisis since the neutralist leaders later became primarily concerned with the dangers inherent in the confrontation itself rather than with the comparative merits of the substantive positions of the opposing sides. For its part, the United States campaigned for nonaligned support by stressing the issue of self-determination and by attempting to engender sympathy for the civilian population of Berlin.[48] Efforts by the Soviet Union to gain nonaligned support, on the other hand, were somewhat more varied, combining both persuasive and coercive approaches. During June and July, the Soviets made an effort to emphasize the essential reasonableness of their program for the future of Berlin and to couple their concrete initiatives in this area with attractive proposals stressing the ideas of neutralizing (West) Berlin, giving it a "free city" status, and making the United Nations a guarantor of the arrangement.[49] In this phase, the Soviets apparently wanted to avoid the image of an incorrigible revisionist whose demands must be met at least on some occasions because of the very incorrigibility from which they emanate. In the aftermath of August 13, however, the Soviet posture in this area shifted markedly. During the later phases of the crisis, the most important and spectacular Soviet move to influence the nonaligned states with regard to the East-West aspects of the Berlin crisis was the decision to resume nuclear testing, which was announced to coincide with the opening of the Belgrade Conference. It now seems highly probable that the Soviets hoped, through this move, to exacerbate the perceived dangers of the crisis and to maximize outside pressures for concessions on the United States as the major participant most likely to be responsive to external influence and to be "reasonable" under the circum-

[48] For an interesting discussion concerning the use of such tactics, see Under-Secretary Chester Bowles' report of August 15 dealing with his recent Asian trip. The text is printed in *DOSB*, XLV, No. 1160 (September 18, 1961), 479-490.

[49] For a discussion of Soviet activities along these lines, see Jean Edward Smith, *The Defense of Berlin* (Baltimore: The Johns Hopkins Press, 1963), p. 237.

stances. As it turned out, the Soviets overplayed this tactic in the aftermath of the Belgrade Conference, and the influence of the nonaligned states on the Western position during this phase of the crisis never became a critical factor in any case.

Cuba, 1962

The Cuban missile crisis can be rather clearly divided into an upswing phase lasting until the Kennedy speech on October 22 and a phase of overt confrontation touched off by the enunciation of the American quarantine policy. The interval between the speech on the evening of October 22 and the official proclamation of the quarantine the next morning was so small that the crisis moved swiftly from upswing to full confrontation.[50] Similarly, there is a clear distinction between the relevant activities of peripheral actors during the two phases.

The Soviet decision to install "offensive" missiles in Cuba and the initial steps designed to implement this decision were taken in almost complete secrecy. The Soviets did in fact coordinate their plans with the Cuban government, but they were quite successful in camouflaging their efforts to implement these plans, at least in the early stages. They evidently hoped to achieve an influential *fait accompli* by revealing the presence of the missiles only after they had become operational. In the week following the first clear-cut verification of the presence of "offensive" missiles in Cuba on October 15, the United States also maintained a veil of secrecy on the subject.[51] There were several reasons for this American posture[52] including: a fear that the Soviets would take some preemptive action if they discovered the level of American information too soon; the perceived need to decide on a response with great dispatch; and the coordination problems that

[50] For a detailed chronology of this shift, see David L. Larson, ed., *The "Cuban Crisis" of 1962: Selected Documents and Chronology* (Boston: Houghton Mifflin, 1963), pp. 314-316.

[51] On the problem of secrecy in this connection, see Roger Hilsman, "The Cuban Crisis: How Close We Were to War," *Look*, Vol. 28, No. 17 (August 25, 1964), 19.

[52] For a discussion of American motives in this area, consult Theodore Sorensen, *Kennedy* (New York: Harper and Row, 1965), p. 676.

would have arisen from consultations with other states. As a result, the United States refrained from informing even its closest allies about the impending confrontation until October 22.[53] The various states were then simply informed of the American decision rather than consulted. A remarkable feature of this procedure during the missile crisis was the relative success of American decision-makers in keeping their secret in the traditionally "leaky" atmosphere of Washington. The informed group remained extremely small, and the American pronouncement on October 22 came as a genuine surprise to the American public (including most Congressmen) as well as to the allies and nonaligned states.

For all these reasons, there was no opportunity for peripheral actors to exercise influence of any kind during the upswing phase of the 1962 crisis. In fact, the degree of impenetrability of the secrecy surrounding the buildup of the Cuban crisis is extraordinary in contemporary international politics. Following the Kennedy speech of October 22, the crisis quickly moved into the phase of full confrontation so that it was too late to think about heading it off.

The positions of previously nonengaged states evolved rapidly following the public announcement of the confrontation. In the first instance, the allies and associates of the two protagonists quickly fell into line behind their leaders, thereby removing themselves from the category of peripheral actors. The Warsaw Pact states, though poorly informed throughout the course of the crisis, sided with the Soviet Union. The Chinese remained aloof, preoccupied as they were with the concurrent Sino-Indian border clash, and played no significant role in the Cuban crisis. On the Western side, the NATO powers, with the partial exception of Canada, came down strongly for the American position. Somewhat more remarkable is the fact that the Latin American states took a clear-cut

[53] Great Britain was a partial exception. By the weekend of October 20-21, David Ormsby-Gore, the British ambassador to the United States, was on the verge of correctly piecing together the nature of the situation. For this reason and because of their close personal relationship, Kennedy took Ormsby-Gore into his confidence that weekend with regard to the crisis.

stand in favor of the United States.[54] On the morning of October 23, the Organization of American States, voted unanimously to back the American position.[55] As a result of these developments, the ranks of potential peripheral actors were considerably reduced.

The states that were ordinarily nonaligned in international politics, on the other hand, attempted immediately to assume the role of moderators in the Soviet-American confrontation over Cuba.[56] They strongly denounced the use of force and directed the bulk of their efforts toward disengaging the two superpowers on any terms.[57] In this effort the leaders of the nonaligned states were joined at least partially by Lester Pearson of Canada. The initiatives of Pope John XXIII also augmented the activities of the moderators. The interest of the Pope in the crisis was dramatically emphasized by the release, on October 25, of a public statement from the Vatican entreating the parties to act in such a way as to protect the well-being of mankind.[58] Though their goal of moderation was perfectly clear, however, the actors in this group found it extremely difficult to do much that would significantly affect the actions of the protagonists in the missile crisis. As a result, they sought to offset their individual helplessness by resorting to the possibility of acting collectively through the United Nations.

The Security Council of the United Nations dealt with the Cuban crisis formally and at considerable length during sessions on October 23, 24, and 25. Here, too, the nonaligned states actively worked for moderation. In formal terms, these efforts resulted in pointed verbal interventions, such as the

[54] On this subject see the discussion in Elie Abel, *The Missile Crisis* (Philadelphia: Lippincott, 1966), pp. 129-32.

[55] The text of the resolution can be found in Larson, ed., *op.cit.*, pp. 64-66. The delegate from Uruguay abstained at the time of the vote due to lack of instructions. Uruguay subsequently recorded its affirmative vote, however.

[56] The Sino-Indian border clash of 1962, which developed concurrently with the missile crisis, limited India to a very small role in the Cuban crisis.

[57] See Henry Pachter, *Collision Course* (New York: Praeger, 1963), pp. 35-36.

[58] For the text of the Vatican's statement, see Larson, ed., *op.cit.*, p. 142.

one by Frank Aiken of Ireland during the October 24 session,[59] and in proposals such as those of the Union of African and Malagasy States[60] outlined on October 25. Moreover, there were numerous informal attempts at behind-the-scenes persuasion in conjunction with the meetings of the Council. The superpowers, however, proceeded systematically to utilize the Security Council as a public debating forum. In the Council, they concentrated their efforts on rhetorical combat without showing any serious interest to use the meetings to find a settlement for the crisis. The forces of moderation in the Council thus found themselves in an extremely ineffectual position.[61] It is interesting to note that the superpowers felt a certain obligation to debate the issues and to justify their positions in the Security Council. But it is also important to point out that the Council failed to produce any significant results with regard to the missile crisis and that it did not meet again to discuss Cuba after Thursday, October 25.

Another force for moderation was provided by the United Nations through the activities of the Secretary-General. Although U Thant had the general backing of the nonaligned states in his activities, he operated largely on his own authority[62] in mapping out his efforts to act as a go-between in Soviet-American interactions during the crisis. Thant's first overt intervention came with his participation in the Security Council meeting of October 24.[63] Beyond this, he attempted to be a relatively formal source of ideas for termination arrangements and a communications link in relations between Kennedy and Khrushchev. This led to his letters of October 24 and 25 to the two leaders.[64] Thant even flew to Havana

[59] For the text of Aiken's statement in the Security Council on October 24, see *ibid.*, pp. 119-120.

[60] The text of the proposal is printed in *ibid.*, pp. 129-130.

[61] On the problems of operating within the framework of the Security Council, consult Pachter, *op.cit.*, p. 41.

[62] For verification see "Cuban Crisis: A Step by Step Review," the *New York Times*, November 3, 1962, pp. 1, 6-7. The relevant portion of the text can be located conveniently in Larson, ed., *op.cit.*, p. 237.

[63] The text of Thant's statement in the Security Council on October 24 is printed in Pachter, *op.cit.*, pp. 209-211.

[64] For the texts of Thant's letters see Larson, ed., *op.cit.*, pp. 112, 144-145, and 146-147.

on October 30 in an ultimately unsuccessful effort to acquire Castro's permission for United Nations inspection of the withdrawal of Soviet missiles from Cuba.[65] Perhaps more important than these overt activities, however, were the efforts of the Secretary-General throughout the week of October 22 to provide an indirect communications link between the Soviet and American missions behind the scenes in New York. As Pachter has put it, "Both parties found it practical to channel suggestions and semiofficial communications through their United Nations ambassadors and to initiate preliminary contacts in discussions with the Secretary General."[66] It is important not to overemphasize the impact of these circumspect efforts on the part of U Thant to exert pressure for moderation. The fact remains, nevertheless, that the Secretary-General was the one peripheral actor who did have a meaningful role, notably in the realm of communications functions, during the Cuban missile crisis.[67]

Conclusion

These case materials generally support the hypothesis that the role of peripheral actors tends to increase following the transition from the upswing phase to the full confrontation phase of a crisis. But this evidence also makes it clear the shift is far more marked in relative than in absolute terms. The almost complete absence of relevant activities on the part of peripheral actors during the upswing phase of these crises produced a setting in which any increase in their roles during the confrontation phase was notable. At one and the same time, therefore, the roles of peripheral actors, though tending to expand with the beginning of the phase of full confrontation, either remained sharply restricted as a determinant of the course of the crisis or became so intangible as to be impossible to assess.

In the crises under discussion, the nonaligned states pro-

[65] A summary of the conversation between Castro and Thant in Havana is printed in Pachter, *op.cit.*, pp. 230-234.

[66] *Ibid.*, pp. 95-96.

[67] For further comments on Thant's role in the 1962 crisis, consult Oran R. Young, *The Intermediaries: Third Parties in International Crises* (Princeton: Princeton University Press, 1967), pp. 324-325.

vided one focal point of external influence. The growth of relevant activities on the part of these states from the first Berlin crisis in 1948 to the Cuban crisis of 1962 strikingly emerges from a review of these cases. Throughout all these crises, nevertheless, the distinction between the upswing phase and the confrontation phase with regard to the activities of the nonaligned states remained clear-cut. In each case, the initiation of a full confrontation acted as a catalyst in drawing the attention of the nonaligned states to the crisis.[68] At the same time, however, there was frequently a distinct delayed reaction effect resulting from the relatively rapid pace of events under conditions of crisis and the problems of the nonaligned states in acquiring adequate information concerning the situation.[69] As a result, these states sometimes found it difficult to match their activities with the realities of the confrontation at any given moment. In addition, the nonaligned states tended to react more often in terms of general pronouncements than in concrete diplomatic initiatives. While the genuine quality of their concern was almost always evident, therefore, the efficacy of their reactions was frequently doubtful. Moreover, during these periods of severe confrontation, the position of the nonaligned states, almost without exception, was based on a general desire for moderation and the avoidance of overt hostilities.[70] The specific proposals of these states, then, were for the most part based far more on fears of escalation and warfare than on any concern with specific arrangements for the future of a disputed area, be it Berlin or the offshore islands in the Taiwan Strait. Though this order of priorities is clearly understand-

[68] The word catalyst, with its implication of a rapid shift, seems fully appropriate. Even in those cases in which the crisis did not flair up with extreme suddenness, such as the two Berlin crises, there was a sharp upsurge of attention on the part of peripheral actors following the shift to a situation of full confrontation.

[69] This problem was perhaps most evident during the Taiwan Strait crisis of 1958. In somewhat less severe forms, however, this is a common difficulty for peripheral actors.

[70] The point here is that the nonaligned states were obviously more concerned with the general dangers of war than with any possibilities of specific gains for themselves. The clarity of this concern with moderation may not, however, characterize crises other than the great-power clashes under analysis in this study.

168

able, it quite frequently reduced the effective influence of the nonaligned states by leading them to advocate somewhat undiscriminating policies of compromise on important substantive issues.

The second major source of external influence during these crises was the United Nations.[71] Here also there was a sharp distinction between the upswing phase and the confrontation phase of a crisis, but, following this transition, the United Nations system as a whole tended to have a greater impact on the course of the crises than the nonaligned states acting independently. Almost without exception, however, the influence of the United Nations did not arise from its formal activities. For various reasons dealing with the paralyzation of the Security Council, problems in convening irregular sessions of the General Assembly, and specific membership gaps,[72] the United Nations encountered severe difficulties in exercising a formal impact on these crises. Only two of the crises, the first Berlin crisis and the Cuban missile crisis, ever came before the Organization on a formal basis. And even in these cases, the formal treatment of the confrontation was characterized more by partisan rhetorical debates than by influential third-party activities.

On the other hand, the United Nations did produce an impact of some significance on these crises in terms of less formal activities. Though these informal roles are somewhat intangible and therefore difficult to pin down, the United Nations exercised some influence on each of the crises on this basis. Each of the clashes became a major topic for discussion in United Nations circles, a process that had some effect in setting the general atmosphere and climate of opinion in which bargaining among the principals took place, at least after the beginning of the confrontation phase. In addition,

[71] The activities of the nonaligned states and the United Nations are, of course, thoroughly intertwined on some occasions. The distinction here is between those activities undertaken by one or more of the nonaligned states acting independently and all the activities organized within the framework of the United Nations.

[72] The most relevant membership gaps are obviously the absence of the People's Republic of China (CPR) and of all representatives of Germany. This became a very influential problem, for example, in the Taiwan Strait crisis of 1958.

the United Nations provided a forum encouraging informal behind-the-scenes contact among the principals during a crisis. In this connection, the formal public activities of the Organization frequently gave a convenient and acceptable excuse for the presence of opposing diplomats, who were then able to communicate with each other on important issues that were not formally before the United Nations.[73] Furthermore, the United Nations was a matrix for semiautonomous activities on the part of the Secretary-General, especially in the area of indirect communication, which were clearly among the most influential activities by peripheral actors on several occasions. While the Secretary-General took some interest along these lines in all of the cases under review, the activities of Thant in the Cuban missile crisis are the outstanding example. In short, these informal roles of the United Nations were not critical determinants of the outcome of any of the crises, but they did have a cumulative impact of some significance in each case.

Several additional points are relevant in assessing the activities of all the peripheral actors. The case materials make it clear that, for most purposes, peripheral actors face severe difficulties in intervening efficaciously even after the confrontation phase of a crisis becomes full-blown. In the first instance, the delayed reaction effect, mentioned above, frequently makes it difficult for peripheral actors to coordinate their initiatives in a precise fashion with the shifting nature of the confrontation, and may even make such initiatives counterproductive in specific situations.[74] In addition, these actors often suffer from problems of inadequate information, lack of coordination among themselves, insufficient sophistication in formulating their initiatives, and inability to time their actions precisely enough to achieve clearcut influence.

[73] The range of specific contacts along these lines, even in the four cases under analysis, is very wide, including a variety of different formats of interaction.

[74] Such initiatives did not, in fact, become critically counterproductive in any of the four cases at hand. The closest approach to such a result was probably in the Taiwan Strait crisis of 1958 in which initiatives on the part of peripheral actors, especially during September, may well have contributed to the persistence of CPR miscalculations. For further discussion of these miscalculations, see *infra* Chap. Eight.

Given the delicate balances of bargaining relationships in a major crisis, these deficiencies are frequently critical.

At the same time, however, it is important to emphasize the function of providing a range of diplomatic options for the protagonists even when *specific* efforts by peripheral actors are unsuccessful. The possibility for diplomatic recourse in the event direct bargaining efforts fail can have a significant influence on the underlying atmosphere in which a crisis is played out, even when none of the external options is utilized during the course of the crisis. In the Taiwan Strait crisis of 1958, for example, some of the informal activities on the part of peripheral actors appear to have played a role of this kind in expanding perceptual horizons about the possibilities for diplomacy.

PART III

TACTICAL EQUATIONS

Introduction

The role of bargaining tactics is of great importance under conditions of crisis just as it is in non-crisis bargaining. There are, however, some tactical problems characteristic of crisis relationships which serve to set crisis bargaining apart from the ordinary course of international bargaining. Straightforward coercive objectives tend to become increasingly central in the development and use of tactics under conditions of crisis. Whereas the use of force is viewed, for the most part, as an alternative to bargaining in non-crisis situations, the application of organized coercion often becomes an integral component of bargaining during crises. This expanded relevance of coercion is fully integrated into the underlying perceptual context in many crisis situations. In addition, bargaining tactics are often greatly affected by the relatively high levels of uncertainty and perceived risk that commonly characterize crisis interactions. These problems arise both from the general fluidity of the underlying setting of most crises and from the heightened interdependence of the individual actors in crisis situations. Furthermore, under conditions of crisis tactical maneuvers must be adapted to the rapid shifts in phase which commonly occur during crises as well as to the relatively short duration of the whole sequence. In this connection, crises are apt to increase perceived time pressures and to emphasize the "one-shot" nature of many tactical maneuvers.

Perhaps the most interesting tactical considerations during crises, from an analytic point of view, are those relating to "strategic" bargaining. Conditions of crisis usually set up influential cross-pressures in this area. In a fundamental sense, crises increase the importance of strategic bargaining by sharply emphasizing the roles of political will and credibly communicated resolve. Because crises are relatively short, coercive, dangerous, and characterized by uncertainty, the importance of superior will and resolve tends to rise significantly in comparison with that of possessing superior capabilities in any physical sense. And highly intangible factors such as will and resolve are peculiarly susceptible to the manipulative approach to interaction, which is the fundamental characteristic of strategic bargaining.

Simultaneously, however, conditions of crisis are apt to cause a number of hindrances for employing strategic bargaining. For example, while this approach to bargaining stresses the importance of credibly communicating key expectations, commitments, and threats to an opponent, conditions of crisis often hamper effective communication. Also, the fact that crises frequently exacerbate the tactical impediments attendant upon all bargaining relationships adds additional complexities to the problems of bargaining strategically under conditions of crisis. Moreover, the uncertainties and risks of crisis interactions increase incentives to act prudentially in the interests of maintaining some freedom of choice, an orientation tending to conflict with efforts to bargain strategically in concrete situations.

This is not to argue that strategic bargaining is likely to decline in importance under conditions of crisis; far from it. Yet under such circumstances bargaining of this kind generally becomes much more complex, delicate, and (frequently) ambiguous than in the ordinary flow of international politics. In addition, efforts to employ strategic bargaining advantageously are apt to become more dangerous, both because the prospects of miscalculation and the difficulties of achieving coordination among the participants are greater and because the destructive consequences of failure to achieve coordination on at least minimal rules of the game can be particularly high under conditions of crisis.

8. Resolve and Prudence

> HYPOTHESIS. Conditions of crisis raise incentives both to demonstrate resolve clearly and to react in a prudent fashion to the dangers of destructive outcomes. The resultant cross-pressures tend to produce bargaining patterns among the principals which are unpredictable and subject to erratic oscillations.

Conditions of crisis are apt to produce a combination of pressures to engage in clear-cut demonstrations of resolve and to undertake risky actions for bargaining purposes on the one hand, and to act prudentially in response to perceived increases in the dangers of destructive outcomes on the other hand. Clear-cut demonstrations of resolve are critical under conditions of crisis for several reasons. Efforts to avoid confrontation do not generally constitute a viable option in such situations. And the problems of achieving effective communication usually multiply during crises. The currency of ordinary diplomatic statements and initiatives is apt to become devalued in the context of an overt and interdependent confrontation unless such efforts are reinforced by more concrete indications of resolve. But concurrent fears of destructive outcomes are also apt to become more influential under conditions of crisis. Force-of-events considerations become more salient, with the result that the confidence of decision-makers in their ability to control the situation tends to decline. Growth of such fears in the minds of decision-makers often leads to a sense of urgency and immediacy about calculations concerning the importance of prudential reactions, calculations which had previously been somewhat remote or obscure. In short, conditions of crisis are apt to stimulate, at one and the same time, incentives to employ organized coercion for bargaining purposes as well as incentives to prevent coercion from taking the form of overt violence.

To make matters more complex, the balances between desires to demonstrate resolve and inhibitions arising from fears of violent destruction may shift along several different axes

177

during the course of any given crisis. Crises, as periods of intensified and highly interdependent interaction, tend to catalyze greater than "normal" changes in attitudes, evaluations, expectations, and moods on the part of all participants. Since these perceptual phenomena tend to shift, in any case, faster than changes in their empirical referents, periods of crisis are often characterized by rapid oscillations with regard to such matters as assessments of the course of the crisis and expressions of concern about the dangers of the situation. These oscillations are apt, in addition, to occur for the most part in asymmetrical patterns, as between the various participants in a crisis. It is frequently the case that asymmetries with regard to these perceptual matters can be manipulated by the participants in a crisis to achieve bargaining advantages. As a result, conditions of crisis tend to be characterized by perceptual fluidity and, frequently, certain types of perceptual confusion that exercise considerable influence on the tactical alternatives and maneuverability available to participants at any given moment.

The impact of these cross-pressures does not generally reduce the overall importance of strategic bargaining during crises. It does, however, tend to unsettle bargaining of this kind and to make it erratic and unpredictable. In this connection, incentives to demonstrate resolve and to react prudently to the dangers of destruction set up competing standards since efforts for the first will emphasize the importance of strategic bargaining under conditions of crisis while pressures for the second will increase incentives to avoid many forms of strategic bargaining, especially those involving the manipulation of risks. Bargaining relations at any given moment during a crisis will contain various characteristics traceable to each of these types of pressure and will reflect the complex interaction between them. At the same time, the specific balances between these pressures in the bargaining activities of any particular participant are apt to shift as a function of: the transition from one phase to another in an unfolding crisis, and changing patterns of perceptual asymmetries between participants with regard to matters of resolve and inhibitory fears.

178

RESOLVE AND PRUDENCE
Berlin, 1948-1949

There are several distinct levels at which to assess the impact of inhibitory fears during the Berlin crisis of 1948-1949. In a general and somewhat undifferentiated sense, the crisis was widely assumed to be extremely dangerous and treated as a serious threat to world peace.[1] Already by June 30, for example, Thomas Hamilton was writing from the United Nations that "It is generally believed that the Berlin dispute constitutes the most serious clash between the United States and the Soviet Union since the end of the war."[2] National officials on all sides showed clear signs of being impressed by the dangers inherent in the situation. Even though they were committed to the tactical offensive in this crisis, the Soviets themselves were sufficiently concerned with the intrinsic dangers of overt violence to exhibit extreme caution in their actions, both in implementing the blockade during the spring of 1948 and in responding to the Western airlift. In Washington, General Clay's telegram of March 5, 1948[3] caused "intense alarm among those . . . who were aware of it."[4] Although the beginnings of the 1948 presidential campaign diverted American attention from the Berlin situation during much of May and the early part of June,[5] concern had again reached a relatively high pitch by July when Clay was reporting that the "Chances of war today [are] about one in four."[6] Moreover, the impact of these generalized fears was even greater in 1948 among the British and French, who were both geographically closer to the actual focus of conflict in Berlin and still showing clear signs of war-weariness in their extreme "reluctance to face any decision which might lead to conflict."[7]

[1] See Charles Saltzman, "The Spotlight on the International Scene," *DOSB*, XIX, No. 485 (October 17, 1948), 498.

[2] Thomas Hamilton, the *New York Times*, June 30, 1948, p. 8.

[3] The text of Clay's telegram of March 5 appears in Jean Edward Smith, *The Defense of Berlin* (Baltimore: The Johns Hopkins Press, 1963), pp. 101-102.

[4] Walter Millis, ed., *The Forrestal Diaries* (New York: Viking, 1951), editor's note, p. 387. See also George Kennan, *Memoirs, 1925-1950* (Boston: Little, Brown, 1967), p. 400.

[5] On this subject see the article by Jack Raymond, the *New York Times*, June 25, 1948, pp. 1, 18.

[6] Millis, ed., *op.cit.*, p. 460.   [7] *Ibid.*, pp. 489-490.

179

Though these general fears were somewhat diffuse and intangible, their impact was substantially heightened by the fact that both sides had powerful incentives to avoid overt hostilities in 1948.[8] Though the Soviet Union was willing to assume the tactical offensive in precipitating the Berlin crisis, it was clearly unprepared for a war of any size at this time. Not only was the Soviet Union without an operational nuclear capability in 1948, it was also still absorbed in efforts to recover from the immense damage it had suffered during World War II. The extreme caution and gradualness with which the Soviets initiated the blockade of Berlin further indicated "that Russia was not prepared to risk war."[9] The Soviets' gingerly response to the Western airlift provided additional confirmation of this posture. On the other hand, the Western powers were also in no position to risk a major military clash on the Continent in 1948. Among other things, Britain and France were preoccupied with internal problems, American armed forces were still substantially demobilized at this time, and the remaining Western forces on the Continent were wholly inadequate for major ground action. Moreover, American domestic politics, especially in connection with the opening phase of the presidential campaign of 1948, were unsettled at this time, a fact exerting growing pressure on President Truman not to "rock the boat" with a serious clash over Berlin.[10] These inhibitions on both sides were attested by the fact that neither side undertook any large-scale or abnormal troop movements or redeployments during the whole period of the crisis.[11]

These general fears were clearly influential in setting the underlying climate of decision-making for all the participants

[8] In contrast to the substantial fears about the dangers of "incidents" (discussed in Chap. Five *supra*), each side appears to have felt relatively confident that the rational interests of its opponent were heavily weighted against a premeditated initiation of large-scale violence over Berlin.

[9] Philip Windsor, *City on Leave* (New York: Praeger, 1963), p. 104.

[10] On the influence of American domestic politics on the posture of the United States in the Berlin crisis, see, for example, Robert Murphy, *Diplomat Among Warriors* (New York: Pyramid, 1965), p. 352.

[11] As will be discussed below, the United States deployed some bombers to Europe during the crisis. Nevertheless, neither side undertook the serious measures of mobilization required to prepare for war.

in the 1948-1949 crisis. But so intangible were they that their impact seems to have been quite limited with regard to day-to-day actions in and around the city of Berlin itself. The really effective inhibitions at this level of concrete activities arose from the possibility that unpremeditated "incidents" might set in motion an uncontrollable chain of events leading to large-scale hostilities. Explicit fears of this sort were expressed repeatedly and at very high levels. Truman, for example, worried about these dangers in very concrete terms,[12] and the actions of the Soviets throughout the crisis suggest a clear awareness of the problem of incidents. Such fears did not, of course, remain constant throughout the whole crisis. In the first instance, awareness of the concrete dangers attendant upon hostile confrontations in and around Berlin developed somewhat slowly during June 1948.[13] And by the end of the summer, as the confrontation settled into rather rigid tactical patterns even though its ultimate outcome was still very much in doubt, there was a noticeable relaxation of tension arising from fears concerning specific incidents.[14] By this time, negotiations concerning Berlin had degenerated into diplomatic wrangling of a *pro forma* nature, and the original tactical confrontation had lost some of its immediate urgency despite the fact that it remained a critical determinant of the ultimate outcome of the crisis. But the summer months, on the other hand, were characterized by intense concern about the dangers of incidents. The picture in this regard was obscured to some extent by the occurrence of several rather rapid perceptual oscillations between pessimism and optimism in assessing the prospects for working out a termination arrangement during the summer. Despite these obscuring shifts, however, the impact of concern about the dangers of incidents—both in connection with activities in the air and land

[12] For an indication of Truman's thinking on the subject, see Harry Truman, *Years of Trial and Hope* (Garden City, N.Y.: Doubleday, 1956), p. 124.

[13] For material on this, consult *ibid.*, pp. 120-124; and W. Phillips Davison, *The Berlin Blockade: A Study in Cold War Politics* (Princeton: Princeton University Press, 1958), pp. 106-110.

[14] For an interesting discussion of these changes of atmosphere, see Percy Winner, "Russia Has a Candidate," *The New Republic*, Vol. 119, No. 14 (October 4, 1948), 21.

corridors to Berlin from the West and in connection with the confused but plainly hostile interactions within the city itself —was widespread and influential during the summer of 1948.

Nevertheless, inhibitions arising from these several types of fear were insufficient to eliminate interest in issues of resolve and processes of strategic bargaining altogether. The specific balances between these problems of resolve and inhibitory fear were simplified considerably in the 1948-1949 crisis, however, by the fact that the fundamental tactical patterns of the crisis were struck at an early stage and, for the most part, simply allowed to run their course over time. In essence, the Soviets chose throughout to stick with a land blockade of Berlin coupled with secondary efforts to undermine morale in the city and to harass the airlift in a cautious fashion. In return, the Western powers tacitly agreed to emphasize the airlift plus secondary moves to maintain morale in Berlin and to implement a counterblockade. Within the framework set by these straightforward underlying patterns, an interesting mixture of efforts at strategic bargaining and clear-cut restraints gradually emerged from the Berlin crisis.

From the outset of the crisis, both sides demonstrated a recurrent interest in the manipulative possibilities of strategic bargaining. Insofar as the blockade of Berlin was directed against the whole German policy of the Western powers as well as toward narrower objectives with regard to Berlin itself, the very process of imposing it was an act of strategic bargaining on the part of the Soviets. Though the Soviets no doubt hoped for a *fait accompli* on the tactical level, they clearly wanted to alter the incentive structure of the Western powers on the larger issues associated with the future of Germany. On the Western side, the dispatching of an armed train toward Berlin from Helmstedt on June 21 was a significant effort to probe the seriousness of Soviet intentions[15] even though no attempt was made to force the train through after it was sidetracked in the Soviet zone of Ger-

---

[15] For the details of this episode involving the dispatch of an armed train, see Philip Jessup, "Review of Allied Action on Berlin Blockade," statement in the United Nations Security Council, October 19, 1948. The text can be found in *DOSB*, XIX, No. 487 (October 31, 1948), 543.

many.[16] Even more important, however, the initiation of the Western airlift, despite the attendant possibilities of interference or dangerous incidents, represented a major venture into the realm of strategic bargaining. While explicit efforts were made to emphasize the nonprovocative nature of the airlift in public statements, the initiation of the airlift importantly changed the underlying bargaining structure of the confrontation.

Even after the crisis moved into the phase of full-blown confrontation at the end of June, both sides continued to show an interest in at least limited ventures into strategic bargaining. The United States, for example, decided on July 1 to dispatch twenty B-29s to Germany and on July 15 to send two additional groups of the planes to British airfields.[17] This move was designed to bolster the credibility of the American commitment to Europe since "The B-29s were known throughout the world as the atomic bombers, and to put a strong force of them into British [and German] bases would be to bring them within striking distance of Moscow."[18] For their part, the Soviets were particularly active during this period in inspiring and organizing strong-arm tactics within the city of Berlin in an effort to undermine popular morale in the Western sectors. The activities of the so-called Markgraf Police, for example, became famous in this context.[19] At the same time, both sides attempted to bargain strategically in the course of the diplomatic negotiations conducted during the summer of 1948. As one writer has put it, "One purpose of the negotiations was to intimidate the other side indirectly by threatening war or a more aggressive use of force. Thus the tone of the diplomatic exchanges was austere and threatening. They spoke of firm intentions, absolute positions and of threats to the peace."[20]

[16] The train stood on a siding in Eastern Germany for three days. It then returned to Helmstedt without incident.

[17] For a discussion of the decision to dispatch the B-29s, see Millis, ed., op.cit., p. 445.

[18] Ibid., p. 456.

[19] On the activities of the Markgraf Police, consult Davison, op.cit., Chap. 4.

[20] Manuel Gottlieb, The German Peace Settlement and the Berlin Crisis (New York: Paine-Whitman, 1950), p. 202.

The constant presence of inhibitory fears did, however, have a substantial impact on these efforts of the participants to bargain strategically. At the most general level, it led at several points to a certain indecisiveness in the interactions among the principals.[21] During the summer of 1948, for example, the United States often "seemed more fearful of the risks than cognizant of the advantages of a firm stand in Berlin."[22] The British and the French, who were even more fearful than the Americans in these terms, were correspondingly more anxious to avoid tactics that might raise the probabilities of armed clashes with Soviet forces. And the Soviets reacted hesitantly even as it began to become apparent, toward the end of the summer, that the airlift was serious and might well succeed in neutralizing Soviet bargaining advantages derived from the blockade.[23]

Even more striking in this connection, however, is the fact that both sides refrained from utilizing a number of specific tactics having considerable potential from the view of strategic bargaining. All of the protagonists were extremely scrupulous in avoiding provocative physical deployments of their garrisons in Berlin. The garrison forces on both sides, in fact, played a significant role in controlling potentially dangerous disturbances within the city on several occasions. For their part, the Western powers ultimately rejected the idea of attempting to open the land routes to Berlin from the Western zones of Germany through the use of armed convoys largely because of fears that such actions would catalyze violent clashes.[24] At the same time, the Soviets were careful to avoid any uses of their ground forces in the Eastern zone of Germany which might have led to violent reactions by the Western powers. Even General Clay was moved to remark on

[21] For some interesting material on this problem, see Smith, *op.cit.*, pp. 108-111.

[22] *Ibid.*, p. 112.

[23] In the early summer, the airlift was looked upon by the Soviets as an annoyance but, in the final analysis, little more than a delaying factor in the operation of their plans for exercising pressure on the Western powers.

[24] For some interesting comments on this decision, see Murphy, *op.cit.*, p. 354.

the meticulousness of the Soviets in this connection.[25] Finally, the Soviets refrained from any serious interference with Western planes in the air corridors over eastern Germany, a fact of great significance both because there were several ways in which the Soviets could have interfered[26] and because the airlift was a critical determinant of the ultimate outcome of the whole crisis. The extent to which the Soviets were restrained by fear of dangerous incidents became especially marked in the later phases of the crisis when they continued to act very cautiously in dealing with the airlift, despite the growing probabilities that it would prove a critical success.

As a result, the crisis was played out to the accompaniment of somewhat muted processes of strategic bargaining. Since the basic tactical patterns of the crisis were set at an early stage, the most influential efforts to bargain strategically occurred during the course of the transition from the upswing phase to the full confrontation phase in the early summer of 1948. In addition, the overall impact of strategic bargaining declined during the summer of 1948 in proportion to the rising influence of fears concerning the dangers of specific incidents. Finally, efforts at strategic bargaining remained sharply circumscribed during the final phases of the confrontation, even when the established tactical patterns began to show clear indications of asymmetry. Since these asymmetries ultimately contributed very substantially to the success of the Western powers toward the end of the confrontation, the Soviet decision during this period not to undertake major new initiatives in the area of strategic bargaining, in particular, was a critical factor determining the final outcome of the crisis.

Taiwan Strait, 1958

Despite the obvious acts of physical violence accompanying the 1958 crisis in the Taiwan Strait, the whole situation was characterized by a marked fear of "war" on all sides (with

[25] See Lucius D. Clay, *Decision in Germany* (Garden City, N.Y.: Doubleday, 1950), p. 374.

[26] For further material on this subject, see *infra* Chap. Thirteen.

185

the possible exception of the Chinese Nationalists).[27] This underlying fear did not, however, prevent the major participants from engaging in a great deal of strategic bargaining on a highly coercive basis. The confrontation therefore assumed the character of a war of nerves, with each side striving to force its opponent to become the first to succumb to the underlying fear of war. In order to analyze the principal developments in this war of nerves, it is necessary to divide the 1958 crisis into several major phases.

The actual decision to initiate the crisis as well as control over the events leading up to August 23 rested primarily with the Chinese Communists.[28] In this regard, it is clear the Chinese People's Republic (CPR)—and certainly the Soviet Union—had no desire to promote a war with the United States in the summer of 1958.[29] At the same time, however, the CPR was willing to run some very real risks in order to probe American resolve in East Asia and, hopefully, to get the best of an important bargaining contest with the United States. In launching their probe against the offshore islands, the Chinese Communists evidently based their bargaining calculations on several key assumptions. First, they calculated that the United States would be at least partially preoccupied with the ongoing Middle Eastern crisis and therefore disinclined to take a firm stand in the Taiwan Strait in the summer of 1958. Second, the CPR hoped that Nationalist resistance to attacks on the offshore islands would be relatively weak and that the resultant indications of weakness would have a depressing effect on Nationalist morale in general.

[27] On this subject consult Donald Zagoria, *The Sino-Soviet Conflict 1956-1961* (New York: Atheneum, 1964), p. 217.

[28] There has been a good deal of debate about the various motives or combinations of motives behind the decision of the CPR to launch a probe in the Taiwan Strait during 1958. The most useful discussions of this subject appear in *ibid.*; Alice Hsieh, *Communist China's Strategy in the Nuclear Era* (Englewood Cliffs, N.J.: Prentice-Hall, 1962); Morton Halperin and Tang Tsou, "The 1958 Quemoy Crisis," Chap. 10 in Morton Halperin, ed., *Sino-Soviet Relations and Arms Control* (Cambridge: M.I.T. Press, 1967); and Harold Hinton, *Communist China in World Politics* (Boston: Houghton Mifflin, 1966).

[29] For verification on this point, see Zagoria, *op.cit.*, p. 208.

This hope was evidently based on assumptions about the likely effectiveness of the CPR's threats of "imminent" invasion[30] and about the probability the United States would put pressure on the Nationalists not to induce a dangerous military confrontation over the offshore islands.[31] Third, the Chinese Communists evidently banked on the proposition that the United States would not make a sharp physical response to actions aimed, in the first instance, against the offshore islands alone.[32] This proposition was based on: the somewhat noncommittal nature of American statements during the preceding period about the relevance of the offshore islands to the defense of Taiwan;[33] the idea that, given the shifting quality of the overall strategic balance, the United States would be deterred from determined local responses by implicit Soviet threats;[34] and the notion that actions aimed ostensibly at the offshore islands could be carried out without fully engaging American prestige. There has been in recent years much debate about Soviet reactions to these initial Chinese calculations.[35] Note, however, that in this initial formulation the probe required no active or clear-cut risk-taking on the part of the Soviet Union. Whatever reservations the Soviets may have had about the plausibility of the Chinese assumptions, it is clear that, at a minimum, they acquiesced at least tacitly in the Chinese decision to initiate the crisis in the first place.[36]

[30] The "imminent" invasion threats of the CPR are discussed in *ibid.*, pp. 210-211.

[31] For information on this point see Halperin and Tsou, *op.cit.*, p. 275.

[32] On this point consult, *inter alia*, Tang Tsou, "Mao's Limited War in the Taiwan Strait," *Orbis*, III, No. 3 (Fall 1959), 339-342.

[33] This arose because of the language of the "Formosa Resolution" of January 29, 1955, which left it to the discretion of the President of the United States to decide, in any specific confrontation, whether the protection of the offshore islands should be considered vital to the defense of Taiwan itself. For the text of the resolution see *DOSB*, XXXII, No. 815 (February 7, 1955), 213.

[34] See Hsieh, *op.cit.*, p. 121.

[35] The most important and controversial elements of the debate are summarized in Zagoria, *op.cit.*; John Thomas, "Soviet Behavior in the Quemoy Crisis of 1958," *Orbis*, VI, No. 1 (Spring 1962), 38-64; and Halperin and Tsou, *op.cit.*

[36] While the joint communiqué issued at the end of Khrushchev's visit to Peking of July 31–August 3, 1958, failed to mention the issue of the

With this background, the 1958 crisis moved into its first major phase of full confrontation. The most critical feature of this phase, which ran roughly from the last days of August to September 6, was the intensity with which the Americans and the Chinese Nationalists acted to disconfirm the initial assumptions of the CPR. Despite some marked restrictions, particularly with regard to the overt use of force, the overall impression created by these reactions was a decisive one. To begin with, the Nationalists reacted with a firmness and determination that made it apparent the defenses of the offshore islands would not simply collapse without a real fight. The combined verbal and physical reactions of the United States also quickly created a powerful impression that the United States would counter any CPR invasion of the offshore islands with American military force.[37] The American verbal response, including a threat to retaliate against the Chinese mainland for any overt attempt to invade Quemoy, was impressive enough. But the crucial feature of the American response was the almost startling speed and decisiveness with which the United States built up its military forces in the area of the Taiwan Strait.[38] Within several days after August 23, actions had been initiated that were ultimately to make the Seventh Fleet the most powerful air-naval striking force in history. Moreover, the American Government proceeded to formulate a series of relatively explicit contingency plans calling for responses to various possible Chinese Communist initiatives based on overt military actions.[39]

At this point, the initial assumptions of the Chinese Communists had been clearly disconfirmed. In fact, the reactions of the Nationalists and the Americans were rapidly making the idea of overt and large-scale hostilities both more real and even less attractive to the CPR than it had been prior to August 23. Under these circumstances, a "reevaluation of

offshore islands, it is generally believed that the CPR's plan for a probe in the Strait was an important topic of discussion during this visit.

[37] On this point see Halperin and Tsou, *op.cit.*, pp. 275-276.

[38] For material on the American buildup, consult Thomas, *op.cit.*, pp. 38-39; and the *New York Times*, September 17, 1958, p. 17.

[39] On the development of American contingency plans, see Dwight Eisenhower, *Waging Peace 1956-1961* (Garden City, N.Y.: Doubleday, 1965), p. 295; and *Business Week*, September 13, 1958, p. 35.

the military situation and of United States intentions appears to have taken place in Peking"[40] in the early days of September and especially in the wake of Dulles' Newport statement on September 4.[41] Indeed there is every indication that *both* the Chinese and the Soviets reacted to these developments with great caution and were essentially in agreement on the necessity of retreating to some extent from the initial lines of the confrontation in order to reduce the dangers of war with the United States.[42] The Chinese Communists as a result quickly introduced a strict policy of avoiding actions that might spark an overt and violent American response.[43] The resultant shifts in the Chinese posture were symbolized by Chou En-lai's statement of September 6 suggesting a resumption of Sino-American ambassadorial talks[44] and by a noticeable lull in the shelling of Quemoy, especially on September 6 and 7. These developments, in effect, marked the close of a major phase of the crisis.

In these early days of September both the Chinese and the Soviets were dismayed about the way the crisis was developing and fundamentally agreed on the need for caution. It now seems probable, however, that this period witnessed the beginning of significant divergences between the views of the two countries, arising, in essence, from a Soviet desire to "backwater" somewhat more rapidly than the Chinese considered necessary. Several factors account for this emerging discord. The Soviets, more than the Chinese, worried about the inherent dangers of the situation and the possibility that a major clash in the Taiwan Strait could escalate into a destructive global war.[45] The Soviet Union was far less committed internationally than the CPR to the probe in the Strait

[40] Hsieh, *op.cit.*, p. 124.

[41] For the text of the Newport statement, see *DOSB*, XXXIX, No. 1004 (September 22, 1958), 445-446.

[42] For an interesting discussion on this point, see Zagoria, *op.cit.*, p. 208.

[43] Halperin and Tsou, *op.cit.*, p. 290.

[44] For the text of the September 6 statement, see Paul Zinner, ed., *Documents on American Foreign Relations 1958* (New York: Harper and Row [for the Council on Foreign Relations], 1959), pp. 440-442.

[45] On Soviet concern about the dangers of violence at this point, see Robert W. Barnett, "Quemoy: the Use and Consequence of Nuclear Deterrence," Harvard Center for International Affairs, March 1960, p. 32; Thomas, *op.cit.*, pp. 49-55, 61; and *Business Week*, September 13, 1958, p. 35.

and therefore less in need of gaining at least a symbolic success from the crisis. A tactical retrenchment at this stage would appear, moreover, as a confirmation of the basic Soviet thesis about the nature of the prevailing strategic balance. As a result, Sino-Soviet disagreement on the crisis began to emerge at this time, but still as a matter of degree rather than qualitative opposition.

At this point the 1958 crisis shifted into a new phase of confrontation lasting roughly from September 6 to October 6. As had been true in the preceding phase, this new phase emerged initially from the bargaining calculations of the CPR. In short, the Chinese refused to abandon their probe in the Strait even after their original assumptions had been proved false. The first phase of confrontation had made the situation important from the point of view of the international image of the CPR and had set in motion a process that was to strengthen the links between the probe and the internal problems of the CPR during this second phase. In addition, the leadership of the CPR began at this time to develop a new bargaining calculus in terms of which to justify a policy of continuing the confrontation. The idea of an artillery blockade of Quemoy began to emerge at this point, with the objective to pin down the Nationalist forces on the islands while keeping the Americans from using force to break the blockade, thus shifting the initiative to employ violence onto the United States.[46] Second, the Chinese began to rely more and more on the notion that, given time, growing pressures of domestic and allied opinion would force the American Administration into a willingness to make significant concessions. The new Chinese calculus, therefore, counted heavily on the idea of stalling in order to let these pressures mount. Third, the CPR leadership came increasingly to believe that important advantages could be reaped by fostering an atmosphere of friction between the Nationalists and the Americans, especially as the latter started to negotiate independently with the

---

[46] On these calculations of the CPR, see Zagoria, *op.cit.*, pp. 215-216; and Tsou, *op.cit.*, p. 344. For a more extended discussion of the CPR's efforts to shift the initiative, see *infra* Chap. Fourteen.

Chinese Communists[47] and (hopefully) to exert pressures on the Nationalists to make significant concessions. The result of this new calculation was a Chinese decision to continue the crisis on a somewhat more restrained basis. The new Chinese objective was to create a situation in which the position of their opponents would inevitably worsen unless they initiated the use of large-scale violence and in which the inhibitions restraining such a move would be great.

Once again, however, the responses of the Americans and the Nationalists disconfirmed the principal assumptions of the CPR's bargaining calculus. Despite a marked cautiousness and restraint in the overt use of force,[48] particularly on the part of the United States, the Americans and the Nationalists ultimately were successful by combining continued firmness with a steady and impressive buildup of physical force in the area. Several aspects of this reaction were of critical importance. First, the two states were able to break the artillery blockade of Quemoy decisively without the initiation of overt violence against the Chinese mainland.[49] Second, the United States demonstrated an impressive willingness to apply force deliberately and proportionally in order both to neutralize CPR actions in the Strait and to deter the Chinese Communists from escalating the conflict further. This posture was made particularly clear both in the utilization of American escorts in the effort to break the blockade of Quemoy and in American willingness to supply Sidewinder missiles to the Nationalist air force to establish decisively Nationalist air superiority in the area of the Taiwan Strait. Third, the American Administration remained adamant in the face of substantial opposition and criticism from domestic opinion, nonaligned states, and certain allies.[50] Despite the debate over

[47] Formal Sino-American talks were actually begun in Warsaw on September 15.

[48] For further discussion concerning overt uses of force in the 1958 crisis, see *infra* Chap. Thirteen.

[49] That is, without raising existing levels of violence and, above all, without necessitating direct American participation in violent exchanges.

[50] For a discussion of the extensiveness of this criticism, see *The Economist*, September 20, 1958, p. 935.

the significance of Dulles' famous press conference of September 30,[51] the relative absence of retreat with regard to the main points in the American negotiating position during the 1958 crisis is remarkable. Fourth, the continuing physical buildup of American forces in the Western Pacific during September 1958 was extraordinarily impressive.[52] This multi-faceted buildup included the supply of "nuclear-capable," eight-inch howitzers to Quemoy, Sidewinder missiles to the Nationalist air force, surface-to-air missiles for Taiwan, large increments of American air and naval power, contingents of marines, and substantial command-and-control facilities. And this buildup began to look more and more impressive as the CPR resorted increasingly to nonphysical bargaining activities during the latter part of September. Fifth, the efforts of the CPR to drive a wedge between the Nationalists and the Americans ultimately proved unsuccessful because the United States shied away from exerting decisive pressure on the Nationalists at the most sensitive points. Though American pressures did deflate, to some extent, the Nationalist myth of a forcible return to the mainland, the United States was ultimately unwilling to coerce Chiang into accepting a compromise arrangement that would weaken the Nationalist position on the offshore islands.[53]

The Soviet position during this later phase of the crisis was also interesting. The opening of this phase was followed immediately by a jump in the Soviet declaratory campaign based primarily on strongly worded protestations of support for the Chinese Communists and on the enunciation of nuclear threats directed toward the United States.[54] Given the devel-

[51] Many writers, both at the time and subsequently, have seen in Dulles' statements at this news conference, which dealt with the question of Nationalist garrisons on the offshore islands, indications of an important shift in the American bargaining position during the 1958 crisis. For further discussion of the significance of this press conference, see *infra* Chap. Twelve.

[52] For information on this subject see, *inter alia*, Malcolm Mackintosh, "The Soviet Attitude," Chap. 8 in Morton Halperin, ed., *op.cit.*, pp. 211-212; and *Business Week*, October 4, 1958, p. 36.

[53] For further discussion of this subject, see *infra* Chap. Twelve.

[54] This Soviet campaign was highlighted by Khrushchev's letters of September 7 and 19 to Eisenhower. The text of the September 7 letter

opments in the preceding phase of the crisis, this shift in Soviet behavior probably was essentially predicated on a growing fear that the United States (perhaps catalyzed by Nationalist actions)[55] would, in effect, reverse the crisis by undertaking major physical strikes against the Chinese mainland.[56] Such a posture was basically consonant with the Chinese objective of strangling Quemoy since it addressed itself, among other things, to the important goal of deterring
the United States from acting to break the blockade with air
strikes against the mainland. But it also allowed the Soviet
Union to restrict its obligations to the Chinese in the crisis
in an effective albeit *de facto* fashion. Despite their rather
bellicose public language, the Soviets came more and more,
as September wore on, to emphasize that their alliance guarantees applied only to situations involving major strikes
against the Chinese mainland and that the CPR itself was
fully capable of handling the civil war aspects of the crisis
without assistance.[57] It now seems quite clear that the Soviets
were by this time increasingly disturbed by the idea that they
could conceivably be trapped in a serious military confrontation with the United States either through inadvertent actions or as a result of Chinese moves that would provoke the
Nationalists and/or the Americans into initiating major strikes
against the mainland. Moreover, the deterrent nature of the
Soviet role during this phase of the confrontation was basically consonant with the Soviet thesis that the strategic balance
was still such in 1958 that the nuclear capacity of the Soviet

can be found in *DOSB*, XXXIX, No. 1005 (September 29, 1958), 499-
503. The text of the September 19 letter, which was formally rejected
by the United States, is printed in the *New York Times*, September 20,
1958, p. 2.

[55] For example, the Nationalists might well have been able to undertake bombing raids against the coastal batteries on the Chinese mainland, which would have been significant enough to raise the level of violence in the crisis but not powerful enough to knock out the coastal batteries decisively.

[56] On Soviet concern along these lines, see Thomas, *op.cit.*, p. 62.

[57] Soviet statements along these lines became steadily more trenchant
during the latter part of September. The shift culminated decisively in
Khrushchev's statement of October 5. For the text of this statement,
which originally appeared in the October 6 issue of *Pravda*, see *CDSP*,
X, No. 40 (November 12, 1958), 18.

Union was usable primarily for deterrent rather than offensive purposes.

Under these circumstances, the Chinese Communists ultimately decided to pull back and to begin disengaging from the crisis. In this connection, Marshal Peng Teh-huai's temporary cease-fire order, issued on October 6,[58] effectively symbolized Chinese recognition of the fact that their second bargaining calculus had been vitiated. The somewhat ambiguous and tortuous Chinese moves following this break are explainable primarily in terms of Chinese efforts to disengage as gracefully as possible and to salvage something of value from the crisis for purposes of domestic explanations and external face-saving.

CPR leaders apparently adopted a two-pronged analysis in deciding to pull back. In the first instance, the Chinese were obviously strongly influenced by the success of the Nationalists, with American assistance, in breaking the blockade of Quemoy without escalating to new levels of violence. This tactical failure, coupled with the evident Chinese fear of escalating the level of violence any further themselves, made the bargaining posture chosen in early September no longer tenable.[59] Furthermore, toward the end of September the Chinese Communists became increasingly worried that the crisis might boomerang by causing a rapid upswing of international pressure and support for a *de facto* formalization of the "two-China" arrangement. To the extent that the CPR continued to put the United States in a politically, though not militarily, embarrassing situation with regard to the Taiwan Strait, pressures seemed likely to grow for the United States to campaign for the acceptance of an arrangement that would split Taiwan and the mainland more effectively than ever by imposing some form of formal internationalization on the offshore islands. As a result, the vehemence with which the Chinese stressed the civil war aspects of the confrontation and the inseparability of the offshore islands question from the whole Taiwan issue began to increase even as

[58] The text of this statement can be found in Zinner, ed., *op.cit.*, pp. 474-476.

[59] For a discussion of these developments see Hsieh, *op.cit.*, p. 129.

they were taking steps to disengage themselves from the crisis they had initiated on August 23.[60]

Berlin, 1961

The Berlin crisis of 1961 can be divided into readily perceived phases with regard to the problems of resolve and prudence. The discontinuities among these phases are relatively distinct. A strong desire by both sides to avoid overt violence over Berlin was evident throughout the 1961 crisis. But perceptions concerning the dangers of overt violence shifted substantially and in asymmetrical patterns during the course of the crisis, thereby leaving considerable leeway for the parties to engage in the processes of strategic bargaining.

From this perspective, the first major phase of the crisis lasted from the Vienna meeting between Kennedy and Khrushchev in early June through approximately the first ten days of August. The Soviets assumed the tactical initiative during this phase and held it for purposes of bargaining. During this period the basic Soviet tactic—just as it had been during the 1958-1959 clash over Berlin—was the *contingent* threat of signing a separate peace treaty with the German Democratic Republic (GDR) as a means of building tension without embarking on irrevocable actions.[61] In 1961, this Soviet threat was emphasized and made to appear particularly graphic by a series of increasingly uncompromising and menacing verbal statements. The basic objective in this connection was to convey a sense of offensive commitment and determination to the West. Similar considerations seem to have motivated Khrushchev's rather flamboyant verbal efforts to sow fears in the minds of visiting Western leaders and diplomats by vividly recounting the Soviet ability to destroy their countries in the event of war.[62] At the same time, the

[60] For a particularly interesting exegesis of the CPR's bargaining calculations during this final phase of the 1958 crisis, see Anna Louise Strong, *New Times*, No. 46, November 1958, pp. 8-11.

[61] The real threat in this connection stemmed not from the idea of a peace treaty in itself, but from the possibility that the promulgation of such a treaty might lead to an effective transfer of control over the access routes to Berlin from the Soviet Union to the GDR.

[62] For comments on this point see Deane and David Heller, *The Berlin Wall* (New York: Walker, 1962), p. 16.

Soviet peace-treaty threat was orchestrated with the proposal that *West* Berlin be transformed into a "free city." Though this proposal in fact contained important "jokers," its public enunciation during the summer of 1961 served the dual function of holding the diplomatic initiative on Berlin and of making it difficult for the West to portray the Soviet position as unreasonable and outrageous.

Throughout this period, the Soviets were evidently encouraged by a feeling that this time Western guarantees of support for Berlin were not ultimately credible.[63] As a result of the sequence of developments discussed in Chapter Four, the Soviets seem to have believed during June and July 1961 that the Western powers were considerably more concerned about the dangers of war over Berlin than they themselves were. They therefore moved strongly after the Vienna conference to play on these Western fears of war. The Soviets also undertook additional steps aimed at probing Western determination on the issue, both by diplomatic means[64] and, later on, by allowing the GDR to experiment with various tentative restrictions in and around Berlin.

During this phase of the crisis there was considerable evidence of genuine perplexity in the West in dealing with the problem of demonstrating resolve without appearing to be dangerously provocative. Especially after the Vienna meeting, there was an increasingly widespread feeling that the problem of political credibility was the key to a successful Western defense of Berlin.[65] Though this concern with credibility became more pervasive as the summer wore on, however, efforts to deal with the problem were hampered by a number of internal difficulties within the West. In the first place, the anxiety of public opinion about the dangers of war over Ber-

[63] For comments on Soviet perceptions to this effect, see Richard Stebbins, *The United States in World Affairs 1961* (New York: Harper and Row [for the Council on Foreign Relations], 1962), p. 82; and Smith, *op.cit.*, p. 245.

[64] For an interesting discussion of Soviet efforts along these lines, see Hans Speier, *Divided Berlin* (New York: Praeger, 1961), pp. 151-152.

[65] For indications of American thinking in this area, consult Arthur Schlesinger Jr., *A Thousand Days* (Boston: Houghton Mifflin, 1965), pp. 390-391.

lin was quite evident in the summer of 1961.[66] And there were substantial disagreements within the Kennedy Administration itself between those who felt that Soviet motives regarding Berlin were basically limited and should be accommodated insofar as possible and those who viewed Soviet aims as fundamentally expansive and argued that the ultimate dangers of war would only be increased by an initial policy of accommodation.[67] There were also at this time sharp differences among the Western allies in their assessments of Soviet motives in Europe and in their views concerning the best way to impress upon the Soviets the credibility of Western commitments in central Europe.

Specific Western efforts to demonstrate the credibility of commitments in Berlin during June and July therefore emerged in an ambiguous context. Nevertheless, a number of efforts were made to bargain strategically in response to the Soviet initiatives on Berlin. A series of verbal statements emphasizing Western firmness and resolve reached a climax with Kennedy's highly publicized speech of July 25 underlining Western commitments and announcing a series of specific decisions affecting defense policy.[68] This Western verbal campaign had the strength of linking the issue of Berlin with larger commitments in Europe, thereby making the credibility problem in the developing crisis a more general issue of the defense of Europe. At the same time, however, Western pronouncements concerning essential rights in Berlin itself were couched almost entirely in terms of *West* Berlin alone, with the result that the Western position regarding East Ber-

[66] This point is discussed in Windsor, *op.cit.*, p. 259.

[67] For an interesting though rather impressionistic discussion of the views of the various factions within the American Administration, consult Smith, *op.cit.*, pp. 293-297.

[68] For the text of Kennedy's speech, see *DOSB*, XLV, No. 1155 (August 14, 1961), 267-273. In this speech, Kennedy announced decisions: (1) to ask Congress for an additional $3,247,000,000 in defense appropriations, (2) to increase the number of men on active service in all three branches of the armed forces, (3) to double and triple draft calls to achieve the previous objective, (4) to ask Congress for authority to call up ready reserves, (5) to delay the deactivization of the B-47 bombers, (6) to retain or reactivate various ships and planes for purposes of sealift and airlift, and (7) to make a new start on civil defense.

lin was even further weakened during this stage of the bargaining.

Moreover, severe disagreements among the Allies produced considerable delays.[69] The Soviet *aide-mémoire* of June 4 was not formally answered until July 17. Weak hints at economic moves such as a trade embargo were not made fully credible. And aside from verbal assurances, the West produced no effective diplomatic counter during this period to the Soviet proposals concerning peace treaties and the idea of making *West* Berlin a "free city." Nor was the American insistence on adopting a favorable attitude toward negotiations on Berlin much help at this stage. The subject was an obvious source of allied disunity.[70] And vague pleas for negotiations tended to conflict from time to time with efforts to demonstrate the credibility of the Western commitment in Berlin, especially when they appeared to take the form of responses to Soviet deadlines on the separate peace treaty issue.

Perhaps the most influential Western bargaining moves during this phase of the 1961 crisis came in American announcements concerning the augmentation of United States armed forces. The idea of proclaiming an emergency mobilization in response to Soviet initiatives on Berlin was ultimately rejected as being more likely to cause serious domestic alarm than to demonstrate international commitment.[71] The United States did, however, make public during this period a series of decisions, culminating in Kennedy's July 25 speech, concerning the buildup of conventional forces in Europe, the adoption of a "flexible response" doctrine, and the augmentation of civil defense programs. In this context, it seems quite plausible to argue that "The display of resolution implicit in the strengthening of United States military capabilities in Europe must have made a painful impression on

[69] For comments on these disagreements and the resultant problems of coordination, see Smith, *op.cit.*, p. 243.

[70] On this point see *The Economist*, August 12, 1961, p. 637.

[71] It was also argued by some that the Soviets would interpret such a proclamation more as a sign of weakness than as a demonstration of resolve. On the debate concerning this proposal see Schlesinger, *op.cit.*, p. 389.

Khrushchev."[72] Nevertheless, the implications of these decisions for the 1961 crisis were two-sided. Though they were indicators of American power in a general sense, these moves also provided clear evidence of a basic rethinking of European defense problems during 1961 and of a concurrent decline in faith concerning the viability of the existing arrangements within the NATO structure.[73] In view of the obvious fact that decisions announced by the United States during the summer of 1961 would take a number of months to implement, the Soviets may well have regarded the public announcement of these decisions as a signal to press for political concessions in central Europe during the hiatus between the loss of faith in one set of NATO defense arrangements and the implementation of a new set.

This process of strategic bargaining over Berlin changed sharply, however, during the short second phase of the 1961 crisis covering the period from early August through approximately August 20. During this phase, the internal GDR crisis came to a head in such a way as to intrude forcefully on the more general East-West conflict. Specifically, both American and Soviet decision-makers were genuinely afraid of the possible consequences of a major blowup within the GDR.[74] The two sides therefore coordinated in taking steps to forestall serious internal uprisings within the country. They accepted, on a *de facto* basis, both the general necessity and the specific timing of the closure of the sector boundary in Berlin on the grounds that the GDR crisis could not be effectively terminated without halting the refugee flow. Moreover, both the United States and the Soviet Union reacted to the fear that their own physical involvement in Berlin during this phase could have dangerous escalatory results. As a consequence, "During the crucial stages of the crisis (August 10-16), both the United States and the U.S.S.R. were noticeably absent from affairs in Berlin. The Soviets left arrange-

---

[72] Arnold L. Horelick and Myron Rush, *Strategic Power and Soviet Foreign Policy* (Chicago: University of Chicago Press, 1966), p. 124.

[73] For a very interesting discussion of this point, see Windsor, *op.cit.*, p. 235.

[74] For an interesting formulation of this point, see Richard Rovere, "Letter from Washington," *The New Yorker*, September 2, 1961, p. 66.

199

ments completely in the hands of the GDR. The United States did the equivalent, keeping its garrison tightly restricted to its barracks. Both avoided the dangerous confrontation which political leaders feared might escalate."[75] In the upshot, therefore, a distinct hiatus in the strategic bargaining of the East-West crisis occurred during this short second phase.

The Western powers played their part during this hiatus with great caution. There was no immediate physical response to the boundary closure either on August 13 or afterwards.[76] On the contrary, the Western reaction was to appeal for calm and to utilize available police forces to maintain order in West Berlin.[77] The Western diplomatic response was also extremely cautious.[78] The first official reaction on August 13 was Secretary Rusk's famous "sigh of relief" statement.[79] No formal Western protest of any kind was forthcoming until August 15 and no high-level diplomatic protest until August 17. At the same time, Willy Brandt's speech of August 16 and his subsequent letter to Kennedy outlining possible Western actions in response to the boundary closure were received with a notable lack of enthusiasm in Washington.[80]

A number of factors were responsible for shaping this cautious response. Western fears of a loss of control in Berlin and the dangerous possibilities of subsequent escalation were both genuine and powerful. The so-called "soft line" approach to the overall crisis was influential in Washington at this time.[81] There was a widespread feeling that nothing the

[75] Jean Edward Smith, "Berlin Confrontation," *The Virginia Quarterly Review*, Vol. 42, No. 3 (Summer 1966), 362.
[76] For discussions of Western attitudes underlying this thinking, consult Windsor, *op.cit.*, p. 240; and Smith, *The Defense of Berlin, op.cit.*, pp. 279, 295.
[77] See Kurt L. Shell, "Berlin," pp. 85-102 in Walter Stahl, ed., *The Politics of Postwar Germany* (New York: Praeger, 1963), p. 99.
[78] For discussion see Smith, *The Defense of Berlin, op.cit.*, p. 271.
[79] The text of Rusk's statement of August 13, 1961, is printed in *DOSB*, XLV, No. 1157 (August 28, 1961), 362.
[80] On the American response to Brandt's actions, see Smith, *The Defense of Berlin, op.cit.*, pp. 282-283.
[81] For discussion of this shift see *ibid.*, p. 295; and Horelick and Rush, *op.cit.*, p. 124.

West could do would save *East* Berlin.[82] The stabilization of the GDR's internal situation might serve to lessen tension in the general East-West confrontation. And in the meantime, it was considered highly important to avoid raising false hopes within East Germany, thereby increasing the dangers of internal uprisings, a development that might follow from various Western efforts to bargain strategically at this juncture.

Under the circumstances of this second phase, the Soviet Union also retreated from its previous efforts to bargain strategically. To begin with, the Soviets acquiesced in Ulbricht's desire to close the sector boundary despite the fact the timing was quite inopportune from their point of view.[83] In the overall East-West crisis, the Soviets would have benefited from a policy of allowing underlying tensions emanating from their earlier threats to mount farther, a policy which they sacrificed in the face of the dangers arising from the internal GDR crisis. At the time of the boundary closure the Soviets manifested clear-cut fears of a repetition of the events of June 1953 and took definite steps to insure against such dangers.[84] They absented themselves physically from Berlin itself in order to minimize the dangers of an East-West military clash. They approved of arrangements for East German forces to occupy East Berlin to maintain order among the people while units of the Soviet Expeditionary Force simultaneously took up positions surrounding the city and dispersed themselves throughout the countryside of the GDR to minimize the possibilities for serious popular uprisings. Once the necessity of stopping the refugee flow was agreed upon, therefore, the Soviets took extensive precautions to see that it was done so as to minimize the risks of an East-West clash. To round out this picture, the Soviets were at pains to make it clear to the West there would be no interference with the access routes

[82] This feeling is outlined in Theodore Sorensen, *Kennedy* (New York: Harper and Row, 1965), p. 593.

[83] On the disadvantages of this timing for the Soviet Union, see Windsor, *op.cit.*, p. 241. The critical shift in the Soviet attitudes with regard to Ulbricht's demands appears to have occurred during the meeting of Warsaw Pact leaders in Moscow on August 3-4.

[84] On this point see, *inter alia*, Shell, *op.cit.*, p. 99.

across East Germany to West Berlin in connection with the closure of the sector boundary. Not only was this policy outlined verbally,[85] it was also evident in the willingness of the Soviets to cooperate with the movement of an American battle group along the autobahn from Helmstedt to Berlin on August 20. In this connection, the Soviets proved willing in the "crunch" to honor a relationship which they were in fact trying to undermine in the general East-West crisis of 1961 by means of strategic bargaining.

Though, in the final analysis, the boundary closure produced some asymmetrical effects, the general propensity of both the Soviet Union and the Western powers to bargain strategically in the crucial days surrounding this event was sharply lowered. Nevertheless, this phase inevitably emerged as nothing more than a short "time-out" in the broader East-West crisis of 1961, which remained very much in evidence and whose principal issues were still far from resolution. The bargaining hiatus could therefore continue temporarily while the dangers of internal uprisings or political collapse within the GDR remained acute, but it could not last indefinitely. The specific processes through which strategic bargaining was resumed in the overall crisis became extremely sensitive.

As it happened, the hand of the West was sharply forced by a rapid and drastic decline in popular morale in *West* Berlin following the events of August 13.[86] In their anxiety concerning the dangers of the internal GDR crisis, the Western powers had at first deemphasized and seriously misjudged the problem of West Berlin morale. As morale began to collapse during the week of August 14, however, the West was faced with a choice of reacting sharply or suffering a major setback in the overall East-West crisis. The result, after some hesitation, was the American decision to send the Johnson-Clay mission to Berlin on August 19-20[87] and to reinforce the

[85] For an important example see the communiqué of the Warsaw Pact powers released by the GDR on the morning of August 13, 1961. The text is printed in *DOSB*, XLV, No. 1158 (September 4, 1961), 400.

[86] For a discussion of popular morale in Berlin at this time, see Smith, *The Defense of Berlin, op.cit.*, pp. 277-287.

[87] The decision to send the Johnson-Clay mission was publicly announced in Washington on August 18.

Western garrison in the city by sending the 1st Battle Group of the 18th American Infantry (approximately 1,500 men) along the autobahn from Helmstedt to Berlin. As a result, Western attention shifted again to the problem of demonstrating resolve and credibility in the East-West crisis. On the other side, the key to Soviet actions at this juncture appears to rest in Soviet assessments of the exact time at which the local situation in Berlin and the GDR had become sufficiently stable to permit a resumption of their principal bargaining endeavor vis-à-vis the West. Tentative Soviet steps to resume the bargaining process were evident already in the Soviet note of August 18[88] complaining about Western efforts to utilize Berlin for purposes of practicing subversion against the GDR and other Eastern European states. Soviet efforts to bargain strategically, however, were resumed in earnest and with serious implications in the Soviet note of August 23.[89] This note effectively marked the beginning of a new Soviet campaign against the Western access routes (and especially the all-important air corridors) to Berlin, and abandonment by the Soviets of their commitment to extreme caution which had been one of the distinguishing features of the short second phase.

With these developments, strategic bargaining resumed a major role in the 1961 crisis, and the clash moved into a third phase. The basic context of the crisis, however, was no longer the same as it had been prior to the boundary closure. Above all, the two major elements of the 1961 crisis were now finally separated, and the most pressing internal problems of the GDR were definitely becoming stabilized.[90] These changes reduced the ability of the Soviets to manipulate the local crisis for their own bargaining purposes vis-à-vis the West and, at least temporarily, put off any possible international negotiations concerning the crisis at a time when the Western powers seemed relatively susceptible to compromise solutions.[91] At the same time, the buildup of pressures for

[88] The text of this note appears in *DOSB*, XLV, No. 1158 (September 4, 1961), 397-400.

[89] For the text see *DOSB*, XLV, No. 1159 (September 11, 1961), 433.

[90] On the resultant changes in the internal problems of the GDR, see Windsor, *op.cit.*, p. 242.

[91] On this point see *ibid.*, p. 241.

negotiations on terms favorable to the Soviet Union was now broken, and the potential scope for East-West negotiations concerning the crisis appeared to narrow. Moreover, Western attitudes with regard to specific moves in and around Berlin began to harden in the aftermath of August 13 despite a somewhat curious public insistence by the United States that negotiations with the Soviets would definitely take place soon. And finally, the developments of the second phase of the 1961 crisis reduced Soviet prospects for major gains in the overall East-West context by creating an appearance that the East would settle for limited gains in the 1961 crisis.[92]

Despite these changes, however, the Soviets had not given up all hopes for significant gains in the crisis. During the third phase, they proceeded to resuscitate the threat of a separate East German peace treaty with its implied threat to the West's position on the access routes. Toward the end of August and during September, they launched an important diplomatic campaign against Western uses of the air corridors. Though this campaign was admittedly limited, it was persistent enough to cause grave concern in the West. The Soviets gave at least limited support during this period to a series of East German actions in Berlin, some of which clearly constituted efforts to circumscribe the Western position in the city even further. Of particular importance in this connection were the so-called "hundred meters" rule dealing with freedom of movement in the area on the Western side of the Wall and the efforts of the GDR to restrict the freedom of access of Allied officials to the Eastern sector of Berlin.[93] Perhaps the single most publicized Soviet bargaining move during this period, however, was the announcement on August 31 (Moscow time) of the Soviet decision to resume nuclear tests in the atmosphere.[94] With this move the Soviets certainly succeeded in

[92] For an interesting formulation of this view, see David Riesman, "Dealing with the Russians over Berlin," *The American Scholar*, Vol. 31, No. 1 (Winter 1961-1962), 24.

[93] For further discussion of these developments, see *infra* Chap. Fourteen.

[94] For the text of the Soviet statement on testing, see *Documents on Disarmament 1961* (Washington: United States Government Printing Office, 1962), pp. 337-348.

raising the general tension level in East-West relations and in increasing, at least temporarily, outside pressures for international negotiations in some form.[95] The move did not, however, succeed either in breaking the will of the West to hold out in Berlin or in reducing the actual physical capacity of the West to hold its ground in the confrontation.

The East-West issues involved in the Berlin crisis thus became increasingly clear while the internal GDR crisis faded from view. By September, nevertheless, it was becoming evident that Soviet fears of touching off overt hostilities were severely hampering any plans for sharp physical moves against either West Berlin or the access routes. At this stage, the Soviets themselves began to show an interest in negotiations on Berlin as time began to undermine the credibility of their separate peace treaty threat. By early October, Khrushchev was evidently becoming convinced that the Western powers would in all probability fight for the key issues of *West* Berlin and access to it. Unwilling to initiate overt violence and increasingly pessimistic about the chances for a diplomatic coup, Khrushchev apparently began to lose hope for major gains in this phase of the crisis. He did not, therefore, terminate efforts at strategic bargaining swiftly and clearly, as the Soviets have done under similar circumstances in certain other crises. There were no doubt still lingering hopes in early October 1961 for a shift in attitudes on the part of the West. As a result, various events of dangerous proportions continued to occur in the Berlin arena for several months. But in retrospect, Khrushchev's withdrawal of the peace-treaty deadline in his speech of October 17[96] to the opening session of the Twenty-second Party Congress, followed by the return of Soviet military personnel to Berlin on October 27, appear to mark the effective termination of serious Soviet hopes for major gains in the Berlin crisis of 1961.

[95] For further comments on the effects of the Soviet statement on the resumption of nuclear tests, see *infra* Chap. Sixteen.

[96] In the course of this speech, Khrushchev stated: "If the western powers show readiness to settle the German problem, then the question of the time of signing a German peace treaty will not be of such importance. We shall then not insist that the peace treaty be signed without fail by 31 December 1961." For the text of Khrushchev's speech, see the *New York Times*, October 18, 1961, p. 16.

205

The Western approach to strategic bargaining during this third phase of the crisis was also marked by ambiguities. In the immediate aftermath of the Johnson mission to Berlin on August 19 and 20, Western positions hardened noticeably and the pattern of Western responses in the confrontation acquired an increased clarity.[97] American resistance to the new Soviet campaign against the air corridors was prompt and sharp. At the same time, Western reactions to new moves in Berlin itself, especially those impinging on the rights of Allied personnel, were characterized by genuine firmness. These reactions included major displays of military force on August 22-23 and on August 25 and the following days. Similarly, the announcement on August 30 that General Clay would return to Berlin in September as President Kennedy's personal representative was widely received as a mark of Western determination. So also was the American announcement on September 9 that a 40,000-troop buildup of American ground forces in Europe would be carried out with all possible dispatch.

As time passed, however, various indications of Western hesitancy began to obscure the firm impressions created during late August and early September.[98] There were growing signs of disagreement between General Clay in Berlin and decision-makers in Washington, coupled with confusing efforts to curtail several of Clay's specific plans to initiate counterpressures in Berlin. In addition, limited Eastern initiatives were allowed to pass without clear Western responses. Toward the end of September there were hints emanating from Washington that the West might consider significant concessions in the interests of negotiating a new international status for West Berlin with the Soviet Union. The juxtaposition of these elements of hesitation with the various indications of firmness mentioned above made the dimensions of the Western bargaining posture somewhat ambiguous.

Nevertheless, the residual Western commitment to hold

[97] On this shift see Smith, *The Defense of Berlin, op.cit.,* p. 299.
[98] For a discussion emphasizing these new elements of hesitancy, see George Bailey, "The Gentle Erosion of Berlin," *The Reporter*, Vol. 26, No. 9 (April 26, 1962), 17-18.

only *West* Berlin and the access routes was intrinsically clearer and more realistically delimited than the Western position vis-à-vis the Berlin question during the earlier phases of the 1961 crisis. The confrontation therefore began to assume the quality described by Philip Windsor: ". . . Khrushchev understood clearly enough that he could not attack West Berlin without the risk of world war, and he knew that he could take any action he chose in East Berlin."[99] In this third phase, East Berlin was no longer a critical factor in the crisis, and the possibility of tying East and West Berlin together to manipulate the risks so as to extract concessions from the West was no longer relevant. In this context, the West was ultimately able to convince the Soviets of the credibility of its residual and minimum commitments in Berlin despite various signs of indecision and faltering during September and early October.

Cuba, 1962

The Cuban crisis of 1962 generated somewhat less confusion concerning bargaining relationships than the other cases. The crisis flared up suddenly without a protracted upswing phase; it moved quickly and decisively from the upswing phase to the confrontation phase; the basic pattern of the confrontation was a relatively straightforward bilateral one; there was only one major phase of confrontation during the crisis, and the whole crisis took place over a short period of time. These qualities of the missile crisis did not reduce the influence of cross-pressures between desires to demonstrate resolve and concern about various dangers. On the contrary, these problems were starkly posed by the very nature of the clash and compressed into a short time period. The starkness with which these problems were posed in the 1962 crisis, however, makes them somewhat easier to analyze in this case than in some of the others.

Even in comparison with other severe crises of the post-war period, the Cuban missile crisis generated extraordinarily sharp and pervasive fears concerning the dangers inherent in the clash. Decision-makers on both sides perceived the dan-

[99] Windsor, *op.cit.*, p. 242.

gers of the situation as being especially immediate and urgent. The Soviet magazine, *New Times*, caught this sense of discontinuity with past crises well in its statement that "The crisis . . . was of a gravity and danger probably unparalleled since World War II. A direct armed clash between the world's two greatest powers seemed imminent, and it would inevitably have triggered a global nuclear-and-rocket war. . . . the tension reached a pitch where one false step could have pushed the world over the brink."[100] This general concern with the dangers of the situation was heightened by widespread feelings that there was an inexorable or uncontrollable dynamic in Soviet-American interactions during the confrontation. As a result, the pressure on both sides to proceed with extreme caution during the week of October 22 was unusually great. In particular, both sides developed an acute anxiety about actions that might lead to the initiation of organized violence or the killing of individual people in any manner whatsoever. With respect to the utilization of strategic bargaining, however, a critical feature of the Cuban crisis of 1962 is that the inhibitions resulting from these pervasive fears had an asymmetrical impact on the actions of the two protagonists.

During the week of October 22, and especially before the tension level of the confrontation began to rise markedly on October 26 and 27, the Soviets made several attempts to engage in strategic bargaining. These efforts were based more on verbalized threats than on concrete actions. In his conversation with William Knox on October 24, for example, Khrushchev outlined several vague threats concerning the use of missiles and talked about the possibilities of retaliating against the American naval blockade by means of submarine attacks.[101] Moreover, during the first part of the week, the Soviets hinted they might attempt to force their cargo ships directly through the blockade. And they repeatedly warned the United States they would counter any specific American acts of violence with massive retaliation.

[100] "Reason Versus Recklessness," *New Times*, November 7, 1962, p. 1.

[101] For material on the Khrushchev-Knox interview, see Roger Hilsman, "The Cuban Crisis: How Close We Were to War," *Look*, Vol. 28, No. 17 (August 25, 1964), 20.

Nevertheless, the sudden flare-up of the 1962 crisis and the starkness of the dangers of nuclear warfare inherent in the confrontation evidently made a great impact on the Soviet leadership. In general, "There is little doubt that Khrushchev and other Soviet leaders were badly scared by the sudden and awesome prospect of nuclear war."[102] Also, the Caribbean arena, far from Soviet-controlled territory and easily accessible to superior American conventional forces, was a bad site for a military showdown from the point of view of the Soviet Union. It is now apparent the Soviets found the American threat to invade Cuba increasingly credible as American invasion forces began to assemble during the week of October 22.[103] In fact, Khrushchev himself subsequently made the reasoning of the Soviet leadership during these days quite clear. In a speech before the Supreme Soviet on December 12, 1962, he argued explicitly that ". . . the Government of the United States continued to aggravate the situation. United States militarist forces were pushing developments towards an attack on Cuba. On the morning of October 27, we received information from the Cuban comrades and from other sources which bluntly said that the invasion would be effected within the next two or three days. We assessed the messages received as a signal of utmost alarm. And this was a well founded alarm.

"Immediate action was needed to prevent an invasion of Cuba and to maintain peace. A message prompting a mutually acceptable solution was sent to the United States President."[104]

At the same time, the Soviets appear to have been caught off guard by the sharpness and speed of American moves on October 22. As one American commentary has put it, "Against this surge of feeling, Khrushchev reacted hesitantly. Twelve hours after Kennedy's speech, the Kremlin issued a cautiously worded statement. Then Khrushchev sent a peace-rattling message to British pacifist Bertrand Russell. Next,

[102] *Newsweek*, November 12, 1962, p. 26.

[103] For an interesting discussion of this point, see *The Economist*, November 3, 1962, p. 433.

[104] The relevant portion of the text of Khrushchev's speech is in Henry Pachter, *Collision Course* (New York: Praeger, 1963), p. 246.

Khrushchev grasped eagerly at a suggestion by U Thant. . . ."[105] Although this statement is worded a little strongly, the hesitancy and indecisiveness of the initial Soviet reaction was clearly reflected in the extreme cautiousness of Soviet actions within the crisis area itself. There were several factors behind this initial indecisiveness. The Soviets apparently still hoped, in the immediate aftermath of October 22, to be able to complete several of their missile installations in Cuba despite the American blockade. Moreover, the naval blockade itself was a delicate issue for the Soviets since any incautious moves in this area might have brought the onus for actually initiating the use of violence during the 1962 crisis onto the Soviet Union.[106]

This initial hesitancy and indecisiveness in the area of concrete actions placed the Soviets in a disadvantageous bargaining position from which they subsequently found it impossible to recover. A remarkable indicator of the effects of inhibitory fear on the Soviets during the missile crisis is the fact they avoided efforts to introduce extraneous questions into the crisis for bargaining purposes, with the exception of their weak and somewhat tardy attempt to exchange the Soviet missiles in Cuba for American missiles in Turkey. In particular, the absence of references to Berlin during the week of October 22 suggests that Soviet concern with the underlying dangers inherent in the Cuban confrontation was highly influential.

On the American side, the level of fear generated by the clash over Cuba was also high. Among American decision-makers, there was a widespread and pervasive, though somewhat undifferentiated, feeling that the probability of violence of some kind arising out of the crisis was very great.[107] More specifically, there was also an evident fear of concrete incidents or inadvertent clashes that could catalyze a major

[105] *Time*, November 2, 1962, p. 16.

[106] For further discussion of the question of the initiative in this context, see *infra* Chap. Fourteen.

[107] For a discussion of this point, see Stewart Alsop and Charles Bartlett, "In Time of Crisis," *Saturday Evening Post*, Vol. 235, No. 44 (December 8, 1962), 15.

war through escalation.[108] Toward the end of the week of October 22, the approach of the time when the United States might be forced to make good its threat to invade Cuba, produced an additional source of worry for the American leadership.[109] Furthermore, on the American side there were grave doubts arising from difficulties in formulating judgments about the probable behavior of the Soviets. Khrushchev had clearly proceeded on the basis of significant misperceptions concerning probable American reactions in his original decision to install "offensive" missiles in Cuba, and it seemed at least plausible the Soviet leadership might make further miscalculations.[110] In addition, American leaders during the week of October 22 were afraid the Soviets would begin to introduce in other parts of the world, especially Berlin, initiatives that would be difficult to counter.

Starting from these several distinguishable strands, American fears reached a high point on October 27.[111] Arriving in Washington on that day, in quick succession, were Khrushchev's letter contradicting his earlier message of October 26,[112] reports of the shooting down of a U-2 over Cuba, and and news of the straying of another U-2 over Soviet territory in the area of the Chukotsk Peninsula. Under the circumstances, both the dangers of inadvertent violence and the impending necessity to launch an invasion of Cuba began to loom larger and larger.

[108] On this problem see the material in James Daniel and John G. Hubbell, "While America Slept," *Reader's Digest*, Vol. 82, No. 491 (March 1963), 279.

[109] For verification of this point see "Cuban Crisis: A Step by Step Review," the *New York Times*, November 3, 1962, pp. 1, 6-7. The text can be located conveniently in Daniel L. Larson, ed., *The "Cuban Crisis" of 1962: Selected Documents and Chronology* (Boston: Houghton Mifflin, 1962), p. 242.

[110] For indications of American concern along these lines, see Sorensen, *op.cit.*, p. 681.

[111] On this point see Elie Abel, *The Missile Crisis* (Philadelphia: Lippincott, 1966), pp. 185-200.

[112] While the Soviet letter of October 26 seemed quite conciliatory, the letter of October 27 introduced the idea of a Cuba-Turkey missile swap. It is still not clear which of these letters was actually composed first in Moscow, but there is no doubt the receipt of the second letter in Washington on the morning of October 27 was something of a blow to American decision-makers.

Though these fears clearly exercised an important inhibiting influence on the United States, there was, at the same time, a strong determination on the American side to go ahead with certain critical efforts at strategic bargaining in any case. The Kennedy Administration was, at this time, acutely sensitive about its international reputation in the wake of earlier East-West encounters involving Cuba, Berlin, and Laos. There was a strong feeling on the American side that the Soviets were seriously violating basic "rules of the game" in international politics with their buildup in Cuba and that a failure to react decisively in this case might well undermine critical patterns of expectations underlying the East-West relationship. The Cuban issue had already been built up as a symbolic case so that the 1962 crisis was widely discussed in terms of "whether, with the whole world looking on, Kennedy would let Khrushchev get away with it."[113]

Given this background, the American leaders clearly felt they had little choice but to react decisively to the Soviet initiatives. The United States began therefore to initiate a series of concrete actions that, along with appropriate diplomatic explanations, produced a powerful impact on the subsequent course of bargaining relationships between the two protagonists in the 1962 crisis. These actions included: the swift implementation of the naval blockade; the stepping up of aerial reconnaissance over Cuba; and, especially, clear-cut signs of mobilization for an early invasion of Cuba. Each of these steps was accompanied by precautionary restrictions designed to reduce the chances of violence breaking out inadvertently. Nevertheless, taken together, they constituted a far more influential program of strategic bargaining than the concurrent verbalized threats of the Soviet Union.

These asymmetries between the protagonists on the matter of strategic bargaining were put to the ultimate test toward the end of the week of October 22. The critical break came on October 26 and 27 when the United States began deliberately to step up its pressures on the Soviet Union despite the continued rise of fears concerning the dangers of overt

[113] I. F. Stone, "The Brink" (a review of *The Missile Crisis* by Elie Abel), *The New York Review of Books*, VI, No. 6 (April 14, 1966), 12.

violence.[114] Measures were taken to push the American invasion preparations more rapidly and prominently. Beginning on October 26, for example, various newspapers began to carry hints about specific plans for air strikes and invasion arrangements.[115] And the government itself began tacitly to foster rumors and "leaks" within the United States and abroad concerning American actions that would follow if the Soviets failed to stop construction on the Cuban missile sites. In addition, the Fomin-Scali contacts, which began on October 26, were used by the American government as a channel for the expression of urgency. On that day, for example, Rusk instructed Scali to report to Fomin that "time was very, very short... no more than two days."[116]

In taking these steps to increase pressure on the Soviet leaders, the Americans were responding, to a considerable degree, to a sense of growing desperation stemming from the fact that the time was fast approaching when the United States would either have to take an irreversible decision to launch an invasion of Cuba or allow the Soviets to call the American bluff on the issue. In this connection, the American decision to step up the pressure on the Soviet Union emerged from a situation in which rising fears were effectively offset by the view (which turned out to be accurate) that the Soviet leaders were even more worried about the dangers of the confrontation than the Americans[117] as well as by assessments of the serious problems of control that would arise if an invasion were, in fact, launched. As it turned out, these final American efforts to bargain strategically had a critical effect on the outcome of the crisis since they convinced the Soviets, once and for all, that the United States would not back down and, in so doing, made an American invasion of Cuba unnecessary in the final analysis. At the same time, however, these final bargaining activities sharp-

---

[114] On this point see "Cuban Crisis: A Step by Step Review," reprinted in Larson, ed., *op.cit.*, p. 239; and Pachter, *op.cit.*, pp. 49-50.

[115] For information on this point see "Cuban Crisis: A Step by Step Review," reprinted in Larson, ed., *op.cit.*, p. 240.

[116] Hilsman, *op.cit.*, p. 20.

[117] For a discussion of the various factors influencing American decision-makers at this point, see *loc.cit.*

ly reemphasized the intricate links between the problems of resolve and fear under conditions of crisis, both within individual states and in relations between states.

Conclusion

The case materials make it clear that the principal participants in the major postwar crises have entered these clashes without any desire to touch off planned or premeditated hostilities. On the contrary, the great powers at least have shown a marked tendency to shy away from overt hostilities in situations where the risks and dangers have been plain from the outset. Moreover, perceptions to the effect that the probabilities of violent exchanges are rising have generally operated as a major source of prudential behavior for all parties during crises. These general fears of war, however, are clearly insufficient to prevent major crises from occurring. During the upswing phase, the parties with the tactical initiative have generally hoped either for a *fait accompli* without touching off a major crisis at all or to structure the bargaining relationship so as to be able to demonstrate that they hold positions of superior strength without having to resort to violence. Once a crisis starts to shift from the upswing phase into the phase of full-blown confrontation, it is too late to terminate it short of a major clash.

Inhibitory fears affecting bargaining under conditions of crisis can be separated into two broad categories. On the one hand, there are the rather general, undifferentiated, and pervasive fears that the dangers of war growing out of a crisis are substantial. Though general fears of this kind were clearly present in each of the crises under analysis, they only became critical determinants of crisis behavior at specific junctures. The Cuban missile crisis, especially, generated influential fears of this kind. The widespread fears arising during the second phase of the Berlin crisis of 1961 also exhibited this quality to a considerable degree. On the other hand, there are the more specific and concrete dangers associated with actual or potential incidents. Concern about the problem of specific incidents was explicitly present and influential in all of the crises under analysis. At the same time, however, the case materials indicate that, all other things being equal, these specific and more *ad hoc* fears are apt to exert a lesser inhibiting effect on efforts at strategic bargaining than the more general and undifferentiated fears when the latter do become influential.

There is also an important distinction to be made between the symmetrical development of fears and various asymmetrical patterns in this area. In general, it is somewhat unusual, but not unheard-of, for clearly effective fears to operate more or less symmetrically and simultaneously on the bargaining calculations of the principal participants in a crisis. The concurrent impact of acute fears on both sides during the short second phase of the 1961 Berlin crisis constitutes a striking example of such simultaneity. Nevertheless, it is more common for fear levels to rise and fall during the course of a crisis in asymmetrical patterns. In this connection, fears and strategic bargaining may be closely interrelated since individual parties frequently attempt to bargain in such a way as to foster the development of asymmetrical patterns of inhibitory fears during crises. Fears therefore tend to be manipulated during the course of a crisis for bargaining leverage as well as to exert an independent inhibitory influence. This complex relationship often produces a "war-of-nerves" relationship in which a major objective is to undermine the opponent's resolve by playing on his fears rather than to demonstrate superior strength in any physical sense. This war-of-nerves phenomenon was clearly in evidence during each of the crises under analysis. It became a particularly critical determinant of the final outcome, however, in the Taiwan Strait crisis of 1958 and the Cuban crisis of 1962.

At this point it is important to note the relevance of a number of essentially structural features whose presence is likely to affect the development of influential asymmetries in the balances between resolve and prudential behavior during specific crises. A party that can hold its position successfully unless the opposing side is willing to assume the responsibility for initiating overt violence tends to have a significant advantage. Then too, the geographical locus of the confrontation in a crisis is apt to affect symbolic perceptions of the clash as well as to determine important logistical asymmetries even in a nuclear context. In addition, a party that can effectively demonstrate that the underlying issues at stake in a crisis are of more fundamental and far-reaching importance to itself than to its opponent can probably translate this asymmetry into advantages in the war of nerves. Obvious differences, moreover, in the types and quantities of military forces that can be brought to bear on a contact point in short order will usually yield important bargaining advantages for the side which is superior in this respect, even though military forces are never employed in any straightforward physical sense during the crisis. A number of such relationships are discussed in depth in Chapters Fourteen and Fifteen. The key point here is that the development of major asymmetries in the war of nerves associated with a crisis is generally the result of several factors interacting with each other.

Specific asymmetries in the area of resolve and prudence are also apt to shift markedly from one phase of a crisis to the next. Though shifts of this kind are generally extraordinarily complex, they tend to be more influential during crises characterized by the existence of several underlying axes of contention than in more straightforward bilateral clashes. Sharp fluctuations in the effective asymmetries produced by the war of nerves were more evident in the Taiwan Strait crisis of 1958 and in the 1961 Berlin crisis, for example, than in the first Berlin crisis or in the Cuban missile crisis. While fear levels certainly shifted over time in the last two cases, the patterns of asymmetries between the participants with regard to resolve and prudence were less obscure and ambiguous here than in the others. In the more complex cases, a succession of major adjustments in basic bargaining calculations as well as tricky transitions from one phase of confrontation to another made the shifting balances in the war of nerves extremely difficult to assess accurately at any given moment and therefore dangerous from the point of view of both the interests of individual participants and the stability of the overall international system.

216

9. Freedom of Choice

HYPOTHESIS. Conditions of crisis raise incentives, at any given moment, to utilize actions and diplomatic formulas designed to divide the issues at stake in ways facilitating the retention of freedom of choice in subsequent phases.

Abstract analyses of bargaining suggest there are many situations in which it is advantageous to employ committal or "bridge-burning" tactics to achieve credibility. Such tactics may at first seem especially relevant to crises in which ordinary verbal procedures are apt to be relatively inadequate in coping with the problems of credibility. Successful employment of these tactics depends, however, on a number of conditions including: the absence of a bargaining context that is ambiguous, confused, or obscured to the point where clear-cut commitments cannot be achieved, and the ability to achieve firm commitments before the opponent does. Moreover, the utilization of committal tactics requires a willingness to employ policies that carry with them a significant "risk of failure"[1] and to make use of expected value calculations with the objective of maximizing gains over time rather than minimizing losses. Above all, committal tactics require an explicit reduction in subsequent freedom of choice since they are based directly on the idea that there are advantages to be gained from reducing the number of options available to the initiator in a public and binding fashion.

Procedures of this kind are therefore apt to be viewed with increasing skepticism under conditions of crisis as a function of: the growth of perceived dangers of highly destructive outcomes; the "one-shot" quality of crisis situations, which may cast doubt on tactics emanating from calculations involving

---

[1] The "risk of failure" concept refers to the facts that committal tactics may not work in a given case and that the failure of such tactics can cause significant damage to the initiator. Committal tactics are especially useful in iterative situations allowing for the possibility to recoup the losses of any given episode and when the maximum losses in a given episode are never so great as to destroy the participants themselves. For further comments on the risk of failure, see Thomas Schelling, *The Strategy of Conflict* (Cambridge: Harvard University Press, 1960), pp. 178-183.

probabilities; and the complexity of crisis interactions, which produces a further decline in the clarity and predictability of events. Under such circumstances decision-makers often shift to concern about the minimization of potential losses in contrast to the maximization of possible gains.

As a result, the desire to retain wide freedom of choice as long as possible and to avoid becoming boxed into irrevocable positions will rise in influence even though this may generate decision rules and demands for actions conflicting with those called for by the desire to achieve clear-cut demonstrations of resolve. Freedom-of-choice considerations are thus apt to have substantial influence in order to retain for one's own side sufficient leeway to withdraw from an unfavorable bargaining situation and in order to allow an opponent as much room as possible for a graceful retreat should the crisis interaction begin to deteriorate for him. Gradual and highly differentiated moves acquire great tactical importance in such an environment. The notion of slicing actions as thinly as possible, for example, is particularly influential in the context of crisis bargaining. Such efforts to preserve freedom of choice may well go against the canons of maximizing expected value in specific situations by overemphasizing relatively improbable outcomes. The resultant orientation toward decision-making, nevertheless, is likely to be perceived as particularly appropriate in handling the urgent and dangerous interactions characterizing major international crises.

Berlin, 1948-1949

The Berlin crisis of 1948-1949, occurring in the tenuous and uncertain political atmosphere of postwar Europe, produced a dangerous and unpredictable situation in which both sides were quite evidently concerned with freedom-of-choice problems. Such concerns were influential with regard to both the gradual and hesitant way the confrontation developed and to the obvious caution with which both sides assessed moves that might precipitate overt military clashes. Concern with freedom-of-choice considerations contributed significantly to the ritualistic quality of much of the bargaining during this crisis.

The roots of contention over Berlin in the postwar period are traceable to the initial occupation arrangements set up in 1945. The source of the 1948-1949 crisis, however, lay in the breakdown of the meeting of the Council of Foreign Ministers in London during November and December 1947.[2] Between December 1947 and the end of March 1948, tension over Berlin began to mount slowly, but neither side was yet prepared to formulate openly the specific issues of the impending crisis. During this period, the Western powers did begin seriously, though still gradually, to coordinate plans for the independent reorganization of the western zones of Germany.[3] Since these developments signified a clear challenge to Soviet objectives in Germany, the Soviet Union tentatively began to probe the determination of the Western powers. As Robert Murphy has put it, "The Russians certainly gave us plenty of warning about the Berlin blockade. During the three months preceding the dissolution of the Allied Control Council, Moscow began cautiously to test the determination of the Western powers to stay in Berlin."[4] The Soviets carefully began to test the possibilities of exercising pressure through the use of trade restrictions.[5] Then in March 1948 the Allied Control Commission for Germany collapsed, though even this development was more a gradual dismantling than a sudden breakdown.[6] In short, the specific actions of both sides during this preliminary phase were ambiguous and ultimately retractable even though the underlying tension level in central Europe was plainly rising.

The actual upswing phase of the 1948-1949 crisis took place from the beginning of April to the end of June. In this crisis, concern with the problem of freedom of choice and interest in highly differentiated bargaining tactics were par-

[2] For an interesting discussion of the origins of the 1948-1949 crisis, see Manuel Gottlieb, *The German Peace Settlement and the Berlin Crisis* (New York: Paine-Whitman, 1950), pp. 178-181.

[3] Serious efforts directed toward the development of separate institutions in Western Germany became quite influential with the opening of the London Conference in January 1948.

[4] Robert Murphy, *Diplomat Among Warriors* (New York: Pyramid, 1965), p. 349.

[5] On these developments consult Gottlieb, *op.cit.*, p. 188.

[6] For verification that this development in fact constituted a gradual dismantling, see *ibid.*, p. 183.

ticularly evident during this phase. This was especially true of Soviet activities, a development attributable to the fact that the Soviet Union held the tactical initiative during most of this period. The tentative step-by-step quality of developments during this upswing phase is evident from the chronology of this period (see Table I).

TABLE I[7]

Soviet Actions	Western Actions
	17 March—Brussels Treaty
20 March—walk-out from Allied Control Council	
30 March—major restrictions on Western rail and highway traffic announced	
	1 April—"little" airlift
3 April—freight routes from Munich and Hamburg closed	3 April—ERP bill signed
13 April—East Berlin police incorporated in Soviet zone police	
	7 June—London recommendations
11 June—all rail traffic to Berlin halted for two days	
16 June—walk-out from Berlin Kommandatura	
	18 June—currency reform for Western zones excluding Berlin
19 June—all passenger traffic to Berlin suspended	
23 June—Warsaw Conference starts; Soviet zone currency reform including Berlin	23 June—Western currency reform for Berlin announced
24 June—complete blockade	
	25 June—airlift begins

[7] This chronology was compiled from a number of sources. Perhaps the single most useful source of dates with regard to this crisis, however, is the chronology compiled by Jean Edward Smith, *The Defense of Berlin* (Baltimore: The Johns Hopkins Press, 1963), pp. 360-375.

In the early part of April, there was a flurry of activity affecting Berlin when the Soviets imposed limited restrictions on Western rail and highway traffic moving across the eastern zone of Germany to Berlin. These actions were met by the so-called "little" airlift, and the situation became relatively tense for a few days. The restrictions in question, however, were ambiguous enough so that the crisis did not acquire major proportions immediately. The Soviets exercised considerable restraint in pursuing the situation at this time.[8] After several additional threatening exchanges during April, tension began to subside. There followed a lull—though none of the basic sources of tension disappeared—during the entire month of May before the upswing of the crisis resumed again in earnest during June. And even during June the Soviets displayed considerable hesitancy and a desire to make their points without assuming an irreversible posture of commitment. They responded to the announcement of the London recommendations on June 7 with some provocative initiatives but without any burning of bridges. It was only after the announcement of the Western currency reform on June 18 and one last futile four-power meeting that the Soviets took the steps that culminated in a full blockade of the land routes to Berlin.

In retrospect, the *primary* objective of the Soviets during the upswing phase of the 1948-1949 crisis was evidently to stop or impede the development of Western reorganization plans for Germany rather than to seize Berlin. As *The Economist* put it, "The Russians . . . made it clear that their measures to restrict traffic into Berlin would keep pace with the progress of the three Western Powers towards an agreed plan for the political and economic reconstruction of their zones of Germany."[9] The Soviets were in fact anxious not to take steps that might precipitate an armed clash over Berlin. They wanted, on the contrary, to take the minimum action necessary to make their concern about developments in western Germany clear to the Western powers. The result was a policy of "isolating Berlin . . . by successive turns of the screw,"[10] coupled with an effort to make individual initiatives

[8] On Soviet restraint during this period, see *The Economist*, April 3, 1948, p. 535.

[9] *The Economist*, July 3, 1948, p. 1.

[10] The *New York Times*, June 10, 1948, p. 1.

as minimal as possible. While the Soviets had clear incentives to utilize Berlin as the pressure point in their efforts to bargain with the West, they also wished to avoid becoming inflexibly committed in this area too early.

The Soviet effort to combine bargaining moves with attention to the problem of freedom of choice was strikingly illustrated in Soviet explanations for the growing restrictions on overland traffic to Berlin during the upswing phase of the crisis. The most important explanation focused on the question of technical difficulties.[11] The Soviets developed this explanation in considerable detail, especially in connection with the Elbe River bridges on the rail line and highway as well as the locks on the canals running toward Berlin. They also began to develop several additional covering explanations for their restrictive bargaining tactics,[12] which included: claims that the Western powers were violating the occupation statutes and that the restrictions were appropriate responses; the argument that additional regulations were necessary because the Western powers were lax in maintaining order on the access routes and particularly in controlling smugglers in these areas; and the complaint that Western authorities were allowing the access routes to be used to introduce spurious currency into eastern Germany, thereby causing inflation in the eastern zone.[13] These explanations were promulgated carefully and unremittingly, and it was not until the publication of the Soviet note of July 14 that actual Soviet bargaining interests in the confrontation began to emerge overtly.[14] From the bargaining view, the critical significance of these

[11] For interesting material on Soviet efforts to construct covering explanations for restrictions on overland traffic to Berlin, see W. Phillips Davison, *The Berlin Blockade: A Study in Cold War Politics* (Princeton: Princeton University Press, 1958), pp. 70-71; and Philip Windsor, *City on Leave* (New York: Praeger, 1963), p. 103.

[12] See also *New Times*, "The 'Berlin Question,'" July 21, 1948, pp. 1-3.

[13] Curiously, the Soviets themselves had attempted to utilize the tactic of currency flooding vis-à-vis the western zones of Germany in the period prior to the blockade.

[14] For the text of the Soviet note of July 14, see Raymond Dennett and Robert K. Turner, eds., *Documents on American Foreign Relations*, Vol. X: *January 1–December 31, 1948* (Princeton: Princeton University Press [for the World Peace Foundation], 1950), pp. 86-88.

circuitous Soviet procedures is that the publicly announced reasons for the blockade were both short-term in nature and essentially legal and subject to withdrawal at any time with relatively little embarrassment. A commentator in *The New Republic* summed it up well at the time in the statement that "the most noticeable aspect of all the Russian acts is that they have at least the appearance of legality, and could be countermanded without serious loss of face."[15]

As the 1948-1949 crisis came to a head with the imposition of the full blockade at the end of June, pressures on the Western powers to assume a more active role on the tactical level level began to grow. These pressures quickly evoked a strong sense of concern with the problems of flexibility and freedom of choice to match that displayed by the Soviets. This development was evident in the hesitancy of the Western powers during the last two weeks of June.[16] Strong feelings that the Western powers should stand up for their rights in Berlin were sharply juxtaposed with clear indications of a desire to avoid becoming too quickly committed to a dangerous and possibly irreversible posture. This tension in fact became the source of friction between local commanders in Germany and the national capitals.[17] The results, however, while somewhat mixed, generally constituted a reassertion of the supremacy of the capitals, which were on the whole inclined to weight the demands of freedom-of-choice considerations more heavily than those of the local commanders.

Initial thinking about the Western airlift emerged, to a significant extent, from a desire to maintain subsequent freedom of choice. At the outset there was no expectation the airlift could supply the city of Berlin indefinitely. The airlift was in fact conceived primarily as a relatively nonprovocative initiative to stall for maneuvering time. Its principal appeal was as a middle course between two more rigid alternatives—a decision to use force to break the land blockade with the attend-

[15] Frederick Ford, "New Marks, Old Mistakes in Berlin," *The New Republic*, Vol. 119, No. 3 (July 19, 1948), 12.

[16] On these developments consult, *inter alia*, Frank Howley, *Berlin Command* (New York: G. P. Putnam's Sons, 1950), p. 200.

[17] For interesting indications of friction along these lines, see *ibid.*, pp. 170-180.

ant risks of violence, and a decision to withdraw from Berlin. The airlift, by putting off irrevocable commitments, offered a chance to retain at least temporarily some subsequent freedom of choice.

Taiwan Strait, 1958

The problem of freedom of choice was an important, though primarily tacit, issue during the 1958 crisis in the Taiwan Strait. In this connection, the contrast between pre-crisis maneuvering and behavior during the crisis itself was particularly striking in 1958. Whereas maneuvering prior to the crisis was marked by considerable diplomatic rigidity and the use of committal tactics, the crisis itself evoked a clear shift toward actions designed to maintain freedom of choice even in the course of simultaneous efforts to impress the opponent with the seriousness of the situation. Interestingly, a shift along these lines was noticeable in the activities of both sides during the 1958 crisis.

The efforts of the Chinese People's Republic (CPR) to avoid becoming inextricably committed to the confrontation were especially striking both because the CPR was the tactical initiator of the crisis,[18] and because the basic bargaining calculations of the Chinese Communists made it imperative to impress their opponents with the firmness of their commitment to the confrontation.[19] Despite these features of the crisis, however, the CPR attempted to maintain loopholes for potential retreat through several separate channels. Above all, the Chinese were for the most part quite careful to employ violence on a withdrawable basis.[20] To begin with, the CPR relied primarily on long-range violence and either abstained from the use of other available techniques of violence against the offshore islands or desisted from their use at the first signs

[18] For this reason, the CPR was especially anxious to project a sense of credibility in its commitment to a posture of not relenting without reaping some significant gains from the confrontation.

[19] For a more extensive analysis of the bargaining calculations of the CPR, see *supra* Chap. Eight.

[20] For a particularly interesting formulation of this point, see *The Economist*, August 23, 1958, p. 582.

of determined opposition.[21] The result was a clear policy of avoiding more direct engagements between opposing forces, which might have developed beyond the ability of the CPR to exercise control over them.[22] In addition, the CPR engaged in clear efforts to graduate the use of force in order to bring to bear enough force to impose a blockade on Quemoy while minimizing the risks of provoking a violent reaction from the United States.[23] The failure of the CPR to organize an invasion fleet opposite the offshore islands was particularly striking in this context.[24] The CPR showed itself unwilling, moreover, to escalate overt military operations against the offshore islands significantly, even when the Nationalists began to succeed in breaking the blockade with American assistance.

Even while launching the crisis, the CPR took political steps to maintain a plausible channel of retreat should that become desirable. Efforts here took the form of moves to cast the United States as the aggressor in the crisis so that a potential CPR withdrawal could be portrayed as an act of praiseworthy restraint. As *The Economist* described it: "They [the Chinese Communists] have left themselves a line of retreat by stressing the idea that it is America alone that is threatening aggression (their own designs on Formosa being classed as a purely domestic matter). As and when they may wish to disengage, they can tell their own people that the aggressor has been foiled, and tell the outside world that they are showing most praiseworthy restraint."[25]

Finally on the Communist side, September produced several interesting efforts by the Soviet Union to protect Soviet freedom of choice in the crisis. These efforts came primarily in Soviet statements stressing the civil war aspects of the crisis so

[21] For a discussion of a number of additional techniques of violence available to the CPR, see Hanson Baldwin, the *New York Times*, September 19, 1958, p. 8.

[22] For a discussion of the CPR's concern with escalatory pressures, see Robert Barnett, "Quemoy: The Use and Consequence of Nuclear Deterrence," Harvard Center for International Affairs, March 1960, pp. 17-18.

[23] For a discussion of this point, see Tang Tsou, "Mao's Limited War in the Taiwan Strait," *Orbis*, III, No. 3 (Fall 1959), especially p. 340.

[24] On this subject see Donald Zagoria, *The Sino-Soviet Conflict 1956-1961* (New York: Atheneum, 1964), p. 210.

[25] *The Economist*, September 13, 1958, p. 817.

as to minimize the coverage of Soviet obligations to the CPR under the terms of the Sino-Soviet defense treaty.[26] The result was, among other things, to create for the Soviets a public excuse to avoid further involvement in the crisis unless the *United States*[27] should launch a major attack against the Chinese mainland. Although the Soviets (like the Chinese) were clearly anxious to deter any American strike against the Chinese mainland, these Soviet efforts to maintain their own freedom of choice in the situation precipitated a growing divergence of interests between the Soviet Union and the CPR toward the end of the crisis.[28]

The United States (and to a much lesser extent the Chinese Nationalists) also demonstrated effective concern with freedom-of-choice issues in the 1958 crisis. First of all, the United States hesitated until a rather late date to commit itself decisively on the question of whether the offshore islands would be deemed to fall within the scope of the Formosa Resolution of January 29, 1955, in the context of the 1958 crisis.[29] During August the United States contented itself with the declaration that the islands were "becoming" more closely related to the defense of Taiwan.[30] Even the famous Newport statement of September 4[31] (as contrasted with the informal briefing given along with it) failed to make a decisive commitment on this issue. The sources of this "wait-and-see" attitude are

[26] For the clearest formulation of this position, see Khrushchev's statement of October 5, which originally appeared in the October 6 issue of *Pravda*. The text can be located conveniently in *CDSP*, Vol. 10, No. 40 (November 12, 1958), 18.

[27] Especially striking is the explicit limitation of the Soviet defensive obligation to the case of a major attack involving outright American participation.

[28] For further material on this point see *supra* Chap. Eight.

[29] The resolution itself left this matter to be decided by the President in the event of a specific confrontation. For the actual language of the resolution, see *DOSB*, XXXII, No. 815 (February 7, 1955), 213.

[30] See, for example, Dulles' letter of August 23 to Thomas Morgan, chairman of the House Committee on Foreign Affairs, in which he stated that "over the last four years the ties between these islands and Formosa have become closer and their interdependence has increased." The text is printed in *DOSB*, XXXIX, No. 1002 (September 8, 1958), 379.

[31] For the text of the Newport statement, see *DOSB*, XXXIX, No. 1004 (September 22, 1958), 445-446.

clear enough in terms of freedom-of-choice considerations.[32] The Eisenhower Administration feared that a definitive commitment to all the offshore islands[33] would lead to an excessively rigid posture and an unacceptable reduction in American freedom of choice, whereas a public statement of commitment to only some (or none) of the islands would invite the CPR to take control of those excluded from the commitment. In retrospect, this American hesitation, based on freedom-of-choice considerations, probably played a role in the initial miscalculations of the CPR about the likelihood of a firm American response to a probe in the Strait.[34]

During the later phases of the 1958 crisis, the United States acted with an acute awareness of freedom-of-choice problems, especially in connection with the efforts to break the Chinese blockade of Quemoy. In this area the United States engaged in a carefully graduated and closely controlled application of force involving extensive efforts to avoid violent initiatives that could touch off overt physical engagements beyond the full control of either side. American efforts both to break the blockade *without* utilizing violent initiatives and actively to restrain the Nationalists from engaging in offensive operations against the Chinese mainland[35] were particularly important in this regard.

At this point, some note should be taken of the efforts of the Chinese Nationalists to maximize their public commitment to retain the offshore islands and, in so doing, to reduce both their own freedom of choice and that of the United States.[36] The principal feature of this campaign was the

[32] For an interesting explanation of American thinking along these lines, see Dwight Eisenhower, *Waging Peace 1956-1961* (Garden City, N.Y.: Doubleday, 1965), pp. 294-295.

[33] There are several major groups of offshore islands which include a large number of very small islands.

[34] On the question of CPR miscalculations along these lines, see also *supra* Chap. Eight.

[35] Offensive action against the mainland became an issue especially in connection with Nationalist agitation for a program of bombing the coastal artillery batteries on the mainland.

[36] For a good factual reconstruction of Nationalist activities along these lines, consult Tang Tsou, "The Quemoy Imbroglio: Chiang Kai-shek and the United States," *Western Political Quarterly*, XXII, No. 4 (December 1959), 1,077-1,078.

augmentation of Nationalist garrisons on the offshore islands to the point where they contained approximately one-third of the Nationalist army, including many of its best units.[37] Nevertheless, the major troop movements involved in this obvious effort to display the rigidity of the Nationalist commitment to the offshore islands took place in the aftermath of the 1954-1955 crisis in the Taiwan Strait and had been completed before the opening of the 1958 crisis.[38] This committal tactic belongs therefore to the rigid postures of the pre-crisis period and serves to enhance the contrast, noted at the outset, between the inflexibility of this period and the clear concern with freedom-of-choice problems which emerged during the crisis itself.[39]

Finally, the process of tacit coordination between the United States and the CPR during the month of September regarding the problem of using physical force coercively but not violently represents an interesting and somewhat delicate display of mutual concern with freedom-of-choice issues. Especially with regard to the blockade of Quemoy, the pattern of interaction that grew out of Chinese Communist abstinence from attacks on American vessels escorting Nationalist supply ships and from the use of available options for escalating the confrontation as the blockade began to fail,[40] together with the efforts of the United States to employ American forces in ways that would minimize the likelihood of provoking violent responses from the CPR, constituted a highly influential case of tacit coordination based on mutual concern with the dangers of overly rigid postures of commitment in a setting al-

[37] Curiously, estimates of the number of Nationalist troops stationed on the offshore islands in August 1958 vary substantially. Most estimates, however, give figures in the 80,000-100,000 range.

[38] For verification of this important point with regard to the timing of Nationalist activities, see Tsou, "The Quemoy Imbroglio," op.cit., pp. 1,077-1,078.

[39] One could say that the failure of the United States to pressure the Nationalists into a reversal of the flow of troops to the offshore islands constituted de facto acceptance of a policy of reducing freedom of choice. Nevertheless, this argument is also primarily relevant to the pre-crisis period since the negative consequences of such a move by the United States would have been far greater during the actual crisis than during the period preceding the 1958 crisis.

[40] On the various options available at the time, see Baldwin, op.cit.

ready characterized by overt hostilities. The restraint exercised by the CPR in this situation was especially critical since American forces, at a number of critical junctures, were operating under explicit orders to shoot back if fired upon.[41] In general, the success of this process of tacit coordination is all the more notable because it occurred simultaneously with a series of substantial violent exchanges between the forces of the Chinese Communists and the Chinese Nationalists.

Berlin, 1961

The Berlin crisis of 1961 produced a number of important efforts to divide issues despite the fact that the problems of maintaining credibility were particularly acute during several of its phases. With the exception of the short phase surrounding August 13 in which the two sides were equally anxious to avoid excessively rigid commitments, however, concern with freedom-of-choice issues was especially characteristic of Eastern activities during the 1961 crisis. This asymmetry appears to be attributable to several distinguishable factors. Western leaders, quite generally, took the view that the Western powers held the defensive side of a defender-challenger relationship in Berlin. They therefore tended to define the fundamental objective of the West in terms of the effort to convince the opponent of the credibility of a sharp Western reaction to various contingencies. Western leaders frequently chose to emphasize, at least verbally, the hardness of Western commitments to Berlin. During the early phases of the crisis, Western thinking about the confrontation tended to focus on preset rather than flexible conceptions concerning the timing and ultimate dimensions of the crisis. As Rovere has put it, "Western planning was based firmly on the assumption that whatever trouble there would be would come from the transfer to Herr Ulbricht's Pankow regime of the remaining Soviet responsibilities in Berlin and East Germany."[42]

The Eastern side, on the other hand, showed considerable

[41] With regard to the orders under which American forces in the Taiwan Strait operated, see Eisenhower, *op.cit.*, pp. 296, 299; and Zagoria, *op.cit.*, p. 215.

[42] Richard Rovere, "Letter from Washington," *The New Yorker,* September 2, 1961, p. 64.

interest in "issue-splitting," especially as an offensive tactic, during several phases of the crisis. This general point must be qualified by the facts that differences between the Soviet Union and the German Democratic Republic (GDR) on the question of freedom-of-choice emerged at several points during the crisis and that the orientation of the Eastern side on these issues shifted significantly from one phase of the crisis to another. Nevertheless, the attention devoted by the Eastern side to the possibilities of dividing the issues at stake was striking in the 1961 crisis.

Throughout most of the period preceding the closing of the sector boundary in Berlin on August 13, the Eastern parties were careful to retain their flexibility by relying ultimately on retractable verbal initiatives and by keeping their more substantive moves tentative. The Soviet Union effectively set the 1961 round of the Berlin confrontation in motion with the conditional ultimatum contained in its June 4 *aide-mémoire*. This initiative, however, was a flexible one: (1) it represented a return to old threats and was therefore not a radical departure,[43] (2) though it constituted an important conditional threat, it did not create a situation in which the Soviets would be compelled to carry out the threat in fact, and (3) the specific terms of the threat were vague enough in the *aide-mémoire* to leave the Soviets considerable leeway to fill in the details on the basis of subsequent Western reactions.[44]

There followed during June and July a series of tentative steps, especially on the part of the GDR, to deal with the growing internal crisis within East Germany while probing Western commitments in a manner designed to avoid direct clashes with the West. From June onward, the GDR began gradually to step up tensions in and around Berlin by imposing new restrictions on travel, currency exchange, and

[43] The main points of the June 4 *aide-mémoire* were for the most part a restatement of the points contained in the Soviet "ultimatum" of November 27, 1958, concerning Berlin.

[44] This was especially the case with regard to the details of the time limit involved. Khrushchev therefore proceeded to utilize his speeches during the succeeding weeks to embroider this and other aspects of the Soviet initiative.

purchases of consumer goods.[45] Such restrictions were imposed only on a gradual basis, however, as no really significant Western responses were forthcoming.[46] During the same period, the GDR began to reduce the contacts between East and West Berlin by restricting intracity communications and by initiating a limited campaign against the "border-crossers" who lived in East Berlin and worked in the West.[47] Moreover, in response to the increasingly critical refugee problem, "the regime tried desperately to stop the flow by every means short of sealing off the sector boundary."[48] Each of these tentative steps was directed primarily toward containing the internal crisis of the GDR. It is especially important to emphasize both the caution with which the GDR acted and the importance which the East German leaders evidently attached to avoiding sharply discontinuous actions that would minimize their maneuverability and possibly catalyze dangerous Western reactions.

As the internal situation within the GDR began to deteriorate rapidly, however, new and more decisive steps were required to handle it. Even at this juncture the GDR continued to act cautiously, carefully observing Western reactions to its step-by-step course leading up to the final closure of the sector boundary. On August 1, the regime imposed important new restrictions on travel into and out of the GDR, but it claimed that this move was required because of the danger of polio being brought into the GDR from West Germany—an obvious device allowing possible retraction of the restrictions in the event Western reactions should make such a move desirable.[49] Then throughout the period between Au-

[45] For a convenient summary of these early Soviet moves, consult the *New York Times*, July 16, 1961, Sect. IV, p. 1.
[46] For a discussion of this relationship see Smith, *op.cit.*, pp. 259-261. The only major Western response during this period was the drafting of the protest note of August 3. Even this response now appears to have been largely perfunctory.
[47] For discussion concerning these developments, see Smith, *op.cit.*, p. 258.
[48] George Bailey, "Dead End at the Brandenburg Gate," *The Reporter*, Vol. 25, No. 4 (September 14, 1961), 25.
[49] That this was only a bargaining device is clear from the fact that the incidence of polio was not abnormally high in the Federal Republic of Germany during this period.

gust 2 and 12, the regime began to accelerate its campaign against refugees and "border-crossers."[50] At the same time, efforts to disseminate stories concerning subversive Western activities emanating from West Berlin were sharply increased, a move whose rationale became clear in the subsequent efforts of the East to justify the closing of the sector boundary in the eyes of the world. Given this progressive buildup, it is probably accurate to argue that "The actual Communist move to close the border on August 13 could have caught the West by no more than tactical surprise."[51] It is certainly true that the Eastern side tested Western responses about as carefully as possible before committing itself to a complete closure, thereby sharply reducing its subsequent freedom to shift its course in Berlin.

The closure of the sector boundary on August 13 did of course constitute a major act of commitment. But even this action was elaborately hedged with devices aimed at minimizing Western reactions and maximizing the remaining freedom of choice available to the East. First, the action was carried out entirely by East German personnel and was begun on a somewhat tentative basis. The use of East German forces provided "the Soviets with a loophole to back out if the West forcibly resisted the building of the Wall."[52] And it is probable that the idea of "commencing with temporary barbed-wire barriers, delaying the construction of the Wall for several days"[53] was at least partly motivated by a desire to maintain an avenue for retreat should the West react sharply. Second, in the immediate aftermath of August 13 the closure of the boundary was clearly billed as a temporary procedure, a posture leaving considerable room for retreat should that course become desirable.[54] Third, the Eastern side

[50] For a step-by-step résumé of these developments, see Deane and David Heller, *The Berlin Wall* (New York: Walker, 1962), pp. 23-31.

[51] Smith, *op.cit.*, p. 265.

[52] Jean Edward Smith, "Berlin Confrontation," *The Virginia Quarterly Review*, Vol. 42, No. 3 (Summer 1966), 362-363.

[53] James L. Richardson, *Germany and the Atlantic Alliance* (Cambridge: Harvard University Press, 1966), p. 286.

[54] For material on this posture see John W. Keller, *Germany, the Wall and Berlin* (New York: Vantage Press, 1964), p. 87, as well as the Soviet note of August 18. For the text of this note, see *DOSB*, XLV, No. 1158 (September 4, 1961), 397-400.

took great care to emphasize that the border had been closed only "in order to bar the way for subversive activity being carried out from West Berlin against the G.D.R. and other countries of the socialist community."[55] Since the move was therefore both temporary and defensive in purpose, it could presumably be rescinded, if this became desirable, by an announcement to the effect that the subversive activities making it necessary had abated. Fourth, the Soviet Union went to great lengths to decouple the closure of the sector boundary both from the issue of the Western right to remain in West Berlin and from the issue of the access routes to the city.[56] The elaborateness of these Eastern efforts to communicate the limited quality of the initiative was particularly striking.[57]

The closing of the sector boundary on August 13 initiated a short period during which the leaders of both sides were strongly influenced by desires to avoid rigid commitments and to safeguard their freedom of choice. The Western powers were impressed by the dangers of overt clashes in Berlin, by the general confusion of the situation, by a feeling that the internal crisis within the GDR created dangers for the West as well as for the Communist bloc, and by a sense that the tensest phase of the East-West confrontation in 1961 was still to come. In the immediate aftermath of August 13, therefore, these powers acted with considerable caution and hesitancy. For the East, on the other hand, the closure of the sector boundary was primarily a defensive move necessitated by the internal crisis of the GDR. As a result, the Soviets, especially, were anxious that this move should not act as a catalyst in bringing the East-West phase of the 1961 crisis

[55] This statement is from the Soviet note of August 18, *DOSB*, XLV, No. 1158 (September 4, 1961), 397. This rather remarkable document was based on the premises that "West Berlin had been transformed into a bed of adventurists, rogues, paid agents, terrorists, and other criminals serving the intelligence services of the entire imperialist world . . ." and that the city had, furthermore, become a base for ". . . economic diversions against the G.D.R." See *ibid.*, p. 398.

[56] For a clear statement of this position, see the Declaration of the Warsaw Pact powers released by the GDR on the morning of August 13. The text of the declaration is printed in *DOSB*, XLV, No. 1158 (September 4, 1961), 400-401.

[57] For a discussion of this point see Smith, *The Defense of Berlin*, *op.cit.*, p. 268.

prematurely to a head. Only when the more general East-West crisis began to come back into focus during the last ten days of August did the Eastern side again find it desirable to employ "issue-splitting" tactics offensively in order to probe Western resolve without destroying its own freedom of choice.

Within Berlin itself, the absence of forcible Western responses to the events of August 13 evidently encouraged the East to initiate new probes designed to influence the overall East-West confrontation.[58] As August proceeded, therefore, Eastern moves began to shift gradually from restrictions on East Berliners and East Germans to actions affecting the rights of West Berliners, foreigners in general, and Allied personnel.[59] In the aftermath of August 13, the GDR began, on a step-by-step basis, to reduce the number of crossing points for entry into East Berlin. Even more important was the gradual and piecemeal progression toward the tightening of requirements with regard to official passes for West Berliners entering East Berlin and toward a policy of insisting that all Allied personnel display their credentials on crossing the sector boundary.[60] Then on August 23 the GDR proclaimed the so-called "hundred-meters" rule purporting to prohibit all movements and activities within a hundred meters of the Western side of the Wall. Significantly, however, a sharply negative Western reaction resulted quickly in the tacit dropping of this rule on the part of the East. In each of these cases, the East took considerable pains to embark on an initiative of some significance, simultaneously leaving itself a clear channel of retreat in the event of a sharp Western reaction.

Similarly, the Soviet Union began a series of probing initiatives regarding the access routes to Berlin in the aftermath of the events of August 13.[61] To begin with, the Soviets

[58] For discussion see *ibid.*, pp. 276-277.

[59] For some interesting material on this shift, with particular reference to the question of freedom of movement within Berlin, consult *The Economist*, August 26, 1961, p. 777.

[60] For the details of developments along these lines, see the Hellers, *op.cit.*, pp. 68-69.

[61] For a particularly interesting discussion of these new Soviet initiatives, see David Binder, "Are We Really Standing Firm in Berlin," *The Reporter*, Vol. 26, No. 6 (March 15, 1962), 20-21.

began a verbal campaign against Western use of the air corridors with their note of August 23.[62] This campaign was interesting from the view of freedom of choice because it was based primarily on verbal probes and because the public reasoning of the Soviets in this instance was based on alleged Western misuses of the air corridors,[63] a procedure carefully designed to offer a plausible channel for backing away from the issue at a later stage. Throughout the remainder of 1961 and into the early months of 1962, the Soviets engaged in various limited acts of physical interference both in the air corridors to Berlin and along the ground routes. On a number of occasions these actions became sufficiently important to play a role in testing Western resolve, but they were never allowed to reach the point where they could effectively commit the Soviet Union to an inflexible or irreversible posture on the Berlin question.

In short, the Soviets attempted during the later phases of the crisis, "by means of constant probing and piecemeal encroachment, to make their own definition of the allied commitment to Berlin."[64] In this endeavor, however, they ultimately met with only limited success. Prior to the closure of the sector boundary, the West had largely sidestepped the problem of dividing issues to retain its freedom of choice by adopting a rather passive position in terms of actions and by failing to make any extended physical response to a number of Eastern initiatives. In the immediate aftermath of August 13, the two sides engaged in a process of *de facto* coordination since they were simultaneously impressed with the desirability of avoiding inflexible postures. Following this brief hiatus, however, two sets of changes occurred to alter the prior relationship. In the new situation that arose after the final division of Berlin, the Eastern side proved ultimately unwilling

[62] For the text of the Soviet note of August 23, see *DOSB*, XLV, No. 1159 (September 11, 1961), 433.

[63] The Soviet allegation in this connection was to the effect that "All kinds of revanchists, extremists, saboteurs, spies, and diversionists are transported from the F.R.G. to West Berlin. For their transport the Western Powers also are using the air corridors. . . ." This statement is from the Soviet note of August 23; see *ibid.*, p. 433.

[64] George Bailey, "The Gentle Erosion of Berlin," *The Reporter*, Vol. 26, No. 9 (April 26, 1962), 18.

to test the residual Western commitments to the point where the West would be forced either to make good its commitments or to give in altogether. In addition, during the later phases of the crisis, the Western powers—and especially the United States—increasingly began to make use of tactical reactions and initiatives that had the effect of putting the ball back in the court of the Eastern side without requiring the use of overt violence.[65] During these phases, therefore, efforts to divide the issues continued to occupy an important tactical position but these efforts were distributed rather evenly between East and West.

Cuba, 1962

The record of the Cuban crisis of 1962 contains some interesting material relating to the question of freedom of choice. However, considerations of this kind did not emerge with any clarity in the period prior to the actual crisis. The original Soviet decision to deploy offensive missiles in Cuba, in fact, suggests a willingness to engage in policies involving relatively rigid commitments. The Soviets evidently hoped the United States would not discover the presence of the missiles before they became operational and that it would therefore be possible to achieve a *fait accompli* with their unveiling. As a result, they allowed their hopes for American inaction[66] to outweigh considerations concerning the preservation of freedom of choice in the event the United States should force a confrontation over the issue. Similarly, the development of American attitudes toward the whole Cuban question during the period preceding the actual crisis suggests a growing sense of commitment and rigidity in this area on the part of the articulate segments of the American public.

Given this background, it is particularly interesting that the importance of maintaining flexibility, options, and freedom of choice became a central theme during the actual period of

[65] Several Western moves of this kind are discussed in greater detail in a later chapter on the "initiative that forces the opponent to initiate." For this discussion see *infra* Chap. Fourteen.

[66] For a suggestive discussion of this point, see *Newsweek*, November 12, 1962, p. 25.

crisis. At virtually every step of the way, the decision-making processes and the actions of both sides demonstrated a strong desire to avoid being "forced to make an irrevocable decision."[67] This orientation was particularly important in the case of American activities during the missile crisis since the United States held the tactical initiative during most of the period of crisis and was therefore in a strong position to determine the general tone of the interaction.

Concern with the problem of freedom of choice was an explicit factor in American decision-making during this crisis. To begin with, it led to a considerable effort to canvass the range of policy alternatives during the week of October 15.[68] As the Wohlstetters have put it, "Before the crisis the alternatives for policy were discussed in terms of a few bare possibilities: a pure American military invasion, a total blockade, or doing nothing. In the crisis it appeared the world was richer in alternatives than had been conceived by extremists of the left or right."[69] At the same time, the various alternatives together with the possibilities of combinations were examined at great length in a conscious effort to analyze the probable consequences of each choice.[70] Moreover, the actual processes used to select and plan for the blockade "route" provide considerable evidence of concern with the goal of avoiding inflexible commitments. The proposition that the American initiative should be both limited and strictly controlled constituted a highly influential argument during the discussions that preceded the October 22 announcement.[71] There were repeated references to prudential behavior, low-key actions, and controlled escalation. And toward the end, when

[67] Henry Pachter, *Collision Course* (New York: Praeger, 1964), p. vi.

[68] For an extended discussion of the effort to canvass the range of policy alternatives, see Elie Abel, *The Missile Crisis* (Philadelphia: Lippincott, 1966), pp. 55-66.

[69] Albert and Roberta Wohlstetter, "Controlling the Risks in Cuba," *Adelphi Paper No. 17* (London: Institute for Strategic Studies, April 1965), p. 18.

[70] For an interesting discussion of this process, see George Ball, "Lawyers and Diplomats" (address delivered on December 13, 1962). The text is printed in *DOSB*, XLVII, No. 1227 (December 31, 1962), 987-991.

[71] For verification of this point see Theodore Sorensen, *Kennedy* (New York: Harper and Row, 1965), p. 688.

the debate had begun to focus on the choice between a blockade and an air strike, arguments of this kind carried enormous weight.[72]

The American Administration chose to initiate its response to the deployment of Soviet missiles in Cuba with a naval blockade, and "the decision made was precisely one that left open a variety of choices."[73] Several aspects of this concern with the maintenance of freedom of choice deserve specification. Great importance was attached to the factor of time. It was deemed critical to avoid precipitate reactions and, therefore, to act in such a way as to allow the protagonists time to consider their moves carefully.[74] Kennedy, for example, was determined ". . . so to pace the events as to give the Soviet leaders time to think out the consequences of each move. His purpose was to avoid putting them in a position where their only response could be, in the President's own words, 'a spasm reaction.' "[75] In addition, the American decision initiated a bargaining process in which both sides demonstrated considerable interest in avoiding actions that would back the opponent into a corner, leaving him little choice but to react violently. As Pachter has expressed it, "At every turning point . . . , both powers always made sure that on the brink of the abyss, the opponent still had room left to move."[76] The United States was particularly concerned to leave the Soviets room to execute a relatively graceful retreat.[77] In fact, the value of making such a retreat relatively painless for the Soviet Union was discussed quite explicitly among American decision-makers.

The American bargaining program in the Cuban crisis of 1962 also contained a built-in, step-by-step process clearly related to concern with the freedom-of-choice problem. One of

[72] On this point see Abel, op.cit., pp. 89-90.

[73] The Wohlstetters, op.cit., p. 19.

[74] For some interesting points on the time factor, see Time, November 2, 1962, p. 26.

[75] Roger Hilsman, "The Cuban Crisis: How Close We Were to War," Look, Vol. 28, No. 17 (August 25, 1964), 19.

[76] Pachter, op.cit., p. 54.

[77] For evidence on the salience of this concern, see Sorensen, op.cit., p. 691.

the critical underpinnings of the naval blockade was the proposition that, if the blockade should prove inadequate, it would still be possible to undertake additional steps that would increase the pressure on the Soviet Union.[78] As George Ball has put it, "the quarantine was conceived as only the first move in a complicated strategy, and, while the details of the quarantine were being worked out, preparations were going forward simultaneously to put in readiness a sequence of other coordinated actions if the weapons were not removed as a result of the initial action."[79] The American response thus combined "a threat that could be executed with a minimal risk, and a slowly ascending sequence of threats which could not be challenged by the Soviet Union without making its position still worse."[80] The United States reacted to the tension between freedom of choice and the maintenance of credibility, therefore, by combining proximate actions based on freedom-of-choice considerations with efforts to maximize the credibility of its contingent threats.[81]

The physical confrontation between the two sides during the week of October 22 was also conducted with evident concern about the importance of maintaining freedom of choice. The United States implemented its naval blockade in a fashion designed to minimize the dangers of precipitate actions and to avoid forcing the hand of the Soviets. There was a pause between Kennedy's speech of October 22 and the official proclamation of the quarantine on October 23. The blockade did not actually become effective until the morning of October 24, and precautions were taken to make its initiation gradual. The original blockade line was moved in closer to Cuba on October 24 in order to provide additional time.[82] American captains received orders to avoid the interception

---

[78] For a good formulation of American thinking with regard to this point, see Fletcher Knebel, "Washington in Crisis: 154 Hours on the Brink of War," *Look*, Vol. 26, No. 26 (December 18, 1962), 50.

[79] Ball, *op.cit.*, p. 990.

[80] The Wohlstetters, *op.cit.*, p. 20.

[81] For an interesting discussion of the development of this posture, see Pachter, *op.cit.*, p. 86.

[82] For information on this alteration see Arthur Schlesinger, Jr., *A Thousand Days* (Boston: Houghton Mifflin, 1965), p. 818.

of opposing ships as long as possible.[83] Similarly, the actual operations of the blockade were conducted in a manner designed to avoid destroying future options. The Soviet tanker *Bucharest* was allowed to pass without boarding on October 25, for example, and it was not until October 26 that the first boarding of an opposing ship occurred.[84]

For their part, the Soviets cooperated extensively with these efforts to buy time and maintain freedom of choice.[85] They turned back those ships that were obviously objectionable to the United States, and they allowed the remaining ships to submit to search procedures without opposition. They took no action against the ships of the blockade by means of either submarines or surface vessels. They made no serious efforts to circumvent the blockade by means of an airlift.[86] And when it became clear that a continuation of work on the missiles in Cuba itself would make an American air strike probable, the Soviets chose to avoid an overt and possibly irreversible clash even though it meant giving in on a critical point.

In general, the Cuban crisis of 1962 suggests that the influence of freedom-of-choice considerations is apt to vary relatively directly with the perceived dangers of a situation. As the Wohlstetters conclude from their analysis of the missile crisis, "Where the alternative is to be ruled by events with such enormous consequences, the head of a great state is likely to examine his acts of choice in crisis and during it to subdivide these possible acts in ways that make it feasible to continue exercising choice."[87] In the 1962 crisis, conceptions of this kind were introduced quite explicitly and they ultimately achieved considerable influence. As a result, freedom-of-choice considerations operated both as a restraint on the actions of the two sides and as a factor raising the premium attached to skillful manipulation of *contingent* threats.

[83] For verification of this point consult Pachter, *op.cit.*, p. 43.

[84] Moreover, the first ship boarded was the *Marucla*, which was registered in Lebanon and only chartered by the Soviet Union.

[85] For a number of examples of Soviet cooperation along these lines, see Abel, *op.cit.*, pp. 141-184.

[86] For material on this point consult Pachter, *op.cit.*, pp. 42-43.

[87] The Wohlstetters, *op.cit.*, p. 19.

Conclusion

Freedom of choice has been a matter of considerable importance in the bargaining of the great powers under conditions of crisis. In general, the case materials suggest that the attention devoted to considerations of this kind varies quite closely with perceptions concerning the likelihood of violent clashes of major proportions. There are, however, a number of factors that can catalyze perceptions of this kind including: the directness and clarity of the confrontation between the protagonists as was the case in Cuba; feelings that the basic situation or context is such that escalatory processes would be difficult to control, as has generally been the case with the clashes over Berlin; and the concomitant presence of subsidiary patterns of violence, as was the case in the Taiwan Strait. Perceptions concerning the likelihood of major clashes arising from all of these sources are likely to vary from one participant to the next so that the concurrent influence of freedom-of-choice considerations may well develop in asymmetrical patterns.

There are several additional sources of asymmetries affecting the impact of incentives to maintain freedom of choice during crises. In the first instance, interest in freedom-of-choice considerations can arise from several different motives. "Issue-splitting" can be employed as an offensive tactic in some situations. On other occasions, issues are divided in response to concern with the dangers of assuming excessively rigid commitments or of adopting irrevocable positions prematurely. In addition, efforts to retain options sometimes emanate primarily from a sense of hesitancy in complex or obscure situations. The case materials suggest that all of these patterns occur regularly in great-power bargaining during crises.

Beyond this, asymmetries with regard to concern over freedom-of-choice considerations are apt to be shaped by offense-defense differentials. The evidence suggests that a party on the defensive, especially at the tactical level, will generally find itself under pressure to employ committal tactics while the side with the initiative is apt to be more concerned with

241

freedom-of-choice considerations both for tactical reasons and because of the probable distribution of responsibility should violence erupt. This relationship is seriously complicated, however, owing to the distinction between offense-defense patterns in broad strategic or substantive terms and in concrete tactical terms. This distinction is important in the present context because the participants in any given crisis do not necessarily array themselves in the same way at both levels. On the contrary, as the Berlin crisis of 1948-1949, the Taiwan Strait crisis, and the Cuban missile crisis suggest, the side that holds an intrinsically defensive position in strategic terms may well hold the tactical initiative during particular phases of the crisis. While freedom-of-choice considerations are apt to be relevant on a widespread basis during crises, therefore, their influence is likely to develop along complex lines.

Finally, asymmetries with regard to freedom-of-choice considerations sometimes arise from divergent relationships between field commanders and central decision-makers. The case materials indicate that local commanders will tend to be particularly impressed with bargaining requirements demanding committal tactics whereas central decision-makers, under the influence of broader perspectives and concern about the dangers of specific crises stemming from an awareness of the interdependence of international politics, usually become advocates of maintaining freedom of choice. A somewhat similar divergence appears to operate in relations between operations officers, even in the capitals, and politically oriented policy-makers. In this context, the fact that the patterns of effective influence, as between these groups, are apt to vary from one state to the next opens up considerable scope for asymmetries in the impact of freedom-of-choice considerations on bargaining under conditions of crisis.

The relevance of freedom-of-choice considerations also tends to vary over time in relation to crises. To begin with, the case materials suggest a relatively clear distinction between pre-crisis maneuvering and activities during crises themselves in this regard. While pre-crisis maneuvering may be somewhat rigid and characterized by committal tactics, there is apt to be a shift toward growing concern with free-dom-of-choice issues as a clear-cut confrontation develops. The Berlin crisis of 1948-1949, nevertheless, constitutes at least a partial exception in this connection since the pre-crisis environment here was peculiarly unsettled and confused because of the existence of a political vacuum in Germany and because the dimensions of the so-called cold war had not yet become clear at this time.

In addition, there appear to be some distinctions with regard to freedom-of-choice considerations between the upswing phase and the full confrontation phase of great-power crises. In general, such considerations are likely to be somewhat more pervasive in the thinking of decision-makers and to operate in more symmetrical patterns during periods of full confrontation. Developments along these lines are apt to occur because of a concomitant shift in motivations underlying interest in efforts to maintain freedom of choice from tactical maneuvering to genuine concern with the dangers inherent in the situation. On the other hand, it is important to emphasize that actions based on freedom-of-choice considerations undertaken during the upswing phase may exercise a considerable impact on the subsequent contours of a crisis because the basic dimensions of international crises are often less settled and more malleable during this phase than during the subsequent phase of full confrontation.

10. Bargaining Impediments

HYPOTHESIS. The impact of bargaining impediments will increase with the onset of a crisis.

Several distinguishable classes of bargaining impediments were outlined in Chapter Two. It is important to emphasize, therefore, that the hypothesis of this chapter does not specify that the impact of *all* bargaining impediments will increase under conditions of crisis. At the same time, there is reason to argue that the overall impact of bargaining impediments, taken together, will be greater during crises than in the ordinary flow of international politics.

A number of the basic qualities of crisis are likely to emphasize the influence of bargaining impediments. Crises are by nature unsettled, rather fluid, and often somewhat confused periods in which bargaining interests tend to be shifting and difficult to define with precision. Crises have a tendency to focus rather intense conflicts onto narrow and sharply defined points of confrontation in ways that circumscribe the room for maneuvering in bargaining. Crises are discrete and highly visible political phenomena which are frequently invested with emotional content and which tend to acquire rigidifying symbolic significance in terms of broader political problems. And crises are apt to be associated with problems of effective understanding and to crystallize certain difficulties of communication in ways that reduce the flexibility of bargaining relations.

Thus, crises are especially likely to exacerbate those impediments that stem from the extended use of bargaining tactics. The difficulties of achieving decommitment are generally heightened by the onset of a direct and highly visible confrontation. The "test-of-strength" aspects of crisis interactions usually make participants particularly sensitive to the goal of projecting images of strength, firmness, and confidence. For this reason, the parties to a crisis are apt to be extremely hesitant to risk any appearance of weakness either by acting in an openly conciliatory fashion or by taking the initiative in a genuine effort to formulate terms for a settlement.

Moreover, the symbolic importance frequently associated with international crises tends to add to these problems by making crisis confrontations critical proving grounds for the bargaining reputations of the participants in their subsequent activities in the international arena.

At the same time, the ambiguities and confusion that often accompany conditions of crisis are likely to compound the rigidities caused by these tactical impediments. And in this connection, there is no *a priori* reason to suppose that the prolongation of a crisis confrontation will result in any reduction of the problems caused by ambiguities and confusion. On the contrary, the mere passage of time in the absence of serious and at least tacitly coordinated efforts to arrive at acceptable termination arrangements may well heighten the impact of doubts, uncertainties, and elements of confusion.

Berlin, 1948-1949

From the perspective of international bargaining, the Berlin crisis of 1948-1949 was strikingly characterized by its prolonged and drawn-out quality, and the general futility of the explicit negotiations that occurred on several occasions during the crisis. An attempt to explain these features of the crisis opens up the question of bargaining impediments directly. And on analysis, it is possible to distinguish a number of impediments that became relevant during the 1948-1949 crisis.

In the first instance, the directness and the focused quality of the confrontation on the ground in Berlin minimized the room for the parties to maneuver. The 1948-1949 crisis developed into a clear-cut example of confrontation over an easily definable piece of territory, which achieves widespread perceptual visibility. As a result, there was little opportunity to terminate the crisis by avoidance or indirect procedures as frequently happens in non-crisis situations.[1] On the contrary, "in Berlin the narrowing margins for compromise gave divergences a more explosive form."[2]

[1] On the concepts of termination by avoidance or indirect actions, see Kenneth Boulding, *Conflict and Defense* (New York: Harper and Row, 1962), Chap. 15.

[2] Manuel Gottlieb, *The German Peace Settlement and the Berlin Crisis* (New York: Paine-Whitman, 1950), p. 173.

Also, the volatility of expectations concerning the consequences of the passage of time operated as a barrier to effective bargaining during this crisis. The Berlin crisis did not
for the most part produce critical difficulties attributable
to shortages of time or excessively fast-moving developments.
The real difficulty with regard to time focused on diverging
assumptions and calculations concerning the incidence of bargaining advantages that would accrue to the parties from
the sheer passage of time. During the early phases of the
crisis, the Soviets were confident the passage of time would
operate to their advantage. On the assumption that the airlift was no more than a temporary expedient, they believed
time would operate primarily as a source of pressure on the
Western states. They were therefore in no hurry to negotiate a settlement of the crisis during these early phases. During the later part of the confrontation, however, the tables
were substantially turned. The airlift succeeded in keeping the
western sectors of Berlin minimally viable. The very existence
of the crisis acquired utility for the Western powers in working out arrangements for Atlantic security and the future of
western Germany.[3] Toward the end of the confrontation,
therefore, these powers became increasingly adamant in refusing to terminate the crisis on anything but highly favorable
terms.

The lengthiness of the 1948-1949 crisis produced additional
bargaining rigidities since it became increasingly difficult for
the parties to relinquish positions the longer they were held
and the more they became publicized. In this connection,
the spotlight of public attention was an important factor. As
James Forrestal put it in July 1948, "these klieg lights bring
the situation into a focus of world opinion which makes it
more and more difficult for the Russians [or the Western

[3] In short, the existence of the confrontation over Berlin was an important factor in the development of positive attitudes among the Western
Europeans toward both NATO and an autonomous West German state.
The possibility that these positive attitudes might begin to deteriorate
following the termination of the Soviet blockade made it seem desirable
to push plans for the development of these Western institutions as rapidly as possible.

powers] to withdraw from a position so publicly taken."[4] This type of rigidity became especially evident later on as the Soviets maintained their position for some time after the elections of December 5 in Berlin and after the success of the airlift during November and December, which were the worst months for flying.[5]

These difficulties were only exacerbated by the tactical problems of projecting a credible image of resolve to the opposition. The situation was particularly acute for the Western powers during this crisis. As Herbert Matthews wrote at the time, "The problem is how to make them [the Soviets] understand that the Western Powers are not bluffing, and to do so with enough tact and diplomacy to give the Soviet Union a chance for graceful withdrawal."[6] Many of the steps taken to emphasize the credibility of commitments, however, also tended to publicize the conflict and to be interpretable as open challenges by the opponent. During the 1948-1949 crisis both sides frequently acted in ways that, in effect, restricted the scope for genuine conciliatory initiatives. The Western powers, in particular, were wary of taking steps that might be utilized by the Soviet Union for propaganda purposes with an eye toward undermining the morale of the Berlin population.[7] Concern along these lines became especially prominent after the Moscow negotiations of August 1948.

Similarly, bargaining impediments arose during this crisis from the fact that the Berlin confrontation quickly acquired symbolic significance for a number of larger issues. In fact, Berlin was widely regarded as an indicator of the subsequent course of the conflict over the future of Germany, Europe, and the cold war. In this sense, the 1948-1949 crisis was in many ways the first great "trial of strength" of the cold war. For the Western powers the crisis became a matter of

---

[4] Walter Millis, ed., *The Forrestal Diaries* (New York: Viking, 1951), p. 460.

[5] With regard to the influence of the weather on the airlift, consult W. Phillips Davison, *The Berlin Blockade: A Study in Cold War Politics* (Princeton: Princeton University Press, 1958), pp. 260-261.

[6] Herbert Matthews, the *New York Times*, June 29, 1948, p. 3.

[7] For some interesting material on the problem of local morale with regard to the 1948-1949 crisis, see Davison, *op.cit.*, pp. 309-320.

prestige and reputation. As Dulles wrote, "They could not, without jeopardy to their position in all of Western Europe, accept the rebuff of Moscow as the last word and acquiesce in the Soviet denial of their right to use the railroad, roads and canals to Berlin."[8] At the same time, the crisis harbored important dimensions of precedent for the Soviets. It is highly probable that the crisis evoked an awareness on the part of the Soviets "that, if the power to squeeze the Western Powers in Berlin were once given up, they might find it impossible to assert a similar grip elsewhere. What they are bargaining for is a position from which they can wage the cold war with the maximum effect and the minimum risk of actual fighting"[9] As a result, concrete events in and around Berlin acquired a kind of ripple effect. As the Berlin confrontation developed into a critical focus of international attention, it quickly began to generate fears that any gestures toward conciliation could easily assume the proportions of a wholesale retreat affecting a wide range of related issues.[10]

Finally, and not surprisingly, these factors taken together produced an emotional investment in the Berlin situation that added to the rigidities of the confrontation. Especially on the Western side, this led to a considerable amount of loose talk about moral obligations. As an American writer put it, for example, "we have morally committed ourselves to stay in Berlin."[11] In retrospect, it is possible to argue that rigid and undifferentiated postures of this kind in fact contributed to Western bargaining strength during the 1948-1949 Berlin crisis by bolstering the credibility of the Western commitment. There is little doubt, however, that emotional rigidities contributed to the somewhat inflexible patterns of bargaining that characterized this crisis.

[8] John Foster Dulles, *War or Peace* (New York: Macmillan, 1953), p. 56.

[9] *The Economist*, October 16, 1948, p. 615.

[10] For examples of thinking of this kind among the Western participants, see Davison, *op.cit.*, Chap. 8. Interestingly, perceptions of this kind became quite prominent during this crisis despite the fact that the now familiar "domino theory" had not yet been formulated in explicit terms at the time.

[11] Frank L. Kluckhohn, "Behind the Scenes in Berlin," *The American Mercury*, LXVII, No. 299 (November 1948), 521.

The underlying conflict in the Berlin crisis was sharp and full-blown. This fact is no doubt more important than the existence of bargaining impediments in accounting for the intensity and duration of the crisis. Nevertheless, the various impediments played a major role both in prolonging the crisis and in determining that the end of the confrontation would come largely through tacit moves rather than through an openly negotiated accommodation. In the end, therefore, diplomatic contacts were used primarily in order to register changes in the situation which emanated from unilateral bargaining sequences.[12]

Taiwan Strait, 1958

The impact of bargaining impediments was relatively heavy during the 1958 crisis in the Taiwan Strait. First of all, the initial bargaining context was a rigid and difficult one. This was the product of accumulated hostility both in relations between the Chinese Communists and the Chinese Nationalists and in relations between the Chinese People's Republic (CPR) and the United States. During the 1958 crisis, this prior history of hostility not only cast a shadow of general unfriendliness over the bargaining, it also accounted for serious limitations on diplomatic contact among the participants, thereby producing significant problems of communication. Beyond these general difficulties, however, a number of more specific bargaining impediments arose during the 1958 crisis.

Several important impediments emanated from aspects of the basic, longer-term confrontation over Taiwan which were severely activated or exacerbated by the specific circumstances of the 1958 crisis. The fact that the parties tended to act on the postulate that the real issues of the crisis were the future status of Taiwan and the future role of the United States in the Western Pacific made it extremely difficult to bargain meaningfully over more specific issues involving the offshore islands. In this sense, the physical confrontation over the offshore islands was only a surface manifestation of deeper

[12] This was particularly true of the agreement announced in New York on May 4, 1949, by whose terms the Soviet blockade was ultimately terminated.

and more fundamental problems.[13] The future status of Taiwan, especially, was a matter involving the actual survival of the Nationalist regime rather than an allocation of values that, however important, would not ultimately raise questions of survival.

A second problem of this type arose from the peculiarities of the triangular relationship among the CPR, the Chinese Nationalists, and the United States in the Western Pacific. In this connection, the 1958 crisis eventually became a serious confrontation of international proportions superimposed on the remnants of an unsettled civil war. As a result it was possible throughout the crisis to muster a majority of two against many plausible solutions for either aspect of the crisis. The two Chinas, for example, were in firm agreement against any arrangement that would seriously alter existing balances with regard to the civil war in the interests of reducing the dangers of international conflict over the offshore islands.[14] At the same time, the United States and the Nationalists joined in opposing local concessions to the CPR which might have produced a negative impact on their prestige or the credibility of their commitments in the broader international arena.[15] And these rigidities were only exacerbated by the Sino-Soviet campaign, during the later phases of the crisis, to portray the whole confrontation as nothing more than a new episode in a continuing civil war.[16] This effort to cause friction in relations between the United States and the Nationalists made the United States more sensitive than ever to Nationalist demands, thereby reducing any chances that might otherwise have existed for an American–Chinese Communist bargain

[13] For an interesting discussion of the links between the different levels of confrontation involved in the 1958 crisis, see Tang Tsou, "Mao's Limited War in the Taiwan Strait," *Orbis*, III, No. 3 (Fall 1959), 335-338.

[14] Acceptance of arrangements designed to internationalize the offshore islands, for example, would have raised problems along these lines by making it considerably more difficult for either China to prosecute its civil war interests vis-à-vis the other.

[15] The relevant commitments in the broader international arena were those having to do with such things as the American system of alliances.

[16] Interestingly, the CPR and the Soviet Union appear to have been motivated in this matter, at least to some extent, by divergent interests. For further discussion of this point, see *supra* Chap. Eight.

aimed at relieving the international tensions associated with the confrontation.[17]

An additional difficulty attributable to the longer-term confrontation between the two Chinas arose from the CPR's absence from various normal arenas of diplomacy, including the United Nations. In 1958 this absence was essentially a procedural rather than a substantive matter since it is hardly likely that membership in the United Nations would have radically altered the CPR's position on the issues of the crisis. Nevertheless, this situation aggravated the communications problems associated with the crisis and made it impossible to make use of some of the facilitative advantages of a multilateral context to alleviate the common rigidities of bilateral contacts under conditions of crisis.[18]

At the same time, the 1958 crisis generated problems *sui generis* that operated to impede serious bargaining. Above all, the crisis led rapidly to the development of incompatible commitments involving matters of prestige.[19] The Chinese Communists, as the initiators of the crisis, were committed to the achievement of at least some tangible gains from the crisis on several counts. They evidently hoped the crisis would undermine the arguments of their Soviet allies concerning the global strategic balance; they desired to utilize the crisis to force recognition of China's emergence as a great power at least in Asia; and, increasingly as the confrontation unfolded, the crisis became linked with domestic problems arising from the simultaneous promulgation of the Great Leap Forward.[20] The United States, on the other hand, found itself in a double bind with regard to the problem of prestige.[21] First,

[17] For additional comments on this subject see *infra* Chap. Twelve.

[18] On the differences between multilateral and bilateral contexts under conditions of crisis, see Oran R. Young, *The Intermediaries: Third Parties in International Crises* (Princeton: Princeton University Press, 1967), especially Chaps. 2 and 3.

[19] For an interesting discussion of these prestige problems, see James Reston, the *New York Times*, September 10, 1958, p. 9.

[20] This, however, is a very ambiguous problem in the context of the 1958 crisis. For additional comments on this subject, see *infra* Chap. Sixteen.

[21] For a particularly interesting formulation of this point, see *The Economist*, October 11, 1958, p. 116.

there was the problem of maintaining the credibility of American alliance commitments without losing too much goodwill among the nonaligned states. Second, the United States came under contradictory pressures from Asian allies afraid that a conciliatory response in this crisis would undermine the value of American guarantees in the future and from European allies afraid that a firm response would touch off major hostilities. Despite these competing pressures, however, the United States (with the support of the Chinese Nationalists) ultimately took a firm stand on the proposition that it would not negotiate any arrangements for the future of the offshore islands under duress.[22] So long as the CPR hoped to gain advantages through the use of violence against the islands, therefore, bargaining difficulties along these lines were apt to increase rather than decrease.

Within this framework of conflicting commitments of prestige, both the Chinese Communists and the Chinese Nationalists acted in ways that further reduced the scope for meaningful compromises with regard to the offshore islands. Increasingly as the crisis progressed, the CPR adopted a policy of insisting that the issues of the offshore islands and Taiwan itself were inseparable,[23] thereby minimizing the prospects for a reduction of international tension in the area through agreement on some form of internationalization for the offshore islands. In fact, the Chinese Communists were strongly opposed to an outcome of this kind, since it would tend to reduce their chances of reuniting China in the future.[24] For their part, the Nationalists supported this policy

[22] For the most part, the United States formulated its position on this issue in terms of the principle that resort to force and violence should not be accepted as a legitimate means of resolving political disputes. See, for example, Eisenhower's language on this point in his address to the nation on September 11, 1958. The text of the address is printed in *DOSB*, XXXIX, No. 1005 (September 29, 1958), 481-484. See especially p. 483.

[23] This was a marked shift from the public position of the CPR during the initial phase of the crisis. On the reasons for this tactical shift, see *infra* Chap. Fifteen.

[24] For a particularly interesting discussion of Chinese thinking along these lines, see Anna Louise Strong, "Chinese Strategy in the Taiwan Strait," *New Times*, No. 46, November 1958, pp. 8-11.

of insisting on the inseparability of Taiwan and the offshore islands. What is more, they proceeded to act in a fashion that emphasized and heightened both the difficulties and the dangers of withdrawal from the islands. And, in the face of this opposition, the United States proved unwilling to force the hand of the Nationalists, first, in connection with preparations for the Warsaw talks[25] and, later, with regard to the idea of thinning out Nationalist garrisons on the off-shore islands. Instead of attempting to focus on negotiable issues, therefore, both Chinas made strenuous efforts to bind the offshore islands to larger issues for which it was evident there were no workable compromises in 1958.

Finally, the recurrent Nationalist idea that a deliberate attempt to broaden the clash through a more active embroilment of the United States might constitute their best remaining hope for a return to the mainland operated as a barrier to serious bargaining on substantive issues between the United States and the CPR.[26] The United States did, in fact, succeed in controlling various Nationalist pressures that could have led to an escalation of overt hostilities during the crisis. Nevertheless, the contingent Nationalist threat to force an escalation of the overt hostilities provided the Nationalists with a workable veto with regard to many of the bargaining concessions the United States might have offered to the CPR.[27] Bargaining between the United States and the CPR, therefore, was impeded by the desire of the United States to avoid putting pressure on the Nationalists in ways that might lead them to exercise their veto power through dangerous physical actions as well as by the rather rigid posture of the CPR.[28]

[25] For information on this point consult Denis Warner, "What Are the Prospects for an Independent Formosa?," *The New Republic*, Vol. 139, No. 18 (November 3, 1958), 13.

[26] For a discussion of this point see Tang Tsou, "The Quemoy Imbroglio: Chiang Kai-shek and the United States," *Western Political Quarterly*, XXII, No. 4 (December 1959), especially 1,085.

[27] It would appear that this threat was more significant in terms of influence on the United States than the concomitant Nationalist threat to reach a political accommodation with the CPR. On the idea of a deal between the two Chinas, see *ibid.*, p. 1,082.

[28] A considerable part of the explanation of the clear-cut failure of the

Berlin, 1961

The influence of bargaining impediments was extensive in 1961, especially in determining the development of the negotiations question during the crisis. In the first instance, the dual nature of the 1961 crisis injected bargaining difficulties into the heart of the confrontation.[29] This duality occasionally opened up possibilities for bargaining tactics by allowing for a division of tactical initiatives and the utilization of trial commitments. On a more general basis, however, it posed serious rigidities. The control problems arising from each segment of the crisis exacerbated those arising from the other. Divergences among the bargaining requirements emanating from the various levels of the crisis made it difficult to formulate coordinated bargaining programs and to communicate them successfully. Above all, the situation posed serious rigidities for the great powers in particular, both because they found their hands forced by the momentum of events in the local arena on several important occasions and because the ultimate responsibility for regulating violence during the crisis devolved onto them despite the fact that they did not possess full control over the actions of some of the local actors.

A somewhat related bargaining impediment in this crisis arose from the continuing link between the specific problem of Berlin and the broader German question. Any clear-cut alteration of the political status of Berlin is apt to have such an extensive impact on the whole German question, at least in symbolic terms, that it is impossible to compartmentalize Berlin from its broader political setting. The intractability of the political problems of central Europe, therefore, almost inevitably operate as bargaining impediments in any dealings concerning Berlin. In 1961, this political link was used

Sino-American talks in Warsaw lies in the peculiarities of this triangular relationship involving the Nationalists, the Communist Chinese, and the Americans.

[29] For a particularly interesting discussion of the dual nature of the 1961 crisis, see Philip Windsor, *City on Leave* (New York: Praeger, 1963), p. 221.

by the Western powers as the basis of tactical efforts to demonstrate the credibility of their commitment to Berlin, but these actions only made the barriers to serious bargaining on Berlin during this crisis more stark. As George Bailey wrote in 1962, "while the allied commitment to Berlin is general, the Communist threats to Berlin are set forth in particulars."[30] As a result, the parties tended to develop their bargaining programs at differing levels of generality, and severe impediments arose with regard to both effective communication and tactical asymmetries or irrelevancies.

These bargaining problems were further aggravated during the 1961 crisis by the fundamental quality of the clash on the issues and the consequent paucity of negotiable subjects.[31] As the American commentator Richard Rovere put it, "There were few changes in the status quo to which we would consent, and it was hard to see what the Soviet Union would give us in exchange for any concessions we might make."[32] The resultant rigidities only became more severe in the aftermath of August 13 as the straightforward East-West aspects of the clash became more prominent and the *de facto* bargaining cushion provided by the existence of intermediate problems disappeared.[33] For all these reasons, bargaining efforts during this crisis tended to acquire the inflexibilities of a campaign designed to force the ratification of one side's demands in contrast to the negotiating behavior characteristic of a genuine search for accommodation. These rigid postures were insistently maintained during the 1961 crisis until the course of events on the ground produced a new relationship of forces (by mid-

[30] George Bailey, "The Gentle Erosion of Berlin," *The Reporter*, Vol. 26, No. 9 (April 26, 1962), 18.

[31] For a discussion of this subject see the *New York Times*, August 27, 1961, Sect. IV, p. 1.

[32] Richard Rovere, "Letter from Washington," *The New Yorker*, September 2, 1961, p. 68.

[33] In a certain sense, the existence of the internal crisis of the GDR and the concrete bargaining problems it engendered served to deemphasize the sharpness of the direct East-West clash over Berlin and the whole German problem during 1961. This bargaining cushion was always circumscribed in its operation, but the whole effect receded quite rapidly in the aftermath of August 13, as the internal crisis of the GDR quickly began to dissipate.

September) which made it virtually impossible to shift to policies aimed at achieving even limited accommodation with any hope of success.[34]

Several sets of tactical impediments exacerbated these basic difficulties during the Berlin crisis of 1961. To begin with, problems of resolve and political prestige played a significant role. During the upswing phase of the crisis, from June until early August, each side strove to make its position credible in ways that tightened the bonds of mutual commitment and generated powerful needs to achieve at least symbolic victory in Berlin. Several additional factors complicated the problem of achieving decommitment in this crisis. The clarity and directness of the actual confrontation made it difficult to handle either by avoidance or by glossing over the clash with ambiguous solutions or substitute arrangements. In addition, the existence of pervasive fears—especially among the Western leaders who were concerned with the problem of projecting an image of defensive credibility—that indications of a willingness to negotiate under pressure or to make concessions would be taken as a sign of weakness blocked the initiation of steps which could have led to decommitment together with a face-saving termination arrangement.[35]

Tactical difficulties also arose during the 1961 crisis from a sharp tendency for assessments of relative bargaining advantages to fluctuate as the crisis unfolded. Among the factors at work in this connection were: the countervailing hopes of each side to initiate serious negotiations at the point of maximum advantage for itself; the frequently inconsistent impact of the different segments of the crisis on these calculations concerning advantages; and the rapidity with which assessments concerning relative bargaining advantages shifted from

[34] This was true even though during September there were verbal indications on both sides of a desire to achieve some sort of political accommodation with regard to Berlin.

[35] Fears of this kind were especially prominent among American decision-makers. American concern with the credibility problem in the 1961 crisis was exacerbated by the insecurity of leading members of the Kennedy Administration arising from the difficulties associated with Cuba, Laos, and Vienna during the spring. For further comments on this concern with the credibility problem, see *supra* Chap. Eight.

one phase of the crisis to the next. Both sides consequently remained wary of any shift from tacit to explicit forms of bargaining throughout the crisis. Each side thus found itself on several occasions in the position of publicly proclaiming a desire to negotiate while dragging its feet in the hopes the balance of bargaining advantages would shift favorably in the near future. A situation never developed in which all the parties simultaneously believed they had more to gain than to lose from the initiation of explicit negotiations.

Finally, the existence of severe coordination problems within each alliance system during the 1961 crisis obscured and confused the development of bargaining relationships between the sides by breaking their continuity. While these problems within the alliances clearly created possibilities for tactical manipulation, they also constituted an important factor in the development of bargaining impediments affecting the termination of the crisis. On the Eastern side, the most important divergences were those involving the German Democratic Republic (GDR) and the Soviet Union.[36] In general, the GDR was anxious to achieve a quick solution for its internal crisis while the Soviet Union frequently desired to play for time in the hopes of improving its bargaining position in the East-West clash—even at the expense of the GDR.

Among the Western powers, on the other hand, the situation was even more confused.[37] Throughout the crisis policy disagreements among these states continued with Britain at one pole, generally pushing for explicit negotiations even at the price of substantial concessions, and France at the other pole, opposing negotiations and calling for a firm stand on the assumption the Soviet Union would ultimately back down from its tactical offensive. At the same time, impending elections in West Germany produced rigidities in the bargaining position of the Federal Republic which made its ultimate espousal of negotiations, but on the basis of virtually impossible condi-

[36] For some interesting comments on these divergences, see Windsor, *op.cit.*, pp. 238-240.

[37] Jean Smith's account, for example, emphasizes the importance of these factors at a number of points. See Jean Edward Smith, *The Defense of Berlin* (Baltimore: The Johns Hopkins Press, 1963), especially Chaps. 12 and 13.

tions, highly predictable. As a result, the United States was left to occupy an uneasy middle position, trying to meld the often contradictory requirements of demonstrating resolve while appearing conciliatory into a meaningful bargaining position—an achievement made all the more difficult by the existence within the American government of diverging schools of thought concerning the crisis whose disagreements were sharp and whose influence fluctuated considerably during the course of the crisis.[38] As a consequence of these problems of coordination, bargaining between the opposing sides during the 1961 crisis frequently took on a disorganized quality. There were times when bargaining between the opposing sides was almost literally suspended while efforts were made to iron out internal problems. Under the circumstances, bargaining positions frequently appeared to shift more *in response* to the unfolding course of events than on the basis of conscious efforts to shape the course of events.

Cuba, 1962

Several sets of bargaining impediments became prominent during the Cuban crisis of 1962, and the overall impact of these impediments was clearly significant. Perhaps the most striking conclusion to be drawn from an analysis of the bargaining impediments in this case, however, is that high-level decision-makers were explicitly aware of the resultant problems and for the most part succeeded in handling them skillfully during the actual period of crisis.

The most serious bargaining problems of the Cuban missile crisis emanated from the process of mutual misperception and miscalculation which led the United States and the Soviet Union into rigid postures of simultaneous commitment with regard to a specific and highly visible point of confrontation. In general, this process is apt to occur from time to time when several parties engage in a relationship characterized by constant maneuvering for relative advantages, the lack of complete information concerning the motivations and expectations of opposing parties, and the presence of a physical environ-

[38] For a discussion of the fluctuating groupings among American decision-makers, consult *ibid.*, pp. 294-297.

ment necessitating interdependent decision-making. In the case at hand, opposing commitments developed obscurely but rapidly became frozen with the American discovery on October 15 of the Soviet move to deploy offensive missiles in Cuba. By the time each side became fully aware of the extent of the other's commitments in the area, it was too late to avoid a major confrontation. And the crisis quickly acquired a built-in rigidity that made the situation like "a rope with a knot in the middle, with President Kennedy pulling on one end and Khrushchev pulling on the other. The more they both pulled, the more the knot would tighten."[39]

Without consciously desiring it, therefore, each side found itself in a position where its prestige was deeply committed in the eyes of the world. The Cuban crisis became a symbolic test of the initiative of the Soviet Union in the international arena and of its ability to carry forward its self-proclaimed struggle against "imperialism."[40] For this reason, "The crisis was one which involved the prestige of the Soviet Union in the eyes of Asia, Africa and Latin America."[41] From the American point of view, on the other hand, the confrontation became both a challenge to the dominant position of the United States in a traditional sphere of influence and a symbolic test of the country's ability to maintain its relative strength in the underlying East-West conflict of the postwar period. The problem of finding a formula for disengagement from the direct confrontation over Cuba without excessive loss of face by either side, therefore, was an extremely difficult one in the 1962 crisis; and the task was further complicated by the spotlight of world attention, which was directed with great intensity on the crisis.

Toward the end of the crisis, as the strength of American determination and the superiority of the military force which

---

[39] The quotation is from Roger Hilsman, "The Cuban Crisis: How Close We Were to War," *Look*, Vol. 28, No. 17 (August 25, 1964), 20. The metaphor of two men pulling on a knotted rope was Khrushchev's.

[40] At the same time, the developments leading up to the 1962 crisis are particularly interesting as an example of the Castro Government's ability to get the Soviet Union committed to the defense of Cuba.

[41] J. W. Burton, *International Relations: A General Theory* (London: Cambridge University Press, 1965), p. 254.

the United States could bring to bear in the Caribbean began to undermine the Soviet position, the bargaining impediments associated with the crisis began to shift increasingly toward the problem of finding a way for the Soviet Union to back down in the face of direct public threats without having to acknowledge its weakness in an intolerably humiliating fashion.[42] Though this problem became a severe one in the Cuban crisis, clear-cut American efforts to preserve options for the Soviets and to allow them an opportunity to retreat relatively gracefully played an important role in providing the Soviets a chance to minimize their public embarrassment.[43] Similarly, Kennedy's policy of avoiding official claims of victory for the United States reduced the rigidities of the situation by assisting the Soviet effort to save face.[44] While American actions were therefore of critical importance in bringing the relationship of mutual commitment with regard to Cuba to a head, the activities of the American Administration also were significant in facilitating the process of decommitment at the end of the crisis.[45]

The 1962 crisis also generated considerable concern about tactical impediments relating to communications problems. Especially during the week of October 22, a widespread sense of urgency led decision-makers to worry about delays in the transmission of messages. Ambiguities such as those surrounding the Soviet letters that reached Washington on October 26 and 27 constituted a potential source of serious misunderstandings and confusion.[46] In an apparent reference to these difficulties, Kennedy himself later emphasized "the dangerous de-

[42] On this subject see Kennedy's American University speech of June 10, 1963. The text of the speech is printed in DOSB, XLIX, No. 1253 (July 1, 1963), 2-6.

[43] For some interesting material on this point, see Theodore Sorensen, Kennedy (New York: Harper and Row, 1965), p. 694.

[44] This important element in the American approach to the later phases of the crisis is discussed in ibid., p. 717.

[45] In fact, a good case can be made that it is the delicate balance of these elements of commitment and facilitation which constitutes the real indicator of skill in the American handling of the 1962 crisis.

[46] It is still not clear, for example, which of these letters was actually composed first in Moscow.

lays, misunderstandings, and misreadings of the other's actions which might occur at a time of crisis."[47] Despite these problems, however, the missile crisis was in fact a striking communications success. While it is true the crisis generated communications problems and relevant leaders were forced to utilize modes of communication that would have been extremely unusual in a non-crisis environment, a more remarkable characteristic of actual period of crisis, especially in contrast with the pre-crisis period, was the relative absence of the problems spelled out by Kennedy.

One communications problem that did prove insoluble during the 1962 crisis arose from the sharp decline in utility of normal channels of diplomatic contact. As soon as the crisis devolved into a public confrontation, both sides began to employ these channels primarily for rhetorical debate and efforts to characterize the clash in black-and-white terms. In the course of these efforts, the parties frequently discarded the usual diplomatic forms, thereby minimizing the opportunities for bargaining arising from the ambiguities and nuances that generally characterize diplomatic exchanges. This problem was particularly evident at the United Nations where the Security Council meetings of October 23, 24, and 25 devolved into relatively useless public displays. But it also hampered the state-to-state channels of bilateral diplomacy. The personal Kennedy-Khrushchev exchanges hence acquired considerable importance as a means of circumventing the bargaining impediment arising from the degeneration of the normal diplomatic channels.

Finally, the missile crisis aroused widespread fears about several potential bargaining impediments that in fact never materialized. There was general concern that one or more naval incidents arising from the blockade might destroy all chances for constructive bargaining. As U Thant put it in his letter to Khrushchev on October 25, "What concerns me most is that such a confrontation and subsequent aggravation of the situation would destroy any possibility of the discussions I have

[47] This statement is from Kennedy's American University speech, *op.cit.*, p. 5.

suggested as a prelude to negotiations on a peaceful settlement."[48] The preparations that the United States was making for a military strike against Cuba, together with the possibility that the Soviets might delay too long in giving in on the question of offensive missiles, caused broad concern about uncontrollable "compulsions" which might somehow force the hands of the superpowers.[49] Fear that a genuine dilemma along these lines might arise appears to have become extensive, especially during the tense hours of October 27.[50] As Arthur Schlesinger has put it, "The compulsions opened up the appalling world of inexorability."[51]

Conclusion

It is sometimes argued that there is a major distinction between international clashes caused by bargaining problems such as misunderstandings, ignorance, or confusion and disputes attributable to more fundamental conflicts. This point is often emphasized in analyses of conflict resolution since clashes of the first type would seem, *a priori*, to offer particularly interesting opportunities for the utilization of various international settlement procedures. The case materials analyzed in this chapter, however, suggest that, at least with regard to crises involving the major powers, bargaining impediments and underlying patterns of substantive conflict tend to develop in conjunction with each other rather than as alternatives. In fact, several of the cases indicate that one of the peculiar problems of crises is their tendency to produce processes of mutual stimulation between substantive conflicts and bargaining impediments. Efforts to achieve termination by emphasizing the distinction between the two types of problem, therefore, are apt to end in frustration.

More specifically, the case materials indicate that the prob-

[48] The text of this letter is printed in Henry Pachter, *Collision Course* (New York: Praeger, 1963), p. 212.

[49] Schlesinger, for example, cites himself as having conceptualized the problem in these terms at the time. See Arthur Schlesinger Jr., *A Thousand Days* (Boston: Houghton Mifflin, 1965), p. 830.

[50] For verification of this point see Elie Abel, *The Missile Crisis* (Philadelphia: Lippincott, 1966), pp. 185-200.

[51] Schlesinger, *op.cit.*, p. 830.

lem of bargaining impediments is related to time factors. Interestingly, though concern with time pressures or shortages was sometimes evident, this factor does not appear to have been a major determinant of the development of bargaining impediments. Several other time factors, however, deserve mention. Crises generally emerge as periods of rapid fluctuation in calculations concerning bargaining advantages. As a result, there is apt to be considerable volatility in the assessments and expectations of the parties concerning relative advantages, a phenomenon which makes it difficult to reach agreement on termination arrangements at any given point in time. In addition, hopes concerning bargaining advantages that may accrue from the sheer passage of time frequently become prominent during crises. In any specific phase of a crisis, therefore, one side or the other may well be satisfied with a prolongation of the confrontation. The case materials suggest, moreover, that sheer prolongation of a crisis often produces rigidities and bargaining impediments regardless of the desires of the parties. The key point here is that positions generally become harder to relinquish as they become invested with emotional commitment and as they are subjected to greater publicity over time.

Bargaining impediments during crises are closely linked to the development of symbolic associations. As the analysis of Chapter Four suggests, crises tend to become focal points for a wide range of international concerns and expectations and therefore to acquire perceived significance for various broader issues. As a result, a crisis is apt to become a symbolic "test of strength" which cannot easily be dealt with in isolation or in terms of its own merits alone. On the contrary, crises frequently call into question alliance commitments, the prestige or political momentum of various actors in the international system, the prevailing rules of the game in international politics, and existing procedures for the management of power. Participants in a crisis, therefore, are often acutely sensitive to indirect or additional consequences of the clash, a posture that often hampers forthright efforts to settle the specific issues underlying the proximate point of confrontation.

A series of related difficulties, which might loosely be labeled tactical problems, appear repeatedly in the case materials as causes of bargaining impediments. Crises, by their very nature, produce points of confrontation characterized by specificity, clarity, and visibility. The resultant clashes are therefore almost inevitably direct ones. For this reason, a number of common techniques of dealing with conflict by means of avoidance, ambiguous agreements, or efforts at routinization are not likely to be applicable under conditions of crisis. Crisis bargaining, in addition, is frequently marked by sharp divergences between the demands of credible commitments and the requirements of efforts to facilitate a nonviolent termination. In short, rigidities tend to arise from a perceived conflict between efforts to project images of resolve and determination and efforts to create a conciliatory environment. Divergences of this kind sometimes add confusion to the bargaining picture by dividing decision-makers on each side into several distinct groupings whose influence is apt to fluctuate in such a way as to produce ambiguities and inconsistencies. Furthermore, crises are frequently characterized by coordination problems among allies on each side which make meaningful bargaining between the sides extraordinarily difficult. While disagreements among allies can often be allowed to ride during non-crisis periods, crises tend to crystallize alliance problems both because they require action rather than mere verbal acquiescence and because they are apt to provide concrete evidence for the competing theses of the various groups within an alliance.[52]

Impediments of this kind tend to be even more influential in complex crises, such as the Taiwan Strait in 1958 and Berlin in 1961, than in relatively straightforward clashes between two more or less unified sides. The very multiplicity of distinguishable interests in complex crises is apt to produce influential sources of ambiguity and confusion. Such cases tend to emphasize conflicts of interest between parties on the same side as well as between the sides. The demands of the local situation may diverge from those of the more general confrontation as

[52] Since crises are by nature relatively complex and multifaceted phenomena, it is generally possible to interpret any given case in a variety of ways. This is especially true when the interpreters view a given case with predispositions toward particular conclusions. As a result, various groups may, at one and the same time, find support for competing theses in the events surrounding a specific crisis.

in the Berlin crisis of 1961. And divergences of interests may generate at least perceived possibilities of deals between individual parties across the principal axis of confrontation as was the case in the Taiwan Strait crisis of 1958. Complexities of this kind undoubtedly increase the scope for unilateral efforts to engage in manipulative bargaining under conditions of crisis. At the same time, however, they tend to exacerbate bargaining impediments barring the way to serious efforts to deal with the underlying issues at stake in a given confrontation.

11. The Relevance of Salience

HYPOTHESIS. The influence of salience as a principle of coordination will rise with the onset of a crisis.

Salience refers to those qualities of a bargaining relationship which exert influence toward the coordination of perceptions and expectations between the parties, especially in the absence of explicit negotiations.[1] Iklé captures the essential element of this notion in his statement that "Among the many alternatives . . . there are often a few which seem particularly prominent to the parties. These focal points are like a notch where a compromise might converge, a resting place where rising demands might come to a halt, or a barrier over which an initial proposal cannot be budged."[2] Salience therefore stems from situational qualities that shape the perceptions and expectations of relevant actors in ways affecting their behavior patterns. Salience is generally conditioned by a variety of cultural conditions and its influence is sometimes open to manipulation or structuring on the part of interested parties. Nevertheless, salience often plays a significant role in efforts to deal with problems of conflict in international politics.

In this context there is reason to argue that salience is likely to be particularly influential under conditions of crisis. Owing to the impact of bargaining impediments and problems of communication, explicit negotiations are frequently either absent or of little utility during the critical phases of international crises. Crises generate both real and perceived problems of control that make the parties anxious to coordinate at least on the development of minimal rules of the game for their encounter even when it is difficult to do so on an explicit basis. Crises, at least among the great powers, generally produce influential fears concerning the dangers of large-scale destruction, a situation tending to reduce the propensities of decision-

[1] For an extensive conceptualization of the notion of salience, consult Thomas Schelling, *The Strategy of Conflict* (Cambridge: Harvard University Press, 1960), Chaps. 2-4.

[2] Fred Iklé, *How Nations Negotiate* (New York: Harper and Row, 1964), p. 213.

makers to utilize risky tactics even in the interests of maximizing potential gains. As a result, decision-makers operating under conditions of crisis are apt to be influenced by cautionary incentives in ways that make them more sensitive to the sway of considerations of salience than would be so were they more inclined to gamble on risky postures.

If this hypothesized relationship between conditions of crisis and the relevance of salience is valid, it would indicate the existence of a significant limitation on the employment of strategic bargaining during crises. The influence of salience generally stems from factors such as naturalness, simplicity, uniqueness, recognizability, tradition, and precedent. And while it is quite possible to alter perceptions based on such factors over time, it is usually quite difficult to do so within the relatively short duration of a given crisis. For this reason, a strikingly salient termination principle or instrumental norm may remain highly visible and relatively unambiguous throughout a crisis despite the effects of tactical efforts at manipulation. Moreover, this line of reasoning suggests that when bargaining activities do affect the bases of salience during a crisis, they are more likely to obscure salient relationships and generate new ambiguities than to lend salience to new principles of coordination or substantive arrangements.

Berlin, 1948-1949

While a number of analysts have discussed the phenomenon of salience in abstract terms, little effort has so far been made to apply the notion to empirical cases in international politics in a systematic rather than illustrative fashion.[3] Analysis of the Berlin crisis of 1948-1949 from the perspective of salience indicates that salience is not a critical determinant of certain important types of international situation, and that some additional conceptualization is needed in applying the notion of salience to cases of international crisis. In particular, it is important to distinguish between substantive solutions or termination arrangements and instrumental rules of the game in ana-

[3] For some interesting points on the relationship between abstract conceptualization and empirical analysis in this area see Thomas Schelling, *Arms and Influence* (New Haven: Yale University Press, 1966), p. vii.

lyzing the relevance of salience under conditions of crisis.

Although the abstract notion of salience has appeared most frequently in connection with substantive problems, the phenomenon was largely irrelevant in these terms during the Berlin blockade since there were no highly salient points or relationships around which pressure for a settlement could coalesce. Moreover, there is little evidence to suggest that decision-makers on either side were extensively influenced by concepts of this kind in their efforts to bargain over Berlin. To a significant extent, the pressure point in Berlin was only a tactical device for getting at the broader problems of Germany and central Europe.[4] The specific contentious issues relating to Berlin were therefore essentially instrumental problems in relation to these broader issues. Also, several of the specific issues of the blockade were commonly perceived in "all or nothing" terms and so were not easily divisible. This was the case with regard to the rights of the Western powers to maintain a presence in the city and with regard to the right of access to Berlin across the eastern zone of Germany. In addition, the circumstances of German defeat and the occupation of Germany had disrupted prior political patterns so extensively that there were no natural, unique or historically sanctioned principles of division obviously relevant to Berlin in 1948.

Under the circumstances, the factors that ultimately determined the termination of the blockade had little to do with perceptions of salience. Eventually, the clash settled into a contest between two opposing bargaining programs. As it happened, the Western position gradually emerged as the stronger not only because of the airlift proved viable in a proximate sense but also because it provided time during which a number of favorable changes in the underlying political context occurred.[5] The termination of the blockade in May 1949 essentially registered important changes in the bargaining positions of the two sides which were factually evident and did not require notions of salience for their formulation.

There was, nevertheless, another set of problems in which

[4] On the links between Berlin and the broader problems of Germany, see *supra* Chap. Eight.

[5] This point is also discussed at greater length in *ibid.*

notions of salience did acquire some relevance during the Berlin crisis of 1948-1949. These problems dealt with the rules of the game on the basis of which the crisis would be conducted in contrast to substantive arrangements for its termination.[6] Interestingly, both sides demonstrated considerable *de facto* concern in coordinating on the development of rules even while adopting relatively rigid postures on the substantive issues. The critical focus for the influence of salience on these instrumental problems during the Berlin blockade was the distinction between coercion and overt violence rather than between persuasion and coercion. A wide range of coercive practices involving East-West contact was sanctioned during the blockade, a development somewhat new at the time but that has since become an accepted norm. The blockade itself, various strong-arm tactics within Berlin, and the utilization of military forces in the airlift, for example, were all conscious applications of organized coercion on a significant scale.

At the same time, both sides went to considerable lengths to coordinate on the development of a norm proscribing direct East-West violence. The Western powers ultimately rejected the idea of breaking the blockade by means of an armed convoy on the basis of reasoning along these lines.[7] The Soviets for their part were careful to restrict interference with Western planes in the air corridors despite the availability of several techniques of interference.[8] And both sides were extremely cautious with regard to any utilization of their garrisons in Berlin which might catalyze overt hostilities. It is a remarkable fact, for example, that the only military casualties during the whole crisis were those resulting from the very early air disaster at Gatow on April 5 and from unambiguous accidents

[6] Interest in this distinction between rules of the game and substantive issues has generally been clearest in the literature on arms control. For examples of such thinking, consult Donald Brennan, ed., *Arms Control, Disarmament, and National Security* (New York: George Braziller, 1961); and Thomas Schelling and Morton Halperin, *Strategy and Arms Control* (New York: Twentieth Century Fund, 1961).

[7] For discussions of this decision see Robert Murphy, *Diplomat Among Warriors* (New York: Pyramid, 1965), p. 354; and Manuel Gottlieb, *The German Peace Settlement and the Berlin Crisis* (New York: Paine-Whitman, 1950), p. 199.

[8] For additional material on this subject, see *infra* Chap. Thirteen.

related to the airlift.[9] In the upshot, the coercion-violence distinction not only achieved considerable salience during the 1948-1949 crisis, it also developed during the course of this crisis into an operative norm that has subsequently had a substantial influence on the quality of East-West interactions on a more general basis.

Taiwan Strait, 1958

Attitudes and positions arising from perceptions of salience were quite evident during the 1958 crisis in the Taiwan Strait. As in other cases, however, the impact of these perceptions was noticeably greater in shaping instrumental rules than in determining substantive arrangements for the termination of the crisis. This uneven pattern of influence emerges clearly from an analysis of the principal problems to which the phenomenon of salience became relevant in the course of the crisis.

Salience played a role in shaping perceptions with regard to at least two sets of substantive problems. In the first instance, considerable support arose for the idea that, regardless of the political details of the crisis at hand, certain geopolitical links between the offshore islands and the Chinese mainland made their separation unnatural. Various explanations were offered in support of this feeling including: (1) the physical proximity of the islands and the mainland, (2) the fact that control of the islands by a hostile power could lead to an effective closure of the important mainland harbors at Amoy and Foochow,[10] (3) the idea that the offshore islands were critical to the mainland for security reasons,[11] and (4) the perceptual

[9] The airlift itself compiled a commendable safety record even by civilian standards. Max Charles sets the figure for deaths in connection with the airlift at fifty-four (*Berlin Blockade* [London: Wingate, 1959], p. 138). W. Phillips Davison, on the other hand, records the figure of forty-eight (*The Berlin Blockade: A Study in Cold War Politics* [Princeton: Princeton University Press 1958], p. 273).

[10] In fact, the Chinese Nationalists had effectively closed the ports of Amoy and Foochow over the years. Interestingly, the Nationalists had relaxed their stand on this issue during the early months of 1958, only a few months prior to the initiation of the 1958 probe by the Chinese Communists.

[11] This issue of security was discussed in several American journals in terms of a hypothetical analogy with the problems that would arise for the United States if Long Island were controlled by a hostile power.

notion that the mainland and the offshore islands (not including Taiwan) formed a natural unity. Soviet journals expounded such views clearly.[12] Nehru enunciated a position based on feelings of this kind. Several highly respected liberal journals in the United States, such as *The New Republic*, developed positions of a similar kind.[13] And *The Economist* spoke of the offshore islands "which most people in the world, including most of America's allies, think belong self-evidently to the mainland."[14] Views along these lines were therefore widespread. They constituted, at least tacitly, a common underpinning for the widely held position in the West that the islands simply were not important enough to risk a major fight. Given this background, it is important to emphasize that considerations of salience were ultimately outweighed by other factors in determining the disposition of the offshore islands during the 1958 crisis. In short, the opposing adamancy of the Chinese Nationalists, coupled with an American unwillingness to force the hand of the Nationalists,[15] proved more influential than the force of salience in this case.[16]

During the later phases of the crisis the Chinese People's Republic (CPR) devoted increasing efforts to a campaign aimed at portraying the clash in the Strait solely as an aspect of civil strife in which American activities amounted to unjustifiable external intervention. In this connection, the CPR attempted to generate salience for an interpretation of the basic nature of the situation which would lead to the conclusion that there was, in fact, no conflict between China and the United States and that American activities therefore amounted to gratuitous and unacceptable interference in a genuine civil

[12] For an interesting example see L. Sedin, "Absurdities of American Policy," *New Times*, No. 38, September 1958, pp. 12-14, especially p. 13.

[13] For an example see the editorial in *The New Republic*, Vol. 139, No. 12 (September 22, 1958), 3-4.

[14] *The Economist*, September 20, 1958, p. 935.

[15] On this subject see O. Edmund Clubb, "Chiang's Shadow over Warsaw," *The Reporter*, Vol. 19, No. 5 (October 2, 1958), 16-17, as well as the discussion in *infra* Chap. Twelve.

[16] In the face of an unyielding political posture backed by substantial physical capabilities, the salience of a particular substantive alternative did *not* become a highly influential factor in determining the actual course of the confrontation.

271

war.[17] This campaign, however, never achieved the desired impact on world opinion for several reasons. To begin with, it was quite clear that the crisis in the Strait had dangerous international implications and that it was therefore a matter of concern to the international community regardless of its *origin*. But above all, it was evident that these arguments constituted a tactical move initiated by the CPR during a relatively late phase of the crisis. In fact, only when its prior physical initiatives had failed to produce the desired results did the CPR turn to these arguments during September, in the hope of salvaging some tangible gains from the crisis through political maneuvering.

The impact of salience on the formulation of instrumental rules, on the other hand, was more substantial during the 1958 crisis. In this context, salience was influential primarily in efforts to formulate restrictions on the utilization of overt violence. The general norm of the cold war, calling for the avoidance of violent contact between forces owned *and* operated by by the United States and the Soviet Union, was clearly in evidence during the 1958 crisis.[18] Owing to various geopolitical factors underlying the crisis, the burden of avoidance in this instance fell primarily on the Soviet Union. The Soviets shouldered this burden both in terms of their general posture and, more specifically, in terms of their policy of avoiding any military preparations or troop mobilizations that would have appeared as efforts to influence the course of the clash in the Strait. The manifestation of this norm of avoidance was particularly interesting in this case because of the clarity and explicitness with which direct Soviet-American contact was distinguished from clashes between proxies or clients employing a wide range of Soviet and American military equipment. Just as evident as the circumspection of the two superpowers toward each other during the 1958 crisis, for example, was the prominence of the air battles between the two Chinas based

---

[17] For an interesting discussion of this position from the Soviet point of view, see M. Sturua, "The Warsaw Talks," *New Times*, No. 40, October 1958, pp. 11-13.

[18] On the development of this norm more generally, consult Morton Halperin, *Limited War in the Nuclear Age* (New York: John Wiley, 1963), pp. 36-37.

largely on a confrontation between American-built F-86s and Soviet-built MIG-17s.[19]

In addition to this rule affecting Soviet-American relations, the 1958 crisis also witnessed the emergence of a salient, though somewhat more complex, norm calling for the avoidance of violent clashes between American and Chinese Communist forces.[20] Successful implementation of this norm posed some delicate problems in 1958, both because force was in fact employed violently (as between the two Chinas) and because the crisis ultimately pitted American and Chinese Communist forces against each other in a coercive and highly interdependent (though nonviolent) fashion.[21] The CPR, nevertheless, was particularly anxious to establish a pattern of nonviolent interaction with American forces because Chinese Communist bargaining strength was *relatively* greater at this level and because violent contacts would produce serious dangers of escalatory sequences that might prove highly destructive to the interests of the CPR. As Robert W. Barnett has put it, the CPR "operation was timed to cause maximum political uproar and was fought with restraint designed to run minimum risk of direct military involvement with United States forces."[22] As it happened, the United States proved willing to support the development of this norm because the dangers of escalatory sequences could involve the Soviet Union in the crisis directly and because it was able to achieve its minimum objectives at lower levels of coercion. The United States therefore cooperated in a program of avoiding Sino-American violence by: exercising considerable control over Chinese Nationalist actions

[19] For a discussion of the importance of these air battles for the course of the whole crisis, see *infra* Chap. Thirteen.

[20] It is especially important in this connection to keep in mind the distinction between coercion in general and specific coercive actions involving violence. During the 1958 crisis, Sino-American relations became highly coercive, but they remained nonviolent throughout the crisis.

[21] The development of this norm in Sino-American relations during the 1958 crisis is even more striking when the background of violent interactions between the two powers in Korea is taken into account. The 1958 probe was initiated little more than five years after the termination of overt hostilities in Korea.

[22] "Quemoy: The Use and Consequence of Nuclear Deterrence," Harvard Center for International Affairs, March 1960, pp. 17-18.

273

that could have catalyzed American involvement in the crisis on a violent basis, and carefully orchestrating the deployment of its own forces in order to minimize the chances of inadvertent Sino-American violence and to maintain the opportunity for the CPR to avoid the initiation of this pattern of hostilities.

Berlin, 1961

Considerations of salience played a circumscribed, though not inconsequential, role during the Berlin crisis of 1961. The fact that the principal participants did not, for the most part, conceptualize the central issues of the crisis in terms of perceptions of salience hampered the operation of this principle of coordination. And in general, the sharpness of the clash over well-defined issues relating specifically to Berlin tended throughout the crisis to emphasize rigidities emanating from conflicting interests rather than possibilities for coordination arising from mutual interests.

With regard to the substantive issues of the crisis, the influence of salience was relevant primarily in the development and implementation during August of a tacit East-West consensus on the necessity of closing the sector boundary in Berlin. During the summer of 1961, it became increasingly apparent that the chances of large-scale and dangerous upheavals within the German Democratic Republic (GDR) were becoming substantial in the absence of arrangements to control the growing exodus of refugees through Berlin. A series of lesser steps to accomplish this objective, carried out during July and the early days of August, were demonstrably inadequate.[23] Under the circumstances, therefore, "The dangers of escalation posed by the continuing refugee exodus required that the East Berlin sector border be sealed."[24] At this point, both East and West coordinated on a tacit but remarkably efficient basis to permit the GDR to achieve this end, despite the fact they were in the midst of a broader and more general confrontation

[23] For a discussion of this point see George Bailey, "Dead End at the Brandenburg Gate," *The Reporter*, Vol. 25, No. 4 (September 14, 1961), 24-25, especially 25.

[24] Jean Edward Smith, "Berlin Confrontation," *The Virginia Quarterly Review*, Vol. 42, No. 3 (Summer 1966), 364.

in Europe. Interestingly, while the closure of the sector boundary seemed inescapable, East-West coordination on this issue had serious disadvantages for both the Soviet Union and the Western powers. Though the drawbacks for the Western powers were more tangible and perhaps ultimately more serious, the negative impact of the events surrounding August 13 on the Soviet bargaining position was far-reaching.[25] Despite these disadvantages, both sides accepted the closing of the sector boundary as the only realistic alternative in a situation perceived as being fraught with grave risks and dangers.

With the exception of this relatively short hiatus during August, salience played only a minor role in the disposition of the substantive issues of the 1961 crisis. Several factors appear to have contributed to this result. The lines of confrontation in this crisis were drawn in such a way that many of the central issues were perceived as essentially dichotomous. As a result, there appeared to be little middle ground in which to formulate acceptable solutions. The long-standing and rigid quality of opposing commitments on many of the key substantive issues[26] sharply reduced the scope for the play of perceptual factors affecting salience. Major divergences in assessments concerning the probable distribution of gains and losses from various alternative outcomes on many specific issues made it difficult to crystallize the components of any given termination arrangement, let alone to portray them in ways that would emphasize their salience. This lack of agreement on assessments of gains and losses stemmed from: the critical influence of implementation processes on final outcomes for many issues; the contingent and unpredictable nature of many factors affecting the Berlin situation; and the interconnectedness of many of the specific issues involved in the Berlin and German problems.

Considerations of salience also played a highly important, though restricted, role in shaping perceptions concerning rules

[25] For further discussion of the consequences of the events surrounding August 13, see *supra* Chap. Eight.

[26] With regard to East-West relations, the principal issues of the 1961 crisis were very similar to those that had arisen in the 1958-1959 period. In particular, the Soviet *aide-mémoire* of June 4, 1961, was strikingly reminiscent of the Soviet "ultimatum" of November 27, 1958.

of conduct during the 1961 crisis. Though this crisis was characterized by serious problems of mutual understanding, both sides were clearly concerned with the dangers that would result from overt East-West hostilities and with the difficulties of maintaining control over a highly interdependent situation in the absence of at least minimal rules. As a result, interest in instrumental norms became quite strong, especially with regard to the distinction between coercion in general and overt violence.

More specifically, several relatively concrete rules of an instrumental nature flowed from this basic pattern of concerns during the 1961 crisis. Both parties consciously sought to avoid direct confrontations of organized Soviet and Western military units in situations where violence might break out inadvertently.[27] Each side therefore relied extensively on proxy forces. During the period surrounding August 13, for example, the Soviets sanctioned the use of GDR forces rather than Soviet military contingents in Berlin itself, though this technically constituted a violation of the occupation statutes.[28] The Western powers relied heavily on West Berlin police to maintain order along the sector boundary so that Western military contingents could be kept safely away from the boundary while the perceived dangers of overt clashes remained high. Moreover, during the most dangerous phases of the crisis, both sides took considerable pains to signal limits on their behavior to the opponent and to avoid dangerous incidents. The Eastern side, for example, went to great lengths to emphasize its intention to decouple the question of the sector boundary in Berlin and the problem of the access routes across the territory of the GDR during the week of August 13.[29] And both sides made clear-

[27] Exceptions to this general conclusion, such as the tank confrontation at the Friedrichstrasse checkpoint on October 27-28, are discussed in later chapters. See *infra* Chaps. Thirteen and Fourteen.

[28] Since the four-power occupation regime placed the whole city of Berlin directly under the authority and control of the four occupying powers, the city was technically off limits for military forces of both the GDR and the FRG.

[29] For examples of this effort see the Declaration of the Warsaw Pact powers released by the GDR on the morning of August 13, in *DOSB*, XLV, No. 1158 (September 4, 1961), 400-401, and the Soviet note of August 18, in *ibid.*, 397-400.

276

cut efforts to maintain impeccable standards of protocol with regard to movements in the access routes during this phase of the crisis,[30] a fact made all the more striking by the relatively frequent occurrence of questionable acts relating to the access routes during other phases of the crisis.

Cuba, 1962

The Cuban crisis of 1962 is another case in which the impact of salience was greater with regard to instrumental rules than in the area of substantive issues. There was, nevertheless, one major substantive area in which perceptions of salience became a significant factor. This area encompassed the issues leading to the formulation of the proposal for a Soviet-American "swap" based on the simultaneous withdrawal of missiles from Cuba and Turkey.

This proposal received its most formal statement in the Soviet letter reaching Washington on October 27. In this letter, Khrushchev stated: "I therefore make this proposal: we agree to remove from Cuba those means which you regard as offensive means; we agree to carry this out and make a pledge in the United Nations. Your representatives will make a declaration to the effect that the United States, on its part, considering the uneasiness and anxiety of the Soviet state, will remove its similar means from Turkey."[31] The basic idea of a missile swap, however, had received growing publicity even before this formal statement from the Soviet Union. The *Manchester Guardian* and the *London Times* carried statements favorable to the idea during the week of October 22. Walter Lippmann endorsed the notion of a swap in his column on October 25.[32] And in general, there was a "favorable reaction in many parts of the world to the Turkey-Cuba trade proposal."[33] Part of this

[30] Perhaps the most striking example of this posture occurred in connection with the movement of an American battle group along the Helmstedt-Berlin autobahn on August 20. For an interesting description of this movement see the *New York Times*, August 20, 1961, pp. 1-2.

[31] The text of the letter is printed in Henry Pachter, *Collision Course* (New York: Praeger, 1963), pp. 217-220. For the quotation see p. 219.

[32] For a discussion of this point see Elie Abel, *The Missile Crisis* (Philadelphia: Lippincott, 1966), pp. 157-158.

[33] This statement is from "Cuban Crisis: A Step by Step Review," the *New York Times*, November 3, 1962, pp. 1, 6-7. The text is conveniently

favorable sentiment no doubt emanated from what C. B. Marshall has labeled "an esthetic hankering for symmetry."[34] But the salience which the proposal achieved stemmed also from more specific considerations. As Pachter has written, "It was received enthusiastically among neutralists and pacifists and even among many Western statesmen. In the United Nations, it was generally approved. It fitted the popular conception that both sides must make a sacrifice. It expressed the widespread feeling that the U.S. was more to blame, for with all his eloquence, Stevenson had not convinced anyone that American overseas bases are different from Communist ones, morally, politically, or militarily. The idea was also pleasing to the numerous strategists of disengagement, from Walter Lippmann to the disciples of Rapacki."[35]

Despite the obvious salience of the idea, however, the proposal for a missile swap came to naught. From the outset, the United States found several powerful reasons to refuse even to consider such a proposal. First, such a swap would not be genuinely symmetrical since acquiescence would constitute an indication that the Soviet Union could score important political gains simply by initiating a series of crises. Second, Kennedy had posed the principal issues in Cuba sharply in order to demonstrate to the Soviets that there were limits to the tolerance of the United States, and he believed a compromise involving Turkey would obscure this point. Third, the notion of a swap was viewed by American decision-makers as requiring an unjustifiable sacrifice of a valued ally. Fourth, the proposal was formally introduced by the Soviets only at an extremely late point in the crisis and under circumstances that made it appear as a last desperate gamble. Pachter has captured the tone of these American reactions well: "To abandon the bases in Turkey under pressure meant to endanger an allied government and to precipitate a not-too-prosperous country

reprinted in David L. Larson, ed., *The "Cuban Crisis" of 1962: Selected Documents and Chronology* (Boston: Houghton Mifflin, 1963), p. 241.

[34] C. B. Marshall, "Afterthoughts on the Cuban Blockade," *The New Republic*, Vol. 147, No. 19 (November 11, 1962), 20.

[35] Pachter, *op.cit.*, p. 53.

into a new crisis. No matter how obsolete the bases might be, they could not be traded now. At stake were Turkey's friendship and the stability of the entire NATO and CENTO system of alliances of which Turkey is a keystone. Khrushchev might think of Castro as a pawn and of Cuba as an object of barter, but the United States could not treat an ally in such a way. Kennedy had precipitated the crisis in Cuba in order to restore the credibility of American defense promises. He could not end the crisis by sacrificing the permanent interests of a powerless ally to the United States' immediate interests. Were Kennedy to agree to the barter of Cuba for Turkey, Khrushchev might next offer to barter British Guiana for Berlin, if by that time a general flight from American alliances did not make all specific threats superfluous. For the stability of peace and for the preservation of the balance of power, it was necessary for America to stand by all her promises."[36]

With regard to the establishment of instrumental rules for the conduct of the crisis, on the other hand, the influence of salience was greater. The Cuban missile crisis suddenly produced a mutual desire for the formulation of clear-cut limits applicable to the confrontation in the Caribbean. There was a certain novelty about this problem in 1962 since the superpowers had never before confronted each other so directly in this part of the world. But the basic pattern of limits worked out in this crisis is familiar from the discussion of the distinction between coercion and violence which was operative in previous crises.

In retrospect, the extent of coercion (including contingent threats of violence) applied during the 1962 crisis seems striking. The circumstances of the crisis itself, however, produced a strong fear among decision-makers on both sides that this was a case in which escalation might well become uncontrollable following the outbreak of violence even on a low level. As a result, both sides went to considerable lengths to avoid violent clashes of any kind.[37] Efforts at coordination to this end

[36] *Loc.cit.*

[37] As it turned out, the heaviest burden of avoiding the outbreak of violence fell on the Soviets. The reasons for this asymmetry were associated with the geographical peculiarities of the point of confrontation and with the efforts of the United States to manipulate the initiative.

were particularly evident with regard to naval activities on the high seas and the aerial reconnaissance activities of the United States. During the whole crisis, the only act of overt violence was the isolated, and still unexplained,[38] shooting down of an American U-2 over Cuba on October 27.

This fear of overt violence was extended during the 1962 crisis to actions that might lead to the killing of individual persons identified with the Soviet Union or the United States as well as to clashes between organized military units. The influence of the resultant prohibition appeared with great clarity, for example, in American debates during the week of October 15 on the alternatives open to the United States. In these debates, one of the most influential arguments against starting with an invasion of Cuba or, especially, an air strike against the missile sites was the perceived importance of avoiding acts that would lead to the killing of individual Russians.[39] Throughout the crisis, each side was at pains to avoid the killing of opposing personnel. Again, the only exception came with the loss of Major Anderson in the shooting down of an American U-2 on October 27.[40] This act itself, however, was received with the sense of shock that generally accompanies the breaking of a clear-cut rule. Moreover, it served to emphasize the remarkable fact that the superpowers were able to conduct a highly coercive and direct confrontation with far-reaching political implications under rules sufficiently stringent to prohibit violence almost entirely.

Conclusion

The case materials analyzed in this chapter make it clear that considerations of salience are frequently of some significance under conditions of crisis. But the evidence also indicates that

[38] The U-2 was brought down by a Soviet-built SAM-2 antiaircraft missile. Whether the decision to do so was made by a local commander or at some higher level, however, remains unclear.

[39] Interestingly, this argument focused specifically on the killing of Russians rather than Cubans. While there is no evident moral justification for this differentiation, the distinction is an important one from the point of view of developing rules of the game in international politics.

[40] For a discussion of this episode, see James Daniel and John G. Hubbell, "While America Slept," *Reader's Digest*, Vol. 82, No. 491 (March 1963), 286.

the overall influence of salience during crises is likely to be sharply restricted. Nor are decision-makers particularly prone to conceptualize important issues during crises in ways that make considerations of salience an explicit ingredient in their deliberations. As a result, the evidence from the cases lends only weak support to the hypothesis set forth at the outset of this chapter.

Within the limits of this general conclusion, nevertheless, it is important to make some additional distinctions. Above all, the case materials make it clear that a distinction between substantive issues and instrumental rules of conduct is called for in analyzing the relevance of salience under conditions of crisis. With relatively few exceptions, the ultimate impact of considerations of salience on substantive issues appears to be sharply limited during crises. These limitations are evidently most extensive with regard to those issues that are most sharply posed and directly contested. Such issues tend to be conceptualized by the parties in dichotomous terms leaving relatively little room for intermediate solutions. At the same time, they are typically perceived by all participants as being so critical to the final outcome of the crisis that no one is willing to gamble on the intrinsically arbitrary distribution of values that may well result from the acceptance of salience as a principle of coordination.[41]

In addition, these limitations on the influence of salience are only exacerbated by the typical interconnectedness of the proximate issues of specific crises and the more general issues of international politics. In short, the symbolic associations commonly evoked under conditions of crisis tend to infuse the specific issues of a given clash with an influence that goes far beyond the immediate arena of the confrontation. For this reason, any given settlement of the proximate issues of a crisis is apt to produce far-reaching consequences affecting the broader issues of international politics. It is hardly surprising, therefore, that the general wariness of states with regard to the

---

[41] Salience is a perceptual phenomenon that may emanate from any of a number of intrinsic qualities. Though a salient arrangement *may* also be a just or equitable one, there is no *a priori* reason to suppose this will be the case in any specific situation. For a discussion of this relationship see Schelling, *The Strategy of Conflict, op.cit.*, Chap. 3.

application of potentially arbitrary principles is likely to be sharply activated even in connection with highly specific or superficially local issues under conditions of crisis.

With regard to instrumental rules, on the other hand, the case materials indicate that considerations of salience are sometimes quite influential. During crises involving the great powers at least, parties too much at odds with each other to accept the relevance of salience in order to reach a settlement with regard to substantive issues, may nevertheless allow themselves to be influenced by such considerations in order to realize a mutual desire to coordinate on the development of at least minimal rules of conduct. In this connection, the evidence suggests there is a positive correlation between the perceived dangers associated with a crisis and the willingness of the parties to be guided by perceptions of salience. Though this link suggests that asymmetries may become important in this area, it also indicates that the overall impact of salience on the development of instrumental rules is likely to rise as a crisis becomes more intense.

As a result, crises frequently produce situations in which the participants are willing to structure their bargaining activities in ways that tend to guarantee the continued existence of their basic relationship but unwilling to grasp opportunities to reach viable settlements affecting the substantive issues at stake in the crisis.[42] Crises are therefore *not* generally played out in the absence of influential rules. They are, however, frequently terminated without important substantive negotiations and on the basis of tacit calculations concerning straightforward bargaining advantages attained by means of actions consonant with the criteria of acceptability established by the instrumental rules operative in the particular case at hand.

With regard to strategic bargaining, the case materials also suggest that the influence of considerations of salience under

[42] This discontinuity appears to be one cause of the tendency noted by many commentators for conflicts to become "frozen" so that the fundamental substantive issues underlying them remain intractable. While agreement on instrumental rules is apt to produce coordination on the goal of terminating clashes that threaten the continued existence of the given arena of interaction, rigidity with regard to substantive issues will tend to make lasting settlements extremely difficult.

conditions of crisis is mixed. With the exception of the period surrounding the closing of the sector boundary in Berlin during the 1961 crisis, salience does not appear to have placed decisive restrictions on efforts to alter positions of relative strength on substantive matters through the utilization of strategic bargaining. The very real impact of salience in instrumental terms, however, does appear to have played a *de facto* role in the development of rules that effectively increased the impact of negative factors taken into account in assessing some specific programs of strategic bargaining. In the Berlin crisis of 1948-1949, for example, sensitivity to the rule against overt violence appears to have been an important negative factor both in the Western decision against using armed convoys for bargaining purposes and in the Soviet decision to restrict efforts to achieve bargaining advantages through various forms of interference in the air corridors. Similarly, the attitudes of the Chinese People's Republic toward the employment of violence against American forces during the 1958 crisis seem to have been shaped at least partly by the tacit development of a rule against Sino-American violence. It is, of course, true that all these restrictions could be justified simultaneously in terms of more tangible interest calculations. The point here, however, is that considerations of salience became an important, not an exclusive, determinant of decision-making with regard to these matters.

12. Political Bargains

HYPOTHESIS. Simple *or* partial bargains that leave many issues to be worked out at a later time are apt to be employed in terminating crises.

Political bargains can take many forms. Such bargains may range from agreements dealing with all the aspects of a given situation in an inclusive and detailed fashion to simple agreements on certain abstract principles to be utilized subsequently as criteria in making decisions on specific issues. Similarly, bargains may be deliberately formulated to avoid particularly difficult issues in the hope of settling others that seem more tractable. Moreover, bargains may range along a spectrum of formality from arrangements based on tacit coordination to provisions spelled out with great explicitness. At the same time, political bargains vary greatly with respect to the question of procedures for their implementation. They may specify the details of a settlement in such a way that the fulfillment of its provisions can be verified on a once-and-for-all basis. They may set up machinery to supervise implementation or to adjudicate disputes arising under the terms of the settlement. Or they may deliberately leave the outcome of certain issues to be settled by the course of events in the future or by the application of more or less arbitrary decision rules operating on some contingent basis.

Various characteristics of international crises, such as the sharpness with which issues are posed, the influence of bargaining impediments, the orientation of salience toward instrumental rather than substantive issues, and the influence of perceived dangers, are all likely to affect the type of bargain that is attainable under conditions of crisis. In general, these conditions are apt to increase the relevance of bargains that are simple and limited in scope. Simple bargains are often more feasible than inclusive or detailed ones in a context characterized by bargaining impediments, problems of communication, and an atmosphere which emphasizes the abrasive elements of the relationship. Above all, simple bargains do not require extensive negotiations on highly specific or detailed issues. For similar reasons, a bargain that is restricted to a few key issues is likely to be attractive during a crisis. In this connection, conditions of crisis are particularly likely to produce bargains that focus on the proximate issues of the clash in contrast to the broader political problems of an area. Moreover, a bargain based on contingent devices may be seized upon as a means of terminating a severe crisis. Such a bargain tends to delay the settlement of at least some of the critical issues at stake, thereby permitting a termination of the actual physical confrontation produced by a crisis. A bargain of this type can sometimes be formulated so as to facilitate efforts at face-saving by making it unclear whether either side is losing any of its essential points. Finally, the various characteristics of crises mentioned above are likely to increase the inclination of the parties to formulate bargains in tacit rather than explicit terms.

As a result, the political bargains arising from a crisis are likely to be oriented more toward the immediate termination of the direct confrontation of opposing forces than toward the settlement of underlying political problems. While a crisis typically produces far-reaching impacts of a general nature on political attitudes, expectations, and bargaining calculations for the future,[1] therefore, it is not apt to generate clear-cut movement toward the settlement of the substantive issues underlying the specific crisis itself.

Berlin, 1948-1949

The basic characteristics of the Berlin crisis of 1948-1949 determined, to a very substantial degree, the process through which it was ultimately terminated. Following the transition from a period of upswing to a situation of full-blown confrontation, the crisis developed into a highly visible clash between two clearly articulated and rather rigid, though nonviolent, bargaining postures. In this context, the passage of time only served to bind the parties more tightly to the basic positions they had assumed initially. The prospects for meaningful negotiations on the substantive issues underlying the clash

[1] For an extended discussion of these effects of crisis, see *supra* Chap. Four.

declined markedly as the confrontation settled into a prolonged contest between opposing postures.[2]

The contacts through which the details of a termination arrangement were ultimately worked out during the spring of 1949 were not part of a genuine effort to arrive at a mutually satisfactory settlement of the basic issues underlying the clash over Berlin. On the contrary, the final bargaining was more nearly a process of registering the gains and losses which were in any case becoming relatively clear from the course of events in Berlin and in the western zones of Germany.[3] Both sides therefore deemed it unnecessary to hold formal negotiations on the subject. Informal contacts through the United Nations and several more indirect channels served as substitutes. The United States, as the leading member of the side that came out on top in the crisis, agreed to procedures for working out a termination arrangement involving secrecy[4] and the utilization of direct Soviet-American contacts. The result was a somewhat ritualized performance well suited to the requirements of registering gains and losses in a situation that posed important problems of face-saving.

A formal announcement indicating that the Berlin confrontation was about to be terminated appeared on May 4, 1949.[5] The bargain on which this announcement was based was a simple and limited one. Specifically, both sides agreed to remove all restrictions imposed on trade and transportation after March 1, 1948.[6] This meant, in effect, the removal of both the

[2] This development became particularly evident following the failure of the military governors in Berlin to agree, in negotiations during the first week of September 1948, on terms and procedures for carrying forth the Moscow negotiations of August.

[3] For further comments on the importance of the unfolding course of events, see *supra* Chap. Eight.

[4] In fact, secrecy was imposed to the point of not informing local commanders in Berlin about the development of termination arrangements. General Clay, for example, was not aware of the Soviet-American contacts at United Nations headquarters in New York during March and April.

[5] The text of this announcement is printed in Jean Edward Smith, *The Defense of Berlin* (Baltimore: The Johns Hopkins Press, 1963), pp. 129-130.

[6] The actual date set for the removal of these restrictions was May 12, 1949.

Soviet blockade of Berlin and the Western counterblockade of the Soviet zone of Germany. In addition, the parties agreed to convene a meeting of the Council of Foreign Ministers, eleven days after the removal of restrictions, to discuss the whole problem of the future of Germany. Nevertheless, the bargain announced on May 4 contained no substantive provisions that would in any way predetermine the conclusions reached at the meeting of the Council of Foreign Ministers. The basic agreement to remove the restrictions on trade and transportation was *not* contingent upon the subsequent negotiation of additional agreements.[7]

The bargain underlying the May 4 announcement contained no further stipulations or guidelines. There was no mention of the currency issue, a subject to which considerable attention had been devoted during the earlier phases of the crisis. Similarly, the announcement offered no guidelines concerning the regulation of interzonal trade in the future. Above all, the agreement was completely silent with regard to the critical but ambiguous problems surrounding the future status of Berlin and access rights to the city from the West. Among other things, this meant that the very existence of the airlift was ignored in the May 4 announcement, and, in fact, the airlift continued to operate for several months after the termination of the blockade.[8] Finally, the termination arrangement contained no provisions for even the most rudimentary machinery designed to prevent the development of a future clash over Berlin. The bargain leading to the termination of the confrontation, then, was a minimal one. As a result, the 1948-1949 Berlin crisis was brought to an end through a process that left most of the important issues underlying the clash unsettled.

In the aftermath of these developments, the Council of Foreign Ministers was actually convened in Paris on May 23, 1949.

[7] In fact, the link between the May 4 agreement and the subsequent meetings of the Council of Foreign Ministers was somewhat obscure at the time. This obscurity was clearly useful as a device for handling some of the bargaining impediments associated with the termination of the blockade. The subsequent course of events, however, made it quite clear that the removal of restrictions was not dependent on specific results from the meetings of the Council.

[8] On the continued operation of the airlift, see Max Charles, *Berlin Blockade* (London: Wingate, 1959), pp. 144-147.

In retrospect, the meetings of the Council clearly served a significant face-saving function since they obscured, to some extent, the exact nature of the bargain that had been struck in terminating the crisis and since they offered both sides a significant international forum in which to air their views concerning the future of Germany. Nevertheless, the Council was unable to reach agreement on any of the important substantive issues at stake so that the meetings ended "in a haze of ambiguity."[9] The two sides simply allowed the underlying issues raised by the crisis to fade out of the spotlight of international attention and to be dealt with on a unilateral and *de facto* basis. This meant that the Soviets tacitly absorbed their losses with regard to the future of Germany and the development of viable security arrangements for the Atlantic area while the Western powers accepted the effective political division of both Berlin and the whole of Germany.

The outcome of the 1948-1949 crisis clearly left open the possibility of another clash focusing on Berlin. This was especially so since the crisis had, in effect, made Berlin a symbolic irritant to the position of the Soviet Union in Eastern Europe. Moreover, both the precariousness of the city's physical situation and the extensive ambiguities surrounding the rights and duties of the occupation powers with regard to Berlin in the aftermath of the 1948-1949 crisis only served to underline the likelihood that the city would become the focal point of any new clash in central Europe involving the United States and the Soviet Union.

Taiwan Strait, 1958

There were several distinguishable points of relaxation during the 1958 crisis in the Taiwan Strait. All of these points, however, were not relevant to the process of terminating the crisis. The events surrounding Chou En-lai's statement of September 6, for example, marked the end of a major phase of the crisis,[10] but they were followed by the development of

[9] Manuel Gottlieb, *The German Peace Settlement and the Berlin Crisis* (New York: Paine-Whitman, 1950), p. 208.

[10] For an interesting discussion of this point, see Donald Zagoria, *The Sino-Soviet Conflict 1956-1961* (New York: Atheneum, 1964), p. 208.

a new bargaining calculus on the part of the Chinese People's Republic (CPR) with the result that the crisis shifted into a new phase. The final termination of the crisis—in contrast to transitions from one phase to another—occurred only during October in the wake of the CPR's decision to accept the failure of its second bargaining calculus.[11] It is the events of this latter period, therefore, that require analysis in this chapter.

Perhaps the most striking feature of the termination process during the 1958 crisis was the total absence of explicit bargains despite the existence of several channels for contact among the participants. The Sino-American ambassadorial talks especially, begun in Warsaw on September 15, failed to produce even the hint of a bargain.[12] On the contrary, the Warsaw talks degenerated into a rhetorical confrontation and never became a forum for meaningful communication.[13] Also, the crisis never came before the United Nations on a formal basis. The absence of formal United Nations involvement stemmed partly from the nonmembership of the CPR, which made direct bargaining within the United Nations virtually impossible, and partly from the unwillingness of both the CPR and the United States to discontinue their futile talks in Warsaw.[14]

[11] For further discussion of the shifts in the CPR's bargaining calculus, see *supra* Chap. Eight.

[12] On the problems associated with the Warsaw talks, see O. Edmund Clubb, "Chiang's Shadow over Warsaw," *The Reporter*, Vol. 19, No. 5 (October 2, 1958), 16-17.

[13] The CPR had virtually no incentives to make far-reaching substantive concessions at Warsaw which would affect the future of the whole situation in the Taiwan Strait. Moreover, insofar as the 1958 probe was failing on a tactical basis, there was no evident advantage for the CPR in admitting this in a public forum. For its part, the United States succeeded in tying its own hands effectively with regard to the Warsaw negotiations by: (1) being rather rigidly committed to a posture of offering no concessions before receiving a promise from the CPR to refrain from further hostilities in the Strait, and (2) promising the Nationalists to avoid any compromises that might "prejudice" their position in the area. On the American demand for a cessation of hostilities, see, for example, Dulles' statements at his news conference on September 9, in *DOSB*, XXXIX, No. 1005 (September 29, 1958), 485-493, especially, p. 492. On the American promises to the Nationalists, consult Clubb, *op.cit.*, p. 16.

[14] The United States adopted a verbal stance of reserving the right to take the issue formally to the United Nations should the talks in Warsaw

Nevertheless, the existence of the United Nations did present certain informal opportunities for contact among the protagonists during the crisis. The relevance of this channel became evident when, in the wake of Dulles' press conference on September 30,[15] a flurry of speculation arose concerning the possibilities for compromises between the United States and the CPR. While this speculation was partly an outgrowth of a strong current of world interest in achieving a negotiated change in the status of the offshore islands, it also arose in response to evidence that efforts had been taking place at the United Nations during the latter part of September to set up indirect communications links between the CPR and the United States.[16] Presently available evidence, however, suggests that Dulles' statements on September 30[17] were essentially tactical shifts designed to give the United States an international image of responsiveness to world opinion on the assumption that neither of the two Chinas would have anything to do with a negotiated change affecting the status of the offshore islands alone. Specifically, he was quite careful to discuss possible American concessions in terms that the CPR would be certain to reject even in the event the United States was willing to force the Nationalists into accepting them. While this set of events remains somewhat ambiguous, therefore, it appears to be explainable more in terms of the tactics of crisis

prove a failure. It is quite clear, however, that the two sides coordinated on a tacit and *de facto* policy of avoiding any overt admission of the failure of the Warsaw talks.

[15] For the text of this news conference, see *DOSB*, XXXIX, No. 1008 (October 20, 1958), 597-604.

[16] For information on these efforts to establish indirect communication, see the *New York Times*, October 10, 1958, pp. 1 and 4, and October 11, 1958, p. 1.

[17] Two of Dulles' statements, in particular, became the objects of considerable attention. First, Dulles indicated the United States considered the earlier decision to build up Nationalist garrisons on the offshore islands an unsound one, despite the fact the United States had not attempted to veto the move. Second, Dulles went on to say that "If there were a cease-fire in the area which seemed to be reasonably dependable, I think it would be foolish to keep these large forces on these islands." The text is in *DOSB*, XXXIX No. 1008 (October 20, 1958), 602.

bargaining than in terms of any genuine interest in terminating the crisis by means of an explicit bargain.[18]

The 1958 crisis was thus ultimately terminated on the basis of tacit coordination. The critical break came early in October when the Chinese Communists, evidently under pressure from the Soviet Union[19] as well as from the United States, concluded that their final bargaining calculus was no longer viable and that under the circumstances further escalation of the confrontation would be both risky and unproductive in terms of bargaining advantages. The CPR therefore issued, on October 6, a unilateral *and* temporary cease-fire order,[20] coupled with a stipulation that the cease-fire would be void unless the United States stopped escorting Nationalist supply convoys en route to Quemoy.[21] The response of the Americans and the Nationalists was twofold. The United States issued a conditional acceptance of the stipulation concerning escorts together with a statement that escorting would be resumed should any actions by the CPR make escorts necessary to supply the offshore islands. In addition, the Nationalists proceeded to use the period of the cease-fire to augment both the supplies and the defenses of the islands to a point where they would be safe against anything but an all-out attack by the CPR. The CPR thereupon extended its unilateral cease-fire, on October 13, for an additional two weeks.[22] As a result, the crisis began to

[18] For further discussion of this point see Richard Stebbins, *The United States in World Affairs 1958* (New York: Harper and Row [for the Council on Foreign Relations], 1959), pp. 325-327.

[19] On this point see Alice Hsieh, *Communist China's Strategy in the Nuclear Era* (Englewood Cliffs, N.J.: Prentice-Hall, 1962), p. 127. Hsieh stresses, in particular, the temporal juxtaposition of Khrushchev's statement of October 5 and the first cease-fire statement issued by the CPR on October 6.

[20] For the text of this statement see Paul Zinner, ed., *Documents on American Foreign Relations 1958* (New York: Harper and Row [for the Council on Foreign Relations], 1959), pp. 474-476.

[21] On this point see the discussions of Zagoria, *op.cit.*, p. 215; and Malcolm Mackintosh, "The Soviet Attitude," Chap. 8 in Morton Halperin, ed., *Sino-Soviet Relations and Arms Control* (Cambridge: M.I.T. Press, 1967), p. 212.

[22] The text of this statement is printed in Zinner, ed., *op.cit.*, pp. 476-477.

dwindle on the basis of a tacit agreement to terminate the physical confrontation without settling the underlying issues.[23] From this point on, the high levels of tension generated during the more acute phases of the crisis fell off rapidly.[24] Even the CPR's brief resumption of shelling, timed to coincide with the arrival of Dulles in Taipei on October 20,[25] failed to stop the dynamic of this "drift" toward termination.

The retreat of the CPR, which cleared the way for a termination of the 1958 crisis, was a tactical move rather than a strategic defeat. While the retreat was, in effect, an acknowledgment of failure to achieve the principal objectives of the 1958 probe, the CPR retained the option to reactivate the confrontation over the offshore islands at any time of its own choosing.[26] Nevertheless, as the party which had initiated the crisis and which was in the position, during October, of taking the most clear-cut steps in the process of terminating the crisis, the CPR was the participant most in need of face-saving devices during this final phase of the crisis. In addition to avoiding any public admission of retreat, therefore, the CPR developed several more specific procedures designed to cover its role in the termination process. First, the cease-fire statements were issued on a temporary and conditional basis: to emphasize that they did not constitute acquiescence to American demands for a "dependable" cease-fire, and to bolster the impression that the CPR held effective control over the outcome of the crisis. Second, the CPR coupled its announcements concerning the cease-fires with its efforts[27] to establish

[23] For a discussion of the termination process in terms of concepts of this kind, see Charles McClelland, Daniel Harrison, Wayne Martin, Warren Phillips, and Robert Young, *The Communist Chinese Performance in Crisis and Non-Crisis: Quantitative Studies of the Taiwan Straits Confrontation, 1950-1964,* Report to the Naval Ordnance Test Station (China Lake), December 14, 1965, p. 44.

[24] For evidence on this point see Stebbins, *op.cit.,* p. 332.

[25] In formal terms, therefore, this resumption of shelling disrupted the CPR's unilateral cease-fire of October 13.

[26] For a discussion of this point see R. F. Wall, "Formosa and the Chinese Offshore Islands," pp. 566-574 in G. Barraclough, *Survey of International Affairs, 1956-1958* (London: Oxford, 1962), especially p. 574.

[27] For evidence of this link see Morton Halperin and Tang Tsou, "The 1958 Quemoy Crisis," Chap. 10 in Morton Halperin, ed., *Sino-Soviet Relations and Arms Control* (Cambridge: M.I.T. Press, 1967), p. 277.

the inseparability of the offshore islands and Taiwan[28] and to generate tension in the relations between the United States and the Nationalists.[29] Each of these themes received its clearest expression, for example, in the Chinese statements of October 6, 13, and 25. Tactical retreat, therefore, was at least partially obscured by the introduction of new political arguments. Third, the CPR's statement of October 25[30] was carefully phrased and timed to create an impression that the CPR was both laying down certain minimum conditions for the termination of the crisis and exercising the praiseworthy restraint of a dominant power prepared to accept a somewhat unpleasant situation on a temporary basis.[31]

As it happened, the United States proved willing to acquiesce in this disguised retreat without making a serious attempt to utilize its success in defeating the CPR's probe to bring pressure to bear for alterations in the underlying political arrangements in the Taiwan Strait.[32] The result was a termination of the actual confrontation which failed to settle the underlying issues raised by the crisis and therefore left much to be worked out in the future.[33] Even with regard to the specific problem of the offshore islands, the result was essentially a reversion to the *status quo ante*. The United States did make some attempts during October to tighten its control over the ability of the Nationalists to initiate the use of overt force in the area.[34] But even here there was no effective American ob-

[28] For an interesting discussion concerning the inseparability of the offshore islands and Taiwan, see Anna Louise Strong, "Chinese Strategy in the Taiwan Strait," *New Times*, No. 46, November 1958, p. 11.

[29] For a summary discussion of the motives of the CPR with regard to this objective, see Tang Tsou, "Mao's Limited War in the Taiwan Strait," *Orbis*, III, No. 3 (Fall 1959), 347.

[30] For the text of the October 25 statement, see *Peking Review*, I, No. 38 (October 28, 1958), 5.

[31] For a discussion focusing on these issues see Stebbins, *op.cit.*, p. 332.

[32] There were at least two major reasons for this acquiescence on the part of the United States. Efforts to exercise pressure along these lines at this time, first, would have generated problems in the domestic politics of the United States, next, would have generated serious friction in relations between the United States and the Chinese Nationalists.

[33] For a discussion of this point see Hanson Baldwin, "Limited War," *The Atlantic*, Vol. 203, No. 5 (May 1959), 41.

[34] For a public manifestation of these efforts see the language of the joint American-Nationalist communiqué released in Taipei on October 23

jection when the Nationalists proceeded to redefine their new undertakings to the United States in such a way as to make their significance extremely ambiguous.

Even while they were terminating the actual crisis, therefore, the major participants engaged in a remarkable process of tacit coordination that led to the preservation of the basic arena of conflict in the Taiwan Strait without drastically altering the balances of strength which had existed prior to the 1958 crisis. By October it had become clear that neither China could gain a major victory from the crisis. The CPR was unable to take the offshore islands by force in the face of determined resistance on the part of both the Nationalists and the United States. The Nationalists, on the other hand, were unable to make significant gains both because of their own weakness vis-à-vis the CPR and because of the restraints placed on their activities by the United States. The only remaining opportunities for significantly altering the status of the offshore islands as a result of the crisis, therefore, involved internationalization or some other form of externally determined and maintained arrangement for the islands. Both Chinas, however, adamantly opposed any settlement along these lines on the grounds that such a development would produce a powerful thrust toward the formalization of a "two-Chinas" situation. The United States, in addition to its inability to pressure the CPR on this issue, was ultimately unwilling to force the hand of the Nationalists on the question both because of the probable ability of the Nationalists to precipitate violent exchanges in which the United States would become involved and because of the residual possibilities of a "deal" between the Chinese Communists and the Chinese Nationalists to thwart such plans for the offshore islands.[35]

As a result, the major parties coordinated, on a *de facto* basis, to preserve the basic arena of conflict while terminating the physical confrontation of the 1958 crisis. Specifically, this coordination was signaled by the simultaneous refusal of the

---

at the end of Dulles' visit. The text is printed in *DOSB*, XXXIX, No. 1011 (November 10, 1958), 721-722.

[35] For a discussion of the possibility of a deal between the two Chinas, see Tsou, *op.cit.*, p. 347.

CPR to comply with American demands for a "dependable" cease-fire and of the United States to force the hand of the Nationalists on such issues as the question of Nationalist garrisons on the offshore islands. In this context, the CPR's temporary resumption of the bombardment of Quemoy on October 20, coincidental with Dulles' visit to Taiwan, effectively destroyed any remaining hopes of achieving significant changes in the status of the offshore islands,[36] thereby guaranteeing the acquiescence of the United States in the *de facto* agreement not to alter the basic arena of conflict in the area.

Berlin, 1961

During the Berlin crisis of 1961, the major parties were unable to arrive at formal or explicit bargains concerning any of the major issues underlying the clash. In fact, they never even succeeded in initiating negotiations that could have produced explicit bargains, despite the professed interest of both sides in doing so, particularly during the later phases of the crisis. This failure to arrive at explicit bargains, however, should not be taken to mean that no bargains at all were struck during the 1961 crisis. On the contrary, the crisis produced distinguishable tacit bargains affecting both the local crisis within the German Democratic Republic (GDR) and the more general East-West clash.

The most decisive bargain of the crisis was the *de facto* agreement leading to the termination of the local crisis within the GDR. This bargain was particularly striking because its implementation required East-West coordination and because it affected substantive as well as procedural issues at the *local* level. The key element of the bargain was the agreement on the necessity of closing the sector boundary in Berlin to stop the exodus of refugees from the GDR. In addition, however, the August actions of the GDR implied:[37] an end to unhin-

---

[36] It was quite widely believed, before this action, that Dulles would attempt to extract genuinely significant concessions from the Nationalists during his visit to Taiwan. In the upshot, the United States contented itself with the limited shifts embodied in the joint communiqué of October 23 and, furthermore, refused to react sharply when the Nationalists began to interpret even these limited changes into obscurity.

[37] For further discussion of these implications, see Smith, *op.cit.*, p.

dered freedom of movement within the city; a definitive disruption of several specific aspects of the postwar agreements governing Berlin; and an end to the "showplace" function of West Berlin. The Western powers proved willing to accept these secondary consequences of the bargain to terminate the local crisis. During the remainder of August, the West contented itself with formal protests on these issues.[38] By September these issues had become settled to the point where Kennedy, in his address at the United Nations, "neither demanded that the right of free circulation be restored in Berlin or that the Wall come down."[39] In return for this acquiescence, however, the Western powers acquired both a measure of tacit consent to the continued presence of Western forces in West Berlin and a tactical situation that was shifting in such a way as to make any decisive disruption of Western access to the city from West Germany increasingly difficult for the East.[40]

The *local* consequences of this bargain were highly influential even though they stemmed from tacit rather than explicit agreements. First of all, the bargain was a critical link in creating the basis for a consolidation of the internal situation of the GDR. The bargain was also a major factor in the development of certain problems affecting the future of West Berlin. These problems focused on:[41] the blow to popular morale in West Berlin caused by the crisis; the emigration of residents of the Western sectors of the city; doubts concerning the economic viability of West Berlin; and uncertainty with regard to the political future of the city. None of these developments had definitive consequences for the economic or political viability of either West Berlin or the GDR. Nevertheless, the effects of this local bargain during the 1961 crisis

---

275; and Kurt L. Shell, "Berlin," pp. 85-102, in Walter Stahl, ed., *The Politics of Postwar Germany* (New York: Praeger, 1963), especially pp. 99-100.

[38] On this point see Smith, *op.cit.*, p. 295.

[39] *Ibid.*, p. 313. For the text of Kennedy's address on September 25, 1961, see *DOSB*, XLV, No. 1164 (October 16, 1961), 619-625.

[40] For further comments on these shifts in the tactical situation, see *supra* Chap. Eight.

[41] For a discussion of these problems, couched in language somewhat too strong, see Smith, *op.cit.*, pp. 7-8.

were asymmetrical to the disadvantage of the Western powers.

The consequences of this asymmetry, however, were strongly conditioned by and ultimately sharply circumscribed by the bargaining process that developed in the more general East-West portion of the 1961 crisis. On this more general level, the ultimate determinants of the final bargain were: the final unwillingness of the Soviet Union to implement its implied threat to turn effective control of the access routes over to the GDR,[42] and the general failure to initiate East-West negotiations relating to the crisis before this weakness of Soviet resolve became apparent. The specific outcome of the crisis, nevertheless, was very much in doubt until the latter part of October. During September and early October, for example, the Western powers evidently came close to offering significant concessions to the Soviet Union in the interests of getting East-West negotiations started.[43] But because of the problems of coordinating policy within the Western alliance and the effects of various bargaining impediments hindering East-West contacts during this period, the Western powers continued to debate the question of concessions until the flow of events both in the actual arena of confrontation and in the Soviet Union had changed the basic context of the crisis so as to make such concessions largely irrelevant. As it happened, the critical break in this delicate balance came with Khrushchev's speech before the opening session of the 22nd Party Congress on October 17.[44] In this speech, Khrushchev, in effect, publicly de-

[42] The unwillingness of the Soviet Union to follow through on this threat began to become clear especially in the aftermath of the events surrounding August 13.

[43] For evidence on this point consult Smith, op.cit., pp. 327-330. Areas in which concessions might have been offered included: (1) the question of de facto recognition of the GDR, (2) the problem of German reunification, and (3) the question of granting formal recognition to the Oder-Neisse line as Germany's eastern boundary.

[44] The fact that this shift in posture was announced at the opening session of the Party Congress seems significant. This is especially so in the light of the evidence suggesting that the Soviets, in reactivating the Berlin question in June, were at least partially motivated by a desire to have some foreign policy success to present to the Party Congress. For the text of Khrushchev's speech of October 17, 1961, see the New York Times, October 18, 1961, p. 16.

fused the Soviet threat to sign a separate peace treaty with the GDR. Some evidence suggests this move may have been informally adumbrated earlier during the Rusk-Gromyko meeting in September.[45] Nevertheless, it was not until Khrushchev's more formal pronouncement on October 17 that it was possible for the Western powers to begin to feel confident that an important change in the Soviet bargaining position had occurred.

Under these circumstances, the tank confrontation of October 27-28 in Berlin, though it generated possibilities for dangerous incidents, actually served to demonstrate that there had been an important shift in the Soviet bargaining position in the crisis and that the Soviets were no longer optimistic about achieving far-reaching gains in this round of the continuing controversy over Berlin.[46] With these developments, therefore, the critical phases of the 1961 crisis came to an end despite the fact that significant bargaining moves and acts of harassment continued to occur in the Berlin arena from time to time during the succeeding months.

In the upshot, the two sides tacitly proceeded to strike a minimal procedural bargain terminating the most acute aspects of the physical confrontation involved in the 1961 crisis without reaching any agreement on the substantive issues at stake. In effect, both sides simply agreed to let matters ride in Berlin for the time being and to avoid actions that would "rock the boat" unduly.[47] They did not in any way commit themselves to a policy of avoiding confrontations over Berlin in the future.

The fact that this bargain was both procedural and sharply

[45] See, for example, Rusk's statement on this point at his press conference of October 18. For the text see DOSB, XLV, No. 1167 (November 6, 1961), 746.

[46] One of the most important results of the tank confrontation was a de facto Soviet acceptance of responsibility for activities in East Berlin, a development that ran directly counter to the implications of the earlier Soviet campaign focusing on the threat to sign a separate peace treaty with the GDR.

[47] In this context, it is worth noting that The Economist was almost certainly wrong in its judgment that "Mr. Khrushchev withdrew his end-of-1961 deadline for signing a peace treaty with East Germany on the understanding that the West would agree to negotiate about Berlin." The Economist, December 9, 1961, p. 1,004.

limited in terms of scope meant that many issues were inevitably left unsettled and much remained to be worked out eventually. The bargain did, nevertheless, produce several *de facto* effects worth noting. First, the 1961 crisis was terminated so inconclusively that Berlin continued to be a focus of periodic probes from the East during the succeeding period. Second, whether the final outcome of the crisis constituted a significant gain for either side is difficult to assess because of the complexity of the situation and the ambiguity of the goals of the parties. In essence, the standoff that developed in the overall East-West portion of the crisis effectively prevented the Soviet Union from exploiting the tactical advantages accruing to the Eastern side in the local arena following the events of August 13.[48] In fact, these local developments produced a solidification of the overall position of the Western powers which contributed to the final outcome of standoff in East-West relations.[49] In the end, therefore, the principal gains from the crisis accrued to the specific interests of the GDR rather than to either side in the overall East-West contest. And the outcome in no sense contained the seeds of an ultimate settlement for the underlying international issues symbolized by the confrontation over Berlin. Third, the procedural bargain struck during the fall of 1961 did, for the immediate future reduce the relevance of several contemporary plans designed to alleviate the basic East-West conflict over Berlin and Germany as a whole. The most prominent plans affected in this way were the idea of negotiating an entirely new political status for Berlin, and the various suggestions focusing on disengagement as the key to a viable political arrangement for central Europe.

Cuba, 1962

The underlying conflict over Cuba that came to a head in the missile crisis of 1962 was rooted in a number of significant but complex issues. Nevertheless, the crisis itself developed

---

[48] A number of efforts to do just this were made during late August and September. But, in the final analysis, these efforts failed to produce any significant additional deterioration in the Western position in Berlin.
[49] For further discussion of this point see *supra* Chap. Eight.

around a specific and relatively well-defined issue—the installation of offensive missiles on Cuban territory by the Soviet Union. Given the initial asymmetries of the situation,[50] the United States was in a position to formulate the specific issues of the confrontation at the tactical level. The American government chose to concentrate on the specific issue of the offensive missiles for both political and tactical reasons.[51] As the crisis shifted to the phase of full-blown confrontation, moreover, other factors came into play to keep the crisis focused on the problem posed by the missiles. This problem constituted the most dramatic aspect of the whole situation. The existence of a high level of tension and perceived danger, especially toward the end of the confrontation, operated to keep attention fixed on the physical clash associated with the missiles. A widespread feeling that the passage of time might drastically alter the situation produced strong pressures on the American side to settle the principal issue quickly without getting involved in ancillary issues.[52] The characteristics of the confrontation itself made it virtually impossible to conduct negotiations of an extended nature.[53] When the two sides reached the point of agreeing on the desirability of a bargain to end the crisis, therefore, they were not prepared to consider anything beyond a limited range of issues directly involved in the immediate confrontation.

As a result, the bargain terminating the 1962 crisis was a highly restricted one. It involved only the United States and

[50] Because the United States discovered the installation of the Soviet missiles in Cuba before they became operational, the Americans held the *tactical* initiative at the outset of the actual crisis of 1962.

[51] In political terms, this formulation was designed to rally the support of the various factions both within the United States and among the allies of the United States. In tactical terms, the focus on the offensive missiles emphasized the issues on which the American position relative to the Soviet position seemed most reasonable and justifiable.

[52] In particular, this feeling arose from a fear that the Soviet missiles in Cuba would become operational. In this context, it is important to note that work on the offensive missiles already in Cuba continued during the first days of the blockade.

[53] The problem here had to do with the setting in motion of sequences of actions that would likely become irreversible within a very short time. For example, American preparations for a strike against the missile installations or an invasion of Cuba had characteristics of this kind.

the Soviet Union on a direct bilateral basis. It was formulated in a simple exchange of letters between Kennedy and Khrushchev on October 27 and 28.[54] And its substantive terms were minimal. The Soviet Union agreed to remove its "offensive" weapons systems from Cuba "under appropriate United Nations observation and supervision."[55] In return, the United States agreed "upon the establishment of adequate arrangements through the United Nations to ensure the carrying out and continuation of these commitments—(a) to remove promptly the quarantine measures now in effect and (b) to give assurances against an invasion of Cuba."[56] The bargain was therefore highly specific in the sense that it dealt only with those concrete matters absolutely essential to terminating the confrontation. At the same time, it was loosely formulated since there was room for significant variation in the interpretation of its terms.

The bargain ending the Cuban missile crisis was striking for its avoidance of a number of important issues. No criteria were supplied to determine whether the Soviet-built, Il-28 bombers in Cuba fell under the heading of "offensive" weapons systems set forth in the bargain. The language of the bargain contained no guidelines relating to the implementation of "observation and supervision" procedures. The timing, format, and exact content of the American noninvasion pledge were left unspecified. And above all, the terms of the bargain were silent on the broader political issues associated with the crisis. In particular, there was no mention of provisions designed to insure the maintenance of general peace and security in the Caribbean area.

The failure of the two sides to deal with these issues was hardly surprising given the tense atmosphere of the crisis and the problems of face-saving involved in its termination. Nevertheless, even in the immediate aftermath of the period of physical confrontation during the week of October 22, two of

[54] The texts of these letters are printed in Henry Pachter, ed., *Collision Course* (New York: Praeger, 1963), pp. 221-226.

[55] These terms were clearly stated in Kennedy's letter to Khrushchev of October 27. For text see *ibid.*, p. 221.

[56] This statement is also from the Kennedy letter of October 27. See *ibid.*, p. 222.

301

these unresolved issues generated serious problems. The question of the Il-28s became a major point of contention since the United States insisted they were "offensive" weapons sytems and had to be removed along with the Soviet missiles.[57] Though the Soviets at first argued they could not comply since the planes actually belonged to the Cubans, the issue ultimately subsided when the Soviets capitulated to American pressure and agreed to force the Cubans into relinquishing them.[58] In addition, difficulties ultimately producing more far-reaching consequences arose over the question of inspection. It now seems clear that the United States and the Soviet Union were essentially in agreement on this issue and were prepared to accept United Nations inspection teams. This agreement reckoned without the Cuban government, however, which proceeded to argue that such inspection would constitute a violation of Cuban sovereignty and refused to allow any inspections to be carried out on Cuban territory.[59] Castro maintained this inflexible position despite the pleadings of U Thant on a special trip to Havana[60] as well as the injection of a number of suggestions for changes in the projected inspection procedures aimed at making them less objectionable to the Cubans.[61] Therefore, the international inspection provisions of the Soviet-American bargain could not be implemented. As an alternative, the United States conducted extensive aerial and naval inspection operations on a unilateral basis. These procedures, however, were not wholly satisfying to many people, particularly in the United States.[62]

The effect of these difficulties was to minimize the lasting significance of the Soviet-American bargain terminating the missile crisis. The Soviet Union did in fact withdraw its offen-

[57] For a discussion of the problem of the Il-28s, see Theodore Sorensen, *Kennedy* (New York: Harper and Row, 1965), pp. 720-721.

[58] For further discussion consult Elie Abel, *The Missile Crisis* (Philadelphia: Lippincott, 1966), pp. 212-213.

[59] On the formulation of the Cuban position, see *ibid.*, p. 210.

[60] See, for example, the record of the Thant-Castro conversations in Havana on October 30, 1962. The most important segments of the conversations are excerpted in Pachter, *op.cit.*, pp. 230-234.

[61] The most important of these suggestions was the idea of using Red Cross personnel in place of United Nations inspectors.

[62] For further discussion of this point see Sorensen, *op.cit.*, p. 722.

sive weapons from Cuba, thereby removing the proximate cause of the 1962 crisis. The United States, however, refused to issue a formal noninvasion pledge in the absence of a Cuban agreement to accept international inspection. Rather, the American government adopted the view that the United States had "no choice but to pursue its own means of checking on military activities in Cuba."[63] Even the proximate issues around which the missile crisis focused, therefore, were never definitively resolved.

Many of the important questions raised by the 1962 crisis were allowed simply to fade away, at least temporarily, without being settled. In a joint letter to the Secretary-General of the United Nations on January 7, 1963, the governments of the United States and the Soviet Union stated that the situation had developed to a point where it no longer required the attention of the United Nations despite the fact that it had not proved possible to settle all the issues raised by the crisis.[64] In the final analysis the Soviet-American bargain in this crisis was far more significant as a device for terminating a specific physical confrontation than as a means for settling the substantive issues underlying that confrontation.

Conclusion

An examination of the case materials in this chapter indicates that the use of simple or partial bargains under conditions of crisis is striking. Several distinguishable types of limitation stand out as typical of bargains arrived at during crises. In the first instance, the issues associated with crises are generally treated in a highly selective fashion. Important issues are frequently either ignored or treated in a peripheral fashion. Bargains emanating from crises are apt to focus on the proximate issues involved in the actual physical confrontation in contrast to the underlying problems associated with the crisis. Even within this framework, there is a tendency to place a heavy emphasis on essentially procedural matters as opposed

[63] This language is from Kennedy's statement to the press of November 20, 1962. The text is printed in Pachter, *op.cit.*, p. 237.

[64] For the text of the letter of January 7, 1963, see David L. Larson, ed., *The "Cuban Crisis" of 1962: Selected Documents and Chronology* (Boston: Houghton Mifflin, 1963), p. 202.

to substantive issues. In the case materials, the only outstanding deviation from these patterns of selectivity is the *local* bargain that emerged in the midst of the overall Berlin crisis of 1961. In addition, the bargains emerging from crises tend to be highly informal. In some cases this means that a bargain is nothing more than a tacit agreement. All of the crises under analysis produced bargains arrived at by relatively indirect means and that were never accorded the acceptance procedures commonly employed in connection with international agreements of a more formal nature. Furthermore, bargains generated during crises are apt to be strikingly silent on the question of guarantee arrangements aimed at preventing a renewal of confrontation. The occurrence of a serious crisis, therefore, seldom leads *directly* to arrangements that have the effect of reducing the probabilities of reactivation in the future. On the contrary, the great powers, at least, have more often shown a tendency to handle crises in such a way as to preserve the basic arena of conflict in an area even while terminating the physical confrontation that has arisen in a specific clash.

The processes of terminating international crises tend to deemphasize the relevance of open negotiations as a procedure for the conduct of bargaining activities. At least this has been the case in crises involving great powers which cannot be forced to enter into negotiations, even on a *pro forma* basis, by the application of superior power. Moreover, even when negotiations relating to the problems of termination do occur during great-power crises, they tend to acquire an extremely restricted nature and to become highly ritualized. This is what happened, for example, in the Berlin crisis of 1948-1949 and the Taiwan Strait crisis of 1958. These difficulties with negotiations however, emphasize several other significant points concerning the processes of striking bargains during international crises. The impact of bargaining impediments is often quite prominent in these processes. Both the substantive content and the format of bargains emerging from crises, therefore, are likely to be shaped by these difficulties. Nevertheless, the great powers have frequently demonstrated remarkable abilities to arrive at bargains of some significance during crises through processes of tacit coordination. Given the conclusions stated above, the use of tacit procedures is hardly surprising. The results achieved through the use of such procedures in such cases as the Taiwan Strait and the Berlin crisis of 1961, however, while obviously limited, were quite striking. Furthermore, because of the problems surrounding negotiations during crises, bargains are apt to be more important as devices for terminating a confrontation by registering the results of strategic bargaining than as procedures for formalizing the results of efforts to achieve mutual accommodation. Crises generally pit opposing bargaining tactics against each other in concrete and well-defined situations. Under these circumstances, bargains usually signify the end of a definable round or episode in a longer-term conflict and indicate the distribution of gains and losses resulting from the round.

All of this emphasizes the contrast between major wars and crises as far as the achievement of international bargains is concerned.[65] Wars tend to disrupt fundamental international relationships in a sharp and drastic fashion. Since they are therefore apt to *destroy* prior patterns of conflict and political balances, they commonly make it necessary to deal with basic political issues within a relatively short space of time. As a result, peace conferences, which inevitably generate an aura of "political engineering," are the classic sequels to wars in international politics. Crises, on the other hand, generally produce fewer opportunities for the development of bargains involving clear-cut and extensive changes in international relationships. Crises are seldom as destructive of existing political patterns as wars. Moreover, the asymmetries in the power positions of the relevant parties are likely to be considerably less decisive in the aftermath of a crisis than in the wake of a war. In contrast to major wars, therefore, crises are not generally followed by extensive and relatively conscious efforts to restructure international relationships so as to minimize the influence of the instabilities of the previous pattern. As a re-

---

[65] Limited wars often occupy the middle ground between major wars and crises with regard to the characteristics of the political bargains they produce. In general, then, the more limited a war, the more its outcome will resemble that of a crisis in this respect.

sult, while crises frequently produce far-reaching impacts on existing patterns of international politics, they are likely to do so in a *de facto* fashion and on a relatively long-term basis. In short, the consequences of crises are more likely to influence the intangible determinants of international politics such as attitudes, expectations, and calculations concerning risks than to produce concrete bargains leading to substantive changes in international relationships on an explicit and short-term basis.

PART IV

FORCE, COERCION, AND VIOLENCE

Introduction

The relationships between the tactical aspects of bargaining and the role of force in international politics are particularly extensive and close during crises. Even when the two sets of phenomena are separated for purposes of analysis, the connections between them should be kept clearly in mind.

A number of concurrent technological and political developments in the postwar period have operated to reduce drastically the physical limitations on the use of force covering large geographical areas with highly destructive effects and to augment the role of essentially political factors as determinants of the modes and patterns in which force is used in the international arena. This changing relationship is, of course, especially evident with regard to developments in the nuclear area, but it is also becoming prominent with regard to a variety of additional developments in such areas as delivery capabilities and technologies that have greatly increased the mobility, firepower, and overall effectiveness of military units at all levels.

One of the most influential consequences of these developments has been their tendency to increase sharply the putative costs of employing armed forces in ways that would lead to large-scale violence, at least *among* the great powers. This in turn has set in motion some important changes in the dominant concepts and images shaping both attitudes and actions with regard to the use of force in international politics. For roughly a century and a half prior to 1945, decision-makers usually operated on the basis of a physical-contest image of international conflict.[1] Disputes or doubts about the relative strength of various powers were ultimately resolved by means

---

[1] This image dates, in effect, from the period of the shift from largely professional armies to military forces composed of ordinary citizens serving limited terms of duty. This shift began on a large scale at the end of the eighteenth century, catalyzed by the developments of the French Revolution. In the ensuing period, the physical-contest image, though not always applied in detail, provided the underlying conceptual structure for the use of force in international politics. Surviving the First World War, the main elements of this image reached a kind of apotheosis during World War II. Simultaneously, however, the Second World War marked the beginning of a decline in the relevance of the physical-contest image of the role of force in international politics.

of overt physical clashes that continued until one side was willing to accept the position of the other or until both sides were exhausted. The decline of physical limitations on the potential destructiveness of military contests, however, has forced important changes in prevailing concepts and images in this area. In this connection, an influential process of conceptual adaptation has begun which focuses primarily on a horizontal shift of concepts with regard to appropriate modes for the employment of force.[2] Increasingly, this shift has led to the development of interest in a wide range of processes through which coercion can be achieved short of large-scale violence within the confines of a nuclear environment.

Under the circumstances, international crises have come increasingly to occupy a critical position at the juncture between the use of violence and the use of diplomacy in primarily persuasive situations. As a result, crises have frequently served both as testing grounds in the development of new procedures for the achievement of coercion in a nuclear environment and as important arenas for the employment of force in nonviolent patterns to attain political objectives.

The following chapters address themselves to several aspects of these emerging patterns of international coercion as manifested under conditions of crisis. It is sometimes possible, for example, to "hypothecate" force—in the sense of deploying military units physically—to achieve advantages by manipulating contingencies affecting the outbreak of violence without actually initiating the use of violence directly. Similarly, there is a growing interest in the systematic analysis of nonviolent techniques of coercion arising from efforts to shape and control important geopolitical features of the arena in which a crisis comes to a head. In general, the current period is witnessing a resurgence of interest in the use of force to affect attitudes, expectations, and resolve rather than to engage in violent or even overtly physical contests with an opponent over specific geographical positions.

[2] There is considerable debate concerning the extent, if any, to which the overall or composite utility of force as an instrument of power in international politics is declining in the contemporary period. The present point about horizontal conceptual adaptation leaves this question open, although it adds another dimension to the question, which is apt to make assessments of change in overall utility extremely difficult.

13. Restraints on the Use of Violence

> HYPOTHESIS. Conditions of crisis will generate highly influen-
> tial restraints on the usability of violence for the achievement
> of political objectives.

Violence refers to the infliction of physical pain on another
party. The term coercion, on the other hand, is commonly applied to *all* activities designed to shape the actions of another
actor against its (individual or collective) will. Coercion,
therefore, does not necessarily involve the use of violence. The
majority of acts of coercion in international politics are in fact
nonviolent. By the same token, violence is not always coercive
either in intent *or* in effect. Violence occasionally occurs without any perceptible link to issues of policy. And it is a relatively common occurrence for the infliction of pain on an opponent
to increase rather than to reduce his resistance to coercion.

It is clear that crises are by nature highly coercive situations. But there is also good reason to argue that conditions of
crisis are apt to sharpen the distinction between coercion and
violence by generating clear-cut and highly influential restraints on the use of violence in any calculated fashion. The
hypothesis of the present chapter refers both to outright
applications of violence and to acts that increase the probability of violence occurring through processes that are beyond
the control of the parties to the crisis.

There are several reasons why the usability of violence for
bargaining purposes tends to be sharply restricted during
crises. International politics in the postwar period have been
characterized by a widespread and influential desire to avoid
large-scale war, especially in situations that could become
nuclear. Under conditions of crisis, however, the prospect of
war becomes increasingly real in the perceptions of decision-
makers with the result that the dangers of large-scale destruction tend to become more sharply defined and pervasive. For
this reason, a crisis is usually a sobering experience in which
the use of violence is linked closely, in perceptual terms, to
the inherent dangers of the situation. In addition, conditions
of crisis tend to reduce the confidence of decision-makers in
their own ability to control escalation in terms of anything but

the most general and clear-cut distinctions. The initiation of violence during a crisis is thus often viewed as a critical breaking point or threshold, and the impact of force-of-events considerations is generally seen as rising sharply following the introduction of violence. These pressures are only heightened by the fact that the general ability of decision-makers to conceptualize the forthcoming course of events within meaningful limits—an ability always rather circumscribed in political contexts—tends to be even more restricted following the outbreak of violence. The incentives for decision-makers to avoid consciously initiating the use of violence are apt to remain strong, therefore, except in hopeless situations, which seldom arise even under conditions of crisis.

These arguments do not suggest that violence will never break out during crises. In any given crisis, incentive to employ violence may still outweigh restraints; efforts to manipulate *threats* of violence may catalyze uncontrollable processes of escalation, and, in general, the probabilities of violence breaking out through inadvertent processes are never likely to be zero. Nevertheless, the restraints on conscious applications of violence are apt to be far-reaching and highly influential under conditions of crisis.

Berlin, 1948-1949

The Berlin crisis of 1948-1949 produced an interesting situation with regard to restraints on calculated uses of violence. In general, both sides had clear interests in avoiding a major war: both sides were unprepared to engage in overt hostilities of major proportions; and neither was willing to accept the physical destruction that might well ensue—an unwillingness heightened by the still vivid memory of the Second World War. The problem of restricting violence, however, was considerably more complicated with regard to specific acts arising out of the physical confrontation in the local arena around Berlin. The very development of a direct physical confrontation made it necessary to live with a situation that was intrinsically risky. Given the existence of a crisis, each side was inevitably under pressure to demonstrate the credibility of its commitments and to maximize its bargaining strength. But these pressures were sharply offset by the dangers of serious incidents occurring in the local arena which might initiate uncontrollable escalation.

The general tone of debate during the 1948-1949 crisis clearly indicates that the dangers attendant upon the use of violence were emphasized strongly. In particular, there was an evident tendency to question the ability of the participants to control escalation once the threshold of overt violence had been passed. In the upshot, though both sides proved willing to employ coercive activities on a relatively large scale, they also demonstrated clear-cut caution with regard to the use of violence. During the course of the crisis, this caution concerning violence led to a number of self-imposed restrictions with far-reaching consequences.

In the first instance, both sides went to considerable lengths throughout the crisis to avoid being the first to use violence or to take steps that would make the outbreak of violence inevitable. On the Western side, this restriction became strikingly evident with regard to the question of using force to break the land blockade of the access routes to Berlin. On June 21, military train No. 20, carrying a strong contingent of armed personnel, set out from Helmstedt in the direction of Berlin.[1] No effort was made to force the issue violently, however, when the Soviets diverted the train onto a siding in eastern Germany. Moreover, both sides made great efforts to avoid the occurrence of violent incidents while the train stood for three days on the siding. Later on, especially during July, the much debated proposal to order a heavily armed convoy to smash its way into Berlin on the ground raised a similar problem. In this case, even though such influential figures as General Clay and Ambassador Murphy favored the proposal,[2] the relevant Western decision-makers ultimately vetoed it primarily on the grounds that a move of this kind might touch off violent

---

[1] For a factual discussion of the circumstances surrounding this initiative, see Philip Jessup, "Review of Allied Action on Berlin Blockade" (Statement in the United Nations Security Council, October 19, 1948). For the text see *DOSB*, XIX, No. 487 (October 31, 1948), 543.

[2] See Robert Murphy, *Diplomat Among Warriors* (New York: Pyramid, 1965), p. 354.

clashes with Soviet forces.[3] The Western decision to rely heavily on the success of the airlift, which was by no means a foregone conclusion during the summer of 1948, constitutes a striking demonstration of the importance attached to the avoidance of violent clashes on the part of the Western powers.

The Soviets also took great care during the crisis to avoid actions that might lead to violence. Given the facts that the airlift was a critical element of the struggle between the two sides and that various types of interference were within the realm of Soviet capabilities, the sharp restrictions the Soviets placed on their efforts to interfere with it are remarkable.[4] These self-imposed limitations are made even more striking by the fact that the possibilities for interference included such activities as radio jamming and the use of barrage balloons, which would have been nonviolent at least in the first instance, as well as more overtly provocative actions such as "buzzing" Western aircraft or carrying out organized maneuvers in the air corridors. In effect, therefore, this situation developed into one in which the notion of the last clear chance of avoidance became highly influential in support of a tacit injunction against the initiation of violence. At the same time, the Soviets meticulously refrained from any serious efforts to use their predominant military strength on the ground in central Europe during the 1948-1949 crisis. Restraint along these lines was both particularly pronounced and extremely influential during the later phases of the crisis as it became increasingly evident that the Western side was gaining the upper hand in the contest between the airlift and the blockade. In this connection, the Western doctrine later to be conceptualized in terms of trip wires and plate glass windows was already beginning

[3] For verification of this point see Manuel Gottlieb, *The German Peace Settlement and the Berlin Crisis* (New York: Paine-Whitman, 1950), p. 199. Interestingly, it is now generally supposed that the Soviets were sufficiently anxious to avoid overt hostilities in 1948 so that a Western move to break the blockade with an armed convoy would have succeeded without touching off large-scale violence.

[4] For interesting discussions of this point see James Reston, the *New York Times*, October 3, 1948, Sect. IV, p. 3; and Frederick Ford, "New Marks, Old Mistakes in Berlin," *The New Republic*, Vol. 119, No. 3 (July 19, 1948), 12.

to operate effectively during the 1948-1949 crisis on a *de facto* basis.

Besides observing this tacit injunction against the initiation of violence, both sides tread cautiously with regard to actions which might raise the perceived dangers of war in a more generalized sense. Throughout the crisis, both sides were circumspect about undertaking unusual mobilizations or movements of troops and military equipment.[5] The United States did seek to demonstrate the credibility of its commitment to the defense of Europe by deploying B-29s to several European airfields.[6] But for the most part both sides conspicuously avoided engaging in activities that would have been both logical and necessary had they been preparing for war, or taking positions on the scene in Germany that would appear unusually provocative. General Clay, for example, emphasized "The care with which the Russians avoided measures that would have been resisted with force."[7] The Western powers too were particularly careful since "The whole success of the airlift and the resistance of West Berlin depended on avoiding a military confrontation."[8] In addition, another striking restriction of this more generalized type arose from the fact that the United States remained silent about its nuclear capability throughout the 1948-1949 crisis. Even though this crisis occurred in the era of the American atomic monopoly, American decision-makers apparently felt they should not attempt to gain bargaining advantages during the crisis from this asymmetry between the capabilities of the United States and the Soviet Union.[9]

[5] On this point see Reston, *op.cit.*, p. 3.

[6] For the background of the American decision to deploy the B-29s in Europe, see Walter Millis, ed., *The Forrestal Diaries* (New York: Viking, 1951), pp. 454-466.

[7] Lucius D. Clay, *Decision in Germany* (Garden City, N.Y.: Doubleday, 1950), p. 374. The adamancy with which the Soviets insisted on the accidental nature of the air disaster at Gatow on April 5, 1948, is also interesting in this connection.

[8] Philip Windsor, *City on Leave* (New York: Praeger, 1963), p. 111.

[9] "Apparently" is employed here since American decision-makers did not make any formal disclaimers concerning the relevance of the effective atomic monopoly of the United States. Nevertheless, there is no evidence to suggest that the atomic monopoly played an important role in American thinking during this crisis.

In addition to these somewhat negative restraints on the use of violence, the Berlin crisis of 1948-1949 also produced, on a number of occasions, tacit coordination among the participants to control situations that might provoke violent clashes. Such activities were particularly evident in connection with the problems raised by popular disturbances within Berlin. It is true that police actions, particularly those of the Markgraf police based in the eastern sector of the city, sometimes played a role in generating inspired disturbances.[10] The opposite, however, was more often true of the actions of the regular military units of the four occupation powers stationed in the city. The presence of troop contingents helped in controlling a number of riots and civil disturbances that threatened to get out of hand and lead to violence. This was clearly the case, for example, with regard to the great rally of September 9, 1948, around the old Reichstag building on the sector boundary between East and West Berlin.[11]

Taiwan Strait, 1958

The 1958 crisis in the Taiwan Strait produced violent exchanges of substantial, though sharply limited, proportions. The use of violence during this crisis fell into several major categories including: the long-range artillery duel over the off-shore islands;[12] the battle for air superiority over the Taiwan Strait; and some light naval actions around the offshore islands and in the Strait itself. Military damage resulting from these hostilities was not severe.[13] Military casualties were not extensive, and damage to fortifications both on the offshore islands and on the mainland was quite moderate. Perhaps the most costly military damage resulted from the loss of aircraft, espe-

[10] For material on these activities see W. Phillips Davison, *The Berlin Blockade: A Study in Cold War Politics* (Princeton: Princeton University Press, 1958), pp. 177-187.

[11] On the September 9 rally consult *ibid.*, pp. 187-190.

[12] The bulk of the artillery bombardment against the offshore islands involved the Quemoy group alone. In fact, the Matsu group, farther north along the coast of the mainland, played only a peripheral role in the main confrontation of 1958.

[13] For some interesting comments on this point, see Dwight Eisenhower, *Waging Peace 1956-1961* (Garden City, N.Y.: Doubleday, 1965), p. 297.

cially by the Chinese People's Republic (CPR).[14] Civilian damage, on the other hand, though largely restricted to the Quemoy islands, was relatively severe.[15] Civilian deaths on the islands may have been as high as a thousand, and damage to civilian property (primarily housing) was extensive.

At the same time, the violence accompanying the 1958 crisis was subjected to several far-reaching restrictions. Only the Chinese Communists and the Chinese Nationalists engaged in outright violence. For the most part, the intensity of violence declined rather than increased over the course of the crisis. In short, the CPR initiated the confrontation phase of the crisis with a sharp outburst whose intensity was never really equaled after the first ten days of the crisis. In addition, the major participants coordinated to prevent violent exchanges from spreading beyond the geographical boundaries set at the outset of the confrontation. As McClelland has put it, "it is notable that the involved parties took care to contain the conflict within the bounds set by the first blow."[16]

These restraints on the use of violence weighed most directly on the two Chinas as the parties actually carrying out acts of violence. In this connection, the restraints observed by the CPR, which held the tactical offensive through much of the crisis, were particularly striking. The Chinese Communists displayed a general air of restraint and marked caution after the initial outburst opening the phase of confrontation.[17] This

[14] Exact losses in this area are not always easy to pinpoint. Available estimates, however, indicate that in the period between July 29 and October 25, thirty Chinese Communist planes were destroyed in battle and six Chinese Nationalist planes were destroyed. These figures do not include planes damaged but not destroyed.

[15] According to the count of the Nationalists, which is generally believed to have been relatively accurate, 474,907 shells struck the Quemoy island group during the first six weeks of the crisis. Because of the solidity of Nationalist fortifications and relatively frequent inaccuracy of CPR targeting, most of the damage caused by the shelling was in the civilian area. For further information on this subject, see Stewart Alsop, "The Story Behind Quemoy: How We Drifted Close to War," *Saturday Evening Post*, Vol. 231, No. 24 (December 13, 1958), 26-27 and 86-88.

[16] Charles McClelland, "Decisional Opportunity and Political Controversy: The Quemoy Case," *Journal of Conflict Resolution*, VI, No. 3 (September 1962), 210.

[17] For further comments of a general nature on this point, see Robert

general impression was strongly buttressed by the willingness of the CPR to impose upon itself a series of specific inhibitions. First, with regard to the offshore islands, the CPR confined itself to long-range bombardment,[18] abstaining almost entirely from efforts to bomb the islands from aircraft and from strafing operations.[19] Second, the CPR not only avoided any attempt to launch an invasion against the offshore islands, it also refrained from making any serious preparations for such a move.[20] Third, Chinese naval activities around the offshore islands and in the Strait, which were never extensive, were brought to early end following the introduction of American vessels in the role of escorts.[21] Fourth, throughout the whole crisis, the CPR confined itself to the use of only a small portion of its air force in actions relevant to the confrontation.[22] Fifth, the Chinese Communists were extremely careful to avoid attacks on American forces (as contrasted with Chinese Nationalist forces) even in delicate and ambiguous situations such as the convoying operations between Taiwan and Quemoy.[23] Sixth, the CPR failed conspicuously to utilize available

---

W. Barnett, "Quemoy: The Use and Consequence of Nuclear Deterrence," Harvard Center for International Affairs, March 1960, pp. 17-18 and 78.

[18] It appears that the coastal batteries were also under orders, for the most part, to target only military installations on the islands, such as the Nationalist gun emplacements, the airstrip on Quemoy, and the facilities at the landing beaches. In fact, however, the islands are very small, and the accuracy of the coastal batteries was not always sufficient to allow for successful discrimination in targeting.

[19] For information on this point see Donald Zagoria, *The Sino-Soviet Conflict 1956-1961* (New York: Atheneum, 1964), p. 208.

[20] For evidence on this subject see *ibid.*, pp. 206-208; and Harold Hinton, *Communist China in World Politics* (Boston: Houghton Mifflin, 1966), p. 266.

[21] For an interesting discussion of this point, see Morton Halperin and Tang Tsou, "The 1958 Quemoy Crisis," Chap. 10 in Morton Halperin, ed., *Sino-Soviet Relations and Arms Control* (Cambridge: M.I.T. Press, 1967), pp. 275-276.

[22] For evidence here see Barnett, *op.cit.*, p. 17; and Zagoria, *op.cit.*, p. 208.

[23] Among other things, American vessels came within the range of at least some of the coastal batteries in the course of their escort duties. Moreover, in view of the relatively poor accuracy of the Chinese shelling, the situation required special care to be sure of avoiding the outbreak of Sino-American violence. On the question of Sino-American restraint in

options for raising the intensity of hostilities even when it became clear that the attempted blockade of Quemoy was failing.[24]

Though their attitudes were ambivalent on the subject, the Chinese Nationalists for the most part matched the restraints on violence observed by the CPR.[25] The Nationalists returned the fire of the mainland artillery only in a limited fashion because they desired to avoid depleting their supplies of ammunition on Quemoy while the blockade remained effective, and they did not want to improve enemy targeting by giving away the exact locations of their own batteries. Far more important, however, the Nationalists refrained from conducting bombing strikes against the mainland either to knock out the coastal batteries opposite the offshore islands or to inflict retaliatory damage on the CPR.[26] An arena in which the Nationalists did conduct serious hostilities, on the other hand, was the contest for air superiority over the Strait. This was, in fact, a critical arena for the Nationalists both because control of the air over the Strait was of great importance to the outcome of the blockade[27] and because this was one of the few areas in which Nationalist forces were a match for those of the CPR.[28] As a result, the 1958 crisis

---

this connection, consult Barnett, *op.cit.*, p. 17; and John Thomas, "Soviet Behavior in the Quemoy Crisis of 1958," *Orbis*, VI, No. 1 (Spring 1962), 39.

[24] These options included: (1) aerial bombing of Quemoy, (2) aerial strafing of both the islands and the supply convoys, (3) the use of various types of naval mines, and (4) more extensive and stronger naval actions. For a discussion of some of these options, see Hanson Baldwin, the *New York Times*, September 19, 1958, p. 8.

[25] For a general discussion of this subject, see Tang Tsou, "The Quemoy Imbroglio: Chiang Kai-shek and the United States," *Western Political Quarterly*, XXII, No. 4 (December 1959), 1,085-1,091.

[26] The restraining influence of the United States appears to have been a factor of great importance in this connection. For additional comments on this point, see *infra*, p. 322.

[27] For a discussion of this point see Tang Tsou, "Mao's Limited War in the Taiwan Strait," *Orbis*, III, No. 3 (Fall 1959), 345.

[28] Nationalist success in this area did not stem from superiority of equipment. In fact, many analysts considered the MIG-17 a superior aircraft to the F-86 Sabrejets which formed the core of the Nationalist air force. The Nationalist edge in the air, which was becoming evident even before the introduction of the Sidewinder missiles on September 24, has generally been attributed to superior training.

was punctuated by a series of air battles between Nationalist F-86 Sabrejets and Communist MIG-15s and -17s which culminated in a decisive Nationalist victory on September 24.[29]

At the same time, the United States and the Soviet Union, each in an allied capacity to one of the Chinese participants, became involved in the problem of restraints on violence with regard to the use of their own forces and with regard to the exercise of influence on the decisions of their allies concerning the use of violence. In this connection, the Soviet posture was particularly forthright. The Soviets made it perfectly clear throughout the crisis that they were anxious to keep their own forces out of the clash.[30] Moreover, they carefully avoided any military moves that could be interpreted as preparations for intervention in the crisis.[31] As a result, the Soviets restricted themselves to some general *verbal* references during the later phases of the crisis to conceivable situations in which force might be used.[32] And they reacted with particular caution to the manipulative American moves involving military force, such as the transfer of Sidewinder missiles to the Nationalists and the deployment of eight-inch howitzers on Big Quemoy.[33] With regard to the exercise of restraint on the CPR, the impact of Soviet cautiousness is somewhat difficult to pinpoint since the evidence suggests that on most issues involving the

[29] Curiously, the September 24 battle appears to have begun as an effort by a numerically superior force of CPR MIGs to trap a group of Nationalist Sabrejets in order to shoot them down or force them deep into CPR airspace. On this aspect of the September 24 battle, see Tsou, "The Quemoy Imbroglio," *op.cit.*, pp. 1,084-1,085.

[30] For verification of this point consult Thomas, *op.cit.*, p. 39.

[31] On this subject consult *ibid.*, p. 58.

[32] These references were formulated with particular clarity in Khrushchev's letters of September 7 and 19 to Eisenhower. For the texts of these letters see, respectively, *DOSB*, XXXIX, No. 1005 (September 29, 1958), 499-503; and the *New York Times*, September 20, 1958, p. 2.

[33] The case of the eight-inch howitzers is particularly important since these weapons are capable of firing both conventional and atomic shells. The United States deployed them to Quemoy in order to offset the superior weight of CPR artillery during the early phases of the crisis. Atomic ammunition was not deployed with the howitzers. At the same time, however, the deployment of these weapons constituted a conditional threat to utilize nuclear weapons should the situation begin to deteriorate seriously. For additional comments on this point, see Zagoria, *op.cit.*, p. 215.

use of force, the Chinese Communists favored a policy of restraint in any case. It is probable, nevertheless, that Soviet caution reinforced the Chinese decision to accept various restraints. In addition the cautious position of the Soviets quite possibly was a factor of some significance in inducing Chinese restraint at several specific junctures, such as the decision to inject a note of relaxation into the crisis at the time of the September 6 statement[34] and the decision not to escalate the level of violence as the blockade of Quemoy began to fail.[35]

The position of the United States regarding the use of violence, on the other hand, was made somewhat ambiguous by the fact that the Nationalists were the weaker party, militarily, in the clash between the two Chinas. The United States proceeded to draw a sharp distinction between the use of its own military forces for purposes of coercion and the use of these forces in a violent fashion.[36] American forces played several important coercive roles. The rapid and extensive buildup of American strength in the area served to intimidate the CPR and to make any ideas of escalation seem unattractive. The use of American ships as escorts was an important factor in breaking the blockade.[37] And direct American assistance to the Nationalist forces in the way of equipment and training played a critical part in offsetting several initial advantages of the forces of the CPR.[38] Nevertheless, the United States did not employ its own forces violently at any time during the crisis.[39]

[34] For additional material on this subject, see Thomas, *op.cit.*, p. 43.

[35] For evidence on this point, see Alice Hsieh, *Communist China's Strategy in the Nuclear Era* (Englewood Cliffs, N.J.: Prentice-Hall, 1962), p. 127.

[36] For discussion see Richard Stebbins, *The United States in World Affairs 1958* (New York: Harper and Row [for the Council on Foreign Relations], 1959), p. 322.

[37] The escort vessels were, however, subject to the important, self-imposed limitation of remaining three miles away from the landing beaches at Quemoy. On the American rationale for this limitation, see Eisenhower, *op.cit.*, p. 297.

[38] American efforts to train Nationalist forces, particularly in the techniques of unloading supplies under fire, were generally successful and of great importance to the program of breaking the blockade by non-violent means.

[39] This was made possible partly through the exercise of great care in the formulation of operational command procedures for American forces in the Far East. On this point see Barnett, *op.cit.*, p. 78. It was also

321

In addition, the United States generally acted as a brake on Nationalist decisions concerning the scope of the violent exchanges that occurred during the crisis.[40] American influence appears to have been crucial in preventing the Nationalists from taking the initiative to carry out bombing strikes against the mainland.[41] The United States also curbed Nationalist ideas of precipitating violence on a broader scale in order to use the crisis to attempt a return to the mainland.[42] Nevertheless, it is important to point out that despite the political influence of these American restraints, the United States was never in a position to exercise complete control over the use of violence by the Nationalists. Moreover, because of the relative weakness of the Nationalists, the United States, despite its general policy of restraint, found itself on several occasions during the crisis in the position of augmenting the military equipment of the Nationalists as an alternative to using violence in its own right. The transfer of Sidewinder missiles to the Nationalists, for example, was an act of considerable importance in assuring Nationalist control of the air over the Strait.[43]

---

made possible, however, by the critical decision of the CPR to back away from the confrontation without escalating the level of violence farther, a decision that relieved American decision-makers of facing the extremely difficult problem that would have arisen if violence had risen to a level at which the Nationalists could not have held out without violent (in contrast to coercive) support from American forces. In fact, American forces operated under contingency plans that called for violent actions under certain circumstances. On this point see Eisenhower, *op.cit.*, p. 295. Nevertheless, any American decision to engage in violent exchanges would have been subject to serious political objections, especially in connection with domestic politics in the United States. For further comments on this point see Tsou, "Mao's Limited War in the Taiwan Strait," *op.cit.*, p. 344.

[40] For a discussion of American efforts along these lines, see Eisenhower, *op.cit.*, pp. 298-299.

[41] For information on this point consult *The Economist*, September 27, 1958, p. 1,003; and *Business Week*, September 27, 1958, p. 168.

[42] This subject is discussed in Tsou, "The Quemoy Imbroglio," *op.cit.*, pp. 1,077-1,078.

[43] For the official American position on the introduction of Sidewinder missiles into the crisis, see Dulles' statements at his news conference of September 30. The text is printed in *DOSB*, XXXIX, No. 1008 (October 20, 1958), 597-604. See especially p. 600.

Berlin, 1961

The question of restraints on the use of violence did not become a critical issue during the early phases of the 1961 Berlin crisis despite the harshness of the verbal exchanges of this period.[44] The question soon acquired major proportions, however, during the days surrounding August 13, and it remained important until the end of the crisis. The most striking evidence of restraint during these phases of the crisis lay in the clear-cut avoidance of overt acts of violence between the two sides and the total absence of military casualties.[45] These outcomes signify the existence of overall attitudes favoring restraints on violence,[46] but they also arose from the exercise of sharp restraints in a number of concrete situations developing out of the physical confrontation on the ground.

The impact of restraints on the use of violence quickly became significant in the events surrounding the closure of the sector boundary in Berlin as general uncertainties on both sides were sharply augmented by fears concerning the possibilities of loss of control. This period was characterized by great caution on the part of all parties, especially in matters of force deployment. Soviet troops were conspicuously kept away from the flashpoint in Berlin throughout this phase of the crisis.[47] In fact, Soviet forces were deployed entirely in East Germany proper during the crisis, primarily for defensive purposes associated with the dangers of uprisings in the German Democratic Republic (GDR). The Soviet armored divisions

[44] In short, during June and July there was no open confrontation or juxtaposition of the physical elements of force which could have precipitated violent clashes. Moreover, the dangers of popular uprisings and mob actions, which later became substantial, were not of critical importance during the early phases of the crisis.

[45] There were, however, some nonmilitary casualties attributable to the crisis. A number of individuals were shot while attempting to flee from East Berlin; several died of injuries sustained in jumps into the western sectors from buildings located in the eastern sector, and there were some lesser injuries sustained in various crowd activities during the course of the crisis.

[46] For further comments of a general nature on this subject, see Jean Edward Smith, "Berlin Confrontation," *The Virginia Quarterly Review*, Vol. 42, No. 3 (Summer 1966), 362, 364.

[47] For verification of this point see *ibid.*, p. 362.

that fanned out to circle Berlin on the night of August 12 were deployed in order to maximize control over events by isolating the city from the hinterlands. Moreover, during most of this period the Soviets were at pains to convey to the West the point that Soviet armed forces would not aggravate the local crisis through acts of physical interference in Berlin. Also, the heavy GDR troop deployment in East Berlin on August 13 was aimed almost entirely inward in an effort to minimize the dangers of popular uprisings in the East.[48] Strictly speaking, the deployment of the GDR forces within the city limits of Berlin was a violation of the occupation statutes for Berlin,[49] but on August 13 the only alternative was to deploy Soviet troops in the city, a course that would have heightened the dangers of East-West clashes besides being detrimental to the Eastern bargaining position.

In the immediate aftermath of the events of August 13, the Western powers made no move whatsoever toward physical resistance in Berlin.[50] The Western garrisons in Berlin were put on alert on August 13, but a specific decision was made not to deploy these troops anywhere near the sector boundary.[51] In fact, West Berlin police forces were mustered along the boundary to control civilians in the western sectors, a move that served as a *de facto* complement to the use of troops for control purposes in the eastern sector. Moreover, Mayor Brandt's suggestion of August 16 for a symbolic show of force along the boundary was sharply rejected by the Western al-

[48] This was done, as *The Economist* put it, "with a show of police and military force directed more against the regime's own subjects than against the indignant west Berliners." This statement appeared in *The Economist*, August 19, 1961, p. 688. For additional comments on the same subject, see Jean Edward Smith, *The Defense of Berlin* (Baltimore: The Johns Hopkins Press, 1963), p. 269.

[49] The West in fact protested this violation verbally in order to maintain the legal posture of the Western powers on the question of Western rights in Berlin but let it pass in all other respects. On this subject see the note, delivered on August 15, of the Western commandants in Berlin to the Soviet commandant. The text of the note is printed in *DOSB*, XLV, No. 1158 (September 4, 1961), 395-396.

[50] On this point consult, *inter alia*, Windsor, *op.cit.*, p. 240 .

[51] For verification of this point see Geoffrey McDermott, *Berlin: Success of a Mission?* (New York: Harper and Row, 1963), pp. 32-33.

lies.[52] There was no Western interference of any kind when the GDR began to replace barbed-wire barriers along the sector boundary with a concrete wall on August 18.[53] And this whole sequence of events led directly to a reduction in the tactical discretion of the local commanders of the Western powers in Berlin.[54]

The influence of caution concerning the dangers of violence went considerably beyond questions of troop deployment during this phase of the crisis. Great care was taken on a number of occasions, for example, to restrict the armaments of troops that might come into direct contact with opposing forces. The men in the GDR forces investing Berlin on the night of August 12 carried only blank ammunition.[55] Similarly, Western forces deployed along the sector boundary later on in August carried "hand grenades" that held only tear gas.[56] This does not mean that live weapons were not close at hand. It does suggest, however, a strong sense of caution with regard to arms, and especially small arms, on both sides of the confrontation. Moreover, there is strong evidence that GDR forces were "under orders to give way should Allied troops intervene"[57] along the sector boundary on the morning of August 13. The GDR

[52] On this point see Smith, *The Defense of Berlin, op.cit.*, p. 274.

[53] *Ibid.*, p. 288.

[54] At the outset of the 1961 crisis, the tactical discretion of the Berlin Command was already considerably more limited than it had been in earlier years. This discretion was, however, reduced even further during the course of the crisis. For additional information on this subject consult *ibid.*, pp. 328-329.

[55] For several reservations concerning the significance of this restraint, however, see Windsor, *op.cit.*, pp. 240-241. Among other things, the officers and NCO's carried usable sidearms and "the tanks and armoured cars were loaded with live shells."

[56] The Hellers relate an interesting incident bearing on this restraint. In the course of the close physical confrontation on August 25, "Communist police . . . sprayed spectators with water cannon and even splashed water at the feet of American soldiers. The impromptu shower baths were stopped when the American soldiers reached for 'hand grenades.'

" 'Our orders are to shoot if attacked by either bullets or water cannon,' one soldier told newsmen. The next day it was announced that the 'hand grenades' merely held tear gas." Deane and David Heller, *The Berlin Wall* (New York: Walker, 1962), p. 72.

[57] Smith, *The Defense of Berlin, op.cit.*, p. 276.

was, of course, extremely hopeful that there would be no significant Western response at this juncture. And it is no doubt reasonable to question whether an Eastern withdrawal could have been easily effected in the event that an East-West firefight had broken out along the sector boundary.[58] Nevertheless, the evidence indicates "that Ulbricht, like Hitler when he ordered the march into the Rhineland, was ready to withdraw at the least sign of opposition"[59] despite the fact that the internal crisis within the GDR had grown to extremely serious proportions by this time.

Sharp restraints on the use of violence and actions that might trigger violent clashes were maintained during the subsequent phases of the crisis. With the resumption of strategic bargaining during the latter part of August, however, the parties showed a new interest in employing force coercively to undermine the resolve and nerve of the opponent. The result was a situation in which extensive restraints were coupled with a number of efforts to manipulate risks without initiating violent clashes. The juxtaposition of these interests became clear in a number of concrete activities.

In the first instance, questions of force deployment remained important during these later phases. The movement of an American battle group into Berlin over the autobahn, for example, was a bargaining move involving significant risks. This move, however, was initiated only after a suitable delay following the events of August 13 and was conducted with great caution by the United States.[60] Moreover, it was greeted with notable circumspection on the part of the Soviets. Similarly, during the later days of August, the Soviets undertook a military buildup along the border between East and West Germany,[61] evidently hoping to demonstrate their determination in the crisis without raising the risks of violence unduly and

[58] For a discussion of the situation in these terms consult Windsor, *op.cit.*, p. 240.

[59] *Loc.cit.*

[60] In particular, the battle group traveled across GDR territory on August 20 with all weapons unloaded. On this point see the *New York Times*, August 20, 1961, p. 2.

[61] The Hellers state that the first reports of such a buildup came on August 19. See the Hellers, *op.cit.*, p. 53.

without, strictly speaking, going back on their statements about avoiding any aggravation of the local situation through physical interference. Perhaps the most striking moves involving force deployment during the later phases of the crisis, however, occurred when the Western powers moved troops and armor up to the Wall on several occasions.[62] The proximate reasons for these shows of force varied,[63] but they were all efforts to demonstrate resolve by manipulating the risks of physical clashes. Both sides acted with marked caution on each occasion when a show of force led to a direct physical confrontation across the sector boundary.[64] Nevertheless, these events were intrinsically dangerous both because the physical juxtaposition of opposing forces generated risks of serious incidents and because the interdependent nature of the resultant confrontations made substantial coordination necessary in order to terminate them without violence.

The problem of controlling the civilian population of Berlin also raised important questions concerning restraints on violence. In particular, the use of tear gas by both sides, as well as the use of water cannon, smoke bombs, and small-arms fire by GDR forces, generated certain dangers of East-West clashes. In fact, these activities were aimed primarily at controlling crowds and therefore stemmed essentially from a desire to reduce the dangers of East-West clashes that might have arisen if mass uprisings had gotten out of hand.[65] Still, the use of these techniques of physical coercion was hazardous on several counts. Given the highly emotional nature of some of the popular demonstrations, the use of physical coercion created a danger of angry and violent mass reactions which could have drawn in troops from both sides. In addition, there was

[62] The most conspicuous moves of this kind occurred on August 21, 23, 25, and October 27-28.

[63] These reasons included such issues as the "hundred-meters" edict and the question of freedom of movement within the whole city of Berlin for Allied personnel.

[64] The tank confrontation during October, which seemed the most dangerous of these confrontations at least superficially, actually involved a critical move in the direction of increased caution with the substitution of Soviet forces for GDR forces within Berlin.

[65] For a discussion of this point see Smith, *The Defense of Berlin,* op.cit., p. 277.

always the possibility that actions intended originally to control civilians could degenerate into dangerous East-West duels.[66] Several minor incidents along these lines involving tear gas and water cannon did in fact occur during the crisis. Moreover, the fact that effective control over such matters rested at least partially at the bottom of the military command structure made such possibilities particularly worrisome.

Finally, the juxtaposition of efforts to manipulate risks and clear-cut caution concerning the initiation of violence was again evident in the Soviet campaign to harass the access routes to Berlin during late August, September, and October.[67] The resultant actions signified a willingness on the part of the Soviets to play a somewhat dangerous game in order to test Western resolve on the access issue. This was especially the case with regard to probes involving the air corridors both because of the special Western sensitivity on the issue of aerial access to Berlin and because of the difficulty of bringing aerial incidents under control should they occur.[68] At the same, all these actions took the form of carefully controlled probes rather than commitments to rigid postures. The Soviets refrained from a number of forms of interference well within their physical capabilities. The resultant contacts were conducted by both sides in such a way that violent exchanges never occurred.

Cuba, 1962

One of the most striking features of the Cuban crisis of 1962 was the extent to which the parties were able to employ coercion for bargaining purposes without actually crossing the threshold into the use of violence. Given the directness of the physical confrontation and the pressures influencing the decisions of the parties in this crisis, the impact of restraints on the use of violence was remarkable. The fact that decision-

[66] For an interesting discussion of this point, see, for example, Windsor, *op.cit.*, p. 246.

[67] For further material on this point consult David Binder, "Are We Really Standing Firm in Berlin?" *The Reporter*, Vol. 26, No. 6 (March 15, 1962), 20-21.

[68] For an interesting discussion of this subject, see Windsor, *op.cit.*, p. 253.

makers placed a conscious and explicit emphasis on the notion of a decline in the usability of violence for bargaining purposes during this crisis was clearly a major determinant of this outcome. Those in control of the action referred repeatedly to the importance of "avoiding the use of violence."[69] As George Ball put it in discussing the requirements for the American initiative, "It had to be a plan that involved the least danger of escalation up an ascending scale of violence."[70]

The impact of these restraints emerged with great clarity in several distinguishable areas during the crisis. In the first instance, the desire to avoid violence played a critical role in the American debate over policy options during the week of October 15. Perhaps more than anything else, considerations along this line tipped the scales in favor of a blockade rather than an air strike or an outright invasion.[71] The blockade seemed desirable in the sense that it offered a chance to avoid the killing of Russians,[72] an act many thought could trigger a more or less uncalculated violent retaliation by Soviet forces.[73] As Hilsman has written, "it was always possible that some local Soviet commander would panic, assume the big war was on, with the Soviet Union itself under attack, and take matters into his own hands."[74] In addition, there was a strong sense among American decision-makers that the initiation of violence over Cuba by the United States would produce widespread negative political repercussions in various parts of the world. Moreover, a general feeling of moral repugnance at the idea

[69] George Ball, "Lawyers and Diplomats" (address delivered on December 13, 1962), in *DOSB*, XLVII, No. 1227 (December 31, 1962), 990.

[70] *Ibid.*, p. 989.

[71] For evidence on this subject see Theodore Sorensen, *Kennedy* (New York: Harper and Row, 1965), pp. 684-685.

[72] On the importance of this factor see "Cuban Crisis: A Step by Step Review," the *New York Times*, November 3, 1962, pp. 1, 6-7. The relevant portion of the text can be located conveniently in David L. Larson, ed., *The "Cuban Crisis" of 1962: Selected Documents and Chronology* (Boston: Houghton Mifflin, 1963), p. 227.

[73] It was generally believed that it would be impossible to carry out a so-called "surgical strike" against the Soviet installations in such a way as to achieve an acceptably high degree of assurance that no offensive missiles would remain in usable condition.

[74] Roger Hilsman, "The Cuban Crisis: How Close We Were to War," *Look*, Vol. 28, No. 17 (August 25, 1964), 19.

of bombing or invading Cuba was influential during the American debate on options. In Sorensen's words, "the nation's basic commitment to tradition and principle was involved. An air strike on military installations in Cuba, without any advance warning, was rejected as a 'Pearl Harbor in reverse.' "[75]

The United States therefore embarked on a program of action based essentially on manipulating the risks of violence rather than initiating violent actions at the outset. It is true this was a program that created a setting in which the possibilities of violent clashes became increasingly vivid and urgent. But given the range of options seriously considered, this program represented a decision in favor of relative caution and restraint.

The influence of sharp restraints on the use of violence was evident in the actions of both sides during the phase of full-blown confrontation that followed the American proclamation of October 22. This influence was particularly clear during the week of October 22 with regard to the naval operations in the Atlantic and the Caribbean, the arena which generated the most immediate dangers of violent clashes during the whole crisis. The fact that overt violence was avoided in connection with these naval operations was by no means accidental. On the contrary, both sides were at considerable pains to proceed with caution. On the same day that the American blockade became effective—October 24—the United States began to take steps to tighten the restrictions on its naval operations as much as possible. At this point, Kennedy "ordered that the navy screen around Cuba should not intercept a Russian ship until absolutely necessary."[76] Elaborate precautions were taken, despite objections from the American Navy,[77] to ensure that every effort would be made to stop Soviet ships with the

[75] Theodore Sorensen, *Decision-Making in the White House* (New York: Columbia University Press, 1963), p. 32. The leading supporter of arguments along these lines in the American Administration appears to have been Robert Kennedy. For evidence on this point see Elie Abel, *The Missile Crisis* (Philadelphia: Lippincott, 1966), p. 88.

[76] Stewart Alsop and Charles Bartlett, "In Time of Crisis," *Saturday Evening Post*, Vol. 235, No. 44 (December 8, 1962), 15.

[77] On the substance of these objections from the navy, see Abel, *op.cit.*, pp. 154-156.

minimum use of force when they actually reached the blockade line. At the same time, the Soviet Union went to great lengths to guarantee the avoidance of a violent clash at sea. Submarines were not used to interfere with the blockade, and no attempt was made to break it with surface vessels. And the Soviets did not try either to form convoys to run the blockade or to evade it in any way. Instead, they abided by the American rules for the blockade and submitted to all the demands of the American Navy. As a result, the blockade went into effect with an almost ritualistic observance of good manners and protocol. The first Soviet ship to reach the blockade line, the oil tanker *Bucharest*, was allowed to pass after only telegraphic communication and without boarding.[78] The first actual boarding did not occur until the morning of October 26. For this ceremony, the United States carefully selected the *Marucla*, a ship registered in Lebanon and manned by a Greek crew which was under charter to the Soviet Union, in contrast to a ship belonging directly to the Soviet Union.[79] Throughout the remainder of the blockade, the two sides continued to act in this proper, though somewhat stylized, manner to minimize the dangers of violent clashes at sea.

The realm of aerial operations constituted another arena characterized by substantial dangers of violent clashes and by the exercise of clear-cut restraints during the 1962 crisis. Given the extensiveness of American aerial surveillance, at both high and low levels, over Cuba during the crisis and the fact that antiaircraft weapons in Cuba were at least partially under the control of junior officers, it is remarkable that only one airplane was shot down during the entire crisis.[80] Even in this case the United States conspicuously avoided a violent

---

[78] On this point see Henry Pachter, *Collision Course* (New York: Praeger, 1963), p. 43. Since it was obvious from visual inspection that the ship was an oil tanker and therefore could not be carrying additional missiles, the United States could afford to exhibit restraint in this case without jeopardizing the credibility of the blockade as a whole.

[79] For information on this decision see Abel, *op.cit.*, pp. 171-172.

[80] This was the American U-2 shot down, evidently by a Soviet "Guideline" (SAM-2) missile, over Cuba on the morning of October 27. On this subject, see especially Pachter, *op.cit.*, p. 51. Though the subject is somewhat controversial, there is little evidence that further significant efforts were made to bring down American aircraft during the crisis.

response, despite the fact that its original contingency plan called for retaliation against a single SAM-site under such circumstances.[81] In fact, under the pressures of an actual case the United States contented itself with a "warning by the Department of Defense that the next time the United States would retaliate by bombarding the Soviet Samsites."[82]

The final tense days of the confrontation produced further indications of influential restraints on the use of violence. The avoidance of a violent incident in connection with the straying of an American U-2 over the Chukotsk Peninsula on October 27 was striking primarily as an indicator of Soviet caution. The matter became tense when "Soviet fighters, based on Wrangel Island . . . scrambled to intercept the intruder. U.S. fighter planes from Alaska were in the air at the moment trying to find the U-2 plane and escort it back safely."[83] The Soviets, however, let the incident pass without violence even though it seems to have put them in a jittery frame of mind.[84] Beyond this, it is now clear that Kennedy was extremely hesitant about shifting to an air strike or an outright invasion of Cuba even during the tensest moments of October 27 when it seemed quite likely that the Soviet response to the preceding events would be unacceptable and when pressures within the United States for such a shift were mounting.[85] As it happened, the acceptable Soviet response on October 28 made it unnecessary to make a final choice in this area. The hesitancy of American decision-makers even under the pressures of extreme commitment, however, constitutes an interesting indication of the influence of restraints on the initiation of violence during the 1962 crisis.[86]

[81] For information on this point see Sorensen, *Kennedy, op.cit.*, p. 713.
[82] Henry Brandon, "An Untold Story of the Cuban Crisis," *Saturday Review*, March 9, 1963, p. 56.
[83] Abel, *op.cit.*, p. 193.
[84] For an interesting commentary on this particular point, see Khrushchev's statement in his letter to Kennedy of October 28, 1962. For the relevant portion of the text, see Pachter, *op.cit.*, p. 225.
[85] For some interesting material on this point, see Sorensen, *Kennedy, op.cit.*, pp. 715-716.
[86] The presence of this hesitancy does *not*, however, mean that Kennedy would have failed to go through with an air strike or an invasion had the crisis developed differently.

Conclusion

An analysis of the case materials in this chapter makes it plain that the use of violence has been subjected to highly influential restraints in the great-power crises of the postwar period. The impact of such limits has been especially striking in crises involving *direct* confrontations between the two superpowers. But limits on the use of violence have not been lacking even when a direct confrontation of this kind has not developed. Moreover, an examination of the cases makes it evident that the development of effective limits has not been a matter of accident. On the contrary, this subject has generally become a matter of explicit concern to decision-makers operating under conditions of crisis. This concern has led to the emergence of a number of distinguishable patterns of action aimed at avoiding violence during crises. Conscious abstinence from particular actions sometimes operates to this end as was the case with: the Western decision not to attempt to break the land blockade of Berlin during the 1948-1949 crisis; the care with which the Soviets avoided serious interference in the air corridors during both Berlin crises; and the conscious efforts of the Chinese Communists to distinguish between American and Nationalist forces during the Taiwan Strait crisis. Another set of procedures for avoiding violence focuses on elaborate and obvious efforts to observe strict protocol in dangerous situations. Both sides coordinated on this rule, for example, with regard to movement in the access routes to Berlin in the immediate aftermath of the events of August 13, 1961. The use of highly stylized or ritualistic procedures constitutes a third route to the avoidance of violence. This was the device through which the two sides coordinated to avoid violence with regard to the American naval blockade during the Cuban crisis of 1962.

The phenomenon of thresholds or "firebreaks" has received a great deal of attention in recent discussions of the use of force in international politics. These notions have generally been employed, however, to distinguish between different levels of violence, as is the case for example with the nuclear threshold.[87] In this connection, a systematic analysis of actual cases of crisis indicates that phenomena of this type are in fact important. The threshold that almost invariably received the greatest attention during these crises was nevertheless the dividing line between nonviolent coercion and violent exchanges. The decision-makers of the two superpowers, especially, appear to be strongly influenced by the idea that this threshold is a particularly critical one. There is, in short, little doubt about the prevalence of fears among these decision-makers that escalatory sequences are apt to be extremely difficult to control once violence has broken out and that beyond this threshold the parties will find it almost impossible to coordinate in order to demarcate clear boundaries between different levels of violence.[88] This is not to say that such fears will be borne out in fact following the initiation of violence in a concrete case. Evidence from cases such as the Taiwan Strait crisis of 1958 suggests quite strongly that they will not necessarily be borne out.[89] The influence of such fears, nevertheless, appears to have been a critical determinant of the important rule that the superpowers should avoid violent con-

[87] For extensive efforts to conceptualize these problems in the nuclear context, see Herman Kahn, *On Escalation, Metaphors and Scenarios* (New York: Praeger, 1965); and Bernard Brodie, *Escalation and the Nuclear Option* (Princeton: Princeton University Press, 1966).

[88] This does not mean that Brodie's analysis of the possibilities of discriminating among various levels of violence is, in fact, unrealistic. It does, however, suggest that many decision-makers *believe* that the possibilities for effective differentiation following the initial use of violence are not very great. And it is clear that the attitudes with regard to such matters which decision-makers bring to crisis situations are generally quite influential. For Brodie's arguments concerning differentiations among levels of violence, see *ibid.*, Chaps. 10 and 11.

[89] This is, in fact, one rather interesting way to retrieve the Brodie position with regard to escalation and escalatory pressures. The Taiwan Strait case is particularly interesting in this connection. Many of the important limits on the use of violence in this crisis were formulated and carried out by the Chinese Communists. Moreover, this was true despite the fact that Chinese Communist decision-makers had quite clearly been exposed to Soviet military doctrines which tended to emphasize the impossibility of differentiating among various levels of violence. For a good statement of Soviet views on the question of escalation, which summarizes positions that were certainly relevant in 1958, see V. D. Sokolovsky, ed., *Military Strategy: Soviet Doctrine and Concepts*, intro. by Raymond Garthoff (New York: Praeger, 1963), Chap. IV.

tact on a direct basis under conditions of crisis. The viability of this rule in concrete cases has, in turn, been critical in allowing these powers to engage in crises with far-reaching political significance on a highly coercive but strikingly non-violent basis.

The importance of the violence threshold has also influenced the actions of states other than the two superpowers. As the Taiwan Strait crisis of 1958 and the actions of the German Democratic Republic (GDR) in the 1961 Berlin crisis indicate, however, lesser powers can disregard this threshold to some extent if the superpowers are sufficiently involved in the situation to assume the ultimate burden of maintaining overall international stability. Several specific aspects of this asymmetry are significant. A lesser power involved in a major crisis is more likely than one of the superpowers to view the situation, literally, as a "life-or-death" matter. This was the case, for example, with the Chinese Nationalists in 1958 and the regime of the GDR in 1961. Next, the very presence of the superpowers is apt to increase the freedom of action of the lesser powers. The case materials strongly suggest that lesser powers, under conditions of crisis, will simply assume that the superpowers will deal with the ultimate problems of maintaining overall international stability. Under such circumstances, the decision-makers of the superpowers have little choice but to contemplate "responsible" postures, at least on a *de facto* basis, when a crisis really becomes dangerous. This relative freedom of action also accounts for the striking bargaining strength that lesser powers often demonstrate vis-à-vis great powers under conditions of crisis. So long as a lesser power is not an absolute satellite of one of the great powers, it can, in effect, gain influence by threatening to complicate severely the task of the great powers in maintaining overall international stability.

Beyond this it is important not to confuse the influence of restraints on the actual use of violence and the relevance of efforts to manipulate the risks of violence for bargaining purposes.[90] Though fears concerning the outbreak of violence cer-

---

[90] For an extensive effort to conceptualize the nature of tactics based on the manipulation of the risks of violence, consult Thomas Schelling, *Arms and Influence* (New Haven: Yale University Press, 1966), Chap. 3.

tainly affect the utilization of such bargaining tactics in important ways, the case materials make it clear that they do not by any means preclude manipulation of this kind entirely. Several specific aspects of the manipulation of risks under conditions of crisis stand out. In all the cases under analysis, manipulative activities of this kind were characteristically conceptualized as alternatives to the actual initiation of violence. In relative terms, therefore, tactics of this kind tend to emerge as essentially cautious acts. The evidence also suggests there is apt to be a correlation between perceived tension in the atmosphere surrounding a crisis and hesitancy in the utilization of manipulative bargaining tactics. This does not mean decision-makers will terminate all efforts along these lines as a crisis becomes more severe, but it does tend to make the parties increasingly sensitive to the dangers of boxing an opposing state into a situation in which it has little choice but to initiate overt hostilities. Finally, asymmetries with regard to willingness to engage in manipulative tactics are apt to be influential determinants of the ultimate outcome of any given crisis. In both the Taiwan Strait crisis of 1958 and the Cuban crisis of 1962, for example, the superior ability of one side to manipulate the risks of violence in a credible fashion *despite* the impact of widespread fears of violence became a critical determinant of the outcome of the confrontation.

14. The Role of Initiative

HYPOTHESIS. Under conditions of crisis, the tactical "initiative that forces the opponent to initiate" tends to become a critical coercive device.

This chapter is concerned with the role of the initiative in international bargaining processes.[1] At the outset, it is important to distinguish between strategic initiatives and tactical initiatives. Initiative at the strategic level refers to efforts aimed at shaping the basic content and the broad directions of the general flow of international politics. Initiative at the tactical level, on the other hand, refers to specific actions aimed at determining the outcome of a particular episode, engagement, or situation occurring within the flow of international politics. Thus the fundamental decision to initiate actions that are likely to precipitate a crisis is generally a strategic problem while specific actions undertaken within the context of an ongoing crisis are usually tactical matters. Though the initiative at both levels may rest with the same party in a given crisis, there is no necessary correlation between the two levels. And it frequently happens that a party in the position of respondent (or defendant) with regard to the underlying strategic issues associated with a crisis will assume the tactical initiative with the regard to concrete issues during the course of the crisis.

There is, in general terms, a presumption in favor of policies that permit an actor to acquire and retain the initiative at the strategic level. This presumption arises from considerations having to do with the ability to define the basic issues in the international arena, the acquisition of political support, the maintenance of morale, and the value of forward momentum in international politics.[2] The situation is significantly different, however, with regard to the tactical initiative, especially under conditions of crisis. There are, as discussed in the

[1] For a rather general discussion of the problem of initiative in bargaining situations, consult Thomas Schelling, *The Strategy of Conflict* (Cambridge: Harvard University Press, 1960), Chap. 5.

[2] The history of postwar international politics, for example, contains many illustrations of the disadvantages associated with a fundamentally defensive orientation at the strategic level.

337

preceding chapter, far-reaching restraints on activities that are likely to bring down on any actor the proximate responsibility for initiating the use of violence during a crisis. Moreover, these restraints are apt to be particularly influential when it is *not* possible for the initiator to argue that the use of violence will produce a *fait accompli* and when, therefore, the actor initiating the use of violence must expect overt hostilities to ensue. But, a passive posture that involves simply waiting for the opponent to undertake clear-cut actions before taking steps to secure one's own position generally leaves much to be desired under conditions of crisis. This is obviously the case for a party with offensive objectives on the strategic level. As a crisis unfolds, however, it is apt to become increasingly true even for a party whose initial position was essentially defensive. Under the circumstances, crises tend to generate, in an acute fashion, problems arising from the desire to employ coercive initiatives for the achievement of political objectives without, at the same time, catalyzing the initiation of violent exchanges.

It therefore becomes an important bargaining objective to project the disadvantages associated with the maintenance of restraints on the use of violence onto the opponent. One of the most successful techniques for achieving this objective is to undertake decisive but nonviolent tactical initiatives aimed at acquiring a position that will guarantee a positive outcome in a given confrontation *unless* the opponent is willing to respond by initiating the use of violence, thereby accepting the political disadvantages associated with the responsibility for the outbreak of violence. Efforts to cut off a garrison from essential provisions without overwhelming it by force or to block critical land or sea passages in such a way that an opponent would have to launch a violent attack in order to advance on a territorial objective, for example, are classic forms of this "initiative that forces the opponent to initiate." The typical complexity of crises, however, can easily play tricks on the participants with regard to tactical initiatives of this kind. For example, a party that believes it has achieved a winning position with an "initiative that forces the opponent to initiate" may overlook or miscalculate certain contingencies and, as a result, suddenly find the tables turned as its opponent employs a new gambit involving a counter initiative of this kind.[3]

Berlin, 1948-1949

The "initiative that forces the opponent to initiate" became a critical feature of the tactical maneuvers undertaken during the Berlin crisis of 1948-1949. In the opening phases of the crisis, the initiative lay with the Soviet Union on the tactical level. During this period, nevertheless, the Soviets chose to exercise the initiative in a circumspect fashion. To understand this development it is necessary to consider the background of the crisis and to assume a broader perspective on the problem of the initiative during this period.

The activities of the Western powers with regard to the future of Germany during the winter and spring of 1948 were somewhat uncoordinated and amorphous. It is unlikely these powers originally conceptualized these activities in terms of a deliberate effort to capture the initiative on the strategic level in central Europe. Nevertheless, Western planning operations during this period ultimately began to focus more and more on the objective of reconstructing the western zones of Germany as an independent state without the eastern zone. Moreover, these activities were capped by the announcement of the London recommendations on June 7 and of the Western currency reform on June 18. As a result, the Soviets evidently began to fear a *fait accompli* in Germany that would be impossible to overturn except through the use of overt force and that would, in turn, constitute a serious challenge to the future position of the Soviet Union in central Europe. In a somewhat obscure fashion and without taking full stock of the probable impact of their moves in the context of East-West relations, therefore, the Western powers began to exercise the initiative with regard to the key problems of central Europe during the early months of 1948.

[3] In employing the "initiative that forces the opponent to initiate," an actor is, among other things, focusing and narrowing the critical nexus of the bargaining relationship in question. If the original initiative fails, therefore, the party that formulated it may find itself severely hampered by the consequent difficulty of shifting the focus of the bargaining relationship onto different issues.

339

These developments constituted the background situation in which the Soviets decided to exercise the tactical initiative by imposing a land blockade on Berlin. Rather than responding with a frontal attack on the Western activities, the Soviets sought to isolate an important point, on which the Western powers were vulnerable, to utilize as a bargaining lever. Moreover, in bringing pressure to bear on this point, the Soviets prudently chose an initiative based on the idea of establishing a stranglehold over Berlin. The blockade was an initiative designed, in effect, to force the problem of choice with regard to the use of violence onto the Western powers. The blockade had another advantage as a coercive initiative since it *apparently* created a situation in which the pressure on the Western powers would increase automatically without any need for further initiatives on the part of the Soviet Union.

The advantages of this Soviet initiative ultimately turned out to be illusory, however, since the blockade was based on a critical miscalculation. In short, the Soviets assumed that a large-scale Western airlift was not a viable possibility.[4] It is probable the blockade would have succeeded in eliciting concessions from the Western powers if this assumption had held. Nevertheless, the ultimate failure of this assumption operated to lock the Soviets into a narrow position that was no longer viable, thereby emphasizing the "tricky" nature of tactics based on the "initiative that forces the opponent to initiate." While an initiative of this kind will appear to be a brilliant success when it works, it may well lock the initiator into an unfavorable pattern of bargaining that is almost impossible to break if it fails.[5]

In this connection, the counterinitiative of the Western powers in meeting the Soviet land blockade with a large-scale airlift appears as a brilliant move. In effect, it shifted the responsibility with regard to the use of violence back to the to the Soviets. For this reason it should be emphasized that

[4] For evidence of this Soviet assumption see D. Melnikov, "The 'Airlift': Legend and Realities," *New Times*, September 15, 1948, p. 9.

[5] The problem here arises from the fact that the original initiator is, to a considerable degree, responsible for both the pattern of bargaining and the ground rules characteristic of a specific situation.

the initiators of the airlift had a far more limited conception of its utility when they began it. In fact, the Western powers initiated the airlift assuming that it could not succeed over the long run and with the more modest hope that it would provide additional time for bargaining.[6] Even on this limited basis the airlift was initiated with considerable hesitancy. It has since become clear, for example, that decision-makers in Washington were at first undecided about the airlift and that the actual decision to begin it was taken by General Clay in Germany.[7] Moreover, the steady introduction of new technology in such forms as the C-54 cargo plane and improved radar during the course of the airlift played a critical, though originally unpredictable, role in the successful expansion and maintenance of the airlift during the summer and fall of 1948.[8]

The airlift became a serious threat to the Soviet bargaining position in the confrontation as the Western powers succeeded in expanding and maintaining it. As time passed, the Soviets began to consider the possibilities for interfering with it. From time to time, they "buzzed" Western planes in the air corridors, and in September 1948 they hinted at plans for coordinated air maneuvers involving the air corridors. Nevertheless, the Soviets exercised striking restraint in this area. While it is probable they could have gotten away with some additional interference with the airlift, the dangers of incidents leading to the outbreak of violence were clear-cut in this arena.[9] As a result, the Soviets refrained from efforts to use several forms of interference that were within their capabilities, thereby offering a striking demonstration of the *de facto* influence of the concept of the last clear chance in an important international situation. The Western initiative in starting the airlift ultimately became a brilliant success. It was, in the

[6] For an interesting discussion of this subject, see Charles J.V. Murphy, "Berlin Air Lift," *Fortune*, November 1948, p. 90.

[7] For additional material on this subject see Lucius D. Clay, *Decision in Germany* (Garden City, N.Y.: Doubleday, 1950), pp. 355-356; and Jean Edward Smith, *The Defense of Berlin* (Baltimore: The Johns Hopkins Press, 1963), pp. 106-110.

[8] For material on this subject consult, *inter alia*, Clay, *op.cit.*, p. 382.

[9] For further discussion see James Reston, the *New York Times*, October 3, 1948, Sect. IV, p. 3; and Frederick Ford, "New Marks, Old Mistakes in Berlin," *The New Republic*, Vol. 119, No. 3 (July 19, 1948), 12.

words of *The Economist*, "like a knight's move in a game of chess; it enable[d] the West to hold its position in Berlin by jumping over the opposing pieces which threaten[ed] it."[10] It was, however, a somewhat haphazard success backed into by the Western powers bit by bit.

The blockade and the airlift illustrate two different forms of the "initiative that forces the opponent to initiate." Insofar as it was designed to affect the German policy of the Western powers, the blockade contained a strong element of compellence.[11] The Soviets were, in effect, attempting to stop ongoing Western activities by exerting pressure at a point where the Western powers were particularly vulnerable. In this connection, the initiative had the *apparent* advantage of containing an automatic tightening process. To affect Western policy outside of Berlin, however, still required an effort to manipulate the political will of the Western powers by establishing a clear link between Berlin and the future of Germany in general. The airlift, on the other hand, was primarily a deterrent initiative. It established a situation in which the Western powers could remain in Berlin on an ongoing basis without initiating the use of violence. The contrast between these two cases lends support to the hypothesis that compellent initiatives are more difficult to utilize successfully than deterrent initiatives.[12] While an obstinate opponent may raise serious problems in a compellent situation, a successful deterrent initiative will establish a position from which the initiator cannot be dislodged without a clear-cut resort to violence.

Taiwan Strait, 1958

The "initiative that forces the opponent to initiate" achieved great significance during the 1958 crisis in the Taiwan Strait. Though the parties did not turn to these procedures on a serious basis during the initial phases of the crisis, the later stages of the confrontation produced reciprocal efforts along these lines which illustrate both the importance and the complexity

10 *The Economist*, October 23, 1948, p. 652.

11 For an extensive effort to conceptualize the notion of compellence, see Thomas Schelling, *Arms and Influence* (New Haven: Yale University Press, 1966), pp. 69-78.

12 For a discussion leading up to this hypothesis, see *ibid.*, pp. 78-90.

of such efforts to manipulate the initiative. In this connection, the Chinese People's Republic (CPR) and the United States became the principal users of the "initiative that forces the opponent to initiate" in this crisis since it was primarily the Sino-American relationship that posed important questions concerning the initiation of violence.[13]

In the 1958 crisis, the CPR became the first to make a major effort to utilize an initiative of the kind with its *de facto* blockade of the Quemoy island group. The essential idea of this blockade was to cut the islands off from all possibilities of resupply on a nonviolent basis. As a result, the Americans would eventually be forced to choose between actions involving the initiation of violence against the armed forces or the territory of the CPR in order to assist the resupply efforts of the Nationalists and a willingness to force the Nationalists into making major concessions with regard to the principal issues of the crisis.[14] It is, of course, true that the CPR engaged in an extensive shelling operation against the islands from the outset of the confrontation. During the first phase of the confrontation, however, the shelling was evidently *not* undertaken to strangle the islands by means of an artillery blockade.[15] In fact, the notion of a blockade became prominent only during the early days of September in the course of the reassessment that followed the decline of Chinese Communist hopes for an early collapse of Nationalist defenses on the islands.

This program of strangulation dragged out over a considerable period of time for several reasons. First, the initiative was ultimately compellent rather than deterrent in nature. Fundamentally, it was designed to force the opponent to give up something rather than to hold a position already in the possession of the initiator. Second, supplies for several months

[13] Since relations between the two Chinas were already characterized by elements of violence, the question here was one of escalation rather than initiation. At the same time, it never seemed probable that the Soviet Union and the United States would become involved in overt hostilities directly between themselves during this crisis.

[14] For a clear explanation of this potential problem, see Donald Zagoria, *The Sino-Soviet Conflict 1956-1961* (New York: Atheneum, 1964), pp. 206-207.

[15] For a more extended analysis of Chinese objectives during this phase of the crisis, see *supra* Chap. Eight.

were already on the islands at the time so that the danger of complete strangulation was not immediate. Third, there were several possible actions to break the blockade without initiating the use of violence between the United States and the CPR which the Nationalists and the Americans could try. Nevertheless, the basic objective of the blockade remained the same over time. In essence, the CPR hoped to shift "to the United States the decision as to whether there would be a direct encounter between American and Communist Chinese forces in Asia."[16]

In the final analysis, however, "the blockade did not work,"[17] and this tactical initiative on the part of the CPR ended in failure, a costly one since the Chinese had become committed to this move and had reduced their overall tactical flexibility in order to push the blockade. In the end, the Nationalists, with extensive American assistance, were able to break the blockade without precipitating Sino-American violence, while the American buildup in the area of the Strait succeeded in intimidating the Chinese Communists with regard to the possibilities of escalating the level of conflict as the blockade began to fail. In effect, therefore, the Americans and the Nationalists were able to counter the initiative of the CPR with an "initiative that forces the opponent to initiate" of their own. But this reversal was not accomplished easily or quickly. In fact, the first attempts to break the blockade were conspicuous failures,[18] and it was not until the end of September that the ultimate outcome of the struggle over the blockade began to become clear.[19]

The program through which the blockade was broken without initiating Sino-American violence involved the coordination of several discrete activities. Beginning on September 7 the United States supplied daylight escorts for Nationalist con-

[16] Tang Tsou, "Mao's Limited War in the Taiwan Strait," *Orbis*, III, No. 3 (Fall 1959), 341.

[17] Zagoria, *op.cit.*, p. 207.

[18] For some interesting factual material on this subject, see Robert W. Barnett, "Quemoy: The Use and Consequence of Nuclear Deterrence," Harvard Center for International Affairs, March 1960, p. 10.

[19] For an important discussion of these developments from the American perspective, see Dwight Eisenhower, *Waging Peace 1956-1961* (Garden City, N.Y.: Doubleday, 1965), p. 302.

voys across the Taiwan Strait and up to a distance of three miles from the beachhead on Big Quemoy.[20] The purposes of escorting were to prevent harassment of the convoys in the Strait itself and to provide a measure of protection by association even in the landing area at Quemoy. Next, the United States supplied critical assistance to the Nationalists in the areas of equipment and training.[21] In the course of the effort to break the blockade, Nationalist forces were provided with more advanced equipment for landing supplies[22] and put through an intensive training program in the techniques of landing supplies under fire.[23] In addition, the Nationalists, again with American assistance, developed a significant program during the month of September of parachuting supplies to the islands. Air drops were particularly important in supplying the smaller islands in the Quemoy group which lie even closer to the mainland than Big Quemoy.[24] The Nationalists

[20] For a statement of the American rationale in adhering to this three-mile limit, see Eisenhower, *op.cit.*, p. 297. Nevertheless, the fundamental point of the limit remains quite ambiguous. Evidently, the three-mile figure was based on traditional concepts concerning the width of the territorial sea. Under the circumstances, however, such considerations would only affect American escort operations insofar as the islands were assumed to be part of the territory of the CPR, an assumption to which the United States clearly did not subscribe in 1958. At the same time, the legal confusion arising from the countervailing claims concerning one China or two Chinas makes this problem even more difficult to sort out. For an unsuccessful effort to clarify the situation, see Dulles' statements at his news conference on September 9. The text of this news conference is printed in *DOSB*, XXXIX, No. 1005 (September 29, 1958), 485-493. Perhaps the most plausible interpretation of the three-mile limit arises from the suggestion that it was essentially a tacit, and only dimly perceived, move by the United States which constituted part of the effort to coordinate on the development of tacit norms concerning the avoidance of Sino-American violence.

[21] On this subject see the comments in Eisenhower, *op.cit.*, pp. 302-303.

[22] This equipment included both "Amtracks" to allow for standoff debarkation of supplies and, ultimately, larger landing craft.

[23] Initially, the unfamiliarity of Nationalist forces with the techniques of landing supplies under fire was a critical problem. The ability of the Nationalists to learn rapidly and on location was a factor of real importance in the effort to break the blockade by nonviolent means.

[24] Eisenhower, for example, has argued that "By the end of the month [September] it appeared that air drop alone could maintain supply levels in essentials." The quotation is from Eisenhower, *op.cit.*, p. 303. While the air drop program clearly acquired considerable importance in the course of the crisis, however, it would appear that this claim for the program is somewhat too extensive.

were able, at the same time, to wage a successful battle for control of the air over the Strait, a factor of considerable importance in making the CPR's options for escalating the level of the conflict unattractive.[25] In this connection, the air battle of September 24, which witnessed the introduction of American-made Sidewinder air-to-air missiles, was a decisive turning point.[26]

By the beginning of October, the success of this carefully orchestrated effort to break the blockade without initiating Sino-American violence was becoming evident. As a result, the locus of decision with regard to the use of violence began to shift back to the CPR. And the Chinese Communists chose not to exercise their options to escalate the level of conflict.[27] Instead they decided to disengage from the crisis before the failure of the blockade became publicly obvious in order to give the appearance of maintaining control over the situation and thereby saving face.[28] The CPR therefore announced the cease-fire of October 6, an important initiative in the direction of deescalation which the United States reciprocated on October 8 by suspending (on a conditional basis) escorts for Nationalist convoys.[29]

The success of the Americans and the Nationalists in this process of trading initiatives was a critical determinant of the final outcome of the crisis from several points of view. Failure to break the blockade would have left the CPR in an

[25] For a discussion of this subject see Tang Tsou, "The Quemoy Imbroglio: Chiang Kai-shek and the United States," *Western Political Quarterly*, XXII, No. 4 (December 1959), pp. 1,084-1,085. Among other things, effective control of the air over the Strait sharply increased the obstacles facing any CPR effort to escalate the level of violence during the later phases of the crisis.

[26] This was the first use of the Sidewinder missile in a combat situation. Its performance in the 1958 crisis, as well as the fact that it is both technologically simple and cheap, has made it a popular weapon ever since.

[27] For a discussion of the options available to the CPR in this connection, see Hanson Baldwin, the *New York Times*, September 19, 1958, p. 8.

[28] For further comments on this procedure, see Charles McClelland, "Decisional Opportunity and Political Controversy: The Quemoy Case," *Journal of Conflict Resolution*, VI, No. 3 (September 1962), 210.

[29] For the text of the American statement of October 8, see *DOSB*, XXXIX, No. 1007 (October 27, 1958), 650.

extraordinarily strong bargaining position.[30] The strangulation of the offshore islands would have proceeded automatically without additional initiatives on the part of the CPR, thereby setting up an ever tightening process. Furthermore, the ability to break the blockade without violently employing American forces was of great importance for the policy of the United States in this crisis. Though the United States had an impressive array of forces in the Strait and contingency plans for their use, the pressures of both domestic and foreign opinion would have made it extremely difficult for the American government to assume the responsibility for initiating Sino-American violence, especially if the resultant actions involved direct strikes against the Chinese mainland.[31]

The struggle over the blockade was the principal focus for efforts to use the "initiative that forces the opponent to initiate" during the 1958 crisis. Notably, however, the United States in particular engaged in several subsidiary activities during the crisis aimed at gaining advantages by manipulating the initiative on the tactical level. The use of the American Seventh Fleet to patrol the Strait—with orders to shoot back if attacked—was, in effect, a means of making any idea of offensive action against Taiwan itself unattractive to the CPR. It is now clear the Chinese Communists did not entertain any idea of attempting an invasion directly against Taiwan during this crisis, but the interposition of the Seventh Fleet in such a way that any invasion attempt would clearly result in a violent American involvement carried with it reassurance value at the time. More important, the American response to the CPR's declaration of September 4, claiming a twelve-mile limit for Chinese territorial waters, illustrates the utility of the "initiative that forces the opponent to initiate" in countering efforts to gain bargaining advantages through the use of verbal threats. American ships simply continued to operate in the waters in question in such a way that the CPR could not enforce its declaration without initiating the use of violence

[30] On this point see also Tsou, "Mao's Limited War in the Taiwan Strait," *op.cit.*, p. 345.

[31] For further discussion of these problems, see *ibid.*, p. 344; and *The Economist*, September 20, 1958, p. 936.

against the ships. Under these circumstances, the CPR chose not to assume the responsibility for such an initiation of violence although this choice carried with it significant costs in terms of political embarrassment and the credibility of Chinese bargaining positions.

Berlin, 1961

During the 1961 Berlin crisis, the "initiative that forces the opponent to initiate" was employed on a number of occasions with significant results. In the early phases of the crisis, the Eastern side attempted to utilize tactical initiatives of this kind in support of its offensive posture with regard to the substantive issues raised by the crisis. As a result, the Western position was generally formulated in defensive terms during this period. Significantly, however, this relationship shifted during the later phases of the crisis as the Western powers began to assume the tactical initiative to consolidate their remaining position with regard to Berlin.

The 1961 crisis emphasizes the importance of distinguishing between diplomatic maneuvers and concrete actions on the ground with regard to the "initiative that forces the opponent to initiate." Especially in the early phases of the crisis, a great deal of diplomatic activity was directed toward shifting the burden of decision to the opponent by acting in such a way as "to place the onus of the risk of escalation on the other" side.[32] Khrushchev, for example, made this clear from the beginning by stressing repeatedly "at Vienna that, if there were military action over Berlin, it would have to be initiated by the United States."[33] At the same time, he was moving to reactivate on a formal basis the earlier Soviet threat to sign a separate peace treaty with the German Democratic Republic (GDR). Similarly, the Western powers attempted throughout to portray their commitments to Berlin in a manner designed to demonstrate that the Soviets possessed the last clear chance to avoid violence in any showdown involving the city. From the point of view of bargaining, the intent of these

[32] Philip Windsor, *City on Leave* (New York: Praeger, 1963), p. 259.
[33] Theodore Sorensen, *Kennedy* (New York: Harper and Row, 1965), p. 587.

diplomatic initiatives was clear. Their impact, however, was never decisive since their effectiveness depended ultimately on complex assessments of the strength of will or resolve underlying them.

Physical actions based on the "initiative that forces the opponent to initiate," on the other hand, are generally more operational and effective since they are less likely to be taken as bluffs and since the probability that a reaction on the part of the opponent will lead to violence is, to a greater extent, beyond the control of the initiator. In short, physical actions are more likely to reduce the room for backing down or failing to carry out an implied threat. The first important use of initiatives of this kind in the 1961 crisis came in a series of Eastern activities accompanying the closing of the sector boundary in Berlin. The large-scale deployment of East German troops within the city and of Soviet troops around the city on the night of August 12-13[34] created a situation in which any significant Western attempt to interfere with the closing of the sector boundary would very likely have led to the outbreak of violence in a way that would have cast the West in the role of initiator of the actual clash.[35] The deployment of armed forces by the East altered the decision-making calculations of the Western powers substantially since the West might otherwise have been able to interfere with the closure of the boundary with relative impunity. This Eastern initiative was particularly hard to deal with from the Western point of view since it was clearly deterrent rather than compellent in nature.[36] As a result, the actions of the East acquired many of the characteristics of a *fait accompli* emphasizing the relative helpless-

[34] For further details see Smith, *op.cit.*, p. 269. The Soviets deployed approximately two armored divisions (from the Soviet Expeditionary Force) in a cordon around the city. GDR forces deployed in East Berlin, though composed of several different types of unit, amounted to approximately a division.

[35] For further comments on this subject see Windsor, *op.cit.*, pp. 240-241; and John Mander, *Berlin: Hostage for the West* (Harmondsworth, Middlesex: Penguin, 1962), p. 113.

[36] At this time, the East made no demands on the West to stop ongoing activities. Eastern forces simply assumed a posture that made it dangerous for the West to attempt to dislodge them.

ness of the West.[37] Although the Western powers themselves had strong interests in stopping the refugee flow by August 13, therefore, the actual Eastern initiative made it impracticable for the West to take any course other than acquiescing in the specific means chosen by the GDR to achieve this end.

In the aftermath of August 13, however, the Western powers responded with several nonviolent initiatives of their own. While these moves did not alter the basic changes in the Berlin situation stemming from the actions of August 13, they were of considerable importance in defining the limits of Eastern gains in the situation and in arresting any further deterioration in the Western position. First, the movement of an American battle group from Helmstedt to Berlin on August 20 was carried out so as to make it difficult for the East to interfere without seriously raising the dangers of violence breaking out. This action was in fact a relatively safe one in the light of explicit Soviet statements emphasizing that the closing of the sector boundary in Berlin in no way affected Western transit rights across East German territory. Nevertheless, the move was significant since it clarified the continued existence of access rights, emphasized the "tripwire" function of Western forces in and around Berlin, and helped to boost popular morale in West Berlin. Second, the quick and firm Western reaction to the proclamation by the GDR of the "hundred-meters" edict on August 23 was a clear example of the use of the "initiative that forces the opponent to initiate" for deterrent purposes. By immediately deploying significant contingents of ground forces right up to the sector boundary, the West achieved in effect a deterrent posture from which it could not be dislodged without the initiation of violence by the East. Since the edict was clearly aimed at probing Western resolve in the aftermath of August 13,[38] this initiative

[37] For further comments on this subject see Hans Speier, *Divided Berlin* (New York: Praeger, 1961), p. 182.

[38] The lack of a sharp Western response to the actions of August 13 evidently generated hopes in the East that the Western powers would also fail to respond sharply to additional and even more extensive initiatives. The East remained very cautious during this phase and no steps were taken that would seriously aggravate the danger of a Western response involving overt violence. Nevertheless, a number of Eastern moves during this phase of the crisis had all the characteristics of probing actions.

helped emphasize the limits of Eastern gains in the confrontation.

During the later phases of the 1961 crisis, the West began to shift, in a limited and sometimes controversial way, to a policy of employing the "initiative that forces the opponent to initiate" in order to consolidate its remaining position in Berlin.[39] Activities of this kind became particularly prominent under the direction of General Lucius Clay, who returned to Berlin on September 19 as the special representative of President Kennedy.[40] Shortly after his arrival, Clay began to experiment with the use of tactical initiatives in the case of Steinstuecken, a small enclave belonging to West Berlin but wholly surrounded by GDR territory and therefore physically isolated.[41] The key initiative in this case came on September 21 when Clay himself entered the enclave by helicopter, flying over GDR territory in the process. Faced with an initiative that could not be effectively countered without accepting a significant chance of initiating violence, the East chose to acquiesce and the enclave remained under the control of West Berlin. In short, having failed to react in the first instance, the East was subsequently forced to accept the use of helicopters on a regular basis to maintain contact with Steinstuecken. While this initiative was hardly critical in substantive terms, it appears, in retrospect, to have been important as a symbol of the continued existence of Western bargaining strength in Berlin.

The most important use of the "initiative that forces the opponent to initiate" during these later phases of the 1961 crisis, however, came in the contest over Western access to East Berlin, which culminated in the tank confrontation at "Checkpoint

[39] This subject, however, always remained a controversial one among decision-makers in Washington. Differences with regard to the utilization of the initiative constituted an important factor separating the factions or groups in Washington.

[40] See George Bailey, "The Gentle Erosion of Berlin," *The Reporter*, Vol. 26, No. 9 (April 26, 1962), 15-19, for a discussion of Clay's tactics during the fall of 1961 as well as for a commentary (though not a very balanced one) on the disagreements that arose between Clay in Berlin and the American leadership in Washington.

[41] For further details on the Steinstuecken episode, consult Smith, *op.cit.*, pp. 310-312.

Charlie" on October 27-28.[42] The bargaining in this instance became particularly complex because it ultimately involved a compellent initiative on the part of the West. On the night of October 22, the GDR began an effort to force American diplomats entering East Berlin to display their credentials before crossing the sector boundary.[43] Rather than submit to these demands, the United States chose to force the situation *physically* by providing American diplomats entering East Berlin with jeep escorts. Since there was some possibility that the East could interfere with these escorts without initiating the use of violence, however, the United States proceeded to deploy ten Patton tanks at the checkpoint to create a situation in which violence might well ensue from any Eastern efforts to molest the jeep escorts.[44] As a result, the GDR guards at the checkpoint were subjected to severe and repeated humiliation, a situation which ultimately led to the counterdeployment of Soviet tanks on the Eastern side of the checkpoint on October 27.[45] Nevertheless, the East was still in a position where it

[42] "Checkpoint Charlie" is the Friedrichstrasse checkpoint. In the aftermath of August 13, it became the only remaining crossing point between East and West Berlin for Allied personnel.

[43] It is important, in this connection, to make a distinction between military and nonmilitary personnel. No move was made at this time to impede the crossing of persons in military uniform. With regard to diplomatic personnel, however, the situation was somewhat ambiguous. The British had, for some time, shown a tendency to be accommodating on the issue of producing diplomatic credentials. The Americans, on the other hand, insisted throughout that diplomatic markings on an automobile should be sufficient to identify the occupants. The October incident began when E. Allan Lightner Jr., the highest ranking American diplomat in Berlin, was stopped at the sector boundary with the demand that he present his credentials.

[44] On the details of the American deployment see the *New York Times*, October 29, 1961, Sect. IV, p. 1.

[45] As George Bailey has written, "After four days of concentrated humiliation produced by American military police forays into East Berlin backed by tanks poised on the sector line, the East German military seemed on the point of panic." Bailey, *op.cit.*, p. 16.

It was at this point that the Soviet armor was deployed, partly to counter the American initiative and partly to ensure that the GDR border guards did not get out of control. The dual basis of this move constitutes a good indication of the complexity of this confrontation. In effect, the American initiative, which ultimately turned out to be an important bargaining success in the context of the overall crisis, assumed both that the Soviets would perceive the nature of the situation correctly and that

could only stop the American forays into East Berlin by assuming the proximate responsibility for actions that would probably have caused an outbreak of violence,[46] a position the Soviets were unwilling to accept. Under these circumstances, the Soviets made the first move to back away from the direct confrontation of tanks on October 28, an initiative which the Americans could afford to reciprocate since it allowed them to make their basic point.

The sequence of actions constituted a critical development in the 1961 crisis for several reasons. First, it clarified the continued existence of the right of free movement for Western personnel within Berlin, a point of some importance in consolidating the remaining Western position.[47] Second, it demonstrated the ultimate responsibility of the Soviet Union for the governance of East Berlin,[48] an admission of critical significance in allowing the West to continue to withhold *de facto* recognition of the GDR in the aftermath of the 1961 crisis.[49] Third, it bolstered the overall credibility of Western bargaining activities with regard to Berlin by giving the West an opportunity to manipulate the risks involved in the confrontation with relatively clear-cut success. As Windsor has put it: "It was in the Western interest to keep tension in Berlin at this moment as high as possible. If the tanks had been prematurely withdrawn, if there had been any indication that the nerves of the local authorities were giving way, there can be

---

the Soviets would move to control it before overt and dangerous actions had occurred.

[46] In short, the last clear chance of avoiding the outbreak of violence still rested primarily with the East. While the Soviet tanks counterbalanced the American tanks, this Soviet response did not help very much in stopping American jeep patrols. Interestingly, this line of reasoning suggests that a desire to remove the situation effectively from the hands of the GDR border forces constituted perhaps the single most important motive behind the Soviet intervention in this situation.

[47] In this connection, it constituted a much more positive step than the Western efforts to draw the line on Eastern gains in Berlin in the immediate aftermath of August 13.

[48] On this point see Smith, *op.cit.*, p. 323. It is important to emphasize that this was the first occasion on which Soviet forces in any form had appeared within Berlin since the onset of the 1961 crisis.

[49] For further discussions of this point, see George Bailey, "The Other Side of the Wall," *The Reporter*, Vol. 25, No. 9 (November 23, 1961), 24; and William Conlon, *Berlin: Beset and Bedeviled* (New York: Fountainhead Publishers, 1963), pp. 203-204.

little doubt that the incidents at the border and in the corridors would have multiplied."[50]

Finally, the Eastern side chose not to attempt what might well have been the most critical and most dangerous "initiative that forces the opponent to initiate" of the 1961 crisis. The reference here is to the situation that would have resulted if GDR guards had simply appeared at the checkpoints on the border between East and West *Germany* on a *de facto* basis and refused to allow passage of Western military traffic until the West agreed to recognize the legitimacy of GDR control over the checking operation.[51] A move of this kind would have put the Western powers in an extremely difficult position. Even though there were large stockpiles of supplies in Berlin in 1961, it would have been far more difficult to supply the city by air then than in 1948-1949[52] since: living standards in the city were far higher in 1961; West Berlin had been extensively integrated into the West German economy in the interim; and it was generally believed that the population of the city had less resistance to privation in 1961. Though an Eastern initiative along these lines would not, therefore, have led to the immediate fall of West Berlin, it might well have forced the West to choose between making major concessions and initiating the use of violence in the long run.[53] Nevertheless, there were several powerful factors behind the Soviet decision against an initiative of this kind. The Soviet Union was unprepared to accept the increased freedom of action that almost certainly would have accrued to the GDR.[54] It was just possible that an airlift might again be successful enough to al-

[50] Windsor, *op.cit.*, p. 250. As it turned out, Soviet actions both in deploying tanks on October 27 and in initiating the withdrawal of armor from the sector boundary on October 28 were of considerable *de facto* importance in signaling the end of the acute phases of the 1961 crisis.

[51] The emphasis on Allied military traffic is important in this connection since the GDR already exercised control over German civilian traffic using the access routes at the time of the 1961 crisis.

[52] For an interesting discussion of this subject see Kurt L. Shell, pp. 85-102 in Walter Stahl, ed., *The Politics of Postwar Germany* (New York: Praeger, 1963), p. 100.

[53] For a clear formulation of this potential problem, see Mander, *op.cit.*, p. 113.

[54] For further discussion of these and related restraints on Soviet behavior, see *infra* Chap. Fifteen.

low the West to hold out, a possibility that raised the unpleasant image of the 1948-1949 crisis for the Soviets. And, in any case, it might have been feasible for the West to respond with a carefully limited use of force sufficient to open the access routes, while leaving the Soviets with a nasty choice between retreating under humiliating circumstances (provided they could still control the GDR at this point) and assuming the responsibility for escalating the level of violence to a point where the clash might have passed beyond the control of either side.

Cuba, 1962

While the record of the Cuban crisis of 1962 is conceptually simpler than that of the other crises under analysis with regard to the "initiative that forces the opponent to initiate," moves of this kind were of considerable importance in determining the outcome of the clash. The 1962 crisis actually stemmed from an attempt by the Soviet Union to pose a serious challenge to the United States through the use of a nonviolent initiative. The Soviets evidently hoped to complete the installation of the missiles in Cuba in secrecy so that the unveiling of operational missiles would be a *fait accompli* to which the United States would be unable to find a satisfactory nonviolent response. The American discovery of this move before the missiles became operational, however, shifted the tactical initiative sharply to the United States. Under these circumstances, the problem of utilizing the initiative became a sensitive issue for the United States, especially since American decision-makers felt torn between an awareness that a sharp reaction to the Soviet activities was important and a real fear of touching off violent exchanges that might rapidly reach uncontrollable proportions.

The American naval blockade was ultimately designed to meet the requirements set by these divergent pressures through a heavy reliance on an "initiative that forces the opponent to initiate." Implementation of the blockade in a sharp and decisive fashion projected an image of strength in the sense that it presented a clear challenge to Soviet activities while maximizing the ability of the United States to "remain master of the alternatives."[55] At the same time, the blockade shifted at least part of the burden of choice about the use of violence to the Soviets by presenting them with the last clear chance to avoid violence in the confrontation at sea.[56] As Daniel and Hubbell have written, "President Kennedy's intention was to present Khrushchev with a situation in which, if war should come, no one would doubt that it was by Khrushchev's choice."[57]

Under the circumstances, the options open to the Soviet Union in responding to the blockade itself were not encouraging.[58] The Soviets could have moved to break the blockade directly by attacking it either with submarines or armed surface vessels. Such a response, however, would have necessitated a clear initiation of violence. On the other hand, the Soviets could have attempted to circumvent the blockade: by evading it; by convoying ships through it; or by simply refusing to halt the cargo ships in the hopes of calling the American bluff. Nevertheless, an attempt to follow any of these options would have raised the probabilities of violent clashes considerably. And the burden of the last clear chance of avoiding violence would have fallen most heavily on the Soviet Union because of the structure of the situation.

The Soviets therefore sought to gain the upper hand in the crisis without breaking the naval blockade. They embarked on an effort to operationalize the missiles already in Cuba on the basis of available matériel and, in so doing, to undermine the American blockade at its most vulnerable point. Given this decision, the Soviets had a clear interest in acting with restraint vis-à-vis the blockade in order to keep the situation under control while they were attempting to operationalize the missiles in Cuba. They therefore proceeded with striking caution in their direct responses to the blockade, contenting themselves with a verbal declaration of its illegality.[59]

[55] Henry Pachter, *Collision Course* (New York: Praeger, 1963), p. 88.
[56] For an interesting formulation of this point, see George Ball, "Lawyers and Diplomats" (address delivered December 13, 1962), text in *DOSB*, XLVII, No. 1227 (December 31, 1962), pp. 989-990.
[57] James Daniel and John G. Hubbell, "While America Slept," *Reader's Digest*, Vol. 82, No. 491 (March 1963), 267-268.
[58] For a good discussion of Soviet options in this context, see Pachter, *op.cit.*, pp. 42-44.
[59] For the Soviet position on this issue see the statement of the Soviet government released on October 23, 1962. The text can be located con-

American efforts to utilize the naval blockade for bargaining purposes illustrate several important problems that may arise in connection with an "initiative that forces the opponent to initiate." In the relatively specific context of the confrontation at sea, the blockade acquired a good deal of the strength of an essentially deterrent initiative. Even here, however, the situation was not without ambiguities. Above all, it was not perfectly clear what would happen if the Soviet ships simply kept advancing, refusing to stop when hailed. This possibility presented at least theoretically the embarrassing prospect that the United States might ultimately have to fire the first shot regardless of which side might be deemed responsible, in terms of the notion of the last clear chance, for initiating the violence.[60] During the period of confrontation, therefore, American decision-makers developed elaborate contingency plans to deal with this problem.[61] Significant suggestions included: the deployment of enough ships to block completely the channels between the Atlantic and the Caribbean;[62] the use of steel cables to trap approaching ships; and various devices for disabling the rudders of oncoming vessels. In the end, the Soviets chose not to test the blockade in these terms, but the problem of stopping approaching ships without using violence was a source of considerable concern to American decision-makers during the week of October 22.

The naval blockade was also designed to serve as a compellent initiative in the context of the overall crisis. However, the requirements of projecting bargaining pressures, critical to the success of a compellent initiative, raised several major problems for the United States in the 1962 crisis. In this case, the key difficulty arose from the absence of an absolutely clear link between the pressure set up by the blockade and the installation of missiles in Cuba.[63] As noted above, the American

veniently in David L. Larson, ed., *The "Cuban Crisis of 1962: Selected Documents and Chronology* (Boston: Houghton Mifflin, 1963), pp. 49-54.

[60] For a discussion of American concern with this problem, see Sorensen, *op.cit.*, p. 687.

[61] On the development of contingency plans, see Elie Abel, *The Missile Crisis* (Philadelphia: Lippincott, 1966), pp. 154-156.

[62] Since there are only five navigable channels leading to Cuba from the Atlantic, it was at least plausible to think of simply blocking them off physically.

[63] On this question of the link between the blockade and the missiles already in Cuba, see Abel, *op.cit.*, pp. 89-90.

move to establish a naval blockade offered the Soviets the option of scrupulously complying with the blockade itself while continuing their efforts to operationalize the missiles already in Cuba. As a result, it ultimately became necessary for the United States to supplement the blockade with a clear-cut effort to manipulate the risks of violence associated with the crisis to coerce the Soviets into complying with American demands for the removal of offensive weapons from Cuba. At this point, the threat of an immediate air strike or an outright invasion of Cuba became critical. In the end, therefore, the naval blockade played an important role in allowing the United States to avoid initiating the use of violence in the 1962 crisis, but it was not sufficient in itself to force the Soviets into agreeing to remove the offensive weapons from Cuba.

Conclusion

An analysis of the case materials in this chapter demonstrates clearly that the "initiative that forces the opponent to initiate" has been a major determinant of the outcomes of the postwar crises. Tactical initiatives of this kind have played important roles in support of both offensive and defensive postures with regard to the fundamental substantive issues involved in international crises. For a party whose position is fundamentally offensive, such initiatives may be designed: to force the opponent into retreat, as was the case with the Chinese artillery blockade of Quemoy in 1958; or to ward off opposing attempts to counter important developments affecting the basic substantive issues at stake, as was the case with the Western airlift in 1948-1949. At the same time, the "initiative that forces the opponent to initiate" has frequently been utilized as a device through which the respondent (or defendant) can turn back opposing offensives or draw a defensible line in a fluid situation. On the whole, the case materials indicate that tactical initiatives of this kind have more often been successful in support of defensive postures at the strategic level than in support of offensive activities. Nevertheless, the evidence makes it clear that this relationship need not hold in all situations.

It is possible to formulate an "initiative that forces the opponent to initiate" in terms of diplomatic moves as well as in terms of concrete actions on the ground. As the case of the twelve-mile limit in the 1958 crisis and the diplomatic maneuvering during the early phases of the 1961 Berlin crisis indicate, however, initiatives of this kind based primarily on diplomatic activities are apt to be extremely weak. In such cases, the initiator heavily depends on a successful projection of last-clear-chance considerations and, therefore, on the opponent's subjective assessment of the firmness of his intentions. The articulation of an initiative of this kind in terms of physical actions, on the other hand, is more characteristic and apt to be more influential. In such cases, the relevant threats are more concretely operational and less implied. The intentions of the initiator gain substance from his actions. There is therefore less room for miscalculation with regard to questions of intent. Moreover, physical actions are apt to reduce the scope for retreat on the part of the initiator, who may thereby achieve a position which an opponent will find difficult to respond to by calling his bluff.

There is also an important distinction between an "initiative that forces the opponent to initiate" which is designed for purposes of compellence and one essentially deterrent in nature. The case materials support the general theoretical conclusion that compellent initiatives are apt to be the more difficult of the two types to utilize successfully.[64] In addition to the fact that compellence requires a positive response while a deterrent initiative requires only abstinence, the evidence from the cases indicates further problems primarily relevant to compellent initiatives. As the naval blockade in the Cuban crisis of 1962 demonstrates, it is sometimes difficult to establish a clear-cut link between the initiative in question and the desired response by the opponent in a compellence situation. Also, compellent initiatives set up greater demands for understanding as well as conscious decisions to acquiesce than is true with deterrent initiatives in which the key requirement is simply the projection of a forbidding image of firmness. From this perspective, the Western actions in the tank confrontation of October 1961 constituted a highly successful case of compellence

[64] The logical reasons underlying this conclusion are set forth in Thomas Schelling, *Arms and Influence, op.cit.*, pp. 69-78.

whereas as the American naval blockade of 1962 was only partially successful. One device that seems particularly interesting as a means of handling the problems of compellence, at least in abstract terms, is the initiative containing an automatic tightening process that does not require additional initiatives. Curiously, however, efforts to utilize devices of this kind in the 1948-1949 crisis and in the 1958 crisis ultimately ended in failure since, in both cases, the *whole* compellent effort was successfully countered by a deterrent initiative spearheaded by the United States.

Throughout the case materials there are indications that the concept of the last clear chance is an important adjunct of the "initiative that forces the opponent to initiate." The primary objective of the initiator is to shift the *responsibility* for any outbreak of violence onto the opponent regardless of which side ultimately fires the first shot. While it is obviously desirable to maximize clarity with regard to the locus of responsibility for the initiation of violence, the evidence suggests that even an ability to achieve a perceptual shift affecting the last clear chance of avoiding violence is apt to be influential under conditions of crisis. The restraint demonstrated by the Soviet Union in responding to the Western airlift in the 1948-1949 crisis and the American naval blockade in the 1962 crisis, for example, provides striking confirmation of the importance of the last clear chance.

Finally, the case materials provide striking empirical evidence of the delicate balances involved in an "initiative that forces the opponent to initiate" and the dangers, mentioned in the opening pages of this chapter, of having such an initiative outdone. In two of the cases under analysis, an initiative of this kind, which had originally seemed very impressive, was decisively topped by the opponent. The sequences in question were the triumph of the airlift over the surface blockade in the 1948-1949 crisis and the breaking of the artillery blockade of Quemoy in 1958 by nonviolent means. Interestingly, in both cases this represented victory for an initiative that was essentially deterrent at the tactical level over a compellent initiative. In addition, the evidence indicates that the failure of an initiative of this kind tends to be very costly for the initiating party. The utilization of such an initiative generally narrows the principal focus of a confrontation and works to establish at least some of the ground rules of the resultant contest. When the tables are turned, therefore, the original initiator frequently finds himself boxed into a situation not only structured to his disadvantage, but whose basic rules he himself has helped to establish.

15. Coercive Uses of Asymmetries

HYPOTHESIS. As alternatives to actions that might precipitate violence during a crisis, efforts to structure the fundamental dimensions and specific issues of the clash in order to utilize or create advantageous asymmetries are apt to become highly influential coercive procedures.

The restraints affecting the use of force under conditions of crisis relate primarily to the usability of violence as an instrument of power. They do not for the most part reduce the coercive interests or intentions of the participants. The search for forceful but nonviolent forms of coercion is therefore apt to be sharply stimulated under conditions of crisis. In this context, one important alternative is a highly coercive form of diplomacy aimed at structuring the basic political context of a crisis and shaping the principal patterns of interaction which develop during a crisis so as to capitalize on various asymmetrical aspects of the relationship for bargaining purposes.[1]

The significance of such efforts to use asymmetries is based, in essence, on the influence that accrues to a party able to control the processes through which the basic dimensions and issues of a crisis are defined. There is within this framework a wide range of possibilities. In general, an alert participant can often influence the development of images and expectations concerning the fundamental nature of the emerging crisis as well as the probable consequences associated with the programs of action open to the opponent in the situation. In short, it is frequently possible to influence underlying thought processes, perspectives, and conceptual frameworks in ways that extensively affect patterns of decision-making with regard to the specific issues of a given crisis.

More specifically, it is possible, in effect, to determine the scope of a crisis by taking steps to define the proximate issues on which it will focus. This is a matter of considerable impor-

---

[1] In the postwar period, the tendency to move toward such bargaining procedures under conditions of crisis was buttressed by the general move toward concepts and images focusing on the use of force on a contingent or hypothecated basis rather than on a direct physical basis.

tance since the breadth or narrowness of a clash, as well as the substantive content of the issues that become its focal point, is apt to be a major determinant of the relative ability of the parties to project resolve and firmness of will on a credible basis. Similarly, geopolitical factors can be utilized to achieve advantageous asymmetries. Above all, it is desirable to control the choice of the final point of contact of a crisis at least in proximate or tactical terms. In general, a contact point that is far from a participant's base of operations or located in a hostile political environment will tend to be disadvantageous for bargaining purposes. In specific tactical terms, moreover, geopolitical peculiarities of a given contact point affecting such matters as communications and transportation frequently generate asymmetries that have a substantial impact on the ultimate outcome of a crisis. Or again, efforts to shape expectations concerning the locus of effective control with regard to such matters as the dangers of escalation can produce influential asymmetries during a crisis. A party that succeeds in projecting onto its opponent the ultimate "responsibility" for keeping escalatory sequences under control, for example, will gain a major advantage in the area of freedom of action.

The parties to any given crisis enjoy only a limited range of choices in attempting to utilize or create advantageous asymmetries; crises are shaped in important ways by the preceding flow of political interactions from which they emerge. Nevertheless, opportunities to use asymmetries are generally extensive enough to provide a highly influential alternative, for purposes of bargaining, to actions that might precipitate the outbreak of violence.

Berlin, 1948-1949

The effectiveness of restraints on the use of violence during the Berlin crisis of 1948-1949 led to an extended search for alternative techniques of exercising coercion. Efforts to structure the clash in ways that would produce advantageous asymmetries became important elements in the bargaining programs of both sides. In the first place, several natural asymmetries were made prominent by the course of the crisis. The fact that the crisis centered on Berlin gave the Soviets a tactical advantage with regard to the distribution of available ground forces and added substantially to the transportation problems of the Western powers. These advantages accrued to the Soviet Union as a function of Soviet control over the tactical initiative during the opening phases of the crisis. They were, however, partially offset by the *de facto* deterrence of Western occupation forces in Berlin.[2] The time factor became another important source of asymmetrical advantages during this crisis. While the Soviet position was aided by the passage of time during the early phases of the crisis, the Western powers benefited asymmetrically from the passage of time as the airlift began to prove successful.[3]

In addition to manipulating specific features of the setting in which a confrontation develops, it is frequently possible to gain bargaining advantages by shaping the fundamental dimensions of a crisis. In the 1948-1949 crisis, this became evident at the outset. The primary Soviet objective in blockading Berlin was to gain leverage with regard to developments affecting all of Germany. While the Soviets were no doubt interested in increasing their control over Berlin, their basic concern in the spring of 1948 was to stop the independent reconstruction of the western zones of Germany.[4] There was, however, no obvious and direct way of dealing with developments in the western zones short of the initiation of violence.[5] As a result, Berlin appeared as an extremely useful pressure point in bargaining about the future of central Europe. For geopolitical reasons, the city could be subjected to a compulsory blockade without using violence; and it seemed reason-

[2] For an interesting development of this point see Frank Howley, *Berlin Command* (New York: G. P. Putnam's Sons, 1950), p. 198. While concepts based on the notions of a tripwire or a plate glass window had not yet been formulated explicitly at this time, the phenomena to which these concepts have subsequently been applied were already operative on a tacit basis.

[3] For additional comments on this subject see *supra* Chap. Eight.

[4] In 1948 Soviet concern with the reconstruction of the western zones of Germany focused on three issues: (1) currency reform, (2) the reorganization of the Ruhr industries, and (3) the projected establishment of an autonomous West German state.

[5] Moreover, the Soviet Union had good reasons to desire to avoid the outbreak of large-scale violence in Europe at this time. For a discussion of these reasons see *supra* Chap. Eight.

able to assume the Western powers would be willing to make significant concessions to avoid losing Berlin altogether.[6] And since the Soviets originally assumed that a large-scale airlift was not a viable option for the Western powers, the acquisition of substantial bargaining leverage through the blockade seemed assured during the early phases of the crisis.

The Western powers were thus faced with a confrontation whose proximate dimensions had been largely determined by the opponent. In this connection, the great success of the Western powers in the 1948-1949 crisis arose from their ability to offset these initial disadvantages by creating new asymmetries rather than by employing violence. The fact that the Western commandants had begun to stockpile essential supplies in Berlin from March 25, 1948,[7] was important since it gave the Western powers a breathing spell in which to maneuver and develop their options, even after the imposition of the full blockade toward the end of June. The critical counterstroke, of course, was the successful initiation and development of an airlift of sufficient proportions to fulfill the minimum needs of the civilian population of Berlin even through the winter months of 1948-1949. At the same time, other Western countermeasures went far beyond the attempt to break the blockade of Berlin. The Western powers proceeded gradually to impose on the whole eastern zone of Germany a counterblockade which became increasingly influential during the course of the crisis.[8] In a sense, therefore, the Western powers moved to redefine the scope of the confrontation in terms that reduced the asymmetrical advantages accruing to the Soviets from the original narrow focus on Berlin.

More specifically, the Soviet decision to focus the confrontation on Berlin produced important asymmetries with regard to force postures. The main advantage of the Soviet gambit

[6] The loss of Berlin would have constituted a large blow to Western morale, and might well have led to a refusal by leaders in the western zones of Germany to accept plans, formalized in the London recommendations of June 1948, for an autonomous West German state.

[7] For the details of this program see Howley, op.cit., pp. 200-201.

[8] There is no doubt the counterblockade was an influential factor, especially toward the end of the 1948-1949 confrontation. But the importance attached to it by writers such as Max Charles seems rather excessive. See Max Charles, Berlin Blockade (London: Wingate, 1959), p. 124.

was that it allowed the Soviet Union to adopt an essentially defensive posture. The Soviets could maintain their stranglehold on the city on a passive basis, and it was up to the Western powers to initiate steps to break it, perhaps increasing the prospects of violence in the process. This relationship prompted *The Economist* to argue during August that "the whole Berlin question looks graver from the Western than it does from the Eastern side."[9] This specific asymmetry with regard to force postures, however, also veered sharply as a result of the success of the airlift. The Western powers demonstrated their ability to stay in Berlin without initiating violence, and the Soviets were put in the position of searching actively for some means to dislodge them. On the question of force postures, therefore, the ultimate success of the airlift ensnared the Soviets in a trap of their own making.

The most important Soviet efforts to redress the asymmetrical advantages accruing to the Western side from the success of the airlift came in a variety of activities aimed at undermining the internal political viability of Berlin itself. Beginning in late August, the Soviets stepped up their efforts to stimulate actions designed to break the morale of the civilian population of Berlin and to reduce the effectiveness of the government and administration of the city.[10] Inspired riots became frequent. Unwarranted arrests and abductions were common. The Berlin City Council was forced to abandon City Hall, located in the eastern sector of Berlin, and to set up a temporary headquarters in West Berlin. Efforts were made to win the support of the population of the western sectors of the city through offers of free food. The fundamental objective of all these activities was to offset the advantages accruing to the Western position from the success of the airlift by turning West Berlin into an empty shell. But this Soviet campaign to create new asymmetries, as their original bargaining program for the crisis began to fail, proved unsuccessful. In short, the morale of the civilian population in the western sectors of Ber-

[9] *The Economist*, August 21, 1948, p. 294.
[10] For a detailed description of these activities see W. Phillips Davison, *The Berlin Blockade: A Study in Cold War Politics* (Princeton: Princeton University Press, 1958), pp. 162-182.

lin held, and government continued to function reasonably effectively in these areas.[11] Nevertheless, these Soviet efforts to counteract the airlift did lead to a *de facto* political division of the city.

Throughout the period of confrontation during the 1948-1949 crisis, the Western powers moved forward in developing new arrangements at the diplomatic level which, in conjunction with the success of the airlift in the local arena, gave the Western side extensive bargaining advantages in the final phases of the crisis. In fact, the Western powers succeeded in emphasizing the symbolic significance of the clash over Berlin so that the crisis became a major impetus behind Western diplomacy during this period.[12] As a result, the West showed a marked ability to make progress in the development of plans for an autonomous West German state and for the organization of coordinated security arrangements for the Atlantic area during the winter of 1948-1949. By the time it became evident that the actual blockade of Berlin would fail, it was also increasingly clear that both an independent West German government and a North Atlantic security pact would come into existence in the wake of the crisis. For this reason, the Soviet position in the local confrontation around Berlin became especially embarrassing during the spring of 1949. In conjunction with the airlift, therefore, Western efforts to gain advantages from the crisis in the diplomatic arena produced influential asymmetries toward the end of the confrontation.

One procedure sometimes used to good effect in efforts to structure asymmetries was conspicuously absent from the bargaining during the 1948-1949 crisis. In short, neither side attempted to introduce issues beyond those associated with the politics of central Europe for purposes of manipulating bargaining advantages. It could be that the perspectives of all the parties were sufficiently Europe-centered at this time to make the possibilities of contextual broadening seem irrelevant or uninteresting. It is worth noting, however, that the period

---

[11] For further material on these points consult *ibid.*, pp. 309-320.

[12] In particular, the crisis spurred activities along two lines: (1) the movement toward the establishment of a separate West German state, and (2) the development of activities to create a Western defense system on a basis broader than that of the Brussels Pact.

spanned by the Berlin crisis was not lacking in other conflicts of significant proportions which could have been drawn in for purposes of bargaining. In particular, the Middle East was in a state of constant upheaval through 1948 and early 1949, and 1948 witnessed a critical turning point in the course of the Chinese civil war.

Taiwan Strait, 1958

The 1958 crisis in the Taiwan Strait was shaped extensively by efforts on the part of all the major participants to gain bargaining advantages by structuring the dimensions and issues of the clash. To understand these efforts, however, it is necessary to keep in mind several confusing features of the patterns of interaction that developed during the crisis. First, the triangular aspects of relations among the Chinese People's Republic (CPR), the Chinese Nationalists, and the United States infused an element of ambiguity into a number of the specific efforts to structure the nature of the confrontation. Second, shifts in the bargaining relationships of the parties from one phase of the crisis to another produced some inconsistencies and contradictions in the efforts of the parties to make use of advantageous asymmetries.

The choice of the offshore islands as the point of confrontation for the 1958 crisis carried with it important implications for bargaining. While in many ways this focus was the logical choice for the CPR,[13] the consequences of this concentration on the offshore islands were by no means entirely favorable to the CPR. The proximity of the offshore islands to the Chinese mainland was clearly beneficial from the point of view of the CPR, and it is also true the Chinese Communists could feel reasonably confident that the United States would not respond to a probe in the Strait with far-reaching retaliatory measures, if for no other reason because of the enormous difficulties of conducting large-scale warfare on the Chinese main-

[13] Among other things, the CPR simply did not have the physical capabilities necessary to assault Taiwan directly with any degree of confidence. Since, however, the leaders of the CPR undoubtedly viewed the continued existence of the Nationalist government on Taiwan as their single most pressing foreign policy problem, it was hardly surprising that they should seek some means of undermining the Nationalist regime.

land. On the other hand, the Nationalists and the Americans together possessed a clear-cut conventional superiority in the area of the Strait itself. Moreover, given the weakness of the naval forces of the CPR and the great advantages of the United States in naval operations, even the small gap of water separating the offshore islands from the mainland constituted an important flaw in the bargaining position of the CPR.

In addition, the possibility of a new crisis focusing on the offshore islands was a contingency that the Nationalists had been consciously preparing for since 1955. Beginning in 1955, the Nationalists had succeeded in building up the fortifications on the offshore islands substantially and, above all, in publicizing the fact that approximately one-third of their army, including many of its best units, was deployed on the islands and committed to their defense.[14] The implications of these earlier moves for bargaining in the 1958 crisis were twofold. First, the movement of a large number of troops to the islands allowed the Nationalists to strengthen the link between the defense of the offshore islands and the defense of Taiwan, publicly to emphasize their commitment to the defense of the offshore islands, and to create a situation in which the loss of the islands would constitute a severe blow to their prestige and morale.[15] As *The Economist* put it, "the Nationalists' redeployment of their forces has radically changed the relationship of the islands to Formosa."[16] Second, the Nationalists hoped that the creation of a vital security link between the offshore islands and Taiwan would effectively force the United States to include the offshore islands within the scope of its defense commitments in the area despite the somewhat ambiguous terms of the Formosa Resolution of January 29, 1955.[17]

[14] For a pointed discussion of the American attitude with regard to this Nationalist policy of building up the garrisons on the offshore islands, see Dulles' statements at his news conference of September 9. The text is printed in *DOSB*, XXXIX, No. 1005 (September 29, 1958), 485-493. See especially pp. 486-487.

[15] For an interesting discussion of Nationalist tactics along these lines, see Tang Tsou, "The Quemoy Imbroglio: Chiang Kai-shek and the United States," *Western Political Quarterly*, XXII, No. 4 (December 1959), 1,077-1,078.

[16] *The Economist*, September 20, 1958, p. 935.

[17] The Formosa Resolution, while it made the American commitment to

Again in the words of *The Economist,* "an attack on the islands now involves a threat to Formosa that the United States could hardly ignore without breaking its political commitments to the Nationalists, even though the American defense authorities still do not consider that it is vital to deny these islands to the Communists."[18] As a result, the probe against the offshore islands was bound to pose difficulties for the efforts of the CPR to gain bargaining advantages in the 1958 crisis through a program of structuring for asymmetries.

Behond these features of the context in which the 1958 crisis unfolded, however, several conscious efforts to create advantageous asymmetries during the opening phases of the crisis deserve mention. In the first instance, the Chinese Communists attempted to orchestrate the initiation of the actual physical confrontation of the crisis so as to maximize their bargaining advantages. The timing of the initiation of the artillery bombardment on August 23 appears to have been significantly influenced by the hope that the United States would be sufficiently preoccupied with the ongoing crisis in the Middle East to be disinclined to take a firm and threatening stand in the western Pacific.[19] Moreover, the initiation of direct confrontation was accompanied by a CPR campaign aimed at drawing a clear distinction between the problem of the offshore islands and the more general problem of Taiwan.[20] This move was clearly a bargaining device since it dovetailed with the requirements of the original bargaining calculus of the CPR and since it certainly did not signify any substantive or long-term interest on the part of the Chinese Communists in separat-

---

defend Taiwan and the Penghus (Pescadores) definite, left it to the discretion of the President to decide, in any given confrontation, whether the defense of the offshore islands should be treated as vital to the defense of Taiwan. For the precise language of the resolution, see *DOSB,* XXXII, No. 815 (February 7, 1955), 213. In this connection, the Nationalists hoped effectively to destroy any possibility that the United States government might arrive at a negative decision on this issue.

[18] *The Economist,* September 6, 1958, p. 750.

[19] For evidence on this point see Donald Zagoria, *The Sino-Soviet Conflict 1956-1961* (New York: Atheneum, 1964), p. 206. There were, of course, other factors affecting the timing of this move.

[20] For some comments on the CPR's subsequent about-face on this issue, see *infra* pp. 375-376.

ing the two issues.[21] In the context of the initial phase of confrontation during the 1958 crisis, this campaign was designed both to undermine the influence of the Nationalists' efforts to commit themselves irrevocably to the defense of the islands, and to place the United States in an embarrassing bind between Nationalist demands for aid in defending the islands and the feelings of others that the offshore islands *alone* were not important enough to warrant a reaction to the Chinese probe which might generate significant risks.

In fact, however, the United States began immediately to counter these efforts of the CPR to gain advantages by controlling the definition of the basic nature of the clash. In this connection, the basic American strategy was to equate the security of the offshore islands with that of Taiwan and consequently with the whole structure of American defense commitments in the western Pacific. There were several important links in this chain of reasoning. To begin with, the American government took the view that, under the circumstances, the loss of the offshore islands would be a severe and perhaps decisive blow to the viability of the Nationalist regime on Taiwan.[22] And, "If the capture of the offshore islands should, in fact, lead to the loss of Formosa, the future security of Japan, the Philippines, Thailand, Vietnam and even Okinawa would be placed in jeopardy and United States vital interests would suffer severely."[23] Thus, the American government adopted an expansionist view of the importance of the offshore islands, a view whose bargaining implications ran directly counter to the separatist position enunciated by the CPR in the early phases of the crisis. Moreover, this expansionist view rapidly became a critical determinant of the American reaction to the initiatives of the CPR, despite the

[21] For further discussion of the bargaining calculations of the CPR, see *supra* Chap. Eight.

[22] For further discussion of this American position, see O. Edmund Clubb, "Chiang's Shadow over Warsaw," *The Reporter*, Vol. 19, No. 5 (October 2, 1958), 17.

[23] The quotation is from Dwight Eisenhower, *Waging Peace 1956-1961* (Garden City, N.Y.: Doubleday, 1965), p. 294. For similar language formulated during the crisis itself, see Eisenhower's address to the American people on September 11, 1958. The text is printed in *DOSB*, XXXIX, No. 5 (September 29, 1958), 481-484. See especially pp. 482-483.

fact that it was criticized from several points of view both within the United States itself and in many other parts of the world.[24] As it happened, the American government succeeded in communicating its commitment to this view convincingly regardless of the realities of the actual situation in the Taiwan Strait.

As the crisis passed into its middle phase of confrontation during the first half of September, the major parties continued to search for structuring devices that would offer bargaining advantages. During this period, the United States was particularly concerned to establish the credibility of its threat to respond with violence to any overt invasion attempt against the offshore islands. This was, in fact, a principal objective of many of the specific moves through which the United States proceeded conspicuously to build up its air-naval strike force in the Taiwan Strait. It was also this objective that produced the public American threat that such an invasion attempt would not remain limited but would, on the contrary, catalyze a far larger military confrontation than the CPR was prepared to handle.[25]

At the same time, American relations with the Nationalists during this period served to enhance the credibility of the American commitment to the defense of the offshore islands.[26]

[24] Some of the criticisms were based on the judgment that the islands were of no real value militarily and that, therefore (regardless of political arguments), the domino theory was inapplicable in this instance. For an example of this position, see Thomas R. Phillips, "The Military Worth of Quemoy," *The Reporter*, Vol. 19, No. 5 (October 2, 1958), 14.

Other critics argued that the position of the Eisenhower Administration placed the United States in a bind in which, on the one hand, it was tied to the actions of the Nationalists while, on the other hand, it was bound to get into political difficulties with both allies and nonaligned states. On this line of criticism see *The Economist*, September 13, 1958, p. 818.

[25] For an important formulation of this American threat, see Eisenhower's address of September 11, 1958. The text appears in *DOSB*, XXXIX, No. 1005 (September 29, 1958), 481-484.

[26] The difficulties for the United States that emerged from this relationship with the Nationalists are discussed elsewhere. The point here is that this admittedly difficult relationship also produced some bargaining advantages for the United States in dealing with the CPR. On this point see also Richard Stebbins, *The United States in World Affairs 1958* (New York: Harper and Row [for the Council on Foreign Relations], 1959), pp. 327-328.

372

The United States, in effect, demonstrated an impressive willingness to support (if not to condone) the *de facto* commitments created in the preceding period by the redeployment of Nationalist troops. Though the issue was obviously a source of great concern, it gradually became clear during this period that the American Administration was not willing to sacrifice its entire position in the confrontation to the objective of controlling the catalytic capabilities of the Nationalists, a fact that also served to demonstrate the seriousness of the American commitment to the defense of the offshore islands.[27]

Similarly, the CPR developed several new ploys of some significance in terms of structuring efforts during this middle phase of the confrontation. On September 4 the CPR issued a formal statement henceforth claiming a twelve-mile limit with regard to its territorial waters.[28] The bargaining significance of this move stemmed from the fact that the Quemoy islands would fall entirely within the territorial waters of the CPR under a twelve-mile limit. The move of September 4 therefore constituted an escalatory threat with regard to the probable response of the CPR to the activities of both Nationalist and American naval vessels in the waters around Quemoy.[29] In effect, the CPR hoped to intimidate the United States with this verbal move *without* having to risk the initiation of potentially dangerous physical actions. The verbal nature of this attempt to achieve an asymmetrical advantage, however, quickly proved its undoing since the unwillingness of the Chinese Communists to back their initiative with physical force allowed

[27] In other words, the posture of the United States on this issue played a role in creating a public impression that the American government would not be scared into submission because of the dangers involved in the confrontation.

[28] The CPR, unlike the Soviet Union, had previously claimed only the traditional three-mile limit. For the text of the CPR's declaration of September 4, see *Peking Review*, I, No. 28 (September 9, 1958), 21. For an interesting discussion of this move from the Chinese point of view, see Liu Tse-yung, "A Major Step to Protect China's Sovereign Rights," *ibid.*, I, No. 29 (September 16, 1958), 11-13.

[29] The idea here was to alarm the Americans and the Nationalists by raising the perceived probability that the CPR would employ violence in harassing American as well as Nationalist vessels operating in the waters around Quemoy.

the United States to call their bluff on the question of a twelve-mile limit.

As September wore on, the CPR began to introduce more and more insistently the argument that the whole affair was only an episode in an ongoing civil war[30] and therefore: there was no conflict between the CPR and the United States; American intervention in the confrontation constituted aggression; and the United States should withdraw and allow the Chinese to settle the clash between themselves. This line of argument was also backed by the Soviets, though for reasons that were only partially the same as those of the CPR.[31] In any case, this shift in argumentation emerged from a desire on the part of the CPR, in the face of a deteriorating situation in the Strait itself, to salvage some gains from the crisis through the manipulation of political expectations. As discussed in Chapter Eight, however, this ploy was ultimately of little utility both because of the manifest international implications of the crisis and because of the tardiness with which the argument was introduced.

Toward the end of the middle phase of confrontation, the position of the Americans and Nationalists began to predominate with the result that the pressure on these parties to seek advantages by structuring the situation declined markedly. As the bargaining position of the CPR deteriorated further during the final phase of confrontation, however, the Chinese Communists initiated several new structuring efforts that, together with their moves to disengage from the physical confrontation of the crisis, were aimed primarily at reducing the losses associated with their decision to back away from the 1958 probe. The actual consequences of these final efforts, nevertheless, were at best equivocal from the view of the CPR.

Toward the end of the crisis the CPR became actively in-

[30] This argument first began to materialize in the CPR's statement of September 6, a statement which in fact marked an important turning point in the crisis. For the text of the September 6 statement, see Paul Zinner, ed., *Documents on American Foreign Relations 1958* (New York: Harper and Row [for the Council on Foreign Relations], 1959), pp. 440-442.

[31] For a discussion of the differences between Chinese and Soviet motives during this phase of the crisis, see *supra* Chap. Eight.

terested in the possibilities of driving a political wedge between the Nationalists and the Americans,[32] an interest pursued simultaneously with the announcement of the unilateral cease-fires during October.[33] The main hope of the CPR in this connection was to wean the Nationalists away from the United States[34] by responding to American activities so as to raise Nationalist fears of a Sino-American deal at Nationalist expense[35] and by hinting to the Nationalists about the possibilities of a deal between the two Chinas that would be better for the Nationalists than partial abandonment by the United States.[36] In the upshot, however, neither the Americans nor the Nationalists were seriously tempted by this ploy, and each party succeeded in giving sufficient reassurances to the other to make the impact of the CPR's efforts relatively small.[37] The Chinese wedge not only proved ineffective, it also made the United States somewhat more sensitive to Nationalist demands for assurance against any actions that might prejudice their interests, thereby effectively destroying any lingering American ideas of terminating the crisis through a compromise with the CPR at the expense of the Nationalists.

The final phase of confrontation also witnessed a complete reversal of the CPR's public posture with regard to the separability of the offshore islands and Taiwan. In direct proportion to their growing concern about the prospects for some form of

[32] For a good general statement on this point, see Stebbins, *op.cit.*, pp. 327-328.

[33] In fact, the most salient efforts on the part of the CPR to pursue this line are encompassed in the statements containing the various cease-fire announcements.

[34] As Tang Tsou has written, the tactic of the CPR was "to wean Nationalist China from her alliance with America rather than to pry the U.S. from the Nationalists." This quotation is from Tang Tsou, "Mao's Limited War in the Taiwan Strait," *Orbis*, III, No. 3 (Fall 1959), 347.

[35] For a discussion of this objective see *The Economist*, October 18, 1958, p. 212.

[36] The notion of a deal between the two Chinas is discussed in Tsou, "The Quemoy Imbroglio," *op.cit.*, p. 1,082.

[37] The joint Nationalist-American communiqué of October 23, for example, contained the following statement: "This aggression and the accompanying Chinese Communist propaganda have not divided them [the two parties], as the Communists have hoped. On the contrary, it has drawn them closer together." The text is printed in *DOSB*, XXXIX, No. 1011 (November 10, 1958), 721.

internationalization for the offshore islands,[38] the Chinese Communists began to place greater stress on the position that no settlement of the problem of the offshore islands was conceivable without a simultaneous settlement of the whole Taiwan question.[39] While this new Chinese position clearly had some utility in terms of its primary objective, it also produced disadvantageous side effects. In particular, this reversal bolstered American bargaining strength in the final phase of the crisis by providing a kind of *ex post facto* justification of the earlier American interpretation of the significance of the crisis in terms of a kind of "domino" effect.[40] As a result, the reaction of the CPR to the prospects of internationalization of the offshore islands stiffened the American stance and therefore undermined even further the assumption in the final bargaining calculus of the CPR that the American government would ultimately prove willing to make significant concessions in order to allay the impact of negative reactions in both domestic and international opinion.[41]

Berlin, 1961

Efforts to gain bargaining advantages by structuring both the underlying dimensions of the clash and the specific issues of the actual confrontation were prominent during the 1961 Berlin crisis. Each side engaged in extensive activities along these lines though, on balance, Western attitudes were somewhat less flexible with regard to such efforts than Eastern atti-

[38] For further comments on the notion of internationalizing the offshore islands, see *supra* Chap. Twelve.

[39] Anna Louise Strong's explanation of the rationale behind this position is particularly interesting. Writing from Peking in late October or early November, she explained: "To take Tsinmentao (Quemoy) at present, without taking Taiwan, would isolate Taiwan and thus assist Dulles in his policy of building 'two Chinas.' It would deprive the Chinese in Taiwan of their hopes of 'return to the mainland,' hopes that Peking will realize for them, but in its own way. It would throw Taiwan on the mercy of Washington. Hence Peking strengthens Tsinmentao and attaches it firmly to Taiwan, hoping later to take them both in a 'package deal.' " This statement is from Anna Louise Strong, "Chinese Strategy in the Taiwan Strait," *New Times*, No. 46, November 1958, p. 11.

[40] For a discussion of this American position in the context of the 1958 crisis, see *supra* Chap. Eight.

[41] For a formulation of these elements in the bargaining calculations of the CPR, see *ibid.*

tudes. In particular, there were no analogues on the Eastern side to the French position that the West should call the Soviets' bluff by doing nothing or to the pressing British concern to get formal negotiations started above all else.

As in the 1948-1949 crisis, the Berlin setting had a number of geopolitical characteristics that provided opportunities for structuring primarily to the East as the side holding the tactical initiative during the early phases of the crisis. The exposed position of the Western powers in Berlin gave the Eastern side a leverage that could be used in defining the scope of the actual confrontation.[42] And the East was able to exercise considerable tactical control over the timing of the crisis from its initiation through its termination. In addition, there were in 1961 some structural asymmetries affecting Berlin itself. In particular, regardless of the formal existence of a four-power regime for all of Berlin, the German Democratic Republic (GDR) was in a position to interfere with freedom of movement between the Eastern and Western sectors of Berlin without initiating or openly inviting the use of violence. Beyond this, the predominance of Eastern conventional forces in the area surrounding Berlin and the relative isolation of the city from the main contingents of NATO forces created important force asymmetries. On the one hand, "because of West Berlin's military and political vulnerability, the U.S.S.R. could mount considerable local pressure even while keeping its risks low and controllable."[43] On the other hand, in the event that open hostilities did break out in Berlin or along the access routes, a situation would have developed in which the West might still have had to assume the proximate responsibility for escalating the conflict to higher levels of force.[44]

[42] For a good formulation of this point see Deane and David Heller, *The Berlin Wall* (New York: Walker, 1962), p. 15.

[43] Arnold Horelick and Myron Rush, *Strategic Power and Soviet Foreign Policy* (Chicago: University of Chicago Press, 1966), p. 118.

[44] John Mander formulates this problem, with some exaggeration, as follows: ". . . if escalation did occur, it is the West that would be required to fire the first—atomic—shot. The West is inferior in conventional strength and can only fight a major action in Europe by using nuclear weapons. The Russians have a choice of weapons: the West has not. Yet it is precisely the West whose public opinion—and internal divisions—

These asymmetries with regard to force postures in 1961 were ameliorated to some extent, however, by the fact that Western conventional forces in Berlin, though small by comparison with Eastern forces in the area, did make the "tripwire" notion credible, at least with regard to major physical initiatives on the part of the Soviet Union.

In conjunction with these asymmetrical advantages attendant upon their ability to specify the actual point of contact for the 1961 crisis, the Soviets also attempted to define the underlying issues of the crisis by threatening to sign a separate peace treaty with the GDR. The signing of a separate peace treaty would not in itself have been detrimental to the Western position in Berlin or in Germany as a whole. The dangers for the West associated with such a treaty arose primarily from the prospects that it would lead to a complete transferral of control over the Berlin access routes to the GDR which in turn might produce irresistible pressures on the Western powers to recognize the GDR on a *de facto* basis, and dangerous or irresponsible East German actions threatening Western access to Berlin. At the time of its reactivation in June 1961, the threat of a separate peace treaty was treated with great seriousness in the West by all except the French.[45] During the early phases of the 1961 crisis, at least, a majority of Western decision-makers evidently believed the Soviets might go through with their threat, leaving the West in the extremely difficult position of having to choose between "seeking an agreement with East Germany alone, or having no agreement at all."[46]

For these reasons, it is particularly important to emphasize that the peace treaty threat was ultimately a somewhat hollow

---

would prevent it from firing the first atomic shot." This quotation is from John Mander, *Berlin: Hostage for the West* (Harmondsworth, Middlesex: Penguin, 1962), pp. 113-114.

[45] As *The Economist* put it in August, "The French have made it plain from the very start that, since the Berlin crisis was of Mr. Khrushchev's choosing, the Western powers had merely to stand firm and call his bluff." The statement appeared in *The Economist*, August 12, 1961, p. 637.

[46] *The Economist*, September 23, 1961, p. 1,137. Whereas many observers in the West subscribed to this view during the early stages of the crisis, it is typical of the British reaction in this crisis to be continuing to emphasize such problems by late September.

one in the sense that the Soviets had, from the beginning of the 1961 crisis, strong and conscious interests in not going through with it. Among other things, a separate peace treaty with the GDR: would have placed a somewhat unstable and untrustworthy satellite in the position of being able to catalyze dangerous East-West clashes;[47] might well have reduced Soviet political control over the GDR substantially by giving the latter freedom both to contemplate deals with West Germany and to blackmail the Soviet Union along these lines with regard to political and economic issues;[48] and would have expended an intrinsically one-shot threat whose use, whatever the consequences, would have destroyed its bargaining functions for the future.[49]

Under the circumstances, the Soviets evidently hoped desperately (though not without reason for encouragement) that the Western powers would relent and make important concessions before the hollowness of the peace treaty threat became apparent. The events surrounding August 13 thus came as a hard blow to the Soviet bargaining position since they necessitated, in effect, a temporary suspension of the peace treaty threat and emphasized the unreliability of the GDR. On August 11, Khrushchev made a last-ditch effort to get Western concessions before the closure of the sector boundary by invoking Soviet prestige, commitment, and "grandeur" in support of the separate treaty threat.[50] Moreover, the Soviets attempted to revive the threat in the wake of the events surrounding August 13. But by this time, both the obvious instability of the GDR and the sheer passage of time were begin-

[47] For useful discussions of this problem see George Bailey, "The Gentle Erosion of Berlin," *The Reporter*, Vol. 26, No. 9 (April 26, 1962), 16; and James L. Richardson, *Germany and the Atlantic Alliance* (Cambridge: Harvard University Press, 1966), p. 290.

[48] For a discussion of this problem see David Riesman, "Dealing with the Russians over Berlin," *The American Scholar*, Vol. 31, No. 1 (Winter 1961-1962), 27.

[49] For an interesting formulation of this point see Richardson, *op.cit.*, p. 290n.

[50] Among other things, Khrushchev spoke rather loosely in this speech about "our fight for the recognition of our grandeur" as a compelling reason for going through with the Soviet threats concerning Berlin. For a useful analysis of this speech, see the *New York Times*, August 12, 1961, p. 1.

ning to undermine the credibility of the separate peace treaty threat. As a result, the threat became gradually more vague and uncertain during September and October as the Soviets tried various ploys to maintain its credibility in a rapidly changing bargaining context.[51] More than any other single event, the relaxation of this threat, symbolized by Khrushchev's speech to the Twenty-Second Party Congress on October 17, signified the impending termination of the 1961 crisis.

In the face of these Eastern efforts to structure the 1961 crisis, the Western powers reacted with an attempt of their own to define the basic dimension of the confrontation to the advantage of the West. Throughout the period in which the issues of the crisis were being formulated, the Western powers sought repeatedly and with some success to make their commitment to the defense of Berlin credible by enlarging the scope of the crisis to cover the whole German question and therefore the fundamental bases of the Western defense system. As Kennedy put it in his key speech of July 25, "The strength of the alliance on which our security depends is dependent in turn on our willingness to meet our commitments to" the Berliners.[52] The symbolic significance of Berlin was therefore emphasized so as to make the clash focusing on the city a test case for the whole structure of Western security arrangements in Europe, a procedure which undoubtedly raised the overall tension level during the 1961 crisis but which also substantially strengthened the tactical position of the Western powers in the confrontation.[53]

[51] For a discussion of this shift see Eugene Rabinowitch, "Berlin and Beyond," *Bulletin of the Atomic Scientists*, XVII, No. 7 (September 1961), 261.

[52] The July 25 speech is printed in *DOSB*, XLV, No. 1155 (August 14, 1961), 267-273. The quotation is from p. 268.

On this subject see also Rusk's statement in an interview on August 20 that "This commitment is one of the great worldwide confrontations between the Sino-Soviet bloc and the free world, and it is of great importance that we make our commitments clear." The text of this statement is printed in *DOSB*, XLV, No. 1159 (September 11, 1961), 434.

[53] During the later phases of the crisis, however, a certain element of ambiguity began to characterize the Western position on this question of commitments. In general terms, Western spokesmen continued to emphasize a broadly symbolic view of Berlin for purposes of credibility. Nevertheless, as the crisis wore on, the Western powers began to move in the

Within the framework established by these broad efforts to determine the dimensions of the 1961 crisis, both sides showed an interest in a number of more specific structuring devices. To begin with, the Eastern side from time to time attempted to gain bargaining advantages by dividing its initiatives between the Soviet Union and the GDR.[54] The bargaining advantages of this procedure were twofold: it allowed the Soviet Union to portray itself as a party acting with praiseworthy restraint and interested in a peaceful settlement of the crisis while the GDR continued to exercise pressure on the West, and it allowed the East to play on Western fears of dangerous or irresponsible actions undertaken by a semiautonomous GDR. This tactical device in fact accounted for some Eastern gains, especially during the early phases of the crisis. As the crisis developed, however, its utility was sharply curtailed both by the emergence of important divergences between the interests of the GDR and the Soviet Union and by the increasing intrusion of the internal crisis of the GDR into Eastern bargaining activities in the East-West context.

Both sides also attempted to utilize the formulation and projection of negotiating positions in such a way as to structure expectations relating to the confrontation. For their part, the Soviets repeatedly attempted to oppose the general and somewhat legalistic Western commitment to Berlin with specific proposals[55] in the hope that such a procedure would suggest a greater understanding of current realities in Berlin than was evident in the Western posture. The Soviet proposals to give *West* Berlin the status of a "free city," furthermore, were probably designed primarily to increase pressures on the West by projecting a superficially attractive plan that would indicate the good intentions of the Soviet Union but that the Western powers would ultimately reject, thus evok-

---

direction of narrowing some of the specific issues at stake in order to reduce the scope for Western concessions should formal negotiations with the Soviet Union be initiated.

[54] For some interesting material on this subject see Jean Edward Smith, "Berlin Confrontation," *The Virginia Quarterly Review*, Vol. 42, No. 3 (Summer 1966), 362-363.

[55] For a particularly interesting formulation of this point, see Bailey, *op.cit.*, p. 18.

ing widespread criticism from outside parties. The Western powers, on the other hand, were somewhat less agile in utilizing structuring devices of this kind. One interesting device that did, in fact, receive some attention grew out of Willy Brandt's suggestion that the Soviet peace treaty threat be countered by a formal Western call for a general peace conference of the fifty-two states that had been at war with Germany in the Second World War.[56] But the Western allies were unable to coordinate sufficiently to utilize diplomatic initiatives of this kind successfully.

In the period of upheaval surrounding the events of August 13, the Eastern side became the somewhat fortuitous beneficiary of an initiative which, as it turned out, fell largely outside the scope of Western contingency plans.[57] In fact, the closure of the sector boundary was primarily a response to the internal crisis of the GDR, which the Soviets regarded as a hindrance to their bargaining efforts in the East-West context. In the event, however, the closure of the sector boundary produced certain tactical advantages for the Eastern side—not from the consequences of the closure for the internal situation of the GDR, which the West was in fact prepared to accept on a tacit basis, but rather from the lag in Western perceptions concerning the significance of these developments for morale in West Berlin and for the subsequent viability of the city in political and economic terms.[58] As a result, the West failed at first to undertake even symbolic countermeasures to draw the line in Berlin and preclude further Eastern gains.[59]

[56] On the idea of a general peace conference see Terence Prittie, the *New York Times Magazine*, August 6, 1961, pp. 7, 53-55. Brandt's suggestion along these lines was made in July. Interestingly, the Soviets, after it became clear the Western powers would be unable to agree on this idea, picked up the proposal and made occasional favorable references to it.

[57] On the question of Western contingency plans see Theodore Sorensen, *Kennedy* (New York: Harper and Row, 1965), p. 594. Though some commentators have argued that the Paris meeting of Western foreign ministers (August 5-7) must have considered this eventuality in general terms, Sorensen is apparently correct in saying there were no precise contingency plans for an Eastern move of this kind.

[58] For comments on these problems see Jean Edward Smith, *The Defense of Berlin* (Baltimore: The Johns Hopkins Press, 1963), pp. 269, 277, 280-281.

[59] On this point see Sorensen, *op.cit.*, p. 593. Western leaders at this point appear to have been so relieved that the Eastern action had not been

In the end, the losses which the Western side sustained by being caught off guard on August 13 were largely recouped by subsequent Western initiatives aimed explicitly at redressing the balance. Nevertheless, this sequence of events appears to have played a significant role in prolonging the period of confrontation, necessitating some risky Western initiatives in the period following August 13, and creating lasting problems for the West in maintaining the viability of West Berlin on a long-term basis.[60]

Throughout the critical phases of the 1961 crisis, the Western powers evidently toyed with the notion of employing economic initiatives as structuring devices that might counter the tactical initiatives of the East as well as offer an alternative to more forceful actions. Despite the apparent success of West German economic threats directed toward the GDR in 1960[61] and the projection of American hints concerning a possible East-West trade embargo,[62] however, the evidence suggests that the idea of using economic sanctions never achieved great influence in the West during the 1961 crisis.[63] In general, the relevant sanctions were not likely to be particularly effective in 1961, might have hurt the West as much as the East, and might have been countered with significant retaliatory actions. More specifically, the use of economic threats as a bargaining

more extensive or overtly dangerous that they at first neglected to pay sufficient attention to the need to draw a clear line in Berlin in order to define the limits of the Eastern position.

[60] Among other things, the handling of the crisis had some effect on the wave of emigration from West Berlin that occurred during the later months of 1961 and the early months of 1962 as well as on the subsequent difficulties in persuading industrial investors to put capital into West Berlin enterprises.

[61] On the use of economic threats by the FRG in 1960, see Smith, *The Defense of Berlin, op.cit.*, p. 228.

[62] The Hellers, for example, state that on August 4 "the United States let it be known that a total trade embargo between the United States and Soviet bloc countries was being considered." This quotation is from Deane and David Heller, *op.cit.*, p. 24. There is little doubt, in this connection, that the memory of the counterblockade during the 1948-1949 crisis was attractive. The sweeping nature of a threat to break off all East-West trade relations, however, makes this development in the 1961 crisis seem somewhat implausible.

[63] For evidence on this point see *The Economist*, August 12, 1961, p. 637.

device in the period surrounding August 13 was rejected for several reasons even though East German trade with West Germany was more important to the former than to the latter. Above all, the Western powers feared that moves along these lines during this period might exacerbate the dangers of internal upheaval within the GDR, a development the Western powers wished to avoid. The GDR undercut the Western powers on this issue, moreover, with an anticipatory threat to counter any Western use of economic sanctions with a total blockade of West German traffic passing into West Berlin over the access routes.[64]

Finally, several activities discussed at greater length in other parts of this study had some bearing on efforts to structure the 1961 crisis to acquire asymmetrical advantages. First, while the attempts of each side to outbid the other with regard to defense buildups during the crisis stemmed largely from the desire to demonstrate resolve, one aspect of the shifting defense picture appears to have played a major role in the timing of the crisis. By reactivating the Berlin clash in the summer of 1961, the Soviets evidently hoped to capitalize on an embarrassed American government's disenchantment with the existing set of doctrines for the defense of Europe and on its hesitancy in formulating or implementing a new policy. As Windsor has put it, "Khrushchev was playing on the very fears of 'escalation' in Europe which the new American administration had revealed in its demands for greater 'flexibility,' and ill-timed reinforcements."[65] Second, the extensive verbal campaigns initiated by both sides, but especially the Soviet Union, during the early phases of the crisis were at least partially aimed at structuring the thinking of the opponent about the fundamental nature of the Berlin conflict and particularly about the dangers of overt hostilities associated with it.[66] Third,

---

[64] On the timing of this threat see Smith, *The Defense of Berlin, op.cit.*, p. 279. The GDR already controlled German civilian traffic flowing into Berlin (i.e. the majority of all traffic using the access routes) and was therefore at least physically in a position to implement such a threat. The access issue associated with the threat of a separate peace treaty focused on the question of "military" traffic under the control of one or more of the Western powers of occupation.

[65] Philip Windsor, *City on Leave* (New York: Praeger, 1963), p. 235.

[66] For additional material on this subject see *infra* Chap. Sixteen.

each side engaged in efforts to muster world opinion against the position of the opponent, albeit with limited success. While the Western powers, led by the United States, attempted to portray the Soviet initiatives as belligerent acts willfully designed to disrupt a fundamentally peaceful situation, the Soviet Union continued to extol the virtues of its various plans for the future of Berlin and to criticize the Western powers for their anachronistic inflexibility in the face of new realities.

Cuba, 1962

Efforts to achieve bargaining advantages by structuring for asymmetries were influential during the Cuban crisis of 1962. The short duration of the crisis made these efforts less prolonged and complex than similar efforts in the other cases under analysis. The clear-cut and extensive influence of restraints on the use of violence in the 1962 crisis nevertheless lent a critical impact to alternative modes of exercising coercion, such as activities aimed at creating advantageous asymmetries.

The Cuban missile crisis arose from a daring Soviet initiative designed to offset the advantages of the United States with regard to the global strategic balance. The exact mixture of Soviet motives that produced the plan to deploy offensive missiles in Cuba is still unclear.[67] Whether the relevant motives were weighted predominantly toward redressing strategic imbalances of a concrete military sort with inferior capabilities or toward efforts to alter the perceived balances of political influence in the third world, however, the strategic initiative of the Soviets in 1962 was clearly aimed at creating advantageous asymmetries. In this connection, the Soviets evidently hoped to achieve an influential *fait accompli* with their initiative by suddenly unveiling a fully operational military capability.[68] But these plans were decisively undermined by the success of American reconnaissance operations in acquiring

[67] Perhaps the best discussion of Soviet motives in this connection is Arnold Horelick, "The Cuban Missile Crisis: An Analysis of Soviet Calculations and Behavior," *World Politics*, XVI, No. 3 (April 1964), 363-389. For additional material see also Albert and Roberta Wohlstetter, "Controlling the Risks in Cuba," *Adelphi Paper No. 17* (London: Institute for Strategic Studies, April 1965).

[68] For some material on this point see *Newsweek*, November 12, 1962, p. 25.

hard evidence concerning the deployment of Soviet missiles in Cuba before the weapons had become operational.[69] As a result, the Soviet Union was caught in a situation in which the United States was able to control the tactical initiative and therefore the choice of a contact point in formulating its response to the strategic initiative of the Soviets.

This led to the American action program announced on October 22. While initial American actions made an open confrontation inevitable and defined the principal point of contact, however, they left the Soviets with the advantage of being able to continue work on the operationalization of the missiles already in Cuba without automatically increasing the probabilities that the actions of the Soviet Union would become the proximate cause of the initiation of violent exchanges. During the first days of direct confrontation, therefore, the Soviets were able to display striking restraint with regard to the American naval blockade while simultaneously moving to undermine its effectiveness by rushing to operationalize the missile emplacements in Cuba. The United States was thus forced to choose between the double embarrassment of accepting the failure of its blockade as well as the success of the Soviet Union in introducing offensive missiles into the western hemisphere or launching new moves designed to destroy the advantages of the Soviet position. In this connection, the ultimate success of the United States in making its threat to launch a violent strike against the missile sites credible to the Soviets became a critical determinant of the final outcome of the crisis.[70]

At the same time, the American success was based on several important efforts to structure for asymmetries as well as on

[69] Whether American intelligence operated efficiently in the period prior to the acquisition of this concrete evidence is a highly controversial and much debated subject. For a particularly interesting and generally balanced discussion of the subject, see Roberta Wohlstetter, "Cuba and Pearl Harbor: Hindsight and Foresight," *Foreign Affairs*, Vol. 43, No. 4 (July 1965), 691-707.

[70] For evidence concerning the credibility of the American threat, see Khrushchev's statements on the subject of his speech to the Supreme Soviet on December 12, 1962. The relevant portions of the text can be found in Henry Pachter, *Collision Course* (New York: Praeger, 1963), p. 246.

the application of clear-cut threats at the actual point of contact. First, the American government chose to define the critical issues of the crisis in ways that highlighted the strongest aspects of the American position. In particular, the American decision to focus the crisis on the issue of the missiles and to deemphasize the broader aspects of the whole Cuban problem contributed to this outcome. Second, the United States succeeded in making a credible case for the claim that the American stakes in the crisis were far higher than those of the Soviets.[71] In this connection, the Americans concentrated on the propositions that the Soviet initiative in Cuba posed a direct threat to the American "heartland," and constituted an open violation of an accepted rule of international politics that *de facto* spheres of influence should be respected. In this perspective, the Soviet action looked like an effort to make a qualitative break with past practices and, what's more, to utilize forbidden types of action in the process. American efforts to define the basic dimensions of the clash, then, were quite influential. They contributed to the development of a surge of hemispheric solidarity in the Americas.[72] They produced a relatively sympathetic reaction to the American position in Europe and even in Africa.[73] And they allowed the United States to hammer on the theme that the predominant American stake in the situation would inevitably force the United States to outbid the Soviet Union in exerting pressure during the missile crisis no matter what the cost.

In more specific terms, the location of the actual point of contact for the confrontation in the Caribbean gave the United States a considerable advantage in the physical use of military forces for coercive purposes without initiating violence. While

[71] On the effort to emphasize the American stakes in the crisis, see Roger Hilsman, "The Cuban Crisis: How Close We Were to War," *Look*, Vol. 28, No. 17 (August 25, 1964), 21.

[72] The unanimity with which the Latin American states supported the basic position of the United States virtually eliminated any possibility for the Soviet Union to manipulate Latin American opinion for bargaining purposes during the 1962 crisis. For an interesting commentary on this subject see Theodore Sorensen, *Decision-Making in the White House* (New York: Columbia University Press, 1963), pp. 24-25.

[73] Several West African states, for example, refused refueling privileges to Soviet aircraft during the period of overt confrontation.

the Soviet initiative would no doubt have been impressive if it had led to a *fait accompli*, the shift of the tactical initiative to the United States in October demonstrated the extensive difficulties associated with efforts to operate within a sphere of influence of an opposing great power. Given the geographical and logistical asymmetries of the situation, the United States was able to achieve important advantages by coupling a deterrent posture at the strategic level with an impressive display of conventional superiority. As Hilsman has put it, "Cuba is far from the sources of Soviet strength. With vastly shorter lines of communication, the United States could apply overwhelmingly preponderant conventional power at the point of contact—Cuba—and do so under an umbrella of nuclear power that foreclosed any possibility of the Soviets trying to use nuclear weapons to redress the imbalance at the contact point. It was this combination of overwhelming conventional power on the spot and adequate nuclear power overall that proved irresistible."[74] In short, the United States succeeded in achieving "escalation dominance" by placing the Soviets in a situation in which they could not improve their bargaining position by raising the level of conflict.[75] As a result, the 1962 Cuban crisis underlined sharply both the importance of forcing direct confrontation at a point of initial advantage and the utility of carefully applied conventional power in controlling escalation even in a nuclear environment.[76]

Finally, a striking gap in the maneuvering to achieve advantageous asymmetries during the Cuban missile crisis was the absence of Soviet efforts to offset the geopolitical advantages of the United States in the Caribbean by introducing the Berlin situation into the picture. There was a widespread feeling at the time among American decision-makers that the Soviets might introduce a blockade of Berlin or some other form of pressure affecting Berlin as a bargaining counter to

[74] Hilsman, *op.cit.*, p. 21.

[75] For a general discussion of the concept of escalation dominance, consult Herman Kahn, *On Escalation: Metaphors and Scenarios* (New York: Praeger, 1965), pp. 23-24, 289-290.

[76] For some interesting comments on this subject see also Sorensen, *Kennedy, op.cit.*, p. 711.

offset their disadvantages in the confrontation over Cuba.[77] Some commentators even suggested that the real motive behind the original Soviet move to deploy offensive missiles in Cuba was a desire to create a "peril point" that would strengthen their bargaining position with regard to Berlin.[78] Nevertheless, the only Soviet attempt to introduce outside issues during the missile crisis was the relatively weak effort on October 27 to push for a Cuba-Turkey missile trade.[79] At the time, this move was quite widely interpreted as an effort to achieve an acceptable termination of the crisis by means of symmetrical compromises. Given the context of the 1962 crisis, however, the move was actually more asymmetrical than symmetrical in nature. In any case, both the tardiness with which the idea of a missile trade was formally introduced and the decisiveness with which the United States rejected it made it impossible for the Soviets to gain any significant bargaining advantages from the move.[80]

Conclusion

The case materials in this chapter make it clear that efforts to structure the fundamental dimensions and specific issues of a clash constitute a highly influential mode of coercion under conditions of crisis. Since activities of this kind frequently focus on relatively intangible matters, however, the achievement of bargaining advantages along these lines requires considerable subtlety. Moreover, since structuring activities can be directed toward any of a number of distinguishable levels of interaction, the quest for advantageous asymmetries often becomes a highly complex process.

At a very general level, it is sometimes possible to influence the formation of images and expectations concerning the un-

[77] For evidence of this feeling see *The Economist*, October 27, 1962, pp. 328, 334.

[78] For an interesting discussion of this idea see Zbigniew Brzezinski, "Cuba in Soviet Strategy," *The New Republic*, Vol. 147, No. 18 (November 3, 1962), 7-8.

[79] That the Soviets failed to make more use of the tactic of introducing external issues for bargaining purposes appears to be, at least partially, a tribute to the credibility and forcefulness of American threats of escalation in the Cuban arena.

[80] For further comments on this point see Pachter, *op.cit.*, pp. 53-58.

derlying qualities of the political context of a crisis. In these terms, the primary objective is to shape the perceptions of all relevant parties concerning the fundamental problem on which a crisis is based. The Chinese Communists, for example, attempted to portray the 1958 crisis as an episode in an ongoing civil war, following their failure to achieve a quick success with their initial bombardment of the offshore islands. Similarly, the Soviets endeavored to define the 1961 Berlin crisis in terms of the general problem of achieving a final peace settlement for Germany. Or again, the United States made a determined effort to cast the Cuban crisis of 1962 as a problem concerning the fundamental rules of the game in international politics whose implications reached far beyond the parochial interests of the United States. In actuality, these efforts met with widely varying degrees of success. Nevertheless, it is clear that the projection of basic perspectives and concepts along these lines can influence the conceptualization of many of the more specific issues associated with a crisis and that there are substantial benefits to be had from successful efforts of this kind.

Significant advantages frequently arise from efforts to control the definition of the proximate issues that become the immediate focus of contention during a crisis. Though the proximate issues are often little more than superficial manifestations of more fundamental problems, their specific formulation is apt to determine, to a considerable extent, the participants' freedom of maneuver during a confrontation. With regard to efforts along these lines, two relatively clear-cut patterns emerge from an assessment of the case materials. In the first instance, the side holding the *tactical* initiative is likely to seek a rather narrow definition of the proximate issues to emphasize the pointedness and credibility of its offensive moves. Thus, the Soviets focused the 1948-1949 and 1961 crises on specific issues connected with the vulnerable contact point of Berlin; the Chinese Communists were careful to distinguish between the offshore islands and Taiwan during the opening phase of the 1958 crisis; and the United States explicitly emphasized the missile issue in 1962 in contrast to the various broader issues associated with Cuba. In short, the objective is to focus the crisis on sharply defined issues in terms of which the opponent is on relatively weak ground. At the same time, the typical reaction of the side which must respond to tactical initiatives of this kind is to formulate the proximate issues of the crisis in considerably broader terms in order to achieve defensive credibility by turning the clash into a symbolic test of its general pattern of international commitments. Thus, the Western powers tried both in 1948-1949 and in 1961 to demonstrate that Berlin was a critical cog in their arrangements for the defense of Europe; and the United States explicitly developed the notion during the 1958 crisis that the offshore islands were an essential element of the overall American security provisions for the western Pacific.

Once the proximate issues on which a crisis will focus have been determined, it immediately becomes important for the parties to demonstrate the critical nature of their interests in these issues. In this connection, the trick is to persuade both the opponent and various peripheral actors that one's own side has a clearly predominant investment or stake in the proximate issues of the crisis. The cases provide illustrations of a number of distinguishable techniques for accomplishing this objective. In some cases, it is possible to emphasize physical links that establish the importance of the issues in question, as the Nationalists did in 1958 by publicizing the fact that a third of their army was stationed on the offshore islands. Then, there are sometimes opportunities to make an influential political commitment to a given outcome that would be costly to break. This was the Soviet objective in emphasizing the separate peace treaty threat in 1961, a tactic which the Soviets attempted to orchestrate by adding a specific time limit to the threat. In addition, an explicit move to stake a country's reputation as a power in international politics on the outcome of the proximate issues of a crisis sometimes serves to create an asymmetrical advantage affecting the overall clash. This was a significant element in the American approach to the Cuban crisis of 1962.

Beyond this, it is useful to distinguish between the somewhat intangible questions of basic context and proximate issues, discussed above, and the physical characteristics of the point of contact in a given crisis. Quite apart from the basic context and proximate issues, the geopolitical features of the actual point of contact are apt to be important determinants of asymmetrical advantages during a crisis. In general, the side holding the tactical initiative in the opening phase of a crisis has the greater opportunity to control the point of contact. An analysis of the cases, nevertheless, indicates this is often a complex matter containing a variety of pitfalls. The Soviets, for example, gained substantial advantages by making Berlin the point of contact in the 1948-1949 and 1961 crises, but on each occasion they failed to foresee certain liabilities associated with this point of contact. Moreover, while it is not difficult to understand why the Chinese Communists chose to make the offshore islands the contact point for the 1958 crisis, this decision generated important problems for the Chinese People's Republic (CPR) at several junctures in the crisis. And more generally, the Soviet initiative in deploying missiles to Cuba in 1962 illustrates the liabilities of neglecting to insure in advance against the dangers of becoming involved in a crisis with an unfavorable point of contact. While the Soviets in fact hoped to complete their strategic initiative in 1962 *without* precipitating a crisis, the shift of the tactical initiative to the United States boxed the Soviet Union into a clash whose contact point was advantageous to the Americans.

Finally, there is a wide variety of more specific structuring devices than can sometimes be employed to advantage during the course of a crisis. A perusal of the case materials indicates the range of options in this area. First, it may be possible to use a crisis confrontation to press related diplomatic initiatives affecting the ultimate outcome of the crisis itself. Second, the introduction of originally unrelated issues may serve to redress an unfavorable bargaining relationship arising from the principal focus of the crisis. Third, both the content and the publication of negotiating positions can sometimes be used as devices for shaping expectations concerning a crisis. Fourth, economic sanctions or threats offer asymmetrical advantages in some situations. Fifth, deliberate and well-timed announcements concerning shifts or buildups in overall defense postures are occasionally usable as devices for structuring bargaining relationships during a crisis. While the range of options is broad, however, the evidence from the cases under analysis makes it clear that specific devices of this kind must be fitted carefully to concrete circumstances if they are to produce significant bargaining advantages.

16. The Determinants of Emphasis

HYPOTHESIS. Conditions of crisis generate strong incentives for decision-makers to manipulate the perceptions of various parties concerning critical aspects of the clash.

The gap between the public pronouncements of decision-makers and impartial factual accounts of events or situations is apt to be relatively great under conditions of crisis. The manipulation of perceptions of events or situations in order to shape the bargaining calculations of other parties is generally an important mode of exercising influence.[1] The fact that conditions of crisis tend to sharpen and emphasize the adversary aspects of relations among the participants, however, makes the pursuit of influence along these lines particularly prominent during crises. The importance of such activities is further heightened by the influence of restraints on direct applications of force during crises since the manipulation of perceptions constitutes an alternative, and less dangerous, mode of exercising influence. Moreover, procedures of this kind can be used during crises to shape the perceptions of domestic audiences where overt coercion is apt to be less acceptable.

The proximate objectives of efforts to manipulate perceptions during crises may vary widely. There are certain circumstances in which a given participant will find it advantageous to play up the dangers or escalatory pressures associated with a crisis. It may be possible, for example, to alarm opposing decision-makers so as to weaken their resolve in specific encounters or to persuade them that it is up to them to control the dangers of violence attendant upon the clash. Furthermore, conscious overemphasis may occasionally be useful in controlling a domestic party or faction bent on forcing the adoption of an excessively hard line in a given crisis. At the same time,

[1] The primary focus of this chapter is therefore quite different from that of the preceding chapter. The manipulation of perceptions refers to efforts designed to control the understanding people have of factual relationships. The idea of structuring for asymmetries, on the other hand, is based on the possibilities of influencing the underlying nature of an interaction process as well as the basic frames of reference and conceptual schemas in terms of which decision-makers think about specific interaction processes.

a policy of systematically underemphasizing the dangers or escalatory pressures of a situation can be useful for a variety of purposes under conditions of crisis. A party preparing to initiate decisive or far-reaching physical actions, for example, may underemphasize the dangers associated with the resultant situation in order to play down the provocativeness or irresponsibility of its impending moves. Or it may utilize such procedures to minimize the impact of popular fears or domestic opposition to the initiation of decisive measures in a dangerous situation. The complexities associated with most crises, moreover, are such that any given participant may well have countervailing incentives with regard to the manipulation of perceptions that will lead it to engage in widely divergent activities in this area either simultaneously or over the various phases of a given crisis.

In general, there is apt to be considerable scope for the manipulation of perceptions under conditions of crisis. Crises frequently clog or degrade some of the more direct channels for the acquisition of information. Decision-makers faced with the tensions and complexities of a crisis must necessarily be selective in dealing with information concerning the clash and may therefore become suggestible with regard to key perceptions in terms of which to interpret major aspects of the situation. Furthermore, crises almost always involve a substantial number of essentially intangible factors. The general absence of both objective criteria and impartial machinery with which to assess such matters as escalatory pressures or the provocativeness of specific actions means there are relatively few clear-cut restraints on the freedom of decision-makers to engage in efforts to manipulate perceptions for bargaining purposes.

Berlin, 1948-1949

The Berlin crisis of 1948-1949 produced substantial, though not extreme, efforts to exercise influence through the manipulation of perceptions. The orientation of the two sides toward such efforts diverged markedly. While the Western powers found themselves seriously cross-pressured in this area, the

Soviet orientation toward the manipulation of perceptions was considerably more straightforward.

There were several factors that produced incentives for the Western powers to underemphasize both the general significance of the crisis and the dangers associated with it. In the first instance, the state of domestic politics in the United States at this time created incentives to underemphasize the crisis. The first really controversial presidential election in the United States in some years was shaping up for November 1948, and it was generally believed that Truman's prospects for election in his own right were poor. The incumbent government was therefore anxious to avoid damaging its already precarious position by becoming involved in a risky confrontation abroad. As Robert Murphy has put it, "If the President were to approve action in Berlin which the voters considered reckless, his election chances would diminish still further."[2] Truman himself was away from Washington on a campaign trip for roughly half of June.[3] The Republican national convention formally nominated Dewey on June 25, the day on which the Berlin airlift was initiated by Clay. Under these circumstances, the hesitancy with which decision-makers in Washington reacted to the shift of the Berlin crisis into the phase of full-blown confrontation was hardly surprising.[4]

In addition to these peculiarly American problems, the Western powers had other incentives to play down the significance of the 1948-1949 crisis. There is considerable evidence to suggest that a continuing sense of war-weariness in Britain and France made these countries reluctant to calculate the full significance of the crisis, an act almost certain to lead to their own direct participation. Even more important, however, was

[2] Robert Murphy, *Diplomat Among Warriors* (New York: Pyramid, 1965), p. 352.

[3] On Truman's campaign trip during June 1948, consult Harry Truman, *Years of Trial and Hope* (Garden City, N.Y.: Doubleday, 1956), p. 188; and Alfred Steinberg, *The Man from Missouri* (New York: G. P. Putnam's Sons, 1962), pp. 313-314.

[4] For a discussion of the impact of domestic politics in the United States on this hesitancy, see Jack Raymond, the *New York Times*, June 25, 1948, pp. 1, 18.

the question of civilian morale in Berlin itself.[5] Efforts to reassure the Berlin population were crucial for success in the crisis from the Western point of view. Such reassurance obviously required a clear demonstration of Western commitment to the defense of Berlin. But it also called for efforts to project a calm view of the situation and to minimize the dangers of the confrontation which might otherwise have been taken as evidence that the Western powers would ultimately be pressured into withdrawal.

There were, nevertheless, other aspects of the clash over Berlin that created incentives for the Western powers to play up the dangers of the situation and the provocativeness of Soviet actions. The Western powers moved in this direction in their efforts to portray the crisis as a challenge to the Western position in all of central Europe and to persuade the Soviets that they would not shrink from the use of force to maintain their position in Berlin. Interestingly, the 1948-1949 crisis produced an early example of the manipulative use of the Munich analogy for purposes of bargaining. Though the analogy between 1938 and 1948 did not stand up well under analysis, the fear of appeasement was used during this crisis to lock the Western powers into a strong stand on Berlin and to convince the Soviets of the necessity for a firm Western stand.[6] The implication, therefore, was that it was up to the Soviets to keep the dangers arising from the clash under control. Furthermore, efforts were made on various occasions to play up the dangers associated with specific incidents involving violence and to emphasize the need for Soviet responsibility in avoiding their occurrence. This procedure was particularly evident with regard to the operations of the airlift.

From the Soviet point of view, on the other hand, incentives concerning the manipulation of perceptions appear to have

[5] For a particularly interesting discussion of civilian morale in Berlin during this crisis, see W. Phillips Davison, *The Berlin Blockade: A Study in Cold War Politics* (Princeton: Princeton University Press, 1958), pp. 162-182.

[6] The use of the appeasement theme among Western decision-makers amounted, during this crisis, to a kind of self-stimulation to the commission of acts of "bridge-burning."

been considerably less mixed. The principal Soviet effort in this area was directed toward undermining resolve and morale on the Western side by portraying the dangers of the situation in strong terms. In the first instance, the Soviets attempted to cause feelings of fear and panic in the Berlin population to discourage the Berliners from holding out against the blockade.[7] This was, for example, a major objective of the Soviet propaganda campaign in Berlin during the crisis, which emphasized the prospects of starvation and the hopelessness of the efforts of the Western powers. An additional aspect of this campaign, which the Western powers found particularly troublesome, was the Soviet tactic of sowing rumors that the United States was about to effect a sudden withdrawal of its personnel from the city. At the same time, the Soviets attempted to manipulate perceptions in the Western capitals concerning the dangers associated with the crisis. The Soviet campaign in this area was the reverse of that conducted by the Western powers. While the Soviet objective in this connection was to achieve advantages by intimidating the Western powers, therefore, the effect of their campaign (together with Western efforts along these lines) was to increase the mutual fears and restraints on the use of force which characterized the crisis. Finally, these Soviet efforts to manipulate perceptions during the 1948-1949 crisis appear to have been essentially free from domestic restrictions, a fact which distinguishes the Soviet efforts along these lines from those of the Western powers during this crisis.

Taiwan Strait, 1958

Efforts to gain bargaining advantages through the manipulation of perceptions remained moderate throughout the 1958 crisis in the Taiwan Strait. Within these limits, however, all the major parties showed some interest in activities along these lines. In general, the Chinese People's Republic (CPR) was most active in this regard during the 1958 crisis, though the tendency of the CPR to shift ground on these issues during the course of the crisis lends a note of ambiguity to this conclusion.

[7] For evidence concerning Soviet efforts along these lines, see Davison, *op.cit.*, pp. 309-320.

A number of commentators, struck by the virtual simultaneity of the onset of the confrontation phase of the 1958 crisis and the public proclamation of the Great Leap Forward,[8] have suggested that the attitudes of the CPR toward both the timing and the conduct of the probe in the Strait were shaped by a desire to achieve internal unity at this time.[9] The thesis here is that the Chinese leadership utilized the resultant "tension and fear of war to induce the Chinese people to make record exertions and to accept the most radical change in their way of life yet attempted."[10] There are, however, serious problems with this interpretation. It does not square with the deliberate cessation of the "liberate Taiwan" campaign during a large part of August.[11] And above all, it is not compatible with the fact that "between August 23, when the shelling began, and September 6 . . . Peking did not let the Chinese public in on the crisis."[12] Moreover, these actions are clearly explainable in terms of the initial Chinese bargaining calculus for the crisis with its emphasis on the idea of undermining the Nationalist position on the offshore islands without fully engaging American prestige.[13] It seems likely, therefore, that the external requirements of bargaining were given precedence over internal propaganda needs by the CPR during the early phases of the crisis.

In the period following September 6, however, the crisis

[8] The overt initiation of the 1958 crisis occurred on August 23. This development was followed on August 29 by the first formal order to initiate the establishment of people's communes within the CPR.

[9] This is, in effect, a specific application of a common general thesis that governments have a tendency to manipulate their foreign relations for internal purposes and that militant external initiatives are often born from a need for increased internal integration.

[10] Harry Schwartz, the *New York Times*, September 14, 1958, Sect. IV, p. 3.

[11] On the cessation of the "liberate Taiwan" campaign, see Donald Zagoria, *The Sino-Soviet Conflict 1956-1961* (New York: Atheneum, 1964), p. 209.

[12] *Ibid.*, pp. 210-211. This statement seems a little too categorical in the light of more recent available evidence. The new evidence does not, however, alter the conclusion that the government of the CPR generally tended to minimize the extent of public notice given to the crisis during this phase.

[13] For further discussion of the bargaining calculations of the CPR, see *supra* Chap. Eight

developed in such a way to make the internal and external needs of the CPR more compatible. Externally, Chinese calculations shifted from hopes for a quick victory to efforts aimed at launching a public outcry against American provocations and mustering world opinion against the position of the United States.[14] This shift was accompanied within China by a variety of efforts to induce massive popular demonstrations and to unite the Chinese population in a "hate America" campaign.[15] Under the circumstances, the propaganda needs associated with both the crisis and the CPR's internal situation began to overlap increasingly so that the same set of activities could be utilized for both purposes. During the later phases of the crisis, therefore, the Chinese government appears to have made some use of the clash for domestic purposes,[16] though external problems probably continued to receive precedence until well into October.

Similarly, Chinese Communist efforts to manipulate perceptions in relations with the Nationalists underwent important shifts during the 1958 crisis. In the early phases of the crisis, the CPR made a substantial effort to undermine the morale of the Nationalists by emphasizing the hopelessness of their position. Both the "liberate Taiwan" campaign during July[17] and the military buildup in Fukien province immediately preceding the crisis[18] were evidently designed to intimidate the Nationalists. In the days following August 23, while the CPR played down the crisis domestically, Chinese coastal radios were active in beaming propaganda toward the offshore islands, threatening an "imminent" invasion[19] and encouraging

[14] For a discussion of this shift see Morton Halperin and Tang Tsou, "The 1958 Quemoy Crisis," Chap. 10 in Morton Halperin, ed., *Sino-Soviet Relations and Arms Control* (Cambridge: M.I.T. Press, 1967), pp. 275-276.

[15] On these efforts to induce popular demonstrations, see Robert W. Barnett, "Quemoy: the Use and Consequence of Nuclear Deterrence," Harvard Center for International Affairs, March 1960, p. 37.

[16] This is, for example, the formulation that Barnett appears to be striving for in his discussion. On this point consult Barnett, *op.cit.*, p. 16.

[17] For material on the "liberate Taiwan" campaign see Zagoria, *op.cit.*, p. 209.

[18] On the dimensions of the CPR's buildup in Fukien province, see *The Economist*, August 23, 1958, pp. 582-584.

[19] The CPR's "imminent" invasion threat was first used on August 27.

defection among the Nationalist garrisons.[20] Here too, however, Chinese Communist efforts underwent a shift during the
later phases of the crisis. As the idea of driving a wedge between the Nationalists and the Americans became increasingly
prominent during September,[21] the propaganda of the CPR began to emphasize the good treatment the Nationalists could
expect if they gave up their reliance on the United States and
voluntarily sought accommodation with the CPR. As a result, Chinese Communist definitions of the enemy began
to focus more and more on the Americans rather than the Nationalists and efforts were made to emphasize both the aggressive nature of American interference in a fundamentally Chinese problem and the political unreliability of the
Americans.

Broadly speaking, Soviet attitudes toward the manipulation
of perceptions during the 1958 crisis followed the shifts in the
efforts of the CPR and require interpretation in terms of Soviet
acquiescence in the basic calculations of the Chinsse Communists. Prior to September 6, the Soviets also played down the
crisis in their public statements. Though this has sometimes
been viewed as a sign of Sino-Soviet disagreement,[22] it now
seems more likely that this early Soviet posture was compatible with Chinese desires.[23] During this period, the Chinese
were hoping for a weak American response, a hope that would
have been made less plausible by a clear-cut Soviet involvement in the situation. Moreover, in the period after September
6 the Soviets swerved to a policy of publicly emphasizing the
provocativeness of the American position and the capacity of
the Soviet Union to defend China in the event of violent interference by the Americans.[24] In essence, this shift appears to

[20] On the hopes of the CPR about the possibility of breaking the
morale of the Nationalist garrisons, see Zagoria, *op.cit.*, pp. 210-211.

[21] For a discussion of this idea see *supra* Chap. Fifteen.

[22] Such a conclusion, at least in part, is the implication from the
interpretations of the crisis set forth in Zagoria, *op.cit.*; and John
Thomas, "Soviet Behavior in the Quemoy Crisis of 1958," *Orbis*, VI,
No. 1 (Spring 1962), 38-64.

[23] For an extensive discussion of the reasoning behind this conclusion,
see Halperin and Tsou, *op.cit.*, pp. 287-289.

[24] The most clear-cut examples of this new Soviet posture are contained
in Khrushchev's letters of September 7 and 19 to Eisenhower. For the

have been compatible with the requirements of the new bargaining calculations of the CPR.[25] Nevertheless, several characteristics of these new Soviet efforts indicate the development of divergences between Soviet and Chinese interests during the later phases of the 1958 crisis.[26] The Soviets were careful to stress only the deterrent function of their new posture while the Chinese could have used more extended support in the struggle over the artillery blockade of Quemoy. In addition, the Soviets used the cover provided by their strong public statements after September 6 to emphasize the limitations on their obligations to the CPR.

Although Nationalist and American efforts to manipulate perceptions during the 1958 crisis were less pervasive, both parties had occasion to operate along these lines with regard to specific issues. From the view of the Nationalists, one defensive issue and one offensive issue became particularly important in these terms. From the outset, the Nationalists lost no opportunity to stress the dangers of an overt attack on the offshore islands together with the serious consequences this would have for the American position in the western Pacific. Here they were largely successful since the American government proved receptive to this interpretation of the situation. During the later phases of the crisis, however, the Nationalists also began to play up the difficulties of breaking the blockade of Quemoy by nonviolent means, at least partially, to justify their demands for the initiation of bombing against the Chinese mainland. This campaign appears to have been associated with Nationalist interests in testing the possibility of using the crisis to realize their hopes of returning to the mainland.[27] Nevertheless, this effort to utilize the manipulation of perceptions for offensive purposes failed since the Nationalists were

texts of these letters see, respectively, *DOSB*, XXXIX, No. 1005 (September 29, 1958), pp. 499-503, and the *New York Times*, September 20, 1958, p. 2.

[25] For a discussion of this shift in the bargaining calculations of the CPR, see *supra* Chap. Eight.

[26] For further comments on the emergence of these divergences, see *ibid.*

[27] On these efforts of the Nationalists see Tang Tsou, "The Quemoy Imbroglio: Chiang Kai-shek and the United States," *Western Political Quarterly*, XXII, No. 4 (December 1959), 1,085.

unable to convince the Americans of the need to bomb the mainland and since they were too heavily dependent on American support to take any chances of alienating the United States.

The principal American efforts to bargain through the manipulation of perceptions during the 1958 crisis fell into two different categories. In the first instance, American decision-makers attempted throughout the crisis to play up both the general dangers associated with the confrontation in the Strait and to persuade the Chinese Communists that it was up to them to exercise control over the risks of Sino-American violence. The rapid buildup of forces in the Strait, the American participation in efforts to resupply Quemoy, and the enunciation of threats of sharp retaliation should American forces come under attack all stemmed at least partially from a desire to manipulate Chinese perceptions in this area. During the later phases of the crisis, on the other hand, the American government engaged in a number of efforts, in the context of American domestic politics, to play down the dangers arising from the confrontation. These efforts were catalyzed by the development of widespread criticism within the United States of the government's handling of the crisis.[28] And they became especially prominent as the political campaign associated with the Congressional elections of 1958 began to get under way.[29] In the end, however, the government's program in this area reached only moderate proportions since the crisis began to subside along lines favorable to the position of the United States before the final weeks of the 1958 campaign.[30]

[28] The sensitivity of the Eisenhower administration along these lines rose sharply in the middle of September following some rather simplified newspaper accounts of the contents of State Department mail on the crisis. For some interesting comments on these issues, see Dulles' news conference of September 30. The text is printed in DOSB, XXXIX, No. 1008 (October 20, 1958), pp. 597-604. See especially pp. 597-598.

[29] Predictions about the prospects of the Republican Party in the Congressional elections were rather dim in any case. For Dulles' efforts to make the case that it was unwise for "current aspects of foreign policy [to] be injected in the campaign," see his news conference of October 14. The text appears in DOSB, XXXIX, No. 1010 (November 3, 1958), pp. 681-688. The quotation is from p. 683.

[30] It is not easy to gauge the impact of the crisis on the outcome of

Berlin, 1961

The Berlin crisis of 1961 produced a number of significant efforts to achieve bargaining advantages through the manipulation of perceptions. In this crisis, such efforts were weighted heavily toward the objective of undermining the resolve of the opponent by playing up the dangers associated with the crisis. Especially in the period between the Vienna meetings in early June and the closure of the sector boundary in Berlin on August 13, both East and West devoted considerable attention to this objective.[31]

While Soviet efforts to manipulate perceptions during the 1961 crisis were relatively unidimensional, they were extensive and vigorously pursued. The Soviets utilized several different instrumentalities in pursuing their interests in this area. In the first instance, Khrushchev himself undertook an extensive series of well-publicized saber-rattling speeches aimed at intimidating his opponents by emphasizing the general dangers of destruction arising from the Berlin situation and by vividly portraying the likely consequences of military exchanges touched off by the crisis.[32] Some of these speeches were general efforts to project a pervasive sense of danger, thereby using "warnings of war to inhibit and restrict the enemy in his political moves."[33] On other occasions, however, the speeches contained more direct warnings specifying options open to the Western powers and designed to increase the weight of negative factors in the Western calculus with regard to these options.[34] Interestingly, this verbal campaign was con-

---

the elections with any precision. The consensus at the time concerning the causes for Republican losses in the 1958 elections, however, emphasized issues of domestic policy far more than questions of foreign policy.

[31] For some interesting comments on this subject, see John R. Dornberg, "Berlin: Consequences of Crisis," *The Nation*, Vol. 193, No. 6 (September 2, 1961), 112.

[32] For evidence concerning Western reactions to these speeches, see Jean Edward Smith, *The Defense of Berlin* (Baltimore: The Johns Hopkins Press, 1963), p. 254; and Deane and David Heller, *The Berlin Wall* (New York: Walker, 1962), p. 16.

[33] Hans Speier, *Divided Berlin* (New York: Praeger, 1961), p. 174.

[34] For Western reactions to these tactics, see, for example, Arthur Schlesinger Jr., *A Thousand Days* (Boston: Houghton Mifflin, 1965), p. 374.

ducted with marked rhetorical abandon and bellicosity.[35] And the level of acerbity and menace contained in Khrushchev's speeches rose steadily as the sequence of events unfolded in the aftermath of the Vienna encounter.[36] It now appears the Soviet leaders had concluded by the end of the Vienna meetings that Kennedy was unsure of his ground in the East-West arena and that his resolve on an issue such as Berlin could be significantly affected by a concerted attempt to manipulate Western perceptions of the dangers associated with the Eastern initiative.[37] In addition, it is likely this verbal campaign was conceived by the Soviets as one means of playing down and obscuring the continuing strategic inferiority of the Soviet Union, at least temporarily, while Soviet pressures on Berlin were being mustered.[38]

At the same time, the Soviets made use of a number of less formal devices in their efforts to manipulate Western perceptions of the dangers involved in the clash over Berlin. Soviet leaders frequently utilized stylized notions of escalation in the realm of nuclear strikes to intimidate Western diplomats. For example, Khrushchev himself "joked" informally with the British ambassador, Sir Frank Roberts, about the number of hydrogen bombs it would take to destroy Britain. And he went out of his way to impress the Greek ambassador with the threat that the Soviet Union would deliberately bomb the Acropolis in the event of war between the Soviet Union and the NATO powers. Another striking example of these informal efforts to shake the resolve of the Western powers occurred when Khrushchev summoned John McCloy, who was in Moscow for informal discussions on questions of disarmament, to Sochi to express his reactions to Kennedy's speech of July 25. At this meeting Khrushchev apparently, "told McCloy emo-

[35] On this point see Smith, *op.cit.*, p. 254; and the Hellers, *op.cit.*, p. 8.

[36] For impressions concerning this development, see *ibid.*, p. 17.

[37] For an interesting interpretation of these aspects of the Vienna encounter, see Thornton Read, "Kennedy and Khrushchev at Vienna" (mimeographed essay), 1967.

[38] For an interesting discussion of this point, see Speier, *op.cit.*, pp. 135-136. While the Soviets were, in 1961, riding a wave of favorable changes in popular perceptions of the strategic balance between the superpowers, there is no doubt that their strategic forces were, during the 1961 crisis, inferior to those of the United States in reality.

tionally that the United States had declared preliminary war on the Soviet Union"[39] and maintained that "the new American military measures constituted an unjustified affront to the Soviet Union, dangerously enhancing the possibilities of total war."[40] Such sentiments were obviously far from the actual Soviet appraisal of the clash over Berlin at the time. But procedures of this kind seemed to constitute sensible bargaining devices designed to exacerbate fears which the Soviets had reason to suppose were already influencing the behavior of opposing decision-makers.

Western efforts to gain advantages through the manipulation of perceptions were less extended but more varied than those of the Soviet Union in the 1961 crisis. In a somewhat restricted fashion, the West also played the game of emphasizing the dangers of war arising from the Berlin crisis and underlining the possible consequences of provocative moves on the part of the opponent. Though these efforts were sometimes hampered by the defensive posture of the Western powers, they were pursued with considerable regularity by the West. Both the format and the content of Kennedy's speech of July 25,[41] for example, illustrate the Western approach to the manipulation of perceptions concerning the dangers associated with the crisis.

The crisis also produced at least one significant instance in which concern about potential overreactions on the part of the American public was an important factor in a decision of the American government to refrain from actions designed to play up the dangers of the crisis for Soviet consumption. The reference here is to the American decision during July 1961 *not* to proclaim a state of national emergency on the grounds that such a step might, among other things, touch off a panicky reaction by the American public.[42]

---

[39] This reaction on the part of Khrushchev is reported by Schlesinger, evidently on the basis of a conversation with McCloy. The quotation is from Schlesinger, *op.cit.*, p. 392.

[40] Smith, *op.cit.*, p. 252.

[41] For the text of Kennedy's July 25 speech, see *DOSB*, XLV, No. 1155 (August 14, 1961), 267-273.

[42] For a discussion of the idea of proclaiming a state of national emergency, see Theodore Sorensen, *Kennedy* (New York: Harper and Row,

Beyond this, the United States, in particular, attempted to manipulate perceptions internationally by emphasizing the view that the Berlin situation was a manufactured crisis and that the Soviet Union was acting as a dangerous "provocateur" in bringing it about. As Kennedy put the case in his July 25 speech: "The world is not deceived by the Communist attempt to label Berlin as a hotbed of war. There is peace in Berlin today. The source of world trouble and tension is Moscow, not Berlin. And if war begins, it will have begun in Moscow and not Berlin. For the choice of peace or war is largely theirs, not ours. It is the Soviets who have stirred up this crisis."[43] This became a pervasive theme in American discussions of the Berlin situation throughout the remainder of the crisis.[44] The Americans attempted to achieve a bargaining edge by playing up the provocativeness of the Soviet position and by fixing the responsibility for the crisis solely on the Soviet Union, even though this meant isolating the specific circumstances of the 1961 clash both from the overall context of East-West relations and from the postwar history of Berlin and Germany.

Cuba, 1962

The Cuban crisis of 1962 produced a number of clear-cut attempts to maintain bargaining strength through the manipulation of perceptions. It should be stressed at the outset, however, that the crisis itself grew out of a situation made already somewhat obscure and ambiguous by the use of manipulative procedures. While the Soviet Union was in fact beginning its deployment of offensive weapons to Cuba, the Soviets became increasingly anxious to convey verbal assurances on the subject to the United States. They were at pains to persuade the Americans that the Soviet Union had no reason to move nu-

---

1965), pp. 589-590. There were other arguments against such a move, including the view of some advisers that the Soviets would interpret it more as a sign of weakness than as a demonstration of resolve.

[43] For the text of this statement see *DOSB*, XLV, No. 1155 (August 14, 1961), 272.

[44] It was, for example, one of Kennedy's principal points about Berlin in his address of September 25, 1961, at the United Nations. The text of this address appears in *DOSB*, XLV, No. 1164 (October 16, 1961), 619-625.

clear-capable weapons to Cuba. As a TASS communiqué of September 11 put it: "Our nuclear weapons are so powerful in their explosive force and the Soviet Union has rockets so powerful to carry these nuclear warheads that there is no need to search for sites for them beyond the boundaries of the Soviet Union."[45] The Soviets also forwarded explicit assurances to the American government, through private channels, that the Soviet Union would refrain from efforts to cause trouble for the United States in the international arena prior to the American elections in November.[46] The Soviets continued these efforts to reassure the United States throughout the period of their arms buildup in Cuba.[47] During the Kennedy-Gromyko meeting in Washington on October 18, for example, this was an important theme the Soviet foreign minister sought to develop.[48]

American leaders tried to counter this Soviet campaign with a series of rhetorical warnings. Kennedy made a number of attempts to convince the world, by verbal means, that the United States would react forcefully to the installation of "offensive" weapons in Cuba. On September 4, for example, he announced that the arms buildup in Cuba did not yet constitute a danger to the United States, but added, "were it to be otherwise, the gravest issues would arise."[49] Then on September 13, Kennedy explicitly linked developments in Cuba with the statement that "this country will do whatever must be done to protect its own security and that of its allies."[50]

At the same time, however, the American Administration was becoming acutely sensitive to the approach of the 1962 Congressional elections in the United States, and to the pros-

[45] The text of this communiqué is printed in Henry Pachter, *Collision Course* (New York: Praeger, 1963), pp. 176-177. The quotation is from p. 177.

[46] For a discussion of this point see Elie Abel, *The Missile Crisis* (Philadelphia: Lippincott, 1966), p. 19. Available evidence suggests that, at the time, this pledge was interpreted primarily in connection with the problem of Berlin.

[47] For evidence on this point see Schlesinger, *op.cit.*, pp. 798-800.

[48] For a summary of the Kennedy-Gromyko conversation on October 18, see Pachter, *op.cit.*, pp. 188-192.

[49] *Ibid.*, p. 176.

[50] *Ibid.*, p. 178.

pects that the domestic opposition would utilize the Cuban issue to good advantage. This concern rose to major proportions following Senator Kenneth Keating's public warnings about the arms buildup in Cuba in early September. By the end of the month, therefore, "The Administration's entire propaganda machine was mobilized to tell the voters that the danger was exaggerated."[51]

Thus, the missile crisis developed in a political setting already somewhat confused by manipulative activities. The United States, for its part, continued to occupy a cross-pressured position with regard to the manipulation of perceptions during the period of direct confrontation. Under the circumstances, Kennedy tried repeatedly to strike a balance among competing demands in this area. As Sorensen has put it, "His warnings on the presence of Soviet missiles in Cuba had to be sufficiently somber to enlist support around the world without creating panic here at home."[52]

As a result, the dangers and the precariousness of the clash in the Caribbean were vividly played up both to the Soviet Union and to other external audiences. Kennedy himself set the tone for this campaign in his key speech of October 22.[53] He characterized Soviet activities in Cuba as provocative and unjustified, and he spoke darkly of the approaching "abyss" of nuclear war. In addition, he went on to issue a sweeping threat to engage in a "full retaliatory response" should the Soviets fail to remove their missiles from Cuba, a threat that stood in marked contrast to the prevailing American doctrines based on the concept of graduated responses.[54] This American campaign to manipulate perceptions was carried forward throughout the week of October 22. In particular, activities of this kind surfaced repeatedly during the meetings of the

[51] Ibid., pp. 18-19.

[52] Theodore Sorensen, Decision-Making in the White House (New York: Columbia University Press, 1963), p. 47.

[53] The text of Kennedy's October 22 speech can be located conveniently in David L. Larson, ed., The "Cuban Crisis" of 1962: Selected Documents and Chronology (Boston: Houghton Mifflin, 1963), pp. 41-46.

[54] For an interesting discussion of this point, see Albert and Roberta Wohlstetter, "Controlling the Risks in Cuba," Adelphi Paper No. 17 (London: Institute for Strategic Studies, April 1965), p. 18.

United Nations Security Council on October 23, 24, and 25.[55] In this context, American representatives drummed on the theme that Soviet activities in Cuba were unprecedented, underhanded, and unjustifiable.

But American leaders at the same time attempted to portray the crisis in different terms for the domestic audience since the primary objective here was to maintain a calm and orderly atmosphere. Again, Kennedy himself set the tone for official presentations in his speech of October 22.[56] No photographs of missile installations in Cuba were shown on television. In describing the potential use of Soviet missiles against American population centers, the word "strike" was deliberately substituted for the phrase "wipe out." Estimates of megatonnage figures for Soviet missiles were carefully avoided. The American naval blockade became a "quarantine" for purposes of public presentation. Similarly, administration leaders maintained their sensitivity to the impending Congressional elections. In general, the proximity of the elections provided an additional incentive to reassure the public about the crisis and to deemphasize the dangers associated with it in domestic presentations. This temporal proximity led American officials to engage in a vigorous effort to undermine and deflate various claims that the administration had timed the initiation of the confrontation phase of the crisis to benefit from it in the November elections.[57]

The Soviets, on the other hand, found themselves less cross-pressured with regard to the manipulation of perceptions during the confrontation phase of the 1962 crisis. In general, they concentrated their efforts to manipulate perceptions on the dangers associated with the crisis in the Caribbean and on the provocativeness of the American initiatives. In the Security Council, for example, the Soviets coupled public denials of the

---

[55] For the texts of Stevenson's statements in the Security Council, see Larson, ed., *op.cit.*, pp. 66-81, 131-136, and 137-141.

[56] On the problems of portraying the crisis for domestic audiences, see Sorensen, *op.cit.*, pp. 698-699.

[57] From the point of view of the Kennedy administration, in fact, the temporal juxtaposition of the crisis and the elections produced more problems than advantages. For further comments on this point see Pachter, *op.cit.*, p. 19.

American charges concerning the installation of offensive weapons in Cuba with a series of counterclaims focusing on the theme that the Americans had willfully brought the world to the brink of nuclear holocaust.[58] In this connection, the fact that the Soviets were genuinely afraid of the dangers engendered by the crisis lent a certain ring of authenticity to their public pronouncements concerning the dangers of violence and destruction. The manipulative aspects of these Soviet activities, moreover, could be pursued with relatively undivided attention since the Soviets were in the position of being able to maintain a general silence with regard to the nature of the crisis for domestic purposes. It was not until after the termination of the crisis that the clash began to emerge as a subject for discussion in Soviet news media.

The Cuban crisis of 1962 was therefore characterized by a marked divergence between the verbal portrayals of the protagonists and their true actions.[59] The resultant duality is captured nicely in Charles Lerche's description of the crisis as "an interesting example of the disparity between rhetoric and action that any major power in the twentieth century must observe. American public statements bristled with determination and menace, but the specific courses of action by the United States left the Soviet Union many convenient and face-saving loopholes. Moscow displayed an equivalent duality, protesting its commitment to the defense of Cuba against American imperialist aggression and its resentment at American missile-rattling, yet all the time acting in a way that would permit the early liquidation of the crisis. The Cuban affair, in other words, was from its very beginning conducted at two levels. . . ."[60]

Conclusion

The evidence from the case materials does not lend clear-cut support to the hypothesis on which this chapter is based.

[58] Zorin's key statement in the Security Council on October 23 provides a particularly clear example of this two-pronged Soviet rebuttal. The text of this statement is printed in Larson, ed., *op.cit.*, pp. 90-102.

[59] For evidence of caution and restraint in the actual actions of the protagonists, see *supra* Chap. Thirteen.

[60] Charles Lerche Jr., *The Cold War . . . and After* (Englewood Cliffs, N.J.: Prentice-Hall, 1965), p. 111.

411

Nevertheless, the case materials do indicate that significant efforts to manipulate perceptions are frequently made under conditions of crisis. In general, activities aimed at manipulating perceptions tend to be concentrated in a relatively small number of the areas to which they could conceivably be applied. Moreover, there is an important contrast between efforts along these lines aimed outward toward foreign audiences and related activities aimed inward toward domestic audiences.

With regard to efforts to manipulate perceptions in the international arena, several patterns are distinguishable. Efforts to alter bargaining calculations by playing up the dangers of war associated with a crisis and the provocativeness of the actions of opposing parties clearly constitute the most important area for manipulation of this kind. Such activities are sometimes aimed at shaking the resolve of opposing decision-makers so as to undermine the credibility of their bargaining positions. The Soviets, for example, embarked on a concerted campaign along these lines during the early phases of the Berlin crisis of 1961. And the American emphasis on the notion of a "full retaliatory response" in the 1962 Cuban crisis was aimed at shaking Soviet resolve. Also, it is occasionally possible to undermine the morale of critical civilian populations by playing up the dangers associated with a crisis. This was the goal of the unsuccessful Soviet effort to destroy the morale of the Berliners in 1948. Furthermore, such activities may also be used to intimidate opposing military forces by emphasizing the hopelessness of their situation. This was the objective of the Chinese Communists in their radio broadcasts to the Nationalist garrisons on the offshore islands during the early part of the 1958 crisis.

Efforts to play up the dangers associated with a crisis may also be utilized to create a backdrop against which other bargaining activities can be more forcefully developed. In particular, the cases suggest that this procedure of emphasizing the negative or dangerous aspects of a situation is apt to be employed as a prelude to offers of positive rewards for actions that would, in effect, change the character of the whole confrontation. This was the procedure the Soviets employed, for example, in conjunction with their offers of food to residents of the western sectors of Berlin who would register in the eastern sector during the 1948-1949 crisis. Similarly, this was the approach of the Chinese Communists in their promises, during the later phases of the 1958 crisis, concerning the good treatment awaiting the Nationalists if they would shift toward the Chinese People's Republic (CPR) and away from the United States.

Another significant international area for the manipulation of perceptions focuses on efforts to muster world opinion in such a way as to project the responsibility for a given crisis onto the opponent. The trick here is to shape perceptions concerning a small number of critical factors that constitute the key to subsequent interpretations of the clash. During the 1958 crisis, for example, the Chinese Communists attempted to project the thesis that there was no Sino-American conflict of any kind, a thesis leading easily to the proposition that American activities during the crisis constituted gratuitous and illegitimate intrusion. Again, during the 1961 Berlin crisis, the United States attempted repeatedly to persuade foreign audiences that Berlin was not a source of tension and that the crisis had been entirely fabricated by the Soviet Union, propositions that served as the basis of a campaign to condemn the Soviets as "provocateurs" and disturbers of international peace and security. And during the Cuban missile crisis, the Americans continually emphasized the idea that the Soviets, in deploying missiles to Cuba, had broken an accepted rule of international politics. As a result, Soviet actions were branded as illegitimate and unjustifiable.

With regard to efforts to manipulate perceptions in domestic arenas, on the other hand, important asymmetries emerge from an analysis of the case materials. In particular, there appears to be a marked contrast between republican and authoritarian political systems in this connection. In the first instance, factional controversy within the decision-making elite is characteristic of both types of system. There is evidence of difficulties along these lines within both the Soviet and American systems, for example, under conditions of crisis.[61] The republican systems, however, demonstrated a much greater sensitivity to domestic

[61] In both the Berlin crisis of 1961 and the Cuban crisis of 1962, for example, internal factional strife appears to have influenced the actions of both sides.

FORCE, COERCION, AND VIOLENCE

public opinion under conditions of crisis. Decision-makers in these systems are apt to be concerned about the volatility and tendency toward overreaction of public opinion.[62] Leaders therefore frequently attempt to play down the dangers of a foreign clash in addressing domestic audiences.[63] In addition, crises are frequently perceived as significant determinants of popular elections, a link sharply affecting the way leaders portray crises for domestic audiences.[64]

The authoritarian systems, on the other hand, demonstrated little sensitivity to popular reactions under conditions of crisis. An external crisis may be used as a device to manipulate popular feelings with regard to domestic issues, as was apparently the case within the CPR during the later phases of the 1958 crisis. But, in general, the regime in an authoritarian system usually has sufficient control over the internal news media so that it can simply suppress information concerning the very existence of a crisis if this seems desirable.[65] A regime of this kind is thus under little pressure to manipulate domestic perceptions concerning specific aspects of a crisis. Whereas republican systems frequently find themselves seriously torn between internal and external interests with regard to the manipulation of perceptions during a crisis, therefore, authoritarian systems are apt to be able to pursue a more consistent course.

[62] In general, popular opinion is apt to fluctuate more rapidly and more radically than elite opinion with regard to foreign policy issues. This appears to be a function of both access to information and conceptual skills. Under conditions of crisis, which place a substantial premium on control and an ability to work at the margins, overreaction can generate significant problems.

[63] In a certain sense, then, public opinion is likely to have an impact on policy-making during crises. This de facto relationship, however, raises questions about the flexibility of republican systems in bargaining under conditions of crisis.

[64] This is especially true of the American system, in which significant elections occur rather frequently. Of the cases under analysis, all but the 1961 Berlin crisis were affected by their temporal association with an American election campaign. Moreover, the 1961 crisis was substantially affected by its juxtaposition with a nationwide election campaign in the Federal Republic of Germany.

[65] The Cuban crisis of 1962, for example, did not become public knowledge in the Soviet Union on a widespread basis until after its termination. Similarly, the Taiwan Strait crisis of 1958 was largely suppressed within the CPR until Chou En-lai's statement of September 6.

414

APPENDICES

Appendix A: Problems of Epistemology

As stated in the Preface, this study has epistemological as well as substantive objectives. Many of the epistemological problems encountered in the analysis have been referred to in the text. It seems useful at this point, however, to clarify the basic context of these epistemological concerns as well as to delineate in greater detail the principal epistemological problems encountered.

The selection of variables and the formulation of hypotheses about empirical phenomena constitute a highly complex process. Hypotheses of the kind set forth in this book emerge from a variety of sources. And there is no doubt that the formulation of hypotheses is one of the most creative aspects of this type of analysis. At the same time, it is essential to match abstract hypotheses with empirical data on a systematic basis. This process of relating hypotheses to empirical data, which may be referred to broadly as the process of substantiation, gives rise to the problems outlined in this appendix.

The present volume suggests that the use of comparative case studies constitutes a fruitful procedure for dealing with the problems of substantiation in many substantive areas within the field of international politics. The use of comparative case studies is an alternative to other procedures based on unstructured generalizations, single case studies, various quantitative procedures, simulation, and so forth. While the body of the study stands as an argument for the advantages of comparative case studies, there are clearly problems associated with the use of this procedure. It is the purpose of this appendix to pinpoint and discuss these problems:

Problems of Definition. In constructing hypotheses about empirical phenomena, it is of critical importance to specify the universe of cases to which the resultant generalizations are said to apply. In the absence of specificity on this point, it is logically impossible to judge whether or not a generalization holds in empirical terms. Specificity with regard to the relevant universe of cases requires, first, one or more definitions sufficiently precise to make it possible to identify cases

417

of the phenomenon under analysis within the broader range of empirical phenomena with confidence. To achieve confidence in identifying cases, it is generally necessary to employ "nominal" rather than "essential" definitions, at least for analytic purposes. This has been the procedure followed in the present study in defining crisis. Under the circumstances, critics may argue that the study is weak because it deals with an uninteresting phenomenon. At this point, however, the debate shifts increasingly from epistemological questions to the more subjective problem of intrinsic interest.

Conditions and Settings. In all theoretical work, it is necessary to specify the conditions under which hypothesized relationships are expected to hold. This requirement raises particularly difficult problems in the field of political science, however, since political phenomena are highly sensitive to changes in many aspects of the setting in which they occur and since the relevant setting frequently changes rapidly and extensively. Compare the problems of analyzing elections or international crises, for example, with those of studying atomic structures or the phenomenon of gravity. As a result, it is especially important to spell out relevant conditions in formulating hypotheses about political phenomena. And since the introduction of conditions is a restrictive process, universes of cases are frequently smaller in the field of political science than they are in the natural sciences.

This argument should not, however, be employed to conclude that empirical generalizations about political phenomena will apply only to a single time period or part of the world. On the contrary, hypotheses about such phenomena can be regarded as applicable whenever their conditions are met despite great divergences in time and place. Moreover, even when all their conditions are not fulfilled, such hypotheses are often useful in generating insights and directing the formulation of new hypotheses. The problems posed for the present study by these considerations concerning conditions and settings are discussed in substantive terms in Chapter Three of the text.

Rigorous Comparison. A major problem in using comparative case studies is the achievement of strict comparisons across individual cases. Among other things, this means that questions must be applied evenly to specific cases and answers compared across cases at least in rough terms. It is one thing to achieve these goals with regard to simple factual matters such as time elapsed or numbers of troops deployed in given situations. It is far more difficult to do so with regard to complex and intangible matters, especially where human perceptions are critically important. Moreover, variations in language, prevailing images, expectations, cultural perspectives, and so forth make these problems of comparison particularly difficult in connection with international activities. There is no obvious or definitive way of handling these problems of rigorous comparison. In analyzing most complex phenomena, a great deal of judgment is necessary in this area. The skill with which such judgments are made is generally a major determinant of the quality and usefulness of any given study.

Organization of Material. There are important choices to be made in the organization of material in empirical studies. In using comparative case studies, the principal choice is between a discrete case organization in which all materials concerning a given case are grouped together, and an analytic organization in which empirical materials are grouped around a series of major hypotheses or sets of questions. There is no *a priori* way of choosing between these patterns of organization outside the context of a specific study. An analytic organization, however, tends to facilitate the substantiation of generalizations concerning regularities in empirical phenomena. Not only does such an orientation lead to the selection of empirical material focusing on the generalizations in question, it also facilitates efforts to handle the problems of comparison discussed above. A discrete case organization, on the other hand, is desirable when the primary goal of analysis is to explain specific cases of a phenomenon which have occurred in the past rather than to develop generalizations concerning regularities in a specified universe of cases.

Operationality and Availability of Data. The problem here is the standard one of acquiring accurate readings for individual variables in empirical cases. The relevant variables are set

419

by the hypotheses whose substantiation is at stake. But there are several common problems in this area in the study of international politics. First, it is frequently difficult to pin down variables with sufficient precision to get accurate and comparable readings for them in specific empirical cases. This problem is particularly great with regard to the perceptual and intangible phenomena that are major factors in bargaining under conditions of crisis. Second, problems of classification and restriction are apt to make it difficult to acquire information about certain aspects of recent events and issues. The specific problems associated with the acquisition of information concerning the postwar crises are discussed in Appendix B.

Confidence Levels. When it is impossible to analyze all members of a specified universe of cases (as it generally is in empirical analyses), proof can never be absolute. Rather than proving empirical generalizations in any absolute sense, therefore, the goal of analysis becomes the maximization of levels of confidence. Confidence, in turn, is a function of the number of cases in a given universe of cases examined, and the accuracy or success with which individual cases are examined. The use of comparative case studies generally constitutes a middle ground between even more extensive examination of a single case and a less developed and less sensitive examination of a larger number of cases, usually on the basis of quantitative procedures. The argument for comparative case studies is based on the proposition that this procedure is apt to reduce both the idiosyncratic results which often characterize single case studies and the problems of acquiring meaningful information on important variables which tend to characterize efforts to examine larger numbers of cases. It is the contention of this study that the use of comparative case studies constitutes an important middle ground in the analysis of many phenomena within the general area of international politics. Whether or not this procedure will yield more fruitful and interesting results than alternative procedures in connection with a particular research project, however, is a matter of judgment which cannot be settled without a close inspection of the problems associated with the application of various procedures to the subject at hand.

There are no easy or definitive solutions for most of these epistemological problems. The success or failure of any given study, therefore, is strongly related to the quality of the judgments concerning these problems which underlie it. Beyond this, it is of critical importance that decisions on such matters be spelled out with sufficient clarity to allow for assessment by analysts other than the author himself. In the absence of such clarity, there is no way to reach meaningful judgments concerning the extent to which a given study succeeds or fails in the effort to substantiate its hypothesized generalizations about empirical phenomena.

Appendix B: A Note on Sources

Empirical analyses of recent events are commonly subjected to criticisms relating to source materials. This is especially true of analyses, such as the present study, which go beyond simple quantitative matters to assess intangible issues. The most important of these criticisms concerns the inadequacy of sources about governmental decision-making before archival materials become available. It is also argued that closeness to events deprives the scholar of the broad historical perspective necessary to use his source materials effectively. Furthermore, the contemporary significance of the matters under analysis, it is often argued, is apt to bias the outlook of the scholar, often unconsciously, so that he cannot treat the materials available to him objectively or impartially.

This appendix attempts to reply to criticisms of this kind as they apply to the present book. In the first instance, it should be noted that extensive materials dealing with the major postwar crises are already available. In fact, it soon becomes evident that more material is available than a single scholar can fully examine. As a result, the debate over source materials shifts immediately from the question of quantity to issues concerning the quality of available material, and the existence of significant gaps in this material. The question of quality is, of course, a serious one, but it is hardly a problem peculiar to efforts to analyze recent events. In short, it is a high-priority task for all scholars to develop criteria with which to judge the quality of the materials available to them. The problem of gaps, on the other hand, is more serious for attempts to analyze recent events. With regard to any given subject there are apt to be specific questions on which material is simply lacking or unsatisfactory. In addition, it is possible to distinguish certain categories of question in terms of which available material is less satisfying then it is for other categories. For example, at any given time there are apt to be at least some important governments whose decision-making processes are difficult to assess with confidence and accuracy.

It is obviously necessary to accept the fact that these problems place limitations on efforts to analyze recent events. It is important, however, not to overemphasize the extent to which these problems are peculiarly limiting for analyses of recent events. It is evident, for example, that both types of difficulty concerning gaps place extensive limitations on the analysis of events occurring in other settings. In fact, these problems mount rapidly as soon as one goes back beyond the modern era or progresses laterally beyond what might be loosely described as the European arena. As a result, it is quite plausible to argue that while the analysis of recent events is hampered by serious gaps in information, there are relatively few time periods and physical settings for which such problems are of lesser significance.

In addition, there are advantages for the scholar who focuses on events occurring in the recent past. First of all, it is clear that events are influenced and shaped by the underlying political atmosphere or context in which they occur as well as by the world views, images, and expectations which are widespread during the period of their occurrence. This is the phenomenon historians often discuss as the "spirit of the age." In general, the acquisition of an accurate and subtle feel for the spirit of an age is a difficult task no matter what time period is involved. The problems of acquiring such a feel, however, are apt to increase with elapsed time and, especially, to become substantially more complex when the period in question passes beyond the realm of living memory.

A related problem concerns the assessment of intangible matters. Information concerning issues or events that were infused with great urgency or emotional content at the time of their occurrence, for example, is apt to lose much of its color, poignancy, and interpretative overtones as time passes and the issues or events in question lose their salience. Under the circumstances, some information is far more "meaningful" than other information for interpretative purposes even though it is no more *accurate* in any formal sense. While it is quite true, therefore, that the perspective of the analyst is apt to increase with the passage of time, it is also true that sensitivity to nuances and the emotional overtones of issues tends to decline as time passes and the events under analysis pass out of the experiential field of the scholar.

For the most part, international issues and events in the contemporary era are subject to far more extensive attention on the part of news media and major opinion groups than they were in the past. Interactions among states are therefore much more widely and extensively publicized than they were in earlier periods. And greater efforts are devoted to the search for information concerning them. This clearly does *not* mean there are no important aspects of international events which are withheld from the public domain for substantial periods. It does mean, however, that the range of questions concerning any specific event which remain completely obscure in the aftermath of the event is now considerably narrower than it was in the past.

Finally, it is important to say a few words about the problems of objectivity and bias. In general, detachment or impartiality is much more a function of the scholar's personality than of the passage of time. While there are obviously problems in detaching oneself from the partial perspectives and attitudes of the recent past, a perusal of the historiography of earlier periods shows that systematic detachment is hardly a hallmark of scholars working on such subjects. In short, the problems of objectivity and bias are common to all endeavors aimed at analyzing past events. Criticisms along this line are more often based on *ad hominem* arguments than on intrinsic or unavoidable qualities of the subject matter under analysis.

In the final analysis, it is unclear whether the problems associated with studies of the recent past impose limitations that are more far-reaching than the limitations attendant upon analyses of earlier periods. It is not the purpose of this appendix to attempt a judgment concerning this complex question. It may, nevertheless, be useful to conclude this discussion with a specific listing of the principal source materials utilized in the present study of bargaining under conditions of crisis.

Available Documents. One obvious source of information is the documentary material currently available. There are still important gaps in the documents, especially with regard to

memoranda concerning governmental decision-making processes. Despite the absence of archival material, however, the
quantity of available documentation on the postwar crises is
impressive. This is particularly true of the Berlin crisis of 1961
and the Cuban crisis of 1962, both of which occurred during
periods in which the attention of news media was focused with
unusual clarity on international problems. The opening of
archival material on the postwar crises will undoubtedly add
substantially to the evidence that is currently available. It
seems probable, however, that the opening of the archives will
be a considerably less important event with regard to the crises
of the postwar period than it has been in the case of events
that occurred in earlier periods.

Participant Accounts. The contemporary tendency for participants in important events to make their reflections available
in written form with little delay makes participant accounts
an important source of information on the postwar crises. Such
accounts tend to enter the public domain earlier than they did
in previous periods. They are frequently more extensive in a
quantitative sense. There is a striking tendency in the contemporary period for officials of the highest rank to engage in
this process of recording *ex post facto* reflections. And participant accounts often have the advantage of interpretative
sensitivity or feel for the atmosphere of decision-making
which is apt to characterize statements recorded relatively
soon after the occurrence of events. There is, of course, considerable unevenness with regard to the availability of materials of this kind. In the contemporary period, for example,
American and British officials have been especially prolific
along these lines.

Current Periodicals. Accounts of unfolding events appearing
in contemporary periodicals constitute an additional source of
information concerning past events. Contemporaneous material of this kind is especially useful in assessing intangible
matters such as the underlying political atmosphere within
which events occur. With regard to the postwar crises, material available in current periodicals is so voluminous that it is
literally impossible to examine it all comprehensively. Major

crises have become so salient and visible in the contemporary period that they have been treated in great detail by publications emanating from many sources and representing a wide range of perspectives. It is therefore necessary to establish criteria with which to make selections within the great bulk of periodical literature. In the present study, the criteria employed focused on: judgments concerning the abilities of individual authors; judgments concerning the reputation of specific periodicals; and the effort to select material in such a way as to consider a wide range of perspectives and outlooks.

Newspapers. With regard to the postwar crises newspapers constitute an especially voluminous source of information. The major newspapers have been in the forefront in the shift of effective attention which has made international crises extremely important focuses of public interest in the contemporary period. The extensiveness of the coverage of the postwar crises in the major newspapers is little short of remarkable in contrast to the amount of attention devoted to international events in similar publications in earlier periods. Moreover, the development of great newspapers that aspire to at least a semblance of objectivity in their reportage of international events is far more characteristic of the contemporary period than of earlier periods.

Monographic Material. In analyzing the postwar crises, it is useful to separate the monographic literature into two categories. First, there are the usual monographic studies by accredited scholars. Such works are particularly valuable as sources of interpretative material. Despite the shortness of the time that has elapsed since the occurrence of the crises under analysis, relatively extensive work of this kind concerning each of the crises dealt with in this study has already been carried out. Second, there is a considerable amount of monographic material that can be described as journalistic reconstruction that focuses primarily on the compilation of factual material concerning important events of the recent past. While such efforts are of limited value as ends in themselves, they are often valuable sources of information for the scholar. In the contemporary period, both the extensiveness and the thoroughness of reconstructions of this kind dealing with salient international events such as the major crises are remarkable. As a result, this material constitutes an important resource for analysis which is frequently either lacking or far less extensive with regard to events that occurred in earlier periods.

Index

Abel, Elie, 92, 165n, 211n, 212n, 237n, 262n, 277n, 302n, 330n, 331n, 357n, 408n
Acheson, Dean, 103n, 122
Acropolis, 405
Adenauer, Konrad, 84, 133
Adzhubei, Aleksei, 131
Afro-Asian bloc, 149
Aiken, Frank, 111n, 166
Alaska, 332
alliances, 50, 54, 264
Allied Control Commission for Germany, 56, 65-66, 120, 219-20
Alsop, Stewart, 210n, 317n, 330n
Amoy, 270
"Amtracks," 345n
analogic reasoning, 35-36
Anderson, Rudolf, 280
appeasement, 397
arms control, 269n
arms race, 23
Aron, Raymond, 25n
asymmetries, 33-34
authoritarian political systems, 413-14

Bailey, George, 206n, 231n, 235n, 255, 274n, 351n, 352n, 353n, 379n, 381n
balance, strategic, 47, 79-80, 85, 87-88, 103, 187, 190, 193-94, 385, 405n
Baldwin, Hanson, 225n, 228n, 293n, 319n, 346n
Ball, George, 90, 141, 239, 329, 356n
bargaining, impediments, 37-39; precedents, 35-36; strategic, 36-41, 175-76, 214-16, 267, 282-83, 305, 326; tactics, 39-41, 175-76 committal: 217
Barnett, Robert W., 71n, 72n, 152n, 189n, 225n, 273, 317n, 318n, 319n, 321n, 344n, 400n
Barraclough, Geoffrey, 76n, 156n, 292n
Bartlett, Charles, 210n, 330n
Bartlett, Ruhl, 67n

Belgrade Conference (1961), 159-60, 162-63
Berlin City Council, 366
Berlin crisis (1948-49), 13-14, 18, 22, 52n, 56, 64-70, 93, 97, 118-23, 143-44, 146, 148-52, 168-69, 179-85, 218-24, 241-43, 245-49, 267-70, 283, 285-88, 304, 312-16, 333, 339-42, 358, 360, 363-68, 383n, 390-92, 395-98, 412-13; Berlin airlift, 121, 151, 179-80, 182-85, 220-21, 223-24, 246-47, 268-70, 287, 314, 340-42, 358, 360, 364-67, 397
Berlin crisis (1958-59), 55, 78-79, 93, 195, 275, 390-92; Soviet ultimatum (November 1958), 57
Berlin crisis (1961), 11, 52n, 56, 57, 79-86, 92-93, 104-109, 114, 130-37, 143-45, 157-63, 195-207, 214-16, 229-36, 241, 254-58, 264-65, 274-77, 283, 295-99, 304-305, 323-28, 333, 348-55, 359-60, 376-85, 404-407, 412-14, 425
Berlin Kommandatura, 120, 220
Binder, David, 234n, 328n
bipolarity, 49-53
Bizerte crisis (1961), 82
Bizonia, 67
Boulding, Kenneth, 25n, 29n, 245n
Bowles, Chester, 162n
Bramuglia, Juan, 150
Brandon, Henry, 110n, 111n, 332n
Brandt, Willy, 68, 200, 324, 382
Brennan, Donald, 269n
British Guiana, 279
Brodie, Bernard, 13n, 334n
Brussels Treaty, 220, 367n
Brzezinski, Zbigniew, 92n, 389n
Bucharest, 240, 331
Bull, Hedley, 25n
Burton, John W., 259n
Butterfield, Herbert, 25n, 48n

Campbell, John C., 150n
Castro, Fidel, 86, 167, 259n, 279, 302

429

Other books published for
The Center of International Studies
Princeton University

Gabriel A. Almond, *The Appeals of Communism*
Gabriel A. Almond and James S. Coleman, editors, *The Politics of the Developing Areas*
Gabriel A. Almond and Sidney Verba, *The Civic Culture: Political Attitudes and Democracy in Five Nations*
Richard J. Barnet and Richard A. Falk, *Security in Disarmament*
Henry Bienen, *Tanzania: Party Transformation and Economic Development*
Cyril E. Black and Thomas P. Thornton, editors, *Communism and Revolution: The Strategic Uses of Political Violence*
Cyril E. Black, Richard A. Falk, Klaus Knorr, Oran R. Young, *Neutralization and World Politics*
Robert J.C. Butow, *Tojo and the Coming of the War*
Miriam Camps, *Britain and the European Community, 1955-1963*
Bernard C. Cohen, *The Political Process and Foreign Policy: The Making of the Japanese Peace Settlement*
Bernard C. Cohen, *The Press and Foreign Policy*
Charles De Visscher, *Theory and Reality in Public International Law*, translated by P. E. Corbett
Frederick S. Dunn, *Peace-making and the Settlement with Japan*
Harry Eckstein, *Division and Cohesion in Democracy: A Study of Norway*
Richard A. Falk, *Legal Order in a Violent World*
Robert Gilpin, *France in the Age of the Scientific State*
Herman Kahn, *On Thermonuclear War*
W. W. Kaufmann, editor, *Military Policy and National Security*
Klaus Knorr, *On the Uses of Military Power in the Nuclear Age*
Klaus Knorr, *The War Potential of Nations*
Klaus Knorr, editor, *NATO and American Security*
Klaus Knorr and James N. Rosenau, *Contending Approaches to International Politics*
Klaus Knorr and Sidney Verba, editors, *The International System: Theoretical Essays*
Peter Kunstadter, editor, *Southeast Asian Tribes, Minorities, and Nations*
Sidney J. Ploss, *Conflict and Decision-Making in Soviet Russia*
Lucian W. Pye, *Guerrilla Communism in Malaya*
James N. Rosenau, editor, *International Aspects of Civil Strife*
James N. Rosenau, *National Leadership and Foreign Policy: A Case Study in the Mobilization of Public Support*
Rolf Sannwald and James Stohler, *Economic Integration: Theoretical Assumptions and Consequences of European Unification*, translated by Hermann F. Karreman
Richard L. Sklar, *Nigerian Political Parties: Power in an Emergent African Nation*
Glenn H. Snyder, *Deterrence and Defense*

Harold and Margaret Sprout, *The Ecological Perspective on Human Affairs, With Special Reference to International Politics*

Thomas P. Thornton, *The Third World in Soviet Perspective: Studies by Soviet Writers on the Developing Areas*

Richard H. Ullman, *Britain and the Russian Civil War, November 1918–February 1920*

Sidney Verba, *Small Groups and Political Behavior: A Study of Leadership*

Karl von Vorys, *Political Development in Pakistan*

Myron Weiner, *Party Politics in India*

E. Victor Wolfenstein, *The Revolutionary Personality: Lenin, Trotsky, Gandhi*

Oran R. Young, *The Intermediaries: Third Parties in International Crises*

438